OXFORD WORLD'S CLASSICS

THE FIRST PHILOSOPHERS

THE PRESOCRATICS were philosophers and scientists who lived and worked in various cities throughout the ancient Greek world, from southern Italy and Sicily to the coast of the Black Sea, from the beginning of the sixth century BCE to the time of Socrates in the late fifth century. Among a number of lesser names, some fifteen major thinkers stand out in this period. Though their work survives only in fragments and in reports from later writers, who were often unsympathetic, as well as far removed in time, enough remains for us to be able to effect a reconstruction with some degree of plausibility, and thus to see that they formed the foundations of Western scientific and philosophical thought. Most of them wrote in prose, and indeed they were among the first prose writers in the West, helping to develop the genre; but some kept to the traditional didactic medium of verse.

THE SOPHISTS were itinerant teachers and writers, dating chiefly from the fifth century BCE. Though they lectured and taught throughout the Greek world, they achieved the most recognition in Athens, which at the time was the centre of culture in Greece. Very little of their original prose survives, and we are largely dependent upon the reports of others, who were often hostile to their enterprise, and upon reflections of their work in contemporary historians, dramatists, and orators. As well as initiating a revolution in education, by offering what was effectively the first Western attempt at higher education, they also made important strides in social, ethical, and political philosophy, and we can now see that the pejorative use of the term 'Sophist', which stems from Plato and Aristotle, is rarely deserved.

ROBIN WATERFIELD was born in 1952. After graduating from Manchester University, he went on to research ancient Greek philosophy at King's College, Cambridge. He has been a university lecturer (at Newcastle upon Tyne and St Andrews), and an editor and publisher. Currently, however, he is a self-employed writer, whose books range from philosophy to children's fiction. He has previously translated, for Oxford World's Classics, Plato's *Republic*, *Symposium*, and *Gorgias*, Aristotle's *Physics*, Herodotus' *Histories*, and Plutarch's *Greek Lives* and *Roman Lives*.

OXFORD WORLD'S CLASSICS

*For over 100 years Oxford World's Classics have brought
readers closer to the world's great literature. Now with over 700
titles—from the 4,000-year-old myths of Mesopotamia to the
twentieth century's greatest novels—the series makes available
lesser-known as well as celebrated writing.*

*The pocket-sized hardbacks of the early years contained
introductions by Virginia Woolf, T. S. Eliot, Graham Greene,
and other literary figures which enriched the experience of reading.
Today the series is recognized for its fine scholarship and
reliability in texts that span world literature, drama and poetry,
religion, philosophy and politics. Each edition includes perceptive
commentary and essential background information to meet the
changing needs of readers.*

OXFORD WORLD'S CLASSICS

═══

The First Philosophers
The Presocratics and Sophists

═══

Translated with commentary by
ROBIN WATERFIELD

OXFORD

UNIVERSITY PRESS

Great Clarendon Street, Oxford OX2 6DP

Oxford University Press is a department of the University of Oxford.
It furthers the University's objective of excellence in research, scholarship,
and education by publishing worldwide in

Oxford New York

Athens Bangkok Buenos Aires Cape Town Chennai
Dar es Salaam Delhi Hong Kong Istanbul Karachi Kolkata
Kuala Lumpur Madrid Melbourne Mexico City Mumbai Nairobi
São Paulo Shanghai Singapore Taipei Tokyo Toronto

Oxford is a registered trade mark of Oxford University Press
in the UK and in certain other countries

Published in the United States
by Oxford University Press Inc., New York

British Library Cataloguing in Publication Data

Data available

Library of Congress Cataloging in Publication Data

Data available

ISBN–13: 978–0–19–282454–7

8

Typeset in Ehrhardt
by RefineCatch Limited, Bungay, Suffolk
Printed in Great Britain by
Clays Ltd, St Ives plc

To the memory of
George Kerferd and Trevor Saunders

CONTENTS

PREFACE AND ACKNOWLEDGEMENTS

So much of our information about the Presocratic philosophers and the Sophists is fragmentary or otherwise obscure that the temptation was to write a book in which the amount of commentary outweighed the amount of translated material. I have resisted this temptation. After a short introduction, each thinker has been allowed to speak as much as possible for himself, or, failing that, at least to be heard, however faintly at times, through the work of ancient commentators. There is a great deal of secondary ancient material, especially about the Presocratics, whose importance was generally recognized in ancient times. It is therefore well beyond the scope of a book such as this to hope for completeness. Rather, my policy has been to translate the majority of the actual fragments themselves, and a small proportion of the ancient testimonia, concentrating on those passages which are both important and relatively clear in their own right (so as to continue to let the thinkers speak for themselves as much as possible), and which seem to me to be relatively faithful to the original thinker or at least to make it plain that they are distorting him, and how they are doing so.

A few scholars are perhaps over-pessimistic about our chances of recovering the thought of the Presocratics and Sophists. In some cases we have enough genuine fragments to test the validity of the secondary testimonia; in some cases the material surrounding shorter fragments can cast light on the original context. Nevertheless, there is an immense amount of discussion among modern scholars about what each of these thinkers really thought. Naturally, scholars prefer to rely as much as possible on the actual fragments themselves, but in the case of none of these first Western philosophers are there ever quite enough of these for us to be able to see the whole picture.[1] In addition, a lot of the fragments are devilishly obscure. The most unsatisfactory aspect of writing this book has been the need to omit a great deal of the

---

[1] However, we may in many cases have a greater proportion of the original work than we might at first imagine. It is likely that the Presocratics' and Sophists' books were not long, but were written in a condensed form, because they were meant to be read out loud to an audience and then expanded by discussion afterwards, as much as they were intended as documents for posterity. This helps to explain the frequent dogmatism of their pronouncements, and also, given that much of what these early thinkers were saying was open to interpretation, this must make our judgement of the distortions of Aristotle and Theophrastus less harsh.

scholarly arguments and counter-arguments which support certain conclusions: when whole books have been written about, say, Heraclitus, Parmenides, and Empedocles, how can one compress the evidence and the deductions from that evidence into twenty or so pages?[2] But that is the necessary policy of this book, and in order to keep to it I have appended longer bibliographies than a volume like this might usually warrant. In the case of the Presocratics and Sophists reference to modern works is indispensable, since many readers will want further guidance. However, let me urge readers to start studying these thinkers simply by thinking for themselves about what any of them might have been meaning. For all the scholarly work that has gone into the area, there is little consensus: your own ideas, based firmly on the available evidence as presented in this book, are as good a way into the thought of the first philosophers as those of the most eminent of academic scholars.

The strategy necessarily adopted in this book, of assigning each thinker his own section, works satisfactorily in the case of the Presocratics, but not quite so well in the case of the Sophists. It helps to show that they were individual thinkers, not members of a school, but a great deal of material that it would be right to call 'Sophistic' is embedded in occasional contexts in other fifth-century writers (especially the historians, Hippocratics, and dramatists), or reflected in fourth-century literature (especially Plato). In the case of the Sophists, then, I strongly recommend supplementing this book by reading the thematic approach to the movement adopted by, say, Guthrie [10], vol. iii, or Kerferd [97].

Work on this book involved a particularly intensive use of libraries. I would like to thank the following Bloomsbury institutions and their staff: the library of the Institute of Classical Studies; the British Library; the library of University College London; the Warburg Institute Library. Individuals to whom I owe thanks for having, in one way or another, eased the process of writing this book, are: Yuri Stoyanov, Stela Tomasevic and Jurgen Quick, Clive Priddle, David and Jane Vaughan, Martin Buckley and Penny Lawrence, Melissa Hawkins, Philip and Briar Maxwell, John Bussanich, and Ingrid Gottschalk. As usual, Judith Luna's combination of patience and clear thinking made her the ideal editor.

---

[2] Vlastos once spoke scathingly of 'the complacent simplifications of the schoolbooks' ([33], p. 304). Let me assure anyone who arrogantly agrees with this that in my experience such simplifications are anything but complacent, and cost a great deal in the way of effort and difficult decisions.

INTRODUCTION

In the last stanza of 'The Gods of Greece' by Friedrich von Schiller (1759–1805), the poet laments the passing of the old gods:

> Yes, home they went, and all things beautiful,
> All things high they took with them,
> All colours, all the sounds of life,
> And for us remained only the de-souled Word.
> Torn out of the time-flood, they hover,
> Saved, on the heights of Pindus.
> What shall live immortal in song
> In life is bound to go under.[1]

The poem perfectly sums up a particular attitude—a Romantic attitude—that at some point *mythos* was replaced by *logos*, the de-souled Word. Although (for reasons that will become clear later) this is not an attitude with which I wholly agree, it does serve as a useful launching-point for discussion.

The Greek word *logos* covers a wide range of meanings. It can mean 'account', in the sense either of 'story', or of 'amount' or 'value', as in 'He is of no account'; it can mean 'word' or 'speech' or 'argument'; it can mean 'proportion', 'principle', or 'formula'; it can mean 'reason', both in the sense of the human rational faculty and in the sense of 'explanation'. In short, it covers a nest of what we might call logical and rational faculties and activities. What Schiller meant, then, was that at some point in history our emotional and intuitive side lost out to such 'de-souled' activities.

Schiller's view is also commonly reflected, though not as an occasion for Romantic mourning, in the standard histories of philosophy. The fact that both Romantics and academics are saying the same

---

[1] Ja sie kehrten heim und alles Schöne
Alles Hohe nahmen sie mit fort,
Alle Farben, alle Lebenstöne,
Und uns blieb nur das entseelte Wort.
Aus der Zeitfluth weggerissen schweben
Sie gerettet auf des Pindus Höhn.
Was unsterblich im Gesang soll leben
Muss im Leben untergehn.

thing constitutes a fascinating case where a truce has apparently
been declared in what Plato described as 'the ancient quarrel
between poetry and philosophy' (*Republic* 607b). Time and again, in
both abstruse academic tomes and more popular histories, we read
how a revolution took place in the ancient Greek world, and how its
first manifestations arose at the beginning of the sixth century BCE.
The thinkers associated with this revolution are known collectively
as the Presocratic philosophers—'Presocratic' because they preceded Socrates in thought, even if the last of them are his contemporaries in time—and they are said to have invented philosophy
and science for the Western world. Here, for instance, is a quotation
from an influential history:[2]

But no uniform picture emerges from all these [Egyptian and Babylonian]
achievements, nor do the separate details coalesce to form a single body of
scientific thought grounded in an all-inclusive philosophical doctrine.
This had to wait for that scientific approach to the study of nature which
was the creation of the Greeks in the sixth century. This approach took
the form of an attempt to rationalize phenomena and explain them within
the framework of general hypotheses. The object aimed at was giving
general validity to the experience obtained from regarding the world as a
single orderly unit—a cosmos the laws of which can be discovered and
expressed in scientific terms.

The fame of the Presocratics has endured well. Even those who
are not aware of them as a group have heard of the obscure aphorisms of Heraclitus, or of Zeno's paradoxes, or of the number-mystic
Pythagoras. But in this book we shall meet others: Thales, Anaximenes and Anaximander, all from the city of Miletus in Asia Minor,
down the coast from Heraclitus' home town, Ephesus; Xenophanes
of Colophon, another town in Asia Minor; Parmenides of Elea (or
Velia) in southern Italy, the first Presocratic to start a recognizable
school of thought, whose first and most important members were his
fellow Eleatic, Zeno, and Melissus from the island of Samos (where
Pythagoras, too, had been born, though he lived half his life in
southern Italy); Empedocles of Acragas in Sicily; Anaxagoras of
Clazomenae in Asia Minor; Democritus of Abdera on the coast of
northern Greece; Diogenes, from Apollonia on the west coast of the
Black Sea. They all lived between about 600 and 400 BCE; Socrates,

---

[2] Sambursky [91], p. 4.

by comparison, lived from 469 to 399. The last of the Presocratics were Socrates' contemporaries, as were the earliest Sophists, whose thought is also covered in this book.

The work of none of the Presocratics or the Sophists remains in its entirety. We have to rely on fragments preserved in later writers and reports about their thought.[3] Some of these reports were written by thinkers with their own agendas, who were implicitly or explicitly unsympathetic or even hostile to the Presocratics; others are the barest summaries of complex views, which often reveal a high degree of incomprehension. Unfortunately, distortion was the name of the game. While we owe an incalculable debt to Aristotle, his pupil Theophrastus, and their successors for preserving discussions of the Presocratics, it has now been established beyond the shadow of a doubt that they viewed their predecessors almost entirely through the lenses of their own philosophies. Here is a single, notorious instance. Aristotle believed that in order to gain an overall perspective on anything, one had to ask four questions about it: What is it made of? What is its origin? What is its purpose? What is its form or appearance? In Aristotelian language, answering the first question gives us the 'material cause' of a thing, then the 'efficient cause', the 'final cause', and the 'formal cause'. When he surveyed his earliest Presocratic predecessors he found them saying something—let us for the moment leave it as vague as possible—about certain material elements, such as water or fire. He found it impossible to resist the idea that they were talking about his 'material cause'; that they were talking about what things were made of. Look, then, at **T8** on pp. 12–13 in which Aristotle discusses Thales. It is clear that he is, however tentatively, claiming that Thales said that everything was made out of water. But is this the case? It is more likely that Thales said that everything started in water, or rests on water, or something like that: there are precedents for either idea in Egyptian or Near Eastern mythology.

Or here is another example. Aristotle has quite high praise for Anaxagoras, famously describing him at one point as 'like a sober man compared to his babbling predecessors' (*Metaphysics* 984[b]17–18), and elsewhere in the same book as 'quite up to date in his thinking' (989[b]6). But these words of praise are reserved for

---

[3] Hence the distinction in the translations that follow between F-texts (fragments) and T-texts (testimonia, or reports).

Anaxagoras only because Aristotle thought that Anaxagoras had intuited certain elements of his own theories. Instead of just talking about the 'material cause', as his predecessors had done, Aristotle thought that, in introducing mind as a motivating factor, Anaxagoras had also introduced an efficient cause, and so had made a considerable advance on his predecessors.

To be fair to Aristotle, he does not disguise the fact that he is presenting a partial picture of his predecessors. He announces his programme close to the beginning of *Metaphysics*: 'Let's take those who were engaged in the study of these matters before us and were concerned to speculate and seek after the truth. For it is clear that they too mention certain first principles and causes. The consideration of their work will also be of some help in our present enquiry, in the sense that either we will discover some other kind of cause or we will have more confidence in the four I have just mentioned' (983^b1–6). In other words, Aristotle makes no bones about the fact that he is studying his Presocratic predecessors only in order to shed light on his own theory of four causes.

Aristotle's pupil, Theophrastus, was even more important in the history of philosophy. The doxographers (the name scholars give to the writers who summarized and discussed the views of earlier thinkers) all depend ultimately on a largely lost book by Theophrastus, called *The Opinions of the Natural Scientists*.[4] Just occasionally, however, we can check what he said against the original; the results are not encouraging. We have not only his account of Plato's theory of the senses, but also Plato's original statements. It is clear that the degree of distortion is extreme.[5] We cannot have confidence that our ancient secondary sources have placed the ideas of their Presocratic predecessors within the right context in any single case. Of course, they might have done in a few cases, but we simply cannot be sure. And sometimes the possibility of distortion is plain to see. Not only is the Aristotelian bias of Theophrastus, as well as of Aristotle himself, obvious, but we can often detect Stoic or Christian bias in later doxographers. Then many of the doxographers were living hundreds

---

[4] This was demonstrated by H. Diels, in his monumental *Doxographi Graeci* (Berlin, 1879). However, it is also likely that there was a rudimentary pre-Platonic doxographic tradition: see Mansfeld, 'Aristotle, Plato, and the Preplatonic Doxography and Chronography', in [29].

[5] See Long [77].

of years after the thinkers covered in this volume (see the Timeline on pp. xliii–xlvi), and may not have had access to the original writings, but were relying on someone else's epitome.

Similar distortions have spoiled the record of the Sophists as well, due in this case not to Aristotle so much as to Plato. One of the avowed purposes of Plato's early dialogues was to defend the memory of his mentor, Socrates—this was an aim he shared with Xenophon and other Socratic writers. He did this by distinguishing him sharply from the Sophists, to the detriment of the latter, who appear as mercenary, and as unconcerned with either logical truth or psychological benefit. At the same time, Plato wanted to delineate the domain and methods of what he saw as philosophy, and to this end he felt impelled to disparage the work of those with rival educational claims—the orators, poets, and, above all, the Sophists. Xenophon succinctly displays the typical prejudice of the Socratics against the Sophists towards the end of his treatise *On Hunting*: 'What surprises me about the Sophists, as they are called, is that although most of them profess to educate young men in virtue, they actually do exactly the opposite. It is not just that we have never *seen* a man become good thanks to the Sophists of today; their writings are also not designed to improve people. Much of their writing is concerned with trivia, which can give young men vain enjoyment, but not virtue. To read it in the hope of learning something is a pointless waste of time; their treatises keep people from doing something useful and teach them things that are offensive. These are serious criticisms, but then the issue is serious; as regards the content of their treatises, my charge is that while they have gone to great lengths over style, they have eliminated the kind of sound views which educate the younger generation in virtue.'

Recovering the thought of the Sophists is also hampered by the fact that Aristotle clearly regarded few if any of them as serious thinkers who deserved his attention. This in turn meant that no doxographic tradition arose in the case of the Sophists as it did for the Presocratics. Apart from a very few original fragments, Plato is our chief source of information—and, as already remarked, he is not a reliable source.

The Presocratics as Scientists

The idea that these thinkers collectively brought something new into
the world, a scientific or proto-scientific attitude, a reliance on *logos*,
is too simple and broad a picture. It is in fact rather naïve to lump all
the Presocratics together as if they were somehow identical, although
it has been a tendency in the history of philosophy from Aristotle
onwards. Nevertheless, it is clear that not all the people standardly
classified as Presocratic philosophers fit comfortably into the Aristotelian mould. They range from shamans like Empedocles, through
mystics like Pythagoras and prophets like Heraclitus, to meta-
physicians such as Parmenides, philosophers such as Anaxagoras,
and proto-scientists like the Milesians and Atomists. To describe
Empedocles as a 'shaman' or Heraclitus as a 'prophet' is not to say
that they could not make valuable contributions towards scientific
or philosophical debate; but it is to say that their emphases and
experiences are not those of a complete scientist or philosopher. But
despite the variety of interests the Presocratics display, there is
something common to them all.

Starting with the broad picture, we should ask what is meant by
the claim that they invented philosophy and/or science. (Strictly,
one should distinguish between those like the Milesians who
brought something scientific into the world, and those like Parmenides or perhaps Heraclitus who reflected upon their predecessors'
scientific work and were therefore philosophers.) We need first an
example of the kind of cosmological work they were doing. Anaximenes of Miletus is typical of the earliest Milesian phase of Presocratic thought, and is fairly easy to summarize without undue
distortion.

Anaximenes said that the prime matter of the universe was air,
and that this could be condensed or rarefied into the various components of the universe. When rarefied it becomes hot and fiery and
forms not just fire itself, but also the fiery heavenly bodies; when
condensed it becomes cold and can be seen as water and ultimately
earth. These four elements form the concentric layers of the universe. Air is and always was in motion, and it was presumably this
motion which in some way initiated the process of condensation and
rarefaction. Of course, having thought up the twin processes of condensation and rarefaction, Anaximenes might just as well have said

that water or one of the other elements was the prime constituent of things, but he chose air because it is apparently all-pervading and can appear to be indefinite, and because we breathe it in and it causes life in us. Our soul is air. The earth and all the heavenly bodies are flat, he said, and float gently on the air like leaves.

So, were Anaximenes and his peers scientists? What does it take to be a scientist? Above all, in today's terms, it takes scientific reasoning—that is, adherence to the scientific method. Paraphrasing Aristotle, whose formulation of the scientific method is as good as any, and better than most, we can describe this as a method of both induction and deduction (or of resolution and composition, as the medieval schoolmen used to call them). The scientist (unless he is a follower of Karl Popper) starts with observation of an event; by a process of induction he reaches explanatory principles; from these principles, facts about the event in question and about related phenomena are then to be deduced. Of course, it is not that simple: it takes a lot of to-ing and fro-ing between observation and theory, refining and correcting both observations and hypotheses. But in this way the scientist has progressed from uncomprehending observation of an event to understanding why the event is as it is. From observation of the pretty spectrum of colours displayed on the wall, he has progressed to understanding that light is in fact composed of rays with different refractive properties.

In other words, scientific reasoning is a combination of forming testable hypotheses to account for observed phenomena (this may take imagination and model-making as well as logic), and of testing and re-testing these hypotheses by experimentation and logic. The resulting hypothesis should explain the observed phenomena in as simple a way as possible, should allow one to predict the behaviour of related phenomena, and should cohere with the body of accepted scientific theories and doctrines. Throughout, everything should be quantifiable, measurable, and testable as far as is possible within the limitations of the technology currently available.

There is absolutely no indication that the Presocratics were scientists in this sense. There is little sign that they undertook experimentation at all; the hypotheses they came up with about the world's formation and constitution were not testable by scientific means; where observation and theory clashed, they invariably preferred theory to observation. They were, in short, dogmatists, not experimental scientists. Of course, it is not entirely fair to criticize the Presocratics for lack of experimentation; after all, a great deal of what interested them was not capable of empirical testing in their day; but that in itself helps to show that they should not be described as scientists in the modern sense of the word.

Even the more scientific relatives of the Presocratics, the Hippocratic doctors,[6] who started working some time in the latter half of the fifth century, tended to use experiment and observation not to test one of their own theories, but either to corroborate a theory or to refute an opponent's theory; also, the subject of their few experiments is rarely the thing itself, the part of the body they are concerned with, but something outside the body, which is supposed to have the same properties as the thing itself inside the body. In other words, simile and analogical thinking rule, as when Empedocles compares human breathing to the action of a device for gathering liquid or when Anaximenes compares lightning to the phosphoresence of water at night cleaved by an oar.

Here are two famous and typical early examples of experimentation. At *On Celestial Phenomena* 358^b-359^a Aristotle tries to support his view that sea water is a mixture of ingredients by describing an experiment in which a wax bottle is let down into sea water; when it is recovered, fresh water is found in it, and Aristotle concludes that the fresh water was percolated through the wax. From this we can conclude either that he never did the experiment himself, but was relying on hearsay, or that the water in the jar came about through condensation; in either case, he was way off the mark.

Again, at *Airs, Waters, Places* 18, preserved in the corpus of works attributed to Hippocrates, the author wants to demonstrate that freezing causes the lightest and finest parts of water to dry up and disappear. He left a bowl of water outside to freeze; when it was thawed again afterwards, he claimed, there was less water than there was originally. From this we can conclude that either some of the water evaporated or was drunk by animals, or he applied heat to thaw the ice and so boiled some away.

---

[6] On the Hippocratics in general, see the ever-increasing series of Loeb texts, with facing English translation, and also: G. E. R. Lloyd (ed.), *Hippocratic Writings* (Harmondsworth: Penguin, 1978); J. Longrigg, *Greek Rational Medicine: Philosophy and Medicine from Alcmaeon to the Alexandrians* (London: Routledge, 1993); E. D. Phillips, *Greek Medicine* (London: Thames and Hudson, 1973).

What evidence do scholars have for their view that the Presocratics, or some of them, were scientists? Here we come to what we may call 'scientific attitudes', as distinct from scientific reasoning or method. A short list of scientific attitudes would consist of the following:

1. The optimistic assumption that the world and its components are comprehensible; this is what Einstein was getting at when he said, 'God may be subtle, but he is not malicious.'

2. The assumption that the human rational mind is the correct tool for understanding the world.

3. Adherence to a particular set of approaches to problem-solving; this involves, for instance, analysing problems into their component parts and then dealing separately with those parts, and starting with simple problems before tackling more complex ones.

4. Tempered curiosity: although curiosity about the world is essential for the scientist, it must not be allowed to lead the investigator into hasty hypotheses or extravagant leaps of the imagination, nor be governed by prejudice in any form.

5. A love of and facility with abstract concepts.

This is where the Presocratics fit in. Some or all of them display at least some of these attitudes. It would, of course, be unreasonable to expect them to be fully fledged scientists in the modern sense of the word but perhaps their adherence to—even invention of—at least some of these scientific attitudes is enough to justify our calling them at least proto-scientists. They tend to fall at the hurdle of tempered curiosity—that is, they tend to rush into what modern scientists would undoubtedly call wild and even visionary speculation—but they were the first to make and explore the consequences of the assumption which is absolutely crucial to the development of science, that the human rational mind is the correct tool for understanding the world. They were reductionists—that is, they formed general hypotheses in an attempt to explain as many things as possible by means of as few hypotheses as possible—and in their theorizing they relied on natural phenomena like air, rather than supernatural phenomena like the traditional Greek gods and goddesses. However, this broad picture must immediately be qualified by the reminder that the Presocratics (some more than others) retained a strong streak of what can only be called mystical thought.

Given the current opposition between reason and irrationality, it is one of the ironies of history that science developed out of partly irrational roots. The kind of cosmology and cosmogony that the Ionians (the three Milesians and Xenophanes) were led to construct with the help of their scientific attitudes then came to be criticized by Parmenides and (if some scholars are right) by Heraclitus, before being reinstated ingeniously by the 'Neo-Ionians' who followed the Eleatics. But in all its phases Presocratic thought was holistic: it was an attempt to give a systematic account of the whole known universe and all its major features.

The Presocratics and their Predecessors

Can it really be said that the Presocratics were the first to assume that the human rational mind is the correct tool for understanding the world? Did people before the Presocratics not think, not use their brains? In what sense did the predecessors of the Presocratics not have or make use of *logos*?

In the history of ideas it is always specious to divide things into a before and an after. It is not the case that with the advent of Thales, or whoever the first true Presocratic philosopher was, a prior world-view suddenly came to an end and evaporated to wherever such views go for an after-life. There is also the question of self-awareness. How would Thales have characterized his own work? It is extremely unlikely that he would have called himself a philosopher or a scientist. It is not clear, then, that he had the means to distinguish what he was doing from what his predecessors were doing. In any case, what follow are the grossest generalizations.

It is plausible to say that every cave and mountain top was sacred; any snake could be a dead relative or a guardian spirit, or bird a manifestation of deity; every stream, river, copse, and settlement had its presiding deity or deities; even individual trees and rocks could be sacred. Meteorological and other large-scale natural phenomena were particularly awesome and divine. While certain places were especially holy (so that cults and eventually shrines and temples grew up there), essentially the whole world was shot through with the sacred, in the form of a plethora of deities, who ruled one's life and required magical rites of propitiation and communication.

This polytheism did in time lead to a degree of systematization. The prime impulse towards such systematization is that, if the divine governs the whole of life, then it must especially govern the special aspects of life. In a largely peasant society like Greece, these are the significant moments of human life, and the main phases and aspects of the agricultural round. In this way, rather than there being a mere plethora of gods, each equal to any other in its particular domain, certain gods start to rise in importance above others, and the latter gods become demoted as local gods, demigods, nymphs, and so on. By and large it may be true to say that the distinction arose between the chief gods being those of natural phenomena which cannot be pinned down to just one spot and the lesser gods being those which belonged to particular localities. However, once a particular god has become prominent, he tends to absorb some of the lesser gods; so we find that Poseidon, for instance, in his capacity as god of the sea, is surrounded by sea-nymphs, who would probably have originally been local deities.

But even though there was now a distinction between prominent gods and lesser gods, there was still an incredible local variation in the number of major deities, their natures, forms, functions, titles, and provinces. The next stage of the process is probably achieved by conquest. As one settlement gains prominence over its neighbours, so its chief deity or deities gain prominence over theirs. The dozen or so major Greek gods—Zeus and his extended family—emerged as a result of this lengthy historical process of simplification due to prominence and conquest. By the time of the epic poet Homer (around 750 BCE), it makes considerable sense to speak of a panhellenic pantheon, consisting of the familiar Olympian deities and their lesser associates, all of whom are by now more or less fully anthropomorphized.

Anthropomorphism is the outstanding characteristic of Homeric religion and hence of Greek religion as a whole. Nor was it a half-hearted anthropomorphism. Not only did the gods have family trees, they also had family squabbles. Being pictured as super-humans, they could not be omnipresent or omniscient. We even hear of the gods washing, walking, eating, drinking, being wounded, and making love. The gods in this respect are just many times more powerful than petty humans; the only utterly irreconcilable gulf between the two species, which makes Homer's *Iliad* a tragic poem, is that the gods are immortal.[7] But for Homer the gods did not have laws, only preferences.

In order to see most clearly how this world-view differs from the one the Presocratics helped to foster, we should look briefly at the work of the epic poet Hesiod (around 700 BCE).[8] In his poem *Theogony* Hesiod exemplifies a spirit of rationalization; he inherited the mass of greater and lesser deities and tried to make some sense of it all. We meet a huge number of individual deities (let alone all the pluralities such as the nymphs), but by the use of family trees, Hesiod attempts to order the unstructured world of the gods. A typical branch of the genealogy is that Night gives birth to Death and Sleep and Dreams; the genealogical model allows Hesiod to group deities and concepts into comprehensible systems.

If we take Hesiod to represent the summit of rationalization as far as the old order is concerned, the main point to notice about him is that he remains an unquestioning pluralist. The spirit of rationalization in him has not made the transition to reductionism; he has not made the leap from *mythos* to *logos*, because he still fully accepts the mythic framework. Not only does he not, of course, display any sign of scientific reasoning, but he scarcely displays any scientific attitudes either. The closest he gets is a concern with abstract concepts, even though they are still disguised as deities.

Just as importantly, Hesiod's divinities are still closely related to cult. That is, they are the kinds of deities with whom an individual human being might strike up a relationship, and whom he or she might hope to sway by means of prayer or sacrifice. Now, the Presocratics were not afraid of talking about gods, but what they tended to divinize was some natural principle or process. Anaximenes, for instance, probably called air divine. Air is an impersonal natural phenomenon, which cannot be affected by sacrifice. Whereas the Greek gods were fickle, and were invoked precisely to account for disturbances in the natural order of things, the Presocratic gods manifest themselves in the operation, not the disturbance, of intelligible law.

---

[7] See J. Griffin, *Homer on Life and Death* (Oxford: Oxford University Press, 1980). Good translations of the Homeric poems include those by Robert Fitzgerald, Robert Fagles, and Richmond Lattimore.

[8] The best translation of Hesiod's surviving poems is by M. L. West (Oxford: Oxford University Press, 1988).

Of course, it was not the case that before the Presocratics Greece was inhabited by 'non-thinking savages leading their lives in accordance with random impulses and mystical associations', as one writer has parodied the fallacy of mythical thinking.[9] Anthropologists have shown time and again that so-called primitive people—people governed by *mythos* rather than *logos*—do think systematically; it is just that they use different systems from the ones with which we are familiar. They have different ideas about what constitutes cause and effect, and about the nature of reality; they think more metaphorically and analogically, more imaginatively and loosely.

But it is enough that there is some kind of difference. The point is that the Presocratics, both in their scientific and in their philosophical modes, ushered in the kind of system with which we are still involved, or perhaps burdened. In other words, the Presocratic revolution was a genuine revolution—a paradigm shift of the first importance. One could say that before the Presocratics the worldview was a kind of projection. All one's awe and fears are projected outwards. It is not that I, an individual human being, am feeling awe of my own accord: it is a deity of some kind out there who is making me feel it. Then along came the Presocratics and said, 'No, there is order in the world. And it is precisely because it is ordered that it can be comprehended by the human mind.' The Sophists picked up on this emphasis on the importance of human beings, and made their message: 'I do it; I can do it.' Then a short while later along came Socrates and made philosophy self-reflective. Instead of just saying, for instance, in the field of ethics, that such-and-such an action is good, he asked, 'What is the good?' Or in science, instead of a concern with the components of the world he asked how we get to know anything about the world.

It is this lack of self-reflection that makes the Presocratic answers (but not their questions) quickly outmoded and liable to criticism; without this self-reflection—that is, without the ability to form a coherent method for their studies, which is the start of true philosophy, and which Parmenides tried to urge upon them—their enquiries were doomed to failure. And so, with Socrates, philosophy had to begin all over again, and to begin with the search for what can

---

[9] Kirk [37], p. 280.

be known, since only that can provide a firm basis for the increase of knowledge.

The Presocratic Revolution and the Sophists

To summarize a complex story in a few words, we can now see that the Presocratics differ both from the preceding world-view and from fully fledged scientism. They differ from their predecessors not so much in the kinds of questions they asked (above all, 'What is the nature of reality?'), but in the kinds of answers they gave—in not adhering to the traditional framework, in assigning the functions of the gods to natural phenomena, in using what we can recognize as logic to reason things through coherently, in forming general philosophical hypotheses and embracing reductionism rather than pluralism, and in an unrestricted, even iconoclastic spirit of enquiry. For the first time they asked and answered searching questions about the distant past of the universe and all its parts. They differ from hard-line scientism in lacking scientific method altogether, and in lacking some scientific attitudes, in being too visionary. They were interested in constructing elegant systems, not verifiable systems. Both Plato (*Theaetetus* 155d) and Aristotle (*Metaphysics* 982^b) rightly held that the springboard for philosophy is a sense of wonder or puzzlement, the irritating need to ask 'Why?'; there can be no doubt that the Presocratics were philosophers in this sense.

In contrast to the list of distinguishing marks that I have just given, it is sometimes claimed that what distinguishes the Presocratics from their predecessors is that they based their conclusions on observation and rational argumentation. This is only partly true. Observation is not a neutral exercise, and so the assessment of results obtained from observation is liable to theoretical prejudice. There is no reason to think that Hesiod and his peers did not use observation, but the way they described what they saw differed from the way the Presocratics expressed their conclusions. As for the idea that the Presocratics were the first to use rational argumentation—to present their theories 'as the conclusions of arguments, as reasoned propositions for reasonable men to contemplate and debate'[10]—all our evidence suggests that this was scarcely true of anyone before

[10] Barnes [15], i. 5.

Parmenides, and so it cannot be a differentiating mark of the Pre-socratics as a whole.

An important chapter in the history of science was initiated or furthered by the anonymous authors of the medical treatises that have come down to us under the name of Hippocrates of Cos. Though dating these treatises is a hazardous business, some of those which we can be reasonably certain were written towards the end of the fifth or beginning of the fourth centuries show signs of an appropriate reaction against some aspects of Presocratic thought. In particular, they reacted against the dogmatism of the Presocratics—and they were right to do so, because medicine must above all else be an empirical science. So, for instance, *On Ancient Medicine* criticizes those who made use of 'arbitrary postulates', such as that everything is made up of hot, cold, wet, and dry—a typical Presocratic theory.[11] In chapter 20 the author of this treatise even singles Empedocles out for criticism: the views of such people are as little relevant to medi-cine as they are to painting, he says. On the other hand, there are also indubitable signs of Hippocratic borrowing from the Presocratics: *On the Art* uses Presocratic terminology to express his scepticism about the evidence of the senses; Empedocles' four-element theory was immensely influential in medicine, where it manifested as the famous four-humour theory (e.g. in *On the Nature of Man*); *On the Sacred Disease* stresses the natural rather than supernatural causes of epilepsy; the first part of *On Fleshes* applies a Presocratic kind of explanation to the origin of parts of the body.

By the end of the Presocratic era, their revolution was incomplete, but well started. It did eventually succeed, of course, and we are its heirs. Its success is the chief reason why it is so difficult to under-stand quite what was going on at the time: we have to try to project ourselves back to a time when for most people rationality was an untrained faculty, rather than the sharp and ubiquitous tool it is today. This kind of revolution takes centuries. Even if the Pre-socratic revolution did succeed eventually, there is good evidence

---

[11] However, it is not perfectly clear that the author of *On Ancient Medicine* is himself free from such postulates. See, for instance, R. A. H. Waterfield, 'The Pathology of Ps.-Hippocrates, *On Ancient Medicine*', in L. Ayres (ed.), *The Passionate Intellect* (New Brunswick, NJ: Transaction Publishers, 1995); R. J. Hankinson, 'Doing Without Hypotheses: The Nature of *Ancient Medicine*', in J. A. López Férez (ed.), *Tratados Hippocráticos: Actas del VII Colloque Internationale Hippocratique* (Madrid, 1992); and works [86]–[88] by G. E. R. Lloyd in the Select Bibliography.

that it was not successful immediately. It was an isolated and specialist phenomenon, of interest only to a few intellectuals. After all,
Greece had only become a literate society a century or so before
Thales, and even in the time of Socrates books were still a rare
phenomenon.[12] Certainly by the time of the Athenian comic poet
Aristophanes, in the last quarter of the fifth century, news had fil-
tered through to the man on the street; otherwise Aristophanes'
scathing comic comments on the new intellectuals would not have
been popular. But news filtering through and being met with
incomprehension does not constitute a successful revolution. Significantly, intellectuals were described as *deinoi*—a word which
simultaneously means both 'clever' and 'terrifying'.

Over the next few centuries, however, we find an increasing number of intellectuals, people whose rational faculties were trained and
exercised, but there was still a solid substrate of superstition in the
overwhelming majority of the population. Nevertheless, in Rome
school education became far more intellectual than the Greek
schools on which they were modelled ever were, and there were in
time enough intellectuals for the apotheosis of rationality to become
redundant. The rational faculty and reasoned argument were now
accepted weapons in the human arsenal. New religions arose (Mith-
raism and Christianity) which were based instead on emotion,
because that was what was now lacking. One of our main sources for
the fragments and opinions of the Presocratics are the writings of
the Christian apologists such as Hippolytus: these early Christian
writers rightly saw the Greek philosophers as their religious rivals.
Emotion was now exalted and rationality, boosted in due course of
time by the Renaissance and the European Enlightenment, could
become the ordinary working tool it now is for us, and the honed tool
of science and logic.

The first heirs of the Presocratics were the Sophists, who lived
and travelled around the Mediterranean, selling their skills, throughout the second half of the fifth century. Like the Presocratics, they
came from all over the Greek world, but (as far as we can tell

---

[12] Is it a coincidence that the development of science and philosophy accompanied
the rise of literacy? Probably not: there is a connection between literacy and the development of abstract thinking. Literacy is not essential for abstract thinking, but it helps;
it speeds up the process of its development, and it allows for leisurely reflection on texts
and ideas.

from our surviving Athenocentric evidence) the focus of their activities was Athens. Protagoras came from Abdera in northern Greece (also the birthplace of Democritus), Gorgias from Leontini in Sicily; Hippias was a native of Elis, near Olympia in the Peloponnese, but, like Gorgias, visited Athens as part of an official delegation; Prodicus came from the island of Ceos, while the brothers Euthydemus and Dionysodorus came from the island of Chios; Thrasymachus came from Chalcedon, opposite Byzantium on the Asian side of the Bosporus. Of the Sophists represented in this book whose names we know, only two were natives of Athens: Callicles (see 'Anonymous and Miscellaneous Texts') and Antiphon.

It might seem puzzling to say that the Sophists were the heirs of the Presocratics, since at first glance the two groups seem to be divided, not united, by their interests. Few of the Sophists (at least, as far as we can now tell from the sparse available evidence) made any, or any significant advances in scientific matters, let alone metaphysics; if one or two of the Presocratics touched on the nature of humans and their institutions, this was still not their focus, and was a ramification of or deduction from their central interests. The Sophists were more interested in language, in all aspects of *logos*, than they were in the nature and origin of the world. However, the Sophists were the immediate heirs of the Presocratic scientific revolution in the sense that, once the Presocratics had made the world at least potentially comprehensible to the human mind, a humanist or anthropocentric emphasis on the importance of human beings was inevitable. The Sophists were the first seriously to raise questions in moral, social, and political philosophy. And, interestingly, this narrower focus of theirs means that their work is more alive to us today than that of the Presocratics, because whereas science has left the speculative answers of the Presocratics far behind, we still debate the kinds of questions in which the Sophists were interested.

Apart from the intellectual background, there were also social factors that helped to give rise to the Sophists. There was an intense mood of optimism in fifth-century Greece, fuelled no doubt by their almost miraculous defeat of the two Persian invasions early in the century; although it would be a vast oversimplification to say that victory over the Persians caused this mood, it was one among a number of factors, the most important of which was technological progress, which tended in the direction of stressing human achievement, rather than human dependence on the gods. It is obvious how Presocratic influence must have played a part in this, and several of the Sophists were agnostics or atheists. Under the influence of this trend, writers as diverse as Sophocles and Thucydides began to hymn humankind. In the mood in which Sophocles wrote the famous choral ode of *Antigone* 332–75, celebrating humanity's achievements, he would instantly have recognized Shakespeare's 'What a piece of work is man!' (*Hamlet* Act 2, scene 2), and ignored its depressive conclusion.

At the same time, in Athens especially, there was far more scope than earlier for an ambitious young man to gain enormous power. Athens was no longer just one parochial small town among many others, but was the ruler of an international federation which fell short in name only of being an Athenian empire. It was hard for the old skills to cope with the new situation. And the finishing touches of Athenian democracy, a noble experiment in truly direct and participatory democracy, gave immense value to the power to speak, to persuade crowds of a point of view. Rhetoric was then, as it is now, a tool of the right to free speech and to a fair trial. It is no wonder that the peripatetic Sophists, who were often teachers of rhetoric and were always teachers of skills useful to gaining civic prominence, were frequent visitors to Athens, where they became an integral part of Pericles' programme of cultural reform. And in addition, the increasing wealth of Athens created a leisured class with the time and inclination to take education more seriously. Standard Greek education was woefully inadequate, focusing on no more than the three Rs and a thorough knowledge of Homer (taught by a *grammatistēs*), knowledge of some lyric poetry and the ability to play a musical instrument (taught by a *kitharistēs*), and sport (taught by a *paidotribēs*). One's education was likely to be complete by one's early teens, and was so little thought of that much of it was in the hands of slaves. What the Sophists offered (until this function was partially taken over in the fourth century by institutions such as Plato's Academy) was a wide range of further educational topics, from martial arts to mathematics, designed to appeal to rich young men. And Protagoras, at any rate, was apparently committed to education not just as a means of making himself rich, if we can believe that when he drew up the constitution of the new colony of Thurii he recommended that every citizen should be taught to read and write at the state's expense. The Sophists delivered public lectures, but their main educational forum was the seminar class of paying private pupils, as depicted in Plato's *Protagoras*. Common teaching methods included the learning of specimen speeches and of antilogical commonplaces, arguing for and against certain forensic and legal topics. They also made themselves available to answer questions, often on an enormous range of subjects. They wrote books, but one gets the impression that where the written word was the main medium for the Presocratics, the spoken word was more important for the Sophists.

There is a recognizable single phenomenon, which deserves to be called the Sophistic movement, but (as we have also found in the case of the Presocratics) it is hard to pin it down, because of the variety of thinkers and their specific interests. Protagoras was a relativist and moderate sceptic who taught rhetoric and supported democratic Athens; Gorgias wrote rhetoric in the grand, poetic style, but also wrote a treatise *On What Is Not*, which was perhaps a parody of Eleatic reasoning; Prodicus was a moral conservative who helped establish a Greek dictionary by distinguishing near synonyms and wrote an anthropological account of the origin of religion; Hippias was a polymath who claimed to be able to answer any question on any subject; and so on. The social context outlined in the last paragraph is actually the best route into understanding the movement as a single phenomenon. There was a need for a new morality, for political theory, for the ability to speak persuasively, and for an education that both went further than the current one, and had the ability to explore some topics in depth; there was a mood of optimism and a dissatisfaction with the vast macrocosmic and transcendental theories of the Presocratics, and a tendency to question the fundamentals of society, so that they were either jettisoned or defended. The word 'Sophist' originally (before Plato and then Aristotle made it a term of opprobrium[13]) had pretty much the same

---

[13] The word was occasionally used pejoratively before Plato, but it was his consistent sneering that established the word as a term of abuse. Plato's reasons for disparaging the Sophists were partly because, as an aristocrat, he was snobbish about their taking money for education, and partly because he thought they reasoned poorly and were not concerned about their students' moral well-being. Above all, though, he wanted to distinguish Socrates from the Sophists. Aristotle's reasons largely focused on their poor logic and superficial argumentation.

implications as our 'teacher': Sophists were, as the name implies, clever, well-educated men (not surprisingly for ancient Greece, there were no female Sophists), who were professionals prepared, for a fee, to impart their skills to others. Even poets could be called 'Sophists', and it is very likely that the Presocratics would have been so described, since the words *philosophos* ('philosopher') and *physikos* ('natural scientist') only became popular in the fourth century. The particular Sophists we are concerned with were itinerant teachers, serving Athens above all, but known to have visited other communities on the Greek mainland and elsewhere (e.g. the Greek communities in Sicily). A professional interest in rhetoric and in education are common features; the sphere of their professional expertise was *logos*, in one or more of the meanings given at the start of this Introduction. But even where their work on *logos* is concerned, there are considerable individual variations of interest.[14]

Why Study the First Philosophers?

Cicero famously said that it was Socrates who called philosophy down to earth from the heavens (*Tusculan Disputations* 5.4.10), but this is too much of a generalization. Not only did a number of the Presocratics comment on human institutions such as religion and politics, and on human psychology, but this was the main thrust of the work of the Sophists. It was the Sophists, then, and not Socrates, who transformed Presocratic reductionism into a kind of humanism, and who earthed Presocratic speculation. But it was Socrates who wiped the slate clean and regenerated philosophy. Few scientists nowadays would recognize the Presocratics as their forefathers, unless they were feeling in a particularly generous mood; few philosophers would allow more than a historical interest to much of the work, and even more of the conclusions, of either the Presocratics or the Sophists. But nearly all philosophers acknowledge Socrates as their ancestor.

However, this is not to say that studying these first philosophers is of merely historical interest. Nor is it just that they are representa-

---

[14] See the summary by E. Schiappa, *Protagoras and Logos: A Study in Greek Philosophy and Rhetoric* (Columbia: University of South Carolina Press, 1991), 81.

tives of a crucial chapter in the evolution of Western thought, and that it is always instructive to look back to where we have come from, both as individuals and as social and intellectual creatures. It is also that for some reason—perhaps because they were the *first*—they can teach us something about the whole nature of human intellectual endeavour.

There is a curious story embedded in the middle of one of Plutarch's many excellent essays (*On the Decline of Oracles* 419b–d). Plutarch was a Greek writer working at the end of the first century CE, and he sets this story somewhat earlier in the century, during the reign of Tiberius in Rome. It concerns the god Pan, who was a nature god in charge of flocks and fertility. He is a lusty, wayward, randy individual. No doubt the story is open to a number of interpretations, but I take Pan's role in it to encapsulate something of the disorderly pluralism of the old gods. Since Pan had the ability to drive people out of their wits—to induce 'panic' in them—he is also an archetype of irrationality. The story goes that a ship under an Egyptian helmsman was becalmed off the island of Paxoi, which lies off the western coast of Greece, just south of Corfu. As they were drifting there, a supernatural voice was suddenly heard from the island, calling the name of the helmsman: 'Thamous! Thamous!' The helmsman did not reply at first, but the third time the voice called his name, he said, 'Here I am. What do you want?' The voice replied, 'When you reach the sea off Palodes'—a place on Paxoi, presumably—'you are to call out, "Great Pan is dead!"' The boat drifted on until they reached Palodes. Thamous did as he had been instructed, but before he had even finished making the announcement—'Great Pan is dead!'—a loud cry of lamentation and bewilderment broke out from all around them, as if many voices were all crying out at once.

This is what Schiller was getting at: the gods have gone. However, while it is true that in broad terms the Presocratics did usher in a revolution, this simple picture needs some important qualifications, which will help to put the Presocratic revolution into perspective, and to explain what they can teach us about human intellectual endeavour in general. In linear time, we build up a simple story of evolution and change, of paradigm shifts, loss of the past—of one thing being replaced by another, in this case of *mythos* being replaced by *logos*. But is this not too simplistic? What, after all, is a myth? The first point to notice is that recent studies have shown that this is the way to ask the question. Rather than asking, 'What is myth?', one can only ask, 'What is *a* myth?', because there are so many different kinds of myths, and so many different kinds of cultures in which they have functioned.

The question is hard to answer, and it is safest to go for a minimalist position, rather than immediately taking on board some high-flown theory. Minimally, then, a myth is a traditional tale. This is a good starting-point, because it reminds us that a myth is a story, and that myths evolve within traditional, often pre-literate societies. Within such societies, a myth also has clear functional relevance to some important aspect of life. But this function is not just to help the society to perpetuate itself, as one school of thought has it; it is to help explain and form consensus reality for that community, and so to help make an individual's experience of life meaningful.

It is true that from the idea that myth explains reality it does not follow that every attempt to explain reality is a myth, but nevertheless it is true that all systems of belief evolve to elucidate the order of things and to make sense of the world. In this sense, science is just as much a myth as anything else; it is a framework or model designed to explain and form reality for those people who accept it—that is, for those people who voluntarily become members of that society—and for only as long as there are enough people to accept it. If this is so, then so far from banishing gods, science has merely been the matrix for a new generation of scientific gods, children of the old gods.[15] One person's *mythos*, then, is another person's *logos*. In introducing one of the eschatological myths with which he ends a few of his dialogues, Plato has Socrates say exactly that. He says, 'I want to tell you a story. You may think it's a *mythos*, but to me it's a *logos*' (*Gorgias* 523a).

A related point is that no replacement is ever perfect, so that *logos* can never entirely replace *mythos*. The world we have made for ourselves is not entirely rational. However much scientism might want to, it does not rule the world, only a little dusty corner of it. However

---

[15]   And the converse is also true: one could also say that *mythos* is just another kind of *logos*. The logic of myth is not Aristotelian logic, but it does follow a peculiar rationale of its own. To repeat: it is important not to fall into the trap of thinking that pre-literate societies were irrational societies.

much we now rely on rationality in our day-to-day lives, it cannot entirely repress the old gods. In every state, however totalitarian, there is always an underground. There is nothing rational about religious faith, which St Paul expressly defined as 'the substance of things hoped for, the evidence of things not seen' (Hebrews 11: 1); there is nothing rational about being overtaken by joy at some scenery or a poem or painting; on the dark side, there is nothing rational about imprisoning a fellow human being within a wall of truck tyres and setting light to him, just because he belongs to another tribe. The old gods of unreason are still there, below the surface, waiting to emerge in horrible ways if they are not allowed to do so in an orderly way.

So we can characterize the Presocratic revolution as a shift from *mythos* to *logos*, if we like, but these terms need using with caution, because there is more overlap between the two domains than might appear at first sight. Although it is uncomfortable to admit it, and many scientists especially try to brush it under the carpet, each of us is a bundle of rational and irrational impulses, and the attempt to divorce the two is as doomed to failure as the attempt to divorce science from mysticism in the Presocratics. In this sense the Presocratic combination of vision and logic is a precise model for two strands of future development in human intellectual endeavour, which should not perhaps have been allowed to separate from each other as far as they sometimes have. Or rather, the attempt to separate them is ultimately unreal, a violation which leads to abominations such as the rape of the planet and the dehumanizing loss of imagination. It is certainly not clear that Schiller was correct in claiming that the *logos* that is with us today is entirely de-souled. And perhaps it is precisely the fact that it has 'soul' that will lead, in some unexpected way, with the help of some modern equivalents to the Presocratics, to the next paradigm shift—not back to the old gods, but to yet another generation of gods. As Homer well knew, the gods in some disguise or other never die.

SELECT BIBLIOGRAPHY

This is a general bibliography; particular bibliographies relevant to each thinker are to be found at the end of the section dedicated to that thinker. In both bibliographies, I have listed both the best and the most recent books, but I have been more selective where articles from academic journals are concerned, while maintaining the purpose of providing the reader with a reasonable spread of views. I mention only those articles which are or are likely to become canonical (or at least which have not been superseded), those whose interpretative thrust is clearly expressed, and those whose focus is wider than, say, the attempt to establish the text of a particular testimonium or fragment, and which are therefore more likely to be of interest to the readers of this volume. There is a fairly large output of articles every year, and any more thorough listing would soon be out of date.

Texts

[1] H. Diels, *Die Fragmente der Vorsokratiker*, 3 vols., ed. W. Kranz, 6th edn. (Zurich: Weidmann, 1951–2).

[2] G. S. Kirk, J. E. Raven, and M. Schofield, *The Presocratic Philosophers*, 2nd edn. (Cambridge: Cambridge University Press, 1983).

[3] M. Untersteiner, *Sofisti: Testimonianze e frammenti*, 4 vols. (Florence: Nuova Italia, 1961–2).

[4] M. R. Wright, *The Presocratics* (Bristol: Bristol Classical Press, 1985).

Translations

[5] J. Barnes, *Early Greek Philosophy* (Harmondsworth: Penguin, 1987).

[6] P. K. Curd and R. D. McKirahan, *A Presocratics Reader* (Indianapolis: Hackett, 1996).

[7] M. Gagarin and P. Woodruff (eds.), *Early Greek Political Thought from Homer to the Sophists* (Cambridge: Cambridge University Press, 1995).

[8] R. K. Sprague (ed.), *The Older Sophists* (Columbia: University of South Carolina Press, 1972).

[9] P. Wheelwright, *The Presocratics* (New York: Macmillan, 1966).

General Histories of Early Greek Philosophy

[10] W. K. C. Guthrie, *A History of Greek Philosophy*, vol. i: *The Earlier Presocratics and the Pythagoreans* (Cambridge: Cambridge University Press, 1962); vol. ii: *The Presocratic Tradition from Parmenides to Democritus* (Cambridge: Cambridge University Press, 1965); vol. iii: *The Sophists and Socrates* (Cambridge: Cambridge University Press, 1969).

[11] T. H. Irwin, *Classical Thought* (Oxford: Oxford University Press, 1989).

[12] R. D. McKirahan, *Philosophy before Socrates* (Indianapolis: Hackett, 1994).

[13] J. M. Robinson, *An Introduction to Early Greek Philosophy* (Boston: Houghton Mifflin, 1968).

[14] C. C. W. Taylor (ed.), *Routledge History of Philosophy*, vol. i: *From the Beginning to Plato* (London: Routledge, 1997).

General Books on the Presocratics

[15] J. Barnes, *The Presocratic Philosophers*, 2 vols. (London: Routledge & Kegan Paul, 1979; single paperback vol., 1982).

[16] P. K. Curd, *The Legacy of Parmenides: Eleatic Monism and Later Presocratic Thought* (Princeton: Princeton University Press, 1998).

[17] D. J. Furley, *The Greek Cosmologists*, vol. i: *The Formation of the Atomic Theory and Its Earliest Critics* (Cambridge: Cambridge University Press, 1987).

[18] E. Hussey, *The Presocratics* (London: Duckworth, 1972).

[19] A. A. Long (ed.), *The Cambridge Companion to Early Greek Philosophy* (Cambridge: Cambridge University Press, 1999).

[20] M. C. Stokes, *One and Many in Presocratic Philosophy* (Washington: Center for Hellenic Studies, 1971).

Collections of Articles

[21] J. P. Anton and G. L. Kustas (eds.), *Essays in Ancient Greek Philosophy* (Albany: State University of New York Press, 1971).

[22] J. P. Anton and A. Preus (eds.), *Essays in Ancient Greek Philosophy*, vol. ii (Albany: State University of New York Press, 1983).

[23] K. J. Boudouris (ed.), *The Sophistic Movement* (Athens: Athenian Library of Philosophy, 1982).

[24] —— (ed.), *Ionian Philosophy* (Athens: International Center for Greek Philosophy and Culture, 1989).

[25] D. J. Furley, *Cosmic Problems* (Cambridge: Cambridge University Press, 1989).

[26] D. J. Furley and R. E. Allen (eds.), *Studies in Presocratic Philosophy*, 2 vols. (London: Routledge & Kegan Paul, 1970, 1975).

[27] G. B. Kerferd (ed.), *The Sophists and their Legacy* (Wiesbaden: Steiner, 1981).

[28] E. N. Lee *et al.* (eds.), *Exegesis and Argument: Studies in Greek Philosophy Presented to Gregory Vlastos* (Assen: Van Gorcum 1973 = *Phronesis*, suppl. vol. 1).

[29] J. Mansfeld, *Studies in the Historiography of Greek Philosophy* (Assen: Van Gorcum, 1990).

[30] A. P. D. Mourelatos (ed.), *The Pre-Socratics: A Collection of Critical Essays* (New York: Doubleday, 1974).

[31] K. Robb (ed.), *Language and Thought in Early Greek Philosophy* (La Salle, Ill.: Monist Library of Philosophy, 1983).

[32] R. A. Shiner and J. King-Farlow (eds.), *New Essays on Plato and the Presocratics* (*Canadian Journal of Philosophy* (Guelph), suppl. vol. 2, 1976).

[33] G. Vlastos, *Studies in Ancient Greek Philosophy*, vol. i: *The Presocratics* (Princeton: Princeton University Press, 1995).

Greek Religion and Myths

[34] W. Burkert, *Greek Religion* (Oxford: Basil Blackwell, 1985).

[35] P. E. Easterling and J. V. Muir (eds.), *Greek Religion and Society* (Cambridge: Cambridge University Press, 1985).

[36] G. S. Kirk, *Myth: Its Meaning and Functions in Ancient and Other Cultures* (Cambridge: Cambridge University Press, 1970).

[37] —— *The Nature of Greek Myths* (Harmondsworth: Penguin, 1974).

[38] M. P. Nilsson, *A History of Greek Religion*, 2nd edn. (London: Oxford University Press, 1949).

[39] R. C. T. Parker, 'Greek Religion', in J. Boardman *et al.* (eds.), *The Oxford History of the Classical World* (Oxford: Oxford University Press, 1986), 254–74.

[40] S. Price, *Religions of the Ancient Greeks* (Cambridge: Cambridge University Press, 1999).

The Predecessors of the Presocratics

[41] F. M. Cornford, *Principium Sapientiae: A Study of the Origins of Greek Philosophical Thought* (Cambridge: Cambridge University Press, 1952).

[42] A. Finkelberg, 'On the Unity of Orphic and Milesian Thought', *Harvard Theological Review*, 79 (1986), 321–35.

[43] H. Frankfort *et al.*, *Before Philosophy: The Intellectual Adventure of Ancient Man* (Chicago: University of Chicago Press, 1946).

[44] A. Laks and G. W. Most (eds.), *Studies on the Derveni Papyrus* (Oxford: Oxford University Press, 1997).

[45] R. D. McKirahan, 'Speculations on the Origins of Ionian Scientific and Philosophical Thought', in [24], 241–7.

[46] O. Neugebauer, *The Exact Sciences in Antiquity*, 2nd edn. (Providence, RI: Brown University Press, 1957).

[47] R. B. Onians, *The Origins of European Thought about the Body, the Mind, the Soul, the World, Time, and Fate* (Cambridge: Cambridge University Press, 1951).

[48] H. S. Schibli, *Pherekydes of Syros* (Oxford: Oxford University Press, 1990).

[49] B. Snell, *The Discovery of the Mind in Greek Philosophy and Literature* (1953; New York: Dover, 1982).

[50] M. C. Stokes, 'Hesiodic and Milesian Cosmogonies', *Phronesis*, 7 (1962), 1–37, and 8 (1963), 1–34.

[51] M. L. West, 'Three Presocratic Cosmogonies', *Classical Quarterly*, 13 (1963), 154–76.

[52] —— *The Orphic Poems* (Oxford: Oxford University Press, 1983).

[53] —— 'Ab Ovo: Orpheus, Sanchuniathon and the Origins of the Ionian World Model', *Classical Quarterly*, 44 (1994), 289–307.

Concept Studies of the Presocratics

[54] H. C. Baldry, 'Embryological Analogies in Pre-Socratic Cosmogony', *Classical Quarterly*, 26 (1932), 27–34.

[55] J. Barnes, 'Aphorism and Argument', in [31], 91–109.

[56] H. Cherniss, 'The Characteristics and Effects of Presocratic Philosophy', in [26], i. 1–28 (first pub. *Journal of the History of Ideas*, 12 (1951)).

[57] F. M. Cornford, 'Innumerable Worlds in Presocratic Philosophy', *Classical Quarterly*, 28 (1934), 1–16.

[58] J. Ferguson, 'The Opposites', *Apeiron*, 3.1 (1969), 1–17.

[59] K. von Fritz, '*Nous, Noein*, and their Derivatives in Pre-Socratic Philosophy (Excluding Anaxagoras)', in [30], 23–85 (first pub. *Classical Philology*, 40 (1945) and 41 (1946)).

[60] E. Hussey, 'The Beginnings of Epistemology: From Homer to Philolaus', in S. Everson (ed.), *Companions to Ancient Thought*, vol. i: *Epistemology* (Cambridge: Cambridge University Press, 1990), 11–38.

[61] W. Jaeger, *The Theology of the Early Greek Philosophers* (London: Oxford University Press, 1947).

[62] J. H. Lesher, 'The Emergence of Philosophical Interest in Cognition', *Oxford Studies in Ancient Philosophy*, 12 (1994), 1–34.

[63] G. E. R. Lloyd, *Polarity and Analogy: Two Types of Argumentation in Early Greek Thought* (Cambridge: Cambridge University Press, 1966).

[64] S. Makin, *Indifference Arguments* (Oxford: Basil Blackwell, 1993).

[65] A. P. D. Mourelatos, 'The Real, Appearances, and Human Error in Early Greek Philosophy', *Review of Metaphysics*, 19 (1965), 346–65.

[66] —— 'Pre-Socratic Origins of the Principle That There are No Origins from Nothing', *Journal of Philosophy*, 78 (1981), 649–65.

[67] —— 'Quality, Structure, and Emergence in Later Presocratic Philosophy', *Proceedings of the Boston Area Colloquium in Ancient Philosophy*, 2 (1986), 127–94.

[68] G. M. Stratton, *Theophrastus and the Greek Physiological Psychology before Aristotle* (London: George Allen & Unwin, 1917).

[69] W. J. Verdenius, 'Notes on the Presocratics', *Mnemosyne*, 3 (1947), 271–89, and 4 (1948), 8–14.

[70] G. Vlastos, 'Equality and Justice in Early Greek Cosmogonies', in [26], i. 56–91, and in [33], 57–88 (first pub. *Classical Philology* 42 (1947)).

[71] —— 'Theology and Philosophy in Early Greek Thought', in [26], i. 92–129, and in [33], 3–31 (first pub. *Philosophical Quarterly*, 2 (1952)).

[72] M. L. West, *Early Greek Philosophy and the Orient* (London: Oxford University Press, 1971).

[73] M. R. Wright, 'Presocratic Minds', in C. Gill (ed.), *The Person and the Mind* (Oxford: Oxford University Press, 1990), 207–25.

Discussion of Sources

[74] H. Cherniss, *Aristotle's Criticism of Presocratic Philosophy* (Baltimore: Johns Hopkins University Press, 1935).

[75] W. K. C. Guthrie, 'Aristotle as Historian', in [26], i. 239–54 (first pub. *Journal of Hellenic Studies*, 77 (1957)).

[76] P. Kingsley, 'Empedocles and his Interpreters: The Four Element Doxography', *Phronesis*, 39 (1994), 235–54.

[77] A. A. Long, 'Theophrastus' *De Sensibus* on Plato', in K. A. Algra *et al.* (eds.), *Polyhistor: Studies in the History and Historiography of Ancient Philosophy* (Leiden: Brill, 1996), 345–62.

[78] S. Makin, 'How Can We Find Out What Ancient Philosophers Said?', *Phronesis*, 33 (1988), 121–32.

[79] J. B. McDiarmid, 'Theophrastus on the Presocratic Causes', in [26], i. 178–238 (first pub. *Harvard Studies in Classical Philology*, 61 (1953)).

[80] C. Osborne, *Rethinking Early Greek Philosophy: Hippolytus of Rome and the Presocratics* (London: Duckworth, 1987).

Presocratic Science

[81] F. M. Cornford, 'Was the Ionian Philosophy Scientific?', in [26], i. 29–41 (first pub. *Journal of Hellenic Studies*, 62 (1942)).

[82] D. R. Dicks, *Early Greek Astronomy to Aristotle* (London: Thames and Hudson, 1970).

[83] —— 'Solstices, Equinoxes and the Presocratics', *Journal of Hellenic Studies*, 86 (1966), 26–40.

[84] C. H. Kahn, 'On Early Greek Astronomy', *Journal of Hellenic Studies*, 90 (1970), 99–116.

[85] G. S. Kirk, 'Sense and Common-Sense in the Development of Greek Philosophy', *Journal of Hellenic Studies*, 81 (1961), 105–17.

[86] G. E. R. Lloyd, *Early Greek Science: Thales to Aristotle* (London: Chatto & Windus, 1970).

[87] —— *Magic, Reason and Experience: Studies in the Origin and Development of Greek Science* (Cambridge: Cambridge University Press, 1979).

[88] —— *Methods and Problems in Greek Science: Selected Papers* (Cambridge: Cambridge University Press, 1991).

[89] D. O'Brien, 'The Relation of Anaxagoras and Empedocles', *Journal of Hellenic Studies*, 88 (1968), 93–113.

[90] —— 'Derived Light and Eclipses in the Fifth Century', *Journal of Hellenic Studies*, 88 (1968), 114–27.

[91] S. Sambursky, *The Physical World of the Greeks* (London: Routledge & Kegan Paul, 1956).

[92] B. L. van der Waerden, *Science Awakening* (Dordrecht: Kluwer, 1975).

[93] M. R. Wright, *Cosmology in Antiquity* (London: Routledge, 1995).

General Books and Articles on the Sophists

[94] R. Bett, 'The Sophists and Relativism', *Phronesis*, 34 (1989), 139–69.

[95] E. R. Dodds, 'The Sophistic Movement and the Failure of Greek Liberalism', in id., *The Ancient Concept of Progress and Other Essays on Greek Literature and Belief* (London: Oxford University Press, 1973), 92–105.

[96] E. A. Havelock, *The Liberal Temper in Greek Politics* (London: Jonathan Cape, 1957).

[97] G. B. Kerferd, *The Sophistic Movement* (Cambridge: Cambridge University Press, 1981).

[98] J. V. Muir, 'Religion and the New Education: The Challenge of the Sophists', in [35], 191–218.

[99] A. Nehamas, 'Eristic, Antilogic, Sophistic, Dialectic: Plato's Demarcation of Philosophy from Sophistry', *History of Philosophy Quarterly* 7 (1990), 3–16; repr. in id., *Virtues of Authenticity: Essays on Plato and Socrates* (Princeton: Princeton University Press, 1999), 108–22.

[100] M. Nill, *Morality and Self-interest in Protagoras, Antiphon and Democritus* (Leiden: Brill, 1985).

[101] J. Poulakos, *Sophistical Rhetoric in Classical Greece* (Columbia: University of South Carolina Press, 1995).

[102] H. D. Rankin, *Sophists, Socratics and Cynics* (London: Croom Helm, 1983).

[103] J. de Romilly, *The Great Sophists in Periclean Athens* (Oxford: Oxford University Press, 1992).

[104] F. Solmsen, *Intellectual Experiments of the Greek Enlightenment* (Princeton: Princeton University Press, 1975).

NOTE ON THE TEXTS

Wherever possible (i.e. except where they fail to include a text), I have translated the texts found in Diels's and Kranz's edition of the fragments and testimonia (number [1] in the Select Bibliography, pp. xxxiv–xl); any places where I differ from the text they provide are marked in the translation with an obelus, which refers the interested reader to the Textual Notes (pp. 337–44). Since Diels/Kranz is an anthology, I have also concluded each extract in the book with a precise reference to the location of the original text in the standard edition, or at least in an accessible edition.[1] However, only in cases where Diels/Kranz fail to include a text should this concluding reference to another edition be taken to imply that I have translated the text of that edition; in all other cases, to repeat, I have translated the text found in Diels/Kranz.

The heading of each translated piece usually also includes a few numbers, which give a conspectus of the numbering of that fragment (F) or testimonium (T) in the most important editions. Thus, for instance, you might find this heading: **F20** (DK 31B17; KRS 348, 349; W 8; I 25). This means that the fragment of Empedocles (whose prefix number is 31 in Diels/Kranz) which is numbered 20 in my translation, is number B17 in Diels/Kranz (in whose edition, by and large,[2] testimonia are signalled by the prefix A and fragments by the prefix B), numbers 348 and 349 in Kirk/Raven/Schofield [2], number 8 in Wright's edition of Empedocles, and number 25 in Inwood's edition.[3] These coded conspectuses will be complex, therefore, only where the thinker has received the benefit of a number of standard editions, whose numbering of fragments differs from that of Diels/Kranz. More normally, you will find only DK and KRS entries, for example: **T12** (DK 12A1; KRS 94). This means that the testimonium of Anaximander numbered 12 in my translation is numbered 1

---

[1] Note the following abbreviation: CAG is *Commentaria in Aristotelem Graeca*, a multi-volumed work by many hands.

[2] Occasionally, when there were further easily distinguishable categories of evidence, such as the lists of Pythagorean *akousmata*, Diels/Kranz went beyond their basic division into A for testimonia and B for fragments.

[3] Bibliographic details of editions of particular thinkers will be found in the bibliographies at the end of each section of the translation.

in Diels/Kranz and 94 in Kirk/Raven/Schofield. Rarely, an entry reads no more than, say, **T23**; this means that the passage does not occur in Diels/Kranz or in any of the standard editions (which in any case are generally editions of the fragments rather than testimonia). The amount of text I have translated in any particular instance, especially where testimonia are concerned, may be longer or shorter than what is to be found in Diels/Kranz or in any other edition.

The following abbreviations have been used:

C	Coxon (Parmenides)
DK	Diels/Kranz [1]
I	Inwood (Empedocles)
K	Kahn (Heraclitus)
KRS	Kirk/Raven/Schofield [2]
L	Lee (Zeno)
M	Marcovich (Heraclitus)
T	Taylor (Atomists)
W	Wheelwright (Heraclitus) or Wright (Empedocles)

Note that some books which count as standard editions preserve the numbering of fragments found in Diels/Kranz, and so do not need a separate code. This goes for Lesher's edition of Xenophanes, Kirk's edition of Heraclitus' cosmological fragments, Robinson's edition of Heraclitus, the editions by Gallop and Tarán of Parmenides, Huffman's edition of Philolaus, and Sider's of Anaxagoras. Note also that although there are in existence some fine editions of some of the Presocratics in languages other than English, I have not given them codes because I decided to restrict my bibliography strictly to the English language. But I should like to mention especially A. Laks's edition of Diogenes of Apollonia (*Cahiers de Philologie*, 9; Lille: Presses Universitaires de Lille, 1983); S. Luria's of Democritus (Leningrad: Scientific Publishers, 1970), J. Bollack's of Empedocles (Paris: Les Éditions de Minuit, 1965–9), and J. Bollack and H. Wismann's of Heraclitus (Paris: Les Éditions de Minuit, 1972). Finally, note that all the works that have been coded are editions of the Greek texts (which invariably include translations); I have not referred in this way to other translations, however widespread their use may have become.

TIMELINE

Among other things, this timeline shows the distance between the original thinkers and some of the doxographers and commentators who reported their views and preserved fragments of their work. But although distance is likely to increase distortion, it must not be thought that a straightforward linear progression of distortion is necessarily the case: Plato was scarcely writing as a historian of philosophy, while Simplicius had many original works by his elbow as he wrote. All dates represent approximate floruits. Scholiasts and most pseudepigrapha are obviously undatable with much certainty. The most important sources are in **bold** type.

PRESOCRATICS & SOPHISTS	DATE BCE	SOURCES
Thales	580	
Anaximander	570	
Anaximenes	550	
Xenophanes, Pythagoras	530	
Heraclitus	500	
Parmenides	490	
Anaxagoras	470	
Zeno	460	
Empedocles	450	Herodotus
Melissus, Protagoras, Leucippus	440	Ion of Chios
Philolaus, Diogenes, Gorgias	430	
Democritus, Prodicus, Hippias, Thrasymachus	420	
Antiphon, Euthydemus, Dionysodorus, Critias	410	
Double Arguments, Anonymus Iamblichi	400	

PRESOCRATICS & SOPHISTS	DATE BCE	SOURCES
	380	**Plato**, Isocrates
	370	Xenophon
	350	**Aristotle**
	340	Xenocrates, Heraclides of Pontus
	330	**Theophrastus**, Arostoxenus
	320	Eudemus, Meno
	310	Dicaearchus
	300	Timaeus of Tauromenium
	290	Anticleides
	270	Callimachus
	200	Ps.-Plato, *Eryxias*
	150	Crates of Mallus
	120?	Apollonius
	100?	Dercyllidas
	90?	Apollodorus the mathematician
	80	Posidonius
	70	Cicero, Lucretius
	60	Philodemus of Gadara
	50?	Ps.-Aristotle, *On the World*
	40	Diodorus of Sicily
	30	Arius Didymus
	20?	Ps.-Aristotle, *On Plants*
	10	Seneca; Dionysius of Halicarnassus
	1	Strabo

PRESOCRATICS & SOPHISTS	DATE CE	SOURCES
	60	Erotian
	80	**Plutarch**
	100	**Aëtius**
	120	Theon of Smyrna
	130?	Ps.-Plutarch, *Letter of Consolation to Apollonius*
	150	Agathemerus, Aulus Gellius
	160?	Ps.-Aristotle, *On Melissus, Xenophanes, and Gorgias*
	170	Herodian, Marcus Aurelius, Galen
	180	Pollux
	190	**Clement**
	200	Alexander of Aphrodisias, **Sextus Empiricus**
	210	Diogenes of Oenoanda, Harpocration
	220	**Hippolytus**
	230?	**Ps.-Plutarch**, *Miscellanies*
	240	Censorinus, Origen
	250	**Diogenes Laertius**
	260?	Achilles Tatius
	270	Porphyry
	280	Aelian
	290	Iamblichus
	300	Eusebius
	310	Ps.-Iamblichus, *The Theology of Arithmetic*
	320?	Ps.-Aristotle, *Puzzles*
	350	Themistius
	360	Didymus the Blind

PRESOCRATICS & SOPHISTS	DATE CE	SOURCES
	400	Augustine
	410	Theodoretus
	440	**John of Stobi**
	450	Hermias
	460	Proclus
	480	Ammonius
	510	**Simplicius**
	520	Philoponus
	790	Elias of Crete
	1000	*The Suda* (lexicon)
	1150	John Tzetzes, Theodorus Prodromus
	1320	Planudes

THE PRESOCRATICS

THE MILESIANS

(THALES OF MILETUS, ANAXIMANDER OF MILETUS, ANAXIMENES OF MILETUS)

It makes sense to group Thales, Anaximander, and Anaximenes together, though the idea that they were a 'school', and formed master-pupil relationships, is certainly a distortion, based on the later desire to systematize which bedevils Presocratic studies in various ways. However, although Miletus was at the time a thriving city-state, it was small enough for all three of these thinkers to have known one another, and for each to have been acquainted with the others' work and ideas. We can pinpoint Thales' date fairly precisely, since we know he was alive at the time of a datable solar eclipse (T1; it was either the eclipse of 28 May 585 or that of 21 September 582 BCE), and it seems likely that the other two were younger contemporaries of his, with Anaximenes younger than Anaximander. If it is wondered why Miletus should have been so important in the history of philosophy, an adequate answer is given by considering its importance as a trade-route with links to the older cultures of Babylon, Egypt, Lydia, and Phoenicia. Ideas always travel with trade. The old civilizations had world-pictures and creation myths vastly different to anything the Greeks had come across. These startling and visionary ideas led a few Milesians to speculate for themselves. Miletus was a wealthy enough city for there to be a literate and leisured class.

The Milesian philosophers belong together because they—or at least Anaximander and Anaximenes, for whom we have just enough evidence— display in a primitive form the reductionist spirit discussed in the Introduction. They were trying to make the world comprehensible, which meant not only severely limiting the number and nature of the factors they used to explain phenomena, but also relying by and large on familiar features of the world, and, most importantly, introducing the idea of cosmic order or natural law. However, what this rather scientific summary of their work fails to capture is the grandeur and splendour of their geometric visions of the universe, which just barely emerge from behind the dry-as-dust writing of the doxographic tradition. In order to have a sense of the Milesian achievement, it is important always to bear the whole in mind, so as to avoid getting bogged down in the details. But this is not to say that the details were unimportant to them: as far as we can tell, they wanted to give a comprehensive picture and explanation of the whole universe, from the largest scale down to everyday phenomena such as rain and mist and rainbows. At the very birth of science and philosophy, the daring of this enterprise is breathtaking. Their distinctive approach is to explain things by looking to their origins, in a biological sense: the world arose by spontaneous generation out of more-or-less undifferentiated matter, which itself has the properties of life and growth.[1]

Our earliest witness to Thales' activities regards him entirely as a practical man, an engineer rather than a speculative thinker (**T2–3**). Even the mathematical discoveries attributed to him are practical aids to drawing up an accurate calendar (**T5**) or navigation (**T6**). He soon became one of the 'seven sages' of Greece, to whom a number of pithy aphorisms were attributed; and in later times he became an archetype of the absent-minded professor (e.g. **T7**). Nevertheless, there is enough evidence for us to be sure that he did come up with a more theoretical set of ideas, involving, above all, some reference to water (**T8–10**). It is very noticeable how hesitant Aristotle is when reporting any of Thales' views, and we cannot know whether Aristotle was putting him in the correct proto-scientific context or, as seems more likely, whether Thales was actually closer to a mythologer, claiming perhaps that the world emerged from a watery swamp at the beginning of time; there are parallels in both Egyptian and Babylonian creation myths. Perhaps he inferred from empirical observation that water was necessary for growth, and Aristotle imposed his own framework on this. Thales also seems to have formulated some kind of religious animism (**T11**). As for the eclipse, it is clear from Herodotus' testimony (**T1**) that Thales did not exactly predict its occurrence, but knew (perhaps from Babylonian records), or more likely guessed, the year in which it was going to happen; however, in the later doxographic tradition this gradually becomes exaggerated, until we read (**T4**) of Thales having developed the ability to predict the exact occurrence of eclipses and other astronomical phenomena.[2]

If we can trust the report of later chroniclers that Anaximander died around 540, he was a younger contemporary of Thales. Again, as with Thales, we find him credited with practical scientific work (**T12–13**), most famously with drawing the first map of the world (which would have been

---

[1] The technical term for this view, sometimes attributed to the Milesians, is 'hylozoism'.

[2] Similarly, Anaxagoras later was credited with predicting the fall of a meteorite! A recently discovered papyrus fragment of a 2nd-cent. CE commentary on Homer's *Odyssey* (*POxy* 3710 col. 2.36–43) implausibly credits Thales (probably on the authority of Aristarchus of Samos, an astronomer of the third century BCE) with a correct account of solar eclipses, as an inference from the fact that they occurred at the time of the new moon. The latter fact may have been known to Thales from Babylonian records, but he is unlikely to have made the inference.

as crudely symmetrical as the historian Herodotus complained at **T14**). Since Thales is also credited with the invention of the *gnomon*, and since it is likely that the Babylonians had been using the device for a long time, the report that Anaximander actually invented it is unreliable.

But apart from these practical achievements, Anaximander also speculated about the origins of the world (**T15**), claiming that it has its source in the boundless (*apeiron*, literally, 'without limits'). Precisely what he meant by this 'boundless' is not clear, and perhaps he did not make it clear himself. Aristotle's claim at **T16** is unhelpful on this score, except to suggest that the boundless might actually have been something like infinite water or infinite air—in other words, that while it may have been boundless spatially (i.e. infinite), it was not indefinite qualitatively. This conforms with other early uses of the Greek word *apeiros*, but is contradicted by Aristotle's own report elsewhere in *Physics* (**T17**), where it appears that Anaximander's *apeiron* was a kind of mixture of opposites—i.e. with none of the oppositely qualified stuffs (early Greeks did not recognize qualities or predicates as distinct from stuffs) being distinct within it. It seems most likely that Anaximander himself said nothing definite about his boundless, seeing it as a spatially (and hence temporally) unlimited, homogeneous, material mass, and leaving Aristotle to fill in the gap in different ways at different times, and also to speculate as to Anaximander's reasons for positing 'the boundless' as the source of all things (**T18–20**). We may catch a glimpse of Anaximander's motivation in **T15** and **T19**: if all the determinate stuffs of the universe, characterized as opposites, can change into one another, it would be wrong to privilege any particular determinate stuff over any other by making it the originating stuff of the universe.

T22 confirms the idea that the *apeiron* is qualitatively indefinite. If Anaximander felt the need to postulate a distinct immediate source for the qualities of the world—a kind of seed or germ that generates the opposites—this suggests that he wanted to preserve the qualitative indefiniteness of the *apeiron* itself. Of course, this raises as many problems as it solves: how does this 'something productive of hot and cold' separate off from the boundless, so that it is something distinct from the boundless? What is it for something to be 'separated off' from something else? At any rate, somehow (in an act which looks like little more than an abstraction of mythical masturbatory genesis by a single male god, especially since the word for 'separate off' can also mean 'secrete') the opposites, the basic elements which make up the world (chiefly, but not exclusively, hot and cold, wet and dry), emerged from the boundless (**T15**).

In **T20** Aristotle seems to suggest that the boundless steers all things even now, in the manner of a purposeful or providential god. It is hard to see how this can be right for Anaximander, since the processes of the universe seem to take place by natural law, without any interference by this boundless god; but it may well be right that Anaximander conceived of the boundless as divine, and felt no need to explain the origin of change and the cosmogonic process because, *qua* divine, the boundless was instinct with life. The idea of natural law is contained in the one fragment of Anaximander, preserved in **T15**. There is constant interplay between the opposite stuffs of the world. Each is seen as giving offence to its opposite, and then as having to pay a penalty to it. At the onset of the hot season, for instance, the cool season gives way, or is overwhelmed by the hot, until it is its turn again. Neither is allowed by Time to commit the injustice of going on for too long.

The Greeks had long believed, except in their more pessimistic moments, that there was a law of compensation in human affairs—that the gods would, sooner or later, belittle a man who rose too high or too fast,[3] but Anaximander extended this law to the world at large, making it a cosmic principle—and, importantly, one that was governed by 'necessity', an abstract, unchanging force, not a bunch of fickle gods. His vision of a universe ordered by cosmic justice was potent, and soon took hold of the Greek imagination. As the Athenian playwright Sophocles would put in the middle of the fifth century: 'Even terrifying and the most mighty forces recognize rights. Winter with its snowdrifts yields to summer with its crops, and the weary round of night makes way for the white-horsed chariot of day, so that she may kindle her light' (*Ajax* 669–73).

Another application of this principle of cosmic equilibrium may be glimpsed in **T21**. Anaximander seems to have believed that the earth was originally covered in water (flood myths are common all over the world, especially in the Middle East), but was drying out and would some day become entirely dry. Since the winds and the consequent motion of the heavenly bodies are also caused by this process of evaporation, at this point the universe would stop moving. This cosmic catastrophe would, we may guess, be followed by another deluge, and the whole process would start again. But these speculations should be tempered first by the fact that Aristotle himself, the source of **T21**, does not name Anaximander (it is only later sources who say that Aristotle had Anaximander in mind when writing this), and second by the fact that such complete flooding and drying out would contravene the principle Anaximander enunciates in his fragment, according to which none of the opposites is allowed to encroach too far. So perhaps Anaximander said that the world was subject to successive periods of increased and decreased sea-levels, which fall short of catastrophe.

In **T15** Theophrastus attributes to Anaximander a belief in a plurality

---

[3] For a famous 5th-cent. story, see Herodotus, *Histories* 3.40; for earlier testimony, see e.g. Hesiod, *Works and Days* 213–73 or Solon, fr. 1.

of worlds, without mentioning whether these are co-existent or successive. In fact, however, Theophrastus is probably wrong on this; given what we have seen about Anaximander's cosmological views, there is no reason for him to posit the existence of more than just this world, which is held more or less in equilibrium for ever. Going back from the present state of the world to the cosmogonical process, it is clear that Anaximander went into some detail about the next stage (T22), which neatly allows him to explain the existence and nature of the heavenly bodies. With a brilliant leap of the imagination, he discussed not only the shape of the world (a drum), but also gave a remarkable explanation why the earth kept its place at the centre of a proportionate and harmonious universe (T23). In short, the world stays where it is because it has nowhere else to go.[4] This is remarkable as an early preference for theory over the evidence of the senses, where the two conflict; for surely the senses would seem to confirm that nothing just hangs in place in mid-air.

T24 and T25 continue the story. Once hot and cold have emerged, hot (seen as fire) surrounds cold (seen as mist or vapour). The cold dries up under the action of heat and forms water and earth. The universe forms concentric rings, with fire on the outside, then mist, then water, which rests on earth. These are not stable elemental rings, but they interact through processes such as evaporation and precipitation. Anaximander's stupendous picture of the finished universe has the earth surrounded by a number of fiery rings, each of which is enclosed and hidden by mist, as a tree is covered by bark, except for an aperture; that aperture—that glimpse into a vast fiery ring—is what we call the sun or the moon or a star. So the moon waxes and wanes as the mist surrounding its fiery ring is driven by a cosmic wind, generated by the sun, to block our view of it; the same goes for solar eclipses too.

Anaximander's universe is symmetrical and harmonious, with the sun furthest from the earth, then the moon, and then presumably the fixed stars (on rings presumably nine times the size of the earth).[5]

---

[4] For a near contemporary view, see the biblical Job 26: 7: 'He hangeth the earth upon nothing.' The kind of argument Anaximander apparently employed, sometimes called an 'indifference argument', was to flourish in Zeno and the atomists (Makin [64]). At *Phaedo* 108e–109a Plato has Socrates allude to this doctrine of Anaximander with distinct approval. A few scholars doubt the attribution of this view to Anaximander and approve the report of Simplicius (*Commentary on Aristotle's 'On the Heavens'* 532.13) that, like Anaximenes, Anaximander believed that the earth was floating on air. But see Schofield in [14], pp. 51–5.

[5] The emphasis on the number 9 may be traditional. Hesiod says (*Theogony* 722–5): 'It would take nine nights and days for a bronze anvil to fall from heaven and on the tenth it would reach earth, and it would take nine nights and days for a bronze anvil to fall from earth and on the tenth it would reach Tartarus.'

Counter-intuitively, the brightness of the sun and the dimness of the stars is probably (unless he gleaned the idea from ancient Iran) what made Anaximander think that the sun was further away from the earth than the stars. Fire, as we have seen, being the lightest element, occupies the outer periphery; the sun is therefore closer to unadulterated fire than the stars are. Anaximander can account to a certain extent for the more regular motions of these heavenly bodies, but he seems to be unaware of the anomalous planets. His recognition that the sun is larger than it seems, and ascription of definite numbers to the distance of the sun and moon from the earth, is a recognition of the mathematics of perspective.

Whereas celestial and meteorological phenomena had in the past been the domain of the gods, Anaximander began (unless **T10** is a reliable report about Thales) the Presocratic trend to explain these phenomena as the product of natural and comprehensible forces (e.g. **T26**). It was precisely this usurpation of the traditional functions of the gods that made this 'modern' thinking suspect to many people. And last, but not least, he seems to have had a vision of the universe as originally consisting of just elemental nature, before the birth of the human race. His description of the origins of humans and other animals is quite remarkable (**T27–28**), but does not allow us to go as far as to call him an evolutionist, a proto-Darwinian, because he seems to be describing no more than the first generation of creatures. It is to be noted how the gestation of the first human beings parallels that of the earth: both are enclosed within a casing before emerging. **T28** looks as though it was an attempt to solve a chicken-and-egg problem: if human babies are not capable of looking after themselves at birth, how were the very first human beings born, and how did they manage to survive?

If Anaximander speculated about the origin of living things, it seems likely that he also had views about the origin of inanimate things, but there is a gap in our surviving evidence. After the four primary regions have taken up their proper places and formed the concentric layers of the universe, we do not know how other particular things were created. Perhaps it was something to do with the interplay of the primary opposites, hot and cold, and wet and dry. Anyway, although our evidence for Anaximenes is less overall than for Anaximander, this gap is securely filled. We have a good idea of how not only the whole universe, but also all the bits and pieces of it were formed in his theory.

We constantly read in our sources that air is the Aristotelian substrate of things, in Anaximenes' opinion (e.g. **T29**). As usual, we need to take such an Aristotelian reading of the Presocratics with a pinch of salt, but in this case, with less salt than in the case of, say, Anaximander. For there can be little doubt that he dreamed up the twin processes of condensation and rarefaction as the means to explain how air became other things. Note, however, that this does not necessarily make air an Aristotelian substrate, rather than just an originative stuff. In Aristotelian theory the substrate, or underlying matter, persists through change. If Anaximenes were an Aristotelian, we would have to attribute to him the belief that this table in front of me is air in another form, greatly condensed. But it seems more likely that Anaximenes actually said that air when condensed turns into earth and so on, which is a different theory altogether. In fact, Anaximenes may have limited the number of things that air itself actually turns into, and left it up to this second order of substances to generate everything else (**T29**).

What drives Anaximenes' theory seems to be the idea that the same laws that operate on the small scale, in the human body, also operate on the large scale, in the universe at large—that the universe is the macrocosm to the human's microcosm (**T30**). We have already met this analogical argument in Anaximander's parallel account of the gestation of the universe and the gestation of the first human beings. For Anaximenes, human beings are given life by air. In Greek terms, this is to say that human beings are animated or ensouled by air; since our soul holds us together (without it, our body perishes), then Anaximenes suggested that it does the same for the whole universe: it surrounds and interpenetrates the whole universe. The whole universe is mobile and alive. And surely another reason for Anaximenes' choice of air as his originative stuff is that it is indistinct and adaptable.

Just as our breath can form clouds of mist and even droplets of moisture, so Anaximenes imagined that the primeval air or wind condensed first as cloud, and then as moisture (**T29**). This moisture then somehow condensed further into earth: did Anaximenes see silt thrown up from a river, or sand from the sea, and think that it was condensed water? Did he see that dust, tiny particles of solid matter, are left behind by raindrops? Did he see stalagmites and stalactites in a cave? At any rate, the whole cosmogonic process was, I think, suggested to Anaximenes by this simple analogy with human breath. Just as human breath is (apparently) colder when compressed and warmer when dilated (**T31**), so air at large can become something colder and more solid when condensed, and something warmer, even fiery, when rarefied. This is an important potential reference to primary and secondary qualities: the primary qualities of air are that it is more or less dense, but these qualities in turn lead it to have the secondary qualities of cold or heat. By implicitly creating a hierarchy like this, Anaximenes reduces the number of factors used to explain the fundamental features of the world, and so makes it more comprehensible. Moreover, if the reference to human breath goes back to Anaximenes, as seems likely, it is noteworthy as an early attempt, not quite to construct an experiment, but to argue by analogy from what can be known through the senses to what is inaccessible to the senses (see also **T40**).

It seems clear from **T32** and **T33** (and one or two other reports, not included here) that Anaximenes said something about the divine in relation to air. Unfortunately, all our reports are very late and unreliable. I find it very unlikely that Anaximenes went so far as to say that the gods emerged from the primeval air, the great god: this seems to confuse Anaximenes with later atomism.[6] Cicero's statement is perhaps closer to the truth, except for his mistake in saying that air was itself created. At any rate, perhaps we can conclude that Anaximenes attributed divinity to air, since it had taken over some of the creative and meteorological functions of the traditional gods, and since, like Anaximander's *apeiron*, air is eternal. It is (as Cicero reports in **T32**, but we could have guessed anyway) always in motion, and so it imparts motion and change to everything else.[7]

The cosmogonic process continues (**T34**): moisture evaporates from the earth and, as it gets lighter, it becomes fiery and forms the heavenly bodies (**T35**). The sun may be a special case (**T34**): perhaps in its case immense winds condensed the evaporating moisture back into earth. There is no real contradiction between seeing the heavenly bodies as leaf-like and as fixed into the ice-like periphery (**T37**, **T39**). In any case, what Anaximenes may originally have said is that the fixed stars are fixed like nails in the periphery, while the sun and moon (and planets, if he recognized any) are floating like leaves. One of the images Anaximenes may well have been wanting to provoke by calling the periphery 'ice-like' is the image of leaves stuck on the surface of frozen water. Of course, the periphery is only ice-like: it cannot actually be ice, because on Anaximenes' scheme of things it is hot out there at the periphery.

As well as explaining the original formation of the universe and its broad features, Anaximenes clearly went in some detail into celestial and meteorological phenomena (**T36**, **T38**, **T40**, **T41**). These testimonia bear witness to his views on earthquakes, thunder and lightning, nightfall, and the rainbow. In the latter case, at least, his opinion is accurate enough (given that 'concentrated air' presumably refers to mist or cloud), as far as it goes: we could not of course expect him to have knowledge of the refraction of light. Other late sources credit him with discoveries such as

---

[6] The atomists and Epicureans wanted to banish superstition by claiming that even the gods were no more than conglomerates of atoms, just as everything else is.

[7] Aristotle complained at *Metaphysics* 988[b] that the Milesians took motion for granted, rather than explaining how it first arose; but for the Milesians the universe was alive, so they saw no need to explain the origins of its living nature. It was only after Parmenides that thinkers felt that motion had to be accounted for.

the true explanation of lunar eclipses, and the fact that the moon's light is reflected sunlight. These are probably not to be trusted.

Thales

T1 (DK 11A5; KRS 64) The Lydians and the Medes even once fought a kind of night battle. In the sixth year, when neither side had a clear advantage over the other in the war, an engagement took place and it so happened that in the middle of the battle day suddenly became night. Thales of Miletus had predicted this loss of daylight to the Ionians by establishing in advance that it would happen within the limits of the year in which it did in fact happen. (Herodotus, *Histories* 1.74.1.5–2.6 Hude)

T2 (DK 11A4; KRS 65) This proposal by Bias of Priene was made to the Ionians after their defeat, but another good proposal had been put to them, even before the conquest of Ionia, by Thales of Miletus, a man originally of Phoenician lineage. He suggested that the Ionians should establish a single governmental council, that it should be in Teos (because Teos is centrally located in Ionia), and that all the other towns should be regarded effectively as outlying demes. (Herodotus, *Histories* 1.170.3 Hude)

T3 (DK 11A6; KRS 66) The story goes that Croesus did not know how his troops were going to cross the river, since the bridges I mentioned were not in existence at the time. But Thales was in the camp, and he helped Croesus by making the river flow on both sides of the army, instead of only to the left. This is how he did it, they say. He started upstream, above the army, and dug a deep channel which was curved in such a way that it would pass behind the army's encampment; in this way he diverted the river from its original bed into the channel, and then, once he had got it past the army, he brought it back round to its original bed again. The immediate result of this division of the river was that it became fordable on both sides. (Herodotus, *Histories* 1.75.4–5 Hude)

T4 (DK 11A17; KRS 76) In his *Astronomy* Eudemus reports . . . that Thales was the first to discover the eclipse of the sun and the fact that the period of its solstices is not always equal. (Eudemus [fr. 94

Spengel] in Dercyllidas *ap*. Theon of Smyrna, *Mathematics Useful for Reading Plato* 198.14–18 Hiller)

T5 (DK 11A3a; KRS 78)

> Victory went to Thales,
> Whose cleverness showed not least in the fact that
> He is said to have measured the tiny stars of the Wain,
> By which the Phoenicians sail.

(Callimachus, *Iambus* fr. 94.1–4 Pfeiffer)

T6 (DK 11A20; KRS 80) In his *History of Geometry* Eudemus attributes this theorem [*the identity of triangles which have one side and two angles equal*] to Thales, on the grounds that the method he is said to have used to demonstrate how far out to sea ships were must have made use of this theorem.*   (Eudemus [fr. 87 Spengel] in Proclus, *Commentary on Euclid* 352.14–18 Friedlein)

T7 (DK 11A9; KRS 72) The story about Thales is a good illustration, Theodorus [*illustrating the detachment of the philosopher from the humdrum reality of the world*]: how he was looking upwards in the course of his astronomical investigations, and fell into a pothole, and a Thracian serving-girl with a nice sense of humour teased him for being concerned with knowing about what was up in the sky and not noticing what was right in front of him at his feet.   (Plato, *Theaetetus* 174a4–8 Duke *et al.*)

T8 (DK 11A12; KRS 85) Most of the original seekers after knowledge recognized only first principles of the material kind as the first principles of all things. For that out of which all existing things are formed—from which they originally come into existence and into which they are finally destroyed—whose substance persists while changing its qualities, this, they say, is the element and first principle of all things . . . However, they disagree about how many of such first principles there are, and about what they are like. Thales, who was the founder of this kind of philosophy, says that water is the first principle (which is why he declared that the earth was on water); he perhaps reached this conclusion from seeing that everything's food is moist, and that moisture is the source and prerequisite for the life of warmth itself (and the source of anything is the first principle of that thing). So, as I say, it was perhaps this that led him to reach this conclusion, and also the fact that the seeds of all things have a moist nature (and water is the first principle of the moist nature of moist things). And there are people who think that those in the dim, distant past who first began to reason about the gods, long before our present generation, shared this conception of the underlying nature; for these poets made Ocean and Tethys the parents of creation, and claimed that the gods took their oath upon water—the river Styx, as the poets call it.* (Aristotle, *Metaphysics* 983^{b}6–32 Ross)

T9 (DK 11A14; KRS 84) Others say that the earth rests on water. This is the oldest account that has been passed down to us today, and they say it was the view of Thales of Miletus, that the earth stays where it is as a result of floating like a piece of wood or something similar (for none of these things is so constituted as to keep its position on air, but they do so on water)—as though the same argument did not apply to the water supporting the earth just as much as to the earth itself. After all, water is just as incapable of staying suspended in mid-air, and is also so constituted as to keep its position only when it is on something. (Aristotle, *On the Heavens* 294^{a}28–294^{b}1 Allan)

T10 (DK 11A15; KRS 88) Thales says that the world is held up by water and rides on it like a ship, and that what we call an earthquake happens when the earth rocks because of the movement of the water. (Seneca, *Questions about Nature* 3.14.1.2–4 Oltramare)

T11 (DK 11A22; KRS 89, 91) Thales too (as far as we can judge from people's memoirs) apparently took the soul to be a principle of movement, if he said that the stone has soul because it moves iron ... Some say that the universe is shot through with soul, which is perhaps why Thales too thought that all things were full of gods. (Aristotle, *On the Soul* 405^{a}19–21, 411^{a}7–9 Ross)

Anaximander

T12 (DK 12A1; KRS 94) Anaximander was the first to discover the *gnomon* and according to Favorinus in his *Universal History* he set one up on the Sundials in Lacedaemon, to indicate solstices and equinoxes. He also constructed a device to mark the passage of the

hours.*   (Diogenes Laertius, *Lives of Eminent Philosophers* 2.1.7–10
Long)

T13 (DK 12A6; KRS 98) Anaximander of Miletus, who studied under
Thales, was the first who dared to draw the inhabited world on a
tablet; subsequently Hecataeus of Miletus, a well-travelled man,
improved the accuracy of this drawing and made it a thing of wonder.* . . . The ancients made the inhabited world round, with Greece
in the centre and Delphi in the centre of Greece, since the navel of
the earth is to be found there.   (Agathemerus, *Geography* 1.1–2
Müller)

T14 (KRS 100) I am amazed when I see that not one of all the
people who have drawn maps of the world has set it out sensibly.
They show Ocean as a river flowing around the outside of the earth,
which is as circular as if it had been drawn with a pair of compasses,
and they make Asia and Europe the same size.   (Herodotus, *Histories* 4.36.2.1–5 Hude)

T15 (DK 12A9, B1; KRS 101) Anaximander said that the first principle and element of existing things was the boundless; it was he who
originally introduced this name for the first principle.* He says that it
is not water or any of the other so-called elements, but something
different from them, something boundless by nature, which is the
source of all the heavens and the worlds in them. And he says that
the original sources of existing things are also what existing things
die back into 'according to necessity; for they give justice and repar-
ation to one another for their injustice in accordance with the ordin-
ance of Time', as he puts it, in these somewhat poetic terms. It is
clear that, having noticed how the four elements change into one
another, he decided not to make any of them the underlying thing,
but something else beside them; and so he has creation take place not
as a result of any of the elements undergoing qualitative change, but
as a result of the opposites being separated off by means of motion,
which is eternal.   (Theophrastus [fr. 226a Fortenbaugh *et al.*] in
Simplicius, *Commentary on Aristotle's 'Physics'*, CAG IX, 24.14–25
Diels)

T16 (KRS 102) Others—the natural scientists without exception—
make something else (one of the things they identify as elements,
such as water or air or something intermediate between them) the

subject of which infinity is predicated.* (Aristotle, *Physics* 203ᵃ16– 18 Ross)

T17 (DK 12A16; KRS 103) The natural scientists fall into two schools of thought. Some make the underlying stuff single, and identify it either with one of the three [*water, air, or fire*], or with some other stuff which is more condensed than fire and more refined than air. Then they have condensation and rarefaction generate everything else, and so they arrive at a plurality of objects . . . Others, however, claim that the one contains oppositions, which are then separated out. This is the view of Anaximander and of those like Empedocles and Anaxagoras whose underlying stuff is simultaneously one and many. (Aristotle, *Physics* 187ᵃ12–23 Ross)

T18 (KRS 106) There are five considerations which particularly lead people to infer that something infinite does exist . . . Third, there is the notion that the only possible explanation for the persistence of generation and destruction is that there is an infinite source from which anything which is generated is subtracted. (Aristotle, *Physics* 203ᵇ15–20 Ross)

T19 (DK 12A16; KRS 105) However, there equally cannot be one simple infinite body, and this is so not only if, as some say, it is an extra body over and above the elements, which acts as the source of the elements, but also on a more straightforward view. Those who suggest that the infinite is not air or water, but this extra body, do so because they want to avoid everything else being destroyed by an infinite element. For the elements are related by mutual opposition (air is cold, for instance, while water is moist and fire is hot), and so if any one of them were infinite, the others would have been destroyed by now. So in fact, they say, there is this extra body which is the source of the elements. (Aristotle, *Physics* 204ᵇ22–9 Ross)

T20 (DK 12A15; KRS 108) Moreover, they take the infinite not to be subject to generation or destruction, on the grounds that it is a kind of principle, because anything generated must have a last part that is generated, and there is also a point at which the destruction of anything ends. That is why, as I say, the infinite is taken not to *have* an origin, but to *be* the origin of everything else—to contain every- thing and steer everything, as has been said by those thinkers who do not recognize any other causes (such as love or intelligence) apart from the infinite. They also call it the divine, on the grounds that it is immortal and imperishable; on this Anaximander and the majority of the natural scientists are in agreement. (Aristotle, *Physics* 203^b7–15 Ross)

T21 (DK 12A27; KRS 132) They say that at first the whole region around the earth was wet, and that part of it began to dry up under the influence of the sun; this evaporating water causes winds and the turnings of the sun and moon, while the rest is the sea. And so they believe that the sea is still in the process of drying up and becoming less, and that eventually, some time in the future, it will all be dry. (Aristotle, *On Celestial Phenomena* 353^b6–11 Bekker)

T22 (DK 12A10; KRS 121, 122) Anaximander says that the earth is cylindrical in shape, and three times as wide as it is deep. He says that, at the point when this universe was created, the part of the eternal which is productive of hot and cold was separated off, and that a kind of sphere of flame emerged from this and grew all around the vapour that surrounds the earth, like bark on a tree. The sun and the moon and the stars came into being, he says, when this fiery sphere broke off and became enclosed in certain circles. (Ps.-Plutarch, *Miscellanies* 2.5–11 Diels)

T23 (DK 12A26; KRS 123) There are some (including, among the thinkers of long ago, Anaximander) who say that the earth stays where it is because of equality. For something which is established in the centre and has equality in relation to the extremes has no more reason to move up than it does down or to the sides; it is impossible for it to move in opposite directions at the same time, and so it is bound to stay where it is. (Aristotle, *On the Heavens* 295^b11–16 Allan)

T24 (DK 12A11; KRS 125, 129) He says that the stars are created as a circle of fire, which is separated off from the fire in the universe and surrounded by vapour. There are breathing-holes—pipe-like channels, as it were—where the stars appear; and so eclipses occur when the breathing-holes are blocked up. The moon appears to wax or wane at different times as a result of the blocking or opening of the channels. The circle of the sun is twenty-seven times the size of the earth, while the circle of the moon is eighteen times the size of the earth. The sun is the highest, and the circle of the fixed stars are the lowest . . . Winds occur when the finest vapours of the mist are separated off, gathered together, and set in motion. Rainfall is the result of the vapour which is sent up from the earth under the influence of the sun. Lightning occurs when wind breaks out and splits the clouds. (Hippolytus, *Refutation of All Heresies* 1.6.4–7 Marcovich)

T25 (DK 12A21; KRS 127) Anaximander says that the sun is equal in size to the earth, but that the circle from which it has its vent and by which it is carried around is twenty-seven times the size of that of the earth. (Aëtius, *Opinions* 2.21.1 Diels)

T26 (DK 12A23; KRS 130) Anaximander says that all these things [*the phenomena of thunderstorms*] are caused by wind: when wind has been enclosed within a dense cloud and compressed, and then breaks out as a result of its fineness and lightness, the rupture causes the noise, and the sundering, in contrast with the blackness of the cloud, causes the flash. (Aëtius, *Opinions* 3.3.1 Diels)

T27 (DK 12A30; KRS 133) Anaximander says that the first living creatures were born in a moist medium, surrounded by thorny barks, and that as they grew older they began to be fitted for a drier medium, until the bark broke off and they survived in a different form. (Aëtius, *Opinions* 5.19.4 Diels)

T28 (DK 12A30; KRS 135) Anaximander of Miletus imagined there arose from heated water and earth either fish or fish-like creatures, inside which human beings grew and were retained as fetuses up until puberty; then at last the creatures broke open, and men and women emerged who were already capable of feeding themselves. (Censorinus, *On Birthdays* 4.7.1–5 Jahn)

Anaximenes

T29 (DK 13A5; KRS 140) Anaximenes of Miletus, the son of Eurystratus, was a companion of Anaximander, and shares his view that the underlying nature of things is single and infinite; however, unlike Anaximander, Anaximenes' underlying nature is not boundless, but specific, since he says that it is air, and claims that it is thanks to rarefaction and condensation that it manifests in different forms in different things. When dilated, he says, it becomes fire, and when condensed it becomes first wind, then cloud, and then, as it becomes even denser, water, then earth, and then stones. Everything else comes from these things. He too makes motion eternal, and in his view motion is the cause of change as well.   (Theophrastus [fr. 226a Fortenbaugh *et al.*] in Simplicius, *Commentary on Aristotle's 'Physics'*, CAG IX, 24.26–25.1 Diels)

T30 (DK 13B2; KRS 160) According to Anaximenes of Miletus,* the son of Eurystratus, air is the first principle of things, since it is the source of everything and everything is dissolved back into it. Just as in us, he says, soul, which is air, holds us together, so the whole universe is surrounded by wind and air (he uses 'wind' and 'air' as synonyms*).   (Aëtius, *Opinions* 1.3.4.1–8 Diels)

T31 (DK 13B1; KRS 143) Anaximenes says that matter in a compressed and condensed state is cold, while in a dilated and 'loose' state (this is more or less exactly how he puts it) it is warm. And so, he says, when people say that man emits both warmth and cold from his mouth, they are not saying anything unreasonable. For breath gets cold when it is put under pressure and condensed by the lips, while when the mouth is relaxed the breath that escapes becomes warm as a result of its being in a rarefied state.   (Plutarch, *On the Primary Cold* 947f8–948a3 Helmbold)

T32 (DK 13A10; KRS 144) Next came Anaximenes, who claimed that air was a god, which had been created, was infinitely huge, and was always in motion.   (Cicero, *On the Nature of the Gods* 1.10.32–4 Plasberg)

T33 (DK 13A10; KRS 146) Anaximenes attributed all the causes of things to infinite air, but he did not deny the existence of gods or have nothing to say about them; however, he believed not that air was made by them, but that they emerged from air.   (Augustine, *The City of God* 8.2.34–6 Dombart/Kalb)

T34 (DK 13A6; KRS 148) Anaximenes says that everything is created by the condensation, as it were, of air, or alternatively by its rarefaction, while motion exists eternally. He says that the first product of the felting* of the air is the earth, which is quite flat, which means that it can therefore ride on the air. The earth is the starting-point for the creation of the sun, moon, and all the other heavenly bodies. At any rate, he says that the sun is earth, but that it has become well and truly heated up as a result of the swiftness of its motion. (Ps.-Plutarch, *Miscellanies* 3.3–8 Diels)

T35 (DK 13A7; KRS 151, 156) According to Anaximenes, the earth is flat and rides on air, and similarly the sun, the moon and all the other heavenly bodies, which are made of fire, ride on the air because of their flatness. He says that the heavenly bodies have come into existence from the earth, as a result of the rising of moisture out of the earth. When this moisture is rarefied, it turns into fire, and the heavenly bodies are composed of this fire, which rises up into the heavens ... He says that the heavenly bodies do not move under the earth, as others have supposed, but around the earth, as a strip of felt moves around one's head; and that the sun is hidden not by being under the earth, but by being concealed by the higher parts of the earth and as a result of its increased distance from us ... Rainbows are created when the sun's rays fall on concentrated air. (Hippolytus, *Refutation of All Heresies* 1.7.4–8 Marcovich)

T36 (DK 13A14; KRS 157) Corroboration of the view that the regions of the earth to the north are highlands is found in the fact that many of the ancient speculators about celestial phenomena held that the sun does not pass under the earth but around it (specifically around this northern region), and disappears and causes night because the land is high in the north. (Aristotle, *On Celestial Phenomena* 354ᵃ27–32 Bekker)

T37 (DK 13A20; KRS 150) Anaximenes, Anaxagoras, and Democritus say that the flatness of the earth is responsible for its staying in place, because it does not cut the air beneath, but rests on it like a lid (as flat bodies obviously do) ... According to these thinkers, thanks to its flatness the earth behaves in the same way in relation to the air beneath it, which does not have enough room to move, and so becomes compressed against the underside of the earth and remains motionless, like the water in a clepsydra.* (Aristotle, *On the Heavens* 294ᵇ13–21 Allan)

T38 (DK 13A15; KRS 153) Anaximenes says that the turnings of the heavenly bodies are due to their being pushed off course by condensed air which repels them. (Aëtius, *Opinions* 2.23.1 Diels)

T39 (DK 13A14; KRS 154) Anaximenes says that the heavenly bodies are fixed like nails into the ice-like periphery; but some say that they are fiery leaves, like paintings. (Aëtius, *Opinions* 2.14.3 Diels)

T40 (DK 13A17; KRS 158) Anaximenes' views coincide with those of Anaximander on these phenomena [*see* **T21** *above*], except that he adds what happens in the case of the sea, which gleams when it is cleaved by oars . . . Anaximenes says that clouds are caused by the increased thickening of the air, and that when air is concentrated even more rain is squeezed out; that hail happens when the water is frozen as it is falling, and snow when a windy ingredient is included in the moisture. (Aëtius, *Opinions* 3.3.2, 3.4.1 Diels)

T41 (DK 13A21; KRS 159) Anaximenes says that when the earth is soaked or dried out, it breaks up, and is shaken when peaks break off under these circumstances and fall down. And that, he says, is why earthquakes happen both during droughts and also during times of excessive rain. For during droughts, as I have said, the earth gets dry and breaks up, and when it becomes saturated by water it falls to pieces. (Aristotle, *On Celestial Phenomena* 365^{b}6–12 Bekker)

E. Asmis, 'What is Anaximander's Apeiron?', *Journal of the History of Philosophy*, 19 (1981), 279–97.

P. J. Bicknell, 'τὸ ἄπειρον, ἄπειρος ἀήρ and τὸ περιέχον', *Acta Classica*, 9 (1966), 27–48.

—— 'Anaximenes' Astronomy', *Acta Classica*, 12 (1969), 53–85.

C. J. Classen, 'Anaximander and Anaximenes: The Earliest Greek Theories of Change?', *Phronesis*, 22 (1977), 89–102.

D. L. Couprie, 'The Visualization of Anaximander's Astronomy', *Apeiron*, 28 (1995), 159–81.

R. M. Dancy, 'Thales, Anaximander and Infinity', *Apeiron*, 22 (1989), 149–90.

D. R. Dicks, 'Thales', *Classical Quarterly*, 9 (1959), 294–309.

J. Engmann, 'Cosmic Justice in Anaximander', *Phronesis*, 36 (1991), 1–25.

A. Finkelberg, 'Anaximander's Conception of the *Apeiron*', *Phronesis*, 28 (1993), 229–56.

—— 'Plural Words in Anaximander', *American Journal of Philology*, 115 (1994), 485–506.

G. Freudenthal, 'The Theory of Opposites and an Ordered Universe: Physics and Metaphysics in Anaximander', *Phronesis*, 31 (1986), 197–228.

D. J. Furley, 'The Dynamics of the Earth: Anaximander, Plato, and the Centrifocal Theory', in [25], 14–26.

H. B. Gottschalk, 'Anaximander's *Apeiron*', *Phronesis*, 10 (1965), 37–53.

U. Hölscher, 'Anaximander and the Beginning of Greek Philosophy', in [26], i. 281–322 (first pub. *Hermes*, 81 (1953)).

C. H. Kahn, *Anaximander and the Origins of Greek Cosmology* (New York: Columbia University Press, 1960).

G. S. Kirk, 'Some Problems in Anaximander', in [26], i. 323–49 (first pub. *Classical Quarterly*, 5 (1955)).

J. Loenen, 'Was Anaximander an Evolutionist?', *Mnemosyne*, 7 (1954), 215–32.

J. Longrigg, 'A Note on Anaximenes, Fragment 2', *Phronesis*, 9 (1964), 1–5.

J. Mansfeld, 'Aristotle and Others on Thales, or the Beginnings of Natural Philosophy', in [29], 126–46 (first pub. *Mnemosyne*, 38 (1985)).

A. Mosshammer, 'Thales' Eclipse', *Transactions of the American Philological Association*, 111 (1981), 145–55.

D. Panchenko, 'Thales' Prediction of a Solar Eclipse', *Journal for the History of Astronomy*, 25 (1994), 275–88.

J. Robinson, 'Anaximander and the Problem of the Earth's Immobility', in [21], 111–18.

D. Roller, 'Thales of Miletus: Philosopher or Businessman?', *Liverpool Classical Monthly*, 3 (1978), 249–53.

P. Seligman, *The 'Apeiron' of Anaximander: A Study in the Origin and Function of Metaphysical Ideas* (London: Athlone Press, 1962).

G. Vlastos, 'Equality and Justice in Early Greek Cosmologies', in [26], i. 92–129, and in [33], 57–88 (first pub. *Classical Philology*, 42 (1947)).

XENOPHANES OF COLOPHON

Xenophanes' place in this book is somewhat precarious. He was primarily a prolific (and very long-lived: **F1**) poet, writing in various metres and various genres, a travelling bard who wandered the Greek world after leaving his native Ionia after the Median invasion of 546 (**F2**). We have over 100 lines of his poetry, only a few of which certainly reflect philosophical interests. The idea that he was either a Pythagorean or the founder of Eleatic monism is mistaken. It is hard to see the grounds for the former claim, and the latter (as in **T1**) is an erroneous inference based on the superficial similarity of his god with Parmenides' 'what-is'. However, Plato's light-hearted claim irredeemably influenced the later doxographic tradition, which frequently attributes to Xenophanes views lifted from Parmenides.

He is best known as the first critical theologian. Where the Milesians had implicitly undermined Homeric religion, Xenophanes made a full frontal assault. The relevant theological fragments (**F3–9**) are mostly self-explanatory. It is clear that he unequivocally rejected Homeric anthropomorphism, and replaced this with a conception of a god whose attributes seem to make him little more than a mind writ large. (I should say that although **F4** and **F5** have no subject, the contexts in which they are preserved guarantee that the subject is this god.) However, it is clear from **F3** that Xenophanes' god is imagined as having a body; it is just that it is not humanoid (see also **F8** in this context). In any case, his god is motionless (**F5**), not just because it would be blasphemous to attribute motion to him, but also because he has no need of movement, since he can move everything else with the power of his mind. Although Homer's Zeus could shake mount Olympus with a nod of his head (*Iliad* 1.528–30), Xenophanes' god has no need to move at all to shake the whole world. He should probably be envisaged as being situated on the periphery of the universe, all around the world, like Anaximander's divine 'boundless';[1] this seems more in keeping with archaic thought than the idea that the god is to be identified with the world; however, it is possible that Xenophanes imagined the world as being imbued with the mind of the god, so that it can direct all things. The rejection of Homeric tales about adultery and so on among the gods presumably means that Xenophanes conceives his god to be good, as well as a being of great power. Finally, given that the god remains 'for ever' in the same place, it is likely that he is conceived as

[1] And also very like the Persian divinity referred to by Herodotus in 1.131.

eternal: **T2**, one of a number of pithy sayings that later became attached to Xenophanes as a well-known sage, is a neat way of expressing the same idea.

What is not so clear, however, is whether Xenophanes was a fully fledged monotheist. Although the mention of 'gods and men' (**F3**) is a formulaic way of expressing emphasis, it would at the very least be extremely casual of Xenophanes to choose this way of expressing emphasis in a context where he was arguing for what would to the Greeks have been the extraordinary concept of monotheism. It seems more reasonable to conclude that Xenophanes' 'one god' is not the only god, but the main god in a pantheon. So, for instance, when he says at the end of one of his non-philosophical fragments (DK 21B1) that 'It is always good to hold the gods in high regard', we have no need to accuse him of hypocrisy, or to suppose that he changed his mind at some point and became a monotheist. He may, like Plato later, have gone no further than decrying the immorality of the gods as traditionally portrayed. In this context, it is interesting that at **T3** ps.-Plutarch applies to all the gods the attributes of **F4**, which most scholars believe apply only to the one supreme god.[2]

Nevertheless, Xenophanes' theology must have seemed extremely shocking to most of his contemporaries, and some aspects of it proved influential, at least on other thinkers, as we shall see in the case of Heraclitus. But his abstract picture of god remained an isolated phenomenon, even among the free-thinking Presocratics. It is tempting to think that Xenophanes' god might have been like the god of the Ionians—a divinization of their cosmogonic principle. But as we shall see, Xenophanes' cosmogonic principle is, or includes, earth, and that his god is not the same as the earth (as Aristotle seems to have thought, to judge by **T4**) is shown by the fact that he moves the earth with his mind. In this sense Xenophanes' god is not as 'advanced' as the Ionian deities. Xenophanes' god is more like a super-abstraction of the Homeric Zeus: he has a location, but it does not seem to be as localized as mount Olympus; he has a body, but it is not anthropomorphic; and he has infinitely more power than Zeus.

Personally, I am not convinced that Xenophanes had a developed cosmogony. It has commonly been argued that he took as his originative substances earth and water (**F11**), but this statement in itself scarcely constitutes an Ionian cosmogony, rather than an expression of the fact that, Xenophanes believed (see below), things emerge from a primordial swamp. As for the alternative statement, **F10**, that everything comes from

---

[2] The most powerful case for reading Xenophanes as a fully fledged monotheist is the one argued for by Barnes ([15], vol. i., ch. 5).

and returns to earth, this may not be a scientific fragment at all, but simply a variation on the English saying, 'Ashes to ashes, dust to dust.' In any case, there is a clash between **F11** and **F12**: one says that things come *from* earth and water, the other that they are made *of* earth and water—two quite different propositions. Moreover, if earth and/or water were cosmogonic principles in the Ionian mould, that would leave us with the strange gap of not knowing how he expected to explain the existence of air and fire; **F14** is not a cosmogonic fragment about the origin of air, but a meteorological fragment about how winds arise (see also **T6**).

Even if he was no cosmogonist, however, Xenophanes did remark on other meteorological phenomena, such as the rainbow (Iris in **F15**), and with less sophistication or imagination than Anaximander and Anaximenes explained the earth's stability by stating that it extends infinitely down below us (**F13**). This raises the question how he would have explained the disappearance of the sun and stars, which were usually thought to rotate under the earth. Here testimonia come to the rescue: Xenophanes apparently believed that the sun (and presumably the other heavenly bodies) is made new each day. This belief in a plurality of suns and moons led, in the doxographical tradition, to the delightful misconception that Xenophanes believed that different regions of the earth had different suns and moons.

However, the constitution of the heavenly bodies remains unclear: are they gathered together from clouds or from 'little pieces of fire' (**T5**)? It has recently been securely established that according to Xenophanes the moon, at any rate, is made out of ignited cloud,[3] and in all likelihood the same goes for the other heavenly bodies. But perhaps the two views found in **T5** are not contradictory; perhaps Xenophanes said that evaporation from the earth causes clouds or mist, that somehow parts of this vapour ignite, and then that the ignited parts gather together and form the sun (and the other heavenly bodies).

T7 records one of the most interesting features of Xenophanes' cosmology. Reflecting on the existence of marine fossils inland, he was led to believe that the earth had once been covered with mud, and had then dried out, but was at the moment gradually becoming soaked again. He seems to imagine that the gradual saturation of the earth causes it to dissolve and slide down into the sea (which may incidentally cause the salinity of the sea: **T8**), until everything is covered by the muddy mixture of earth and sea. Then the process of drying out begins again, and life begins again—from earth and water, as **F12** says.

Xenophanes' most remarkable contribution to philosophy is contained

---

[3] See Runia in the bibliography below.

in the fragments with which I end the sequence, in which he reflects on the limitations of human knowledge. Xenophanes was probably led to these remarks by reflection on his theology: having conceived of the divine as super-intelligent, the traditional contrast between the powers of gods and those of men will have led him to belittle men's knowledge and intelligence (cf. **F3**: god is completely different from man): all we can have is belief, not knowledge (**F16** l. 4). This applies explicitly to his own views as well as anyone else's; in fact it is possible that **F17** came close to the end of a philosophical poem (supposing there to have been one), and was therefore a comment on everything that had gone before. Above all, we are limited by the fact that our experience is limited (**F18**). Nevertheless, by diligent research we can improve our epistemic situation (**F19**), so that there is gradual overall progress; but research is what it takes, not wild speculation. In **F20** he lampoons Pythagoras (that it is a lampoon is guaranteed by the context: Diogenes Laertius preserves this fragment among those of other satirists who poked fun at Pythagoras), either for his theory of metempsychosis or for his claim to be able to recognize a human soul in the yelping of a puppy, but in either case for making unverifiable claims. This is in keeping with Xenophanes' more cautious approach to cosmogony and cosmology.

Undoubtedly the most important reason why Xenophanes pointed out the limitations of human knowledge is the one enunciated in the first two lines of **F16**; indeed, many of his theological comments can also be seen as having the same purport. All the usual ways in which the Greeks assumed they could obtain knowledge about the gods are criticized: the gods do not visit us in human guise (as often in Homer), because they do not have human bodies; the gods' will is not made manifest through portents like rainbows, because these are purely natural phenomena; the gods are not as the poets or other experts have described; and in any case no one can know if an inspired utterance is accurate. In short, as **F3** insists, the main god, at least, is so unlike us humans that we cannot really lay claim to any reliable knowledge about him.

Xenophanes' ideas are based more on common sense and observation (e.g. of fossils) than his Ionian predecessors. His vision is less splendid, but more solidly based. This aspect of his character may also be glimpsed in his non-philosophical fragments, where in a cosy fashion he praises the conventional virtues of piety, duty towards one's native city, and a life of moderation. But this caution also gave rise to a degree of scepticism, particularly about matters relating to the gods. Xenophanes was no thoroughgoing sceptic: he was as concerned as any of his opponents to give an accurate description of phenomena and the gods, and he was certain that honey tasted sweet; but he was aware of the limitations of human knowledge of the most important and remote things. We cannot attain infallible knowledge, and we are limited by the experiences we happen to have encountered. Enquiry can improve matters (**F19**), but even so we will never attain certainty about the big questions of life. This thesis in turn depends on a thesis about the senses: Xenophanes is implicitly saying that the reason we will never attain certain knowledge is that the information we receive through our senses is incapable of taking us there. And so his philosophical successors took up various positions on the reliability of the senses, some (Parmenides, Melissus) claiming that the senses are useless, while intelligence or divinely granted insight gives them a fast track to the truth which Xenophanes found so elusive, others (e.g. Heraclitus, Empedocles) arguing for cautious use of the senses.

F1 (DK 21B8; KRS 161)

> Already my thoughts have been tossed here and there in Greece
> For sixty-seven years; and that's not all:
> From my birth till then there were twenty-five more,
> If I know how to speak truly about these things.

> > (Diogenes Laertius, *Lives of Eminent Philosophers*
> > 9.19.1–4 Long)

F2 (DK 21B45)

> > I tossed myself about, travelling from city to city.
> > (Erotian, *Notes on Hippocrates' 'On Epidemics'* 102.23–4
> > Nachmanson)

T1 (DK 21A29; KRS 163) [*A visitor from Elea is speaking*] And our Eleatic tribe, beginning with Xenophanes or even earlier, tell us tales in their stories on the assumption that what people call 'all things' are really one. (Plato, *Sophist* 242d4–7 Duke *et al.*)

F3 (DK 21B23; KRS 170)

> > One god, greatest among gods and men,
> > In no way similar to mortal men in body or in thought.

> (Clement, *Miscellanies* 5.109.1 Stählin/Früchtel)

F4 (DK 21B24; KRS 172)

> > Complete he sees, complete he thinks, complete he hears.

> (Sextus Empiricus, *Against the Professors* 9.144.4 Bury)

F5 (DK 21B26, B25; KRS 171)

He remains for ever in the same place, entirely motionless,
Nor is it proper for him to move from one place to another.
But effortlessly he shakes all things by thinking with his mind.

(Simplicius, *Commentary on Aristotle's 'Physics'*,
CAG IX, 23.11–12, 20 Diels)

F6 (DK 21B11; KRS 166)

Homer and Hesiod have attributed to the gods
Everything that men find shameful and reprehensible—
Stealing, adultery, and deceiving one another.

(Sextus Empiricus, *Against the Professors*
9.193.3–5 Bury)

F7 (DK 21B14; KRS 167)

But mortals think that the gods are born,
Wear their own clothes, have voices and bodies.

(Clement, *Miscellanies* 5.109.2
Stählin/Früchtel)

F8 (DK 21B15; KRS 169)

If cows and horses or lions had hands,[†]
Or could draw with their hands and make things as men can,
Horses would have drawn horse-like gods, cows cow-like gods,
And each species would have made the gods' bodies just like their
own.

(Clement, *Miscellanies* 5.109.3 Stählin/Früchtel)

F9 (DK 21B16; KRS 168)

Ethiopians say that their gods are flat-nosed and black,
And Thracians that theirs have blue eyes and red hair.*

(Clement, *Miscellanies* 7.22.1 Stählin/Früchtel)

T2 (DK 21A13) The people of Elea asked Xenophanes whether or
not they should sacrifice to Leucothea and mourn for her. The
advice he gave them was not to mourn for her if they took her to
be divine, and not to sacrifice to her if they took her to be
human. (Aristotle, *Rhetoric* 1400^{b}6–8 Ross)

T3 (DK 21A32) Concerning the gods, he declared that there is no hierarchy among them, since it is sacrilege for any of the gods to have a master; and none of them is in the slightest need of anything; and they see and hear as a whole, rather than partially.   (Ps.-Plutarch, *Miscellanies* 4.9–11 Diels)

T4 Xenophanes was the first of these monists (for he is said to have been Parmenides' teacher), but he did not express himself clearly and in fact seems not to have grasped either of these concepts [*either what Aristotle sees as the formal monism of Parmenides or the material monism of Melissus*]. Rather, gazing up at heaven as a whole, he declared that the One is God.   (Aristotle, *Metaphysics* 986^{b}21–5 Ross)

F10 (DK 21B27)

　　Earth is the source of all things, and all things end in earth.
　　　　　　　　　　　　　　　　　　(Aëtius, *Opinions* 1.3.12 Diels)

F11 (DK 21B29; KRS 181)

　　All that is created and grows is no more than earth and water.

　　　　　　　(Philoponus, *Commentary on Aristotle's 'Physics'*,
　　　　　　　　　　　　　　　　　　CAG XVI, 125.30 Vitelli)

F12 (DK 21B33; KRS 182)

　　　　　　For we are all created from earth and water.
　　　　　　(Sextus Empiricus, *Against the Professors* 10.314.8 Bury)

F13 (DK 21B28; KRS 10, 180)

　　Plainly, the upper limit of the earth, here at our feet,
　　Abuts the aither; but below it stretches on without limit.

　　　　　　(Achilles, *Introduction to Aratus' 'Phaenomena'*
　　　　　　　　　　　　　　　　　4.34.13–14 Maass)

F14 (DK 21B30; KRS 183)

　　　　The sea is the source of water and the source of wind;
　　　　For there would be no wind without the great sea,†
　　　　Nor flowing rivers, nor rainfall from the aither.
　　　　No, the great sea is the creator of clouds, winds,
　　　　And rivers.

　　　　　　(Crates of Mallus [fr. 32a Mette] in the Geneva
　　　　　　　　　　　Scholiast on Homer's *Iliad* 21.196)

F15 (DK 21B32; KRS 178)

> And the one called Iris is also a cloud,
> Purple, red, and yellow to the sight.

> (Scholiast BLT on Homer's *Iliad*
> 11.27, Dindorf 3.457)

T5 (DK 21A40; KRS 177) Xenophanes says that the sun is made up of ignited clouds. In his *The Opinions of the Natural Scientists* Theophrastus writes that it is made up of little pieces of fire which are assembled out of the moist exhalation and assemble the sun.   (Theophrastus [fr. 232 Fortenbaugh *et al.*] in Aëtius, *Opinions* 2.20.3 Diels)

T6 (DK 21A46) Xenophanes says that meteorological phenomena are caused in the first instance by the warmth of the sun. For when moisture is drawn up from the sea, the sweet part of it separates off as mist because of its fineness, forms clouds, and falls as rain when it is subjected to felting; and winds are caused by the evaporation.†   (Aëtius, *Opinions* 3.4.4 Diels)

T7 (DK 21A33; KRS 184) Xenophanes believes that the earth is becoming mixed with the sea and that it will eventually be dissolved by the moist. He adduces the following evidence: shells are found inland and in the mountains; in the quarries at Syracuse the impression of a fish and seaweeds† has been found; on Paros the impression of a bay-leaf has been found buried in stone; and on Malta there are slabs of rock made up of all kinds of sea-creatures. He says that these came about a long time ago, when everything was covered with mud, and that the impression became dried in the mud. He claims that the human race is wiped out whenever the earth is carried down into the sea and becomes mud, that then there is a fresh creation, and that this is how all the worlds have their beginning.   (Hippolytus, *Refutation of All Heresies* 1.14.5–6 Marcovich)

T8 (DK 21A33) He says that the sea is salty because of all the various ingredients that flow together in it.   (Hippolytus, *Refutation of All Heresies* 1.14.4.1–2 Marcovich)

F16 (DK 21B34; KRS 186)

Indeed, there never has been† nor will there ever be a man
Who knows the truth about the gods and all the matters of which I
    speak.

For even if one should happen to speak what is the case especially
well,
Still he himself would not know it. But belief occurs in all matters.

(Sextus Empiricus, *Against the Professors* 7.49.4–7 Bury)

F17 (DK 21B35; KRS 187)

Let these things be believed as approximations to the truth.

(Plutarch, *Table Talk* 746b7 Sandbach)

F18 (DK 21B38; KRS 189)

If the god had not made yellow honey, they would have said
That figs were much sweeter.

(Herodian, *On Peculiar Speech* 41.5 Lentz)

F19 (DK 21B18; KRS 188)

The gods did not intimate all things to men straight away,
But in time, through seeking, their discoveries improve.*

(John of Stobi, *Anthology* 1.8.2 Wachsmuth/Hense)

F20 (DK 21B7; KRS 260) [*about Pythagoras*]

Once, they say, he was passing by when a puppy was being thrashed,
And he took pity on it and spoke the following words:
'Stop! Do not beat the dog! It is, in fact, the soul of a friend of
mine.
I recognized it when I heard its voice.'

(Diogenes Laertius, *Lives of Eminent Philosophers*
8.36.12–15 Long)

S. Darcus, 'The *Phren* of the *Noos* in Xenophanes' God', *Symbolae Osloenses*, 53 (1978), 25–39.

M. Eisenstadt, 'Xenophanes' Proposed Reform of Greek Religion', *Hermes*, 102 (1974), 142–50.

A. Finkelberg, 'Studies in Xenophanes', *Harvard Studies in Classical Philology*, 93 (1990), 104–67.

—— 'Xenophanes' Physis, Parmenides' Doxa, and Empedocles' Theory of Cosmogonical Mixture', *Hermes*, 125 (1997), 1–16.

H. Fränkel, 'Xenophanes' Empiricism and his Critique of Knowledge', in [30], 118–31.

P. Keyser, 'Xenophanes' Sun on Trojan Ida', *Mnemosyne*, 45 (1992), 299–311.

J. H. Lesher, *Xenophanes: Fragments* (Toronto: University of Toronto Press, 1992).

A. P. D. Mourelatos, ' "X is Really Y": Ionian Origins of a Thought Pattern', in [24], 280–90.

J. A. Palmer, 'Xenophanes' Ouranian God in the Fourth Century', *Oxford Studies in Ancient Philosophy*, 16 (1998), 1–34.

D. Runia, 'Xenophanes on the Moon: A Doxographicum in Aëtius', *Phronesis*, 34 (1989), 245–69.

A. Tulin, 'Xenophanes Fr. 18 DK and the Origins of the Idea of Progress', *Hermes*, 121 (1993), 129–38.

HERACLITUS OF EPHESUS

In the case of Heraclitus of Ephesus, we are blessed for the first time with a large number of fragments, and cursed by their enigmatic obscurity, which was already notorious in ancient times (and which has led to quite a high degree of textual corruption of the fragments). It is even possible that Heraclitus did not write a coherent treatise, but a series of longer and shorter aphorisms, suitable for an oral culture, which frequently rely on metaphor and paradox. This makes pinning his thought down extremely hard, which is presumably (since he was a consummate stylist) the result he intended. Under these circumstances, it seems safest to group his fragments by theme or family resemblance, and gradually to see if anything more systematic can be made out of them. It is hardly going too far to say that divergent interpretations of Heraclitus' thought can be reached simply by grouping different fragments together, but at the same time it is true that Heraclitus builds resonances into his sayings, by repeating the same or similar words and phrases, and these resonances come into play whatever order we impose on the fragments.[1]

There are several recurring themes. The first concerns what Heraclitus calls 'the *logos*', and people's incomprehension of it. The *logos* is something one can hear (**F1**), and yet it is not simply Heraclitus' own 'account' of things, since he distinguishes himself from it in **F10**, and it predates his or any account of it in **F1**. It speaks through him, then, and at the same time it is responsible for events on earth. It comes from the world at large, and is presumably what entitles Heraclitus to describe the world as 'wise' in **F4**. The whole world is intelligent and alive, and speaks to the wise man subtly, communicating its inner nature and enabling him to model himself on it. The best I can do to encompass most of the range of Heraclitus' meanings is 'principle',[2] but this loses the idea of speaking/hearing, which may still be prominent, in that Heraclitus may have conceived of this 'principle' as something spoken eternally by the universe, for those with ears to hear, and reflected, more or less accurately, in the teaching of sages such as himself.

---

[1] The phenomenon of resonance would be a little clearer had I translated *all* the fragments. I translate only about half—though nearly all those that are philosophically important, and (as it happens) nearly all those in which resonances occur.

[2] Compare the fragment of Heraclitus' near contemporary, the philosophical comic playwright, Epicharmus of Syracuse: 'The *logos* guides men and keeps them always on the straight and narrow. A man has reasoning, but there is also divine *logos*. Human reasoning is born from the divine *logos*' (DK 23B57.1–3).

These first fragments (up to **F8**) reveal Heraclitus in prophet mode, castigating people for their failure to wake up to reality. Like Xenophanes and Philolaus, Heraclitus draws a line between the truth, which is accessible only to divine understanding, *qua* eternal, and mere human comprehension (see also **F19**); yet we can, presumably, attain the divine understanding required. The combination of **T1** and **F5** shows that (like the modern mystic G. I. Gurdjieff) Heraclitus calls our normal waking state 'sleep', and is urging us to wake up to a higher understanding. The *logos*, like the whole world, is common—accessible to all—and yet we fail to see what is right before our eyes: this is the implication of **F5** and **F6**.

According to the truth of the *logos*, all is one and there is proportion or harmony throughout the world. This leads us into a second set of fragments (**F13–20**), which illustrate various ways in which there is coincidence or even identity of opposites. Either they are part of the same continuum (e.g. **F13–14**), or they are relative in some way or another (**F15–16**). Relativity is another common theme in Heraclitus (**F17–19**). Somewhat pedantically, Aristotle complains (e.g. at *Physics* 185^{b}19–25, *Metaphysics* 1012^{a}24–6) that Heraclitus breaks the law of non-contradiction, and in identifying opposites makes every statement true. But what is important to Heraclitus is precisely that things change from day to day and from context to context.

Although the *logos*, the truth of things, is common (i.e. universal and universally apprehensible), it is different from anything else (**F11**); although it is common, it is unfamiliar and unexpected (**F9**). Since the apprehension of things like the underlying harmony of the world requires reflection, not just naïve reliance on the senses (**F24–5**), it is not surprising to find Heraclitus casting doubt on the senses (**F27**). His scepticism is not absolute, though: the senses are still all we have (**F28**, **F29**), but the data with which they supply us require judicious assessment. **F26** refers simultaneously to the ambiguity of sensory evidence and the ambiguity of Heraclitus' own sayings. The way to truth is perhaps suggested by **F30** and **F31**, where Heraclitus reveals his own methodology ('I searched for myself') and suggests that we can all do the same, and will all come up with the same result: the common *logos*. At any rate, note the difference in methodology between the judicious use of the senses and introspection recommended by Heraclitus, and the 'wide learning' for which he condemns Pythagoras (**T1** and **T2**, on p. 95).

The underlying unity of things, according to **F4** and **F32**, can be called 'god', or 'the divine law' (**F12**). This is to say, by Milesian convention, that it is the ultimate reality of things. And yet in antiquity Heraclitus was famous for stressing the flux of things, rather than this stability. Indeed, Plato thinks of him entirely as a teacher of the metaphysical doctrine of flux, and constantly opposes him to unitarians like Parmenides. The main evidence for Heraclitus' teaching on flux is given in **F33–6** (assuming that 'dying' in **F36** is a metaphor for change), and **T3–4**. The solution to the apparent contradiction between flux and stability may be that Heraclitus actually taught the underlying unity and stability of things at a deeper level, the level underlying flux which is accessible to divine reason. The river is single, despite its flux; dying and living are a single continuum. As well as actual physical flux, there is the epistemic flux implied by the emphasis on relativity that we have already noted. This of course relates to Heraclitus' scepticism about the evidence of the senses: there is nothing on the face of the world that we can securely grasp or base our moral opinions on; so we had better wake up and look to the underlying stability and unity of things.

At one point, with tantalizing obscurity, this underlying unity is described as 'back-turning, like a bow or a lyre' (**F21**). Obviously, the strings of a bow or a lyre would not maintain their tension in one direction if there was not an equal tension in the opposite direction. This seems to be what Heraclitus is getting at, especially in his emphasis on opposites in the world. They tend in opposite directions, but are actually essential to each other, and this tension is in fact another way of hinting at the underlying unity or connectedness of the world. The idea of tension leads naturally into yet another possible description of the underlying connectedness of things as a kind of war (**F22, F23**).

We now come to the most puzzling aspect of Heraclitus' thought. A number of fragments make some cosmological mention of fire (**F32, F36–40**). On the one hand, fire seems to be another symbol of constancy in change, like 'war' above: while seeming to be in motion, there is still the unity of the fact that it remains fire, and the proportionate balance between the flames and the fuel. On the other hand, fire also at times seems close to being a Milesian *arkhē* or divinized elemental principle; this, of course, is how Aristotle took it (*Metaphysics* 984ᵃ7), and we can judge from **F10** that Heraclitus was a monist. But **F38** tells strongly against the idea that fire is an Aristotelian substrate, since what is important about commercial exchange is precisely that I come away with goods, not gold: gold does not outlast the exchange. In any case, fire for Heraclitus does not seem to be unlimited (as Anaximenes' air is, for instance), but he does sometimes speak as if it were a constituent of things. We should think of this fire not as the fire in our grates, but as the pure fire or aither of the upper heavens. Broadly, he seems to divide the matter of the world into fire, water (sea), and earth, with all three interacting in a way that preserves their original equilibrium, and changing into one another: fire becomes water by gradual condensation (**T8**), sea becomes earth and fire (as witnessed by the phenomenon of lightning, which Heraclitus may have thought rose up from the sea to the upper fire of the universe, rather than striking downwards), and so on. But, assuming that in **F39** 'thunderbolt' is a form of fire, fire plays the dominant role (this is also perhaps the implication of **F41**). Heraclitus must have been impressed with the destructive power of fire, and also its role in preserving life, through warmth. Fire is itself a paradox, and serves as both a symbol and a major constituent of the paradoxical world.

F40 is the only one of Heraclitus' fire fragments which could easily be interpreted as implying that, at some stage, the world will be consumed by fire; **F36** would imply this too, if the 'measures' Heraclitus speaks of are understood in a temporal sense. The periodic destruction of the world by fire was Stoic doctrine, and they commonly (but not universally) looked back to Heraclitus as their predecessor in this respect. Cosmic conflagration is also the context in which Hippolytus preserves this particular fragment. This is a difficult issue, with various scholars arguing for or against the attribution of the doctrine to Heraclitus. On the one hand, the general tenor of Heraclitus' thought seems to be that there is harmonious give and take between the major stuffs of the world—fire, water, and earth—and it is hard to see how the idea that the world is periodically overwhelmed by fire fits in with this. On the other hand, fire clearly does occupy a special place in Heraclitus' thought, and is not just on a par with earth and water. In addition to late Stoic doctrine, there is also the unequivocal evidence of Aristotle in **T5** and **T6**, which clearly attributes to Heraclitus a belief in the cyclical destruction and renewal of the world. On balance—but it is a fine balance—I suppose that Heraclitus may have believed in a periodic cosmic conflagration.[3]

The pure fire in the heavens is replenished, according to **T8**, by evaporation from the sea. These gaseous evaporations are ignited and form the heavenly bodies. If the sun is renewed each day (by these evaporations), as **T7** tells us, presumably the same goes for the other heavenly bodies as well. Although we have little or nothing in the way of astronomical fragments (e.g. **F42**), Diogenes Laertius' report in **T8** seems pretty authoritative and accurate.[4] Heraclitus was considerably less interested in astronomical and meteorological matters than his predecessors; he had a universal message to convey, and seems to have spent only a little time

[3] However, if the word translated 'order' in **F36** is to be translated 'the world' (as it certainly could be in slightly later Greek), that would be unequivocal evidence that Heraclitus did *not* believe in periodic universal conflagration, or indeed in cosmogony, since he would be saying that the world was eternal.

[4] On the daily renewal of the sun, compare Xenophanes **T5**.

indicating how it applied in various domains—astronomy, politics, ethics, and so on.

Given the dominance of fire, it is perhaps not surprising to find that it constitutes and explains the functioning of the dominant part of humans—the soul; he may have inferred the hot nature of soul from the fact that de-animated corpses turn cold. Typically, though, Heraclitus expresses this idea in a teasing and elliptical fashion. It is only because we know that the three major stuffs of the world are earth, water, and fire, that we recognize in **F44** the replacement of 'fire' with 'soul'. Water is the source of soul because (as Aristotle noted at *On the Soul* 405ᵃ) for Heraclitus the stuff of soul was the same as the stuff exhaled by water; and we know from **T8** that the light, dry exhalations from the sea form the pure kind of fire that is found in the upper regions of the universe. So again, soul is fire, or at least light, bright, and fiery. **F45** and **F47** fit into this framework straightforwardly, but **F48** is more mysterious. Perhaps Heraclitus conceived of soul as a fragment of the fire at large in the universe (see Xenophon, *Memorabilia* 1.4.8 and Plato, *Philebus* 29a-c). **F46** implies that a degree of asceticism may be necessary to avoid moistening the soul. However, as **F44** reminds us, soul/fire emerges out of water, and therefore there is a cycle of death and rebirth for soul. Much of **F49** is obscure, but the idea that when dreaming we kindle a light for ourselves shows the connection between not just sensation and light, but cognition and the internal fire which is our soul. The innovatory notion that the soul is responsible for cognition is also, of course, suggested by **F27**. This is also the theme of **T9** (which we may take to be basically accurate). This enables us to tie up a couple of loose threads. We know from **F1** that the *logos*, the 'principle', governs things; we know from **F39** that fire guides things; we now know that our soul is fiery, and it is reasonable to think that it governs the otherwise insensate body. Our human soul, then, when properly dry and fiery, like a beam of light (**F47**), is in touch or even in communion with the fiery nature of the principle which governs the universe as a whole. In this sense, as **F48** hints, the soul is co-extensive with the universe as a whole.

Heraclitus' teaching on the soul did not stop with its fiery constitution and relation to the governing fire of the *logos*. He believed that good people would be repaid with a better lot in the afterlife (**F50–2**)—or perhaps that they were the only ones who gained an afterlife, while other souls perish as water (**F44**). But what is a good person? **T10** seems to suggest that Heraclitus subscribed to a traditional Homeric code. His reputation in antiquity was as a haughty aristocrat, and this may perhaps be borne out by the few fragments which reflect on political matters (**F53–8**; see also **F7**), especially if the 'insolence' referred to in **F58** is the insolence of democratic intentions (but this fragment may just be a general ethical recommendation of moderation) and if the 'animals' of **F59** are symbols for a 'lower' type of human. It seems to me that **F55** and **F12** are the crucial political fragments: his hierarchical, meritocratic politics is merely a reflection of the hierarchy he perceived in the universe at large. Thus the deliberate ambiguity of **F54** falls into place: in a political context, one should obey the one leader; in a cosmic context, one should hearken to the one, the *logos*. By relating politics and perhaps ethics to his larger, metaphysical framework, Heraclitus earns a place as the first systematic moral philosopher.

Finally, since the *logos* is divine, it comes as little surprise to find Heraclitus in **F61–4** continuing Xenophanes' criticism of conventional religion and some of its beliefs and practices. **F64** was considered particularly shocking, but once Heraclitus had made the soul the true self (he was the first philosopher to do so), it naturally followed that once the soul has left the body, the corpse is totally worthless. But in general his criticism is not as far-reaching as that of Xenophanes. He still acknowledges at least some divinities (**T11**, and see also the use of Apollo in **F26** and Zeus in **F4**) and, just as the implication of **F62** may be that there is a proper way to conduct mystery initiations, so the implication of **F61** could be that there is a correct way to purify oneself and pray to the gods. His divinized *logos* is like the Intelligence or *nous* of later Greek philosophy: a somewhat anthropomorphized way of explaining the apparent orderliness of the world. The Greek word *kosmos* ('universe', 'world') originally meant 'orderly arrangement' (as in **F36**). But his rejection of external guardian spirits (**F60**) has profound consequences: we make our own destinies. In a world of flux and hidden stability, of war and hidden peace, we choose to be one of the sleepers or to wake up.

F1 (DK 22B1; KRS 194; W 1; M 1; K 1) But of this principle which holds forever people prove ignorant, not only before they hear it, but also once they have heard it.* For although everything happens in accordance with this principle, they resemble those with no familiarity with it, even after they have become familiar with the kinds of accounts and events I discuss as I distinguish each thing according to its nature and explain its constitution. But the general run of people are as unaware of their actions while awake as they are of what they do while asleep.* (Sextus Empiricus, *Against the Professors* 7.132 Bury)

F2 (DK 22B78; KRS 205; W 61; M 90; K 55) Unlike divine nature, human nature lacks sound judgements. (Origen, *Against Celsus* 6.12.13–14 Koetschau)

F3 (DK 22B41; KRS 227; W 120; M 85; K 54) The one wise thing is to know, in sound judgement, how everything is guided in every case.[†] (Diogenes Laertius, *Lives of Eminent Philosophers* 9.1.7–8 Long)

F4 (DK 22B32; KRS 228; W 119; M 84; K 108) The one and only wise thing is and is not willing to be called by the name of Zeus. (Clement, *Miscellanies* 5.115.1 Stählin/Früchtel)

F5 (DK 22B34; W 55; M 2; K 2) In their ignorance after having listened they behave like the deaf. The saying 'Though present they are absent' testifies to their case. (Clement, *Miscellanies* 5.115.3 Stählin/Früchtel)

T1 (DK 22B89; W 15; M 24; K 6) Heraclitus says that the universe for those who are awake is single and common, while in sleep each person turns aside into a private universe.* (Ps.-Plutarch, *On Superstition* 166c5–8 Babbit)

F6 (DK 22B2; KRS 195; W 2; M 23; K3) And so one ought to follow what is common.[†] Although the principle is common, the majority of people live as though they had private understanding. (Sextus Empiricus, *Against the Professors* 7.133.4–7 Bury)

F7 (DK 22B104; W 91; M 101; K 59) What intelligence or insight do they have? They trust the people's bards and take for their teacher the mob, not realizing that 'Most men are bad, few good.'* (Proclus, *Commentary on Plato's 'First Alcibiades'* 256.2–5 Segonds)

T2 (DK 22B42; W 93; M 30; K 21) He said that Homer deserved to be expelled from the competition and thrashed, and Archilochus as well.* (Diogenes Laertius, *Lives of Eminent Philosophers* 9.1.8–10 Long)

F8 (DK 22B72; W 64; M 4; K 5) They tend away from that with which they are in the most continuous contact.[†] (Marcus Aurelius, *To Himself* 4.46.5–6 Haines)

F9 (DK 22B18; KRS 210; W 19; M 11; K 7) If you do not expect the unexpected, you will not find it, since it is trackless and unexplored. (Clement, *Miscellanies* 2.17.4.4–5 Stählin/Früchtel)

F10 (DK 22B50; KRS 196; W 118; M 26; K 36) It is wise for those who listen not to me but to the principle to agree in principle that everything is one.   (Hippolytus, *Refutation of All Heresies* 9.9.1.3–4 Marcovich)

F11 (DK 22B108; W 7; M 83; K 27) I have heard a lot of people speak, but not one has reached the point of realizing that the wise is different from everything else.   (John of Stobi, *Anthology* 3.1.174 Wachsmuth/Hense)

F12 (DK 22B114; KRS 250; W 81; M 23; K 30) Those who speak with intelligence must stand firm by that which is common to all,* as a state stands by the law, and even more firmly. For all human laws are in the keeping of the one divine law; for the one divine law has as much power as it wishes, is an unfailing defence for all laws, and prevails over all laws.   (John of Stobi, *Anthology* 3.1.179 Wachsmuth/Hense)

F13 (DK 22B88; KRS 202; W 113; M 41; K 43) It makes no difference which is present: living and dead, sleeping and waking, young and old. For these changed around are those and those changed around are again these.   (Ps.-Plutarch, *Letter of Consolation to Apollonius* 106e3–6 Babbit)

F14 (DK 22B60; KRS 200; W 108; M 33; K 103) Road: up and down, it's still the same road.*   (Hippolytus, *Refutation of All Heresies* 9.10.4.6 Marcovich)

F15 (DK 22B61; KRS 199; W 101; M 35; K 70) Sea: water most pure and most tainted, drinkable and wholesome for fish, but undrinkable and poisonous for people.   (Hippolytus, *Refutation of All Heresies* 9.10.5.3–4 Marcovich)

F16 (DK 22B110, 111; KRS 201; W 52, 99; M 44, 71; K 67) It is not better for men to get everything they want. Disease makes health pleasant and good, as hunger does being full, and weariness rest.   (John of Stobi, *Anthology* 3.1.176, 177 Wachsmuth/Hense)

F17 (DK 22B9; W 102; M 37; K 71) Donkeys would prefer refuse to gold.   (Aristotle, *Nicomachean Ethics* 1176ª7 Bywater)

F18 (DK 22B13b; M 36; K 72a) Pigs prefer filth to clean water. (Clement, *Miscellanies* 1.2.2.3–4 Stählin/Früchtel)

F19 (DK 22B79; W 105; M 92; K 57) A man is thought as foolish by a supernatural being as a child is by a man. (Origen, *Against Celsus* 6.12.14–15 Koetschau)

F20 (DK 22B126; W 22; M 42; K 49) Cool things become warm, warm things cool down, moist things dry out, parched things become damp.[†] (John Tzetzes, *Notes on Homer's 'Iliad'* 126.17–19 Hermann)

F21 (DK 22B51; KRS 209; W 117; M 27; K 78) They are ignorant of how while tending away it agrees with itself—a back-turning harmony, like a bow or a lyre. (Hippolytus, *Refutation of All Heresies* 9.9.2.2–4 Marcovich)

F22 (DK 22B80; KRS 211; W 26; M 28; K 82) It is necessary to realize that war is common, and strife is justice, and that everything happens in accordance with strife and necessity.[*] (Origen, *Against Celsus* 6.42.21–3 Koetschau)

F23 (DK 22B53; KRS 212; W 25; M 29; K 83) War is father of all and king of all. Some he reveals as gods, others as men; some he makes slaves, others free. (Hippolytus, *Refutation of All Heresies* 9.9.4.4–7 Marcovich)

F24 (DK 22B54; KRS 207; W 116; M 9; K 80) Harmony: non-apparent is better than apparent. (Hippolytus, *Refutation of All Heresies* 9.9.5.3 Marcovich)

F25 (DK 22B123; KRS 208; W 17; M 8; K 10) The true nature of a thing tends to hide itself. (Themistius, *Speeches* 5.69b3 Dindorf)

F26 (DK 22B93; KRS 244; W 18; M 14; K 33) The lord whose oracle is in Delphi neither speaks nor suppresses, but indicates. (Plutarch, *On the Failure of the Oracles at Delphi These Days to Use Verse* 404d12–e1 Babbit)

F27 (DK 22B107; KRS 198; W 13; M 13; K 16) Eyes and ears are bad witnesses for men if they have souls which cannot understand their language. (Sextus Empiricus, *Against the Professors* 7.126.8–9 Bury)

F28 (DK 22B55; KRS 197; W 11; M 5; K 14) The things I rate highly are those which are accessible to sight, hearing, apprehension. (Hippolytus, *Refutation of All Heresies* 9.9.5.6 Marcovich)

F29 (DK 22B7; W 58; M 78; K 112) If everything were smoke, the nostrils would tell things apart. (Aristotle, *On the Senses* 443ᵃ23–4 Bekker)

F30 (DK 22B101; KRS 246; W 8; M 15; K 28) I searched for myself.* (Plutarch, *Against Colotes* 1118c7 Einarson/de Lacy)

F31 (DK 22B116; W 9; M 23e; K 29) Everyone has the potential for self-knowledge and sound thinking. (John of Stobi, *Anthology* 3.5.6 Wachsmuth/Hense)

F32 (DK 22B67; KRS 204; W 121; M 77; K 123) God: day/night, winter/summer, war/peace, fullness/hunger.† He changes like fire† which, when mixed with spices, is named according to the savour of each. (Hippolytus, *Refutation of All Heresies* 9.10.8.5–6 Marcovich)

F33 (DK 22B12; KRS 214; M 40; K 50) On those who step into the same rivers ever different waters are flowing. (Arius Didymus, fr. 39 Diels)

F34 (DK 22B91; W 31; M 40; K 51) 'It is impossible to step twice into the same river,' as Heraclitus says . . . 'It scatters and regathers, comes together and dissolves, approaches and departs.' (Plutarch, *On the E at Delphi* 392b10-c3 Babbit)

T3 (DK 22B49a; W 110; M 40) Heraclitus the obscure says, 'We step and do not step into the same rivers, we are and are not.'* (Heraclitus Homericus, *Homeric Questions* 24.10–12 Oelmann)

T4 (DK 22A6; KRS 215) Heraclitus says somewhere that everything gives way and nothing is stable, and in likening things to the flowing of a river he says that one cannot step twice into the same river. (Plato, *Cratylus* 402a8–10 Duke *et al.*)

F35 (DK 22B21; W 16; M 49; K 89) Dying is all we see when asleep; sleep is all we see when awake.† (Clement, *Miscellanies* 3.21.1.3–4 Stählin/Früchtel)

F36 (DK 22B30; KRS 217; W 29; M 51; K 37) Order was not made by god or man.† It always was and is and shall be an ever-living fire, flaring up in regular measures and dying down in regular measures.*   (Clement, *Miscellanies* 5.104.2 Stählin/Früchtel)

F37 (DK 22B31; KRS 218; W 32, 33; M 53; K 38, 39) The turning-points of fire: first sea, and of sea half is earth, half lightning.* Sea drains off† and is measured into the same principle as before it became earth.   (Clement, *Miscellanies* 5.104.3 Stählin/ Früchtel)

F38 (DK 22B90; KRS 219; W 28; M 54; K 40) Everything is a compensation for fire† and fire is a compensation for everything, as goods are for gold and gold for goods.   (Plutarch, *On the E at Delphi* 388e1–4 Babbit)

F39 (DK 22B64; KRS 220; W 35; M 79; K 109) Thunderbolt steers everything.   (Hippolytus, *Refutation of All Heresies* 9.10.7.4–5 Marcovich)

F40 (DK 22B66; W 72; M 82; K 121) Fire on its approach will judge and condemn everything.   (Hippolytus, *Refutation of All Heresies* 9.10.7.2–3 Marcovich)

F41 (DK 22B16; W 73; M 81; K 122) How can anyone be overlooked by that which never sets?   (Clement, *The Pedagogue* 2.99.5.5 Mondésert/Marrou)

T5 (DK 22A10) All thinkers agree that the world had a beginning, but some claim that, having come into existence, it is everlasting, while others claim that it is just as destructible as any other natural formation, and others (like Empedocles of Acragas and Heraclitus of Ephesus) that it alternates between sometimes being in the state we find it now and sometimes being in a different state—that is, in the process of being destroyed—and that this process continues nonstop.   (Aristotle, *On the Heavens* 279^b12–17 Allan)

T6 (DK 22A10) Nor can one of the elements—fire, for instance—be infinite: for there is the general consideration, quite apart from any of them being infinite, that it is impossible for the whole universe (even if it were finite) to be or to become just one of the elements—as Heraclitus says that at some time everything becomes fire.   (Aristotle, *Physics* 204^b35–205^a4 Ross)

T7 (DK 22B6; KRS 225; W 36; M 58; K 48a) The sun, according to Heraclitus, is new each day.* (Aristotle, *On Celestial Phenomena* 355ª13–14 Bekker)

F42 (DK 22B3; W 37; M 57; K 47) The sun is as broad as a human foot. (Aëtius, *Opinions* 2.21.4 Diels)

F43 (DK 22B94; KRS 226; W 122; M 52; K 44) The sun will not overstep its measures, or else the Furies, the allies of Justice, will find it out.* (Plutarch, *On Exile* 604a10–12 de Lacy/Einarson)

T8 (DK 22A1; KRS 224; M 61) As it is condensed, fire becomes moist, and then as it is further compressed it becomes water, and as water solidifies it turns into earth; this is the 'road downward'. Then again earth dissolves and gives rise to water, which is the source for everything else, since he attributes almost everything to the process of exhalation from the sea; this is the 'road upward'. Exhalations take place from the earth as well as from the sea; some exhalations are bright and clean, while others are dark. Fire is fed by the bright ones, moisture by the others. He does not give a clear description of the periphery, but there are bowls in it, with their hollow side turned towards us. In these bowls the bright exhalations gather and produce flames, which are the heavenly bodies.* The brightest and hottest of these flames is that of the sun. The rest of the heavenly bodies are further away from the earth, and so are less bright and emit less heat. Closer to the earth is the moon, which travels through a region which is impure, but the sun moves† in a translucent and untainted region. The sun maintains a proportionate distance from us, which is why it gives us more heat and light. Solar and lunar eclipses occur when the bowls are turned upwards; the monthly phases of the moon occur as its bowl gradually turns in on it. Day and night, months, annually recurring seasons, and years, rain and wind and so on, all depend on the various exhalations. For instance, when the bright exhalation is ignited in the circle of the sun it causes daylight, but when the opposite kind of exhalation is dominant the result is night; and summer is the result of an increase in warmth arising from the brightness, winter of an increase in moisture arising from the darkness. He has nothing to say about the nature of the earth, nor about the bowls either. (Diogenes Laertius, *Lives of Eminent Philosophers* 9.9–11 Long)

F44 (DK 22B36; KRS 229; W 49; M 66; K 102) Death for souls is the birth of water, death for water is the birth of earth, and earth is the source of water, and water is the source of soul. (Clement, *Miscellanies* 6.17.2 Stählin/Früchtel)

F45 (DK 22B117; KRS 231; W 48; M 69; K 106) When a man is drunk he is guided, stumbling and ignorant of his route, by an immature child, because he has a moist soul.   (John of Stobi, *Anthology* 3.5.7 Wachsmuth/Hense)

F46 (DK 22B85; KRS 240; W 51; M 70; K 105) The reason it is hard to fight against passion is that it buys what it wants at the expense of the soul.   (Plutarch, *Life of Coriolanus* 22.2.5–6 Perrin)

F47 (DK 22B118; KRS 230; W 46; M 68; K 109) A dry soul, a beam of light, is wisest and best.[†]   (John of Stobi, *Anthology* 3.5.8 Wachsmuth/Hense)

F48 (DK 22B45; KRS 232; W 42; M 67; K 35) You will not be able to discover the limits of soul on your journey, even if you walk every path; so deep is the principle it contains.* (Diogenes Laertius, *Lives of Eminent Philosophers* 9.7.6–8 Long)

F49 (DK 22B26; KRS 233; W 65; M 48; K 90) During the night a man kindles a light for himself. Just as when dead-but-alive, with sight extinguished, he contacts death, so when asleep-but-awake, with sight extinguished, he contacts sleep.*[†]   (Clement, *Miscellanies* 4.141.2 Stählin/Früchtel)

T9 (DK 22A16; KRS 234; M 116) According to Heraclitus, we become intelligent by drawing in this divine reason, and although we become forgetful when asleep, we regain our intelligence as soon as we wake up. For since when we are asleep the sensory channels are closed, mind-in-us is separated from its natural union with what surrounds us (the only lifeline, so to speak, which is preserved being connection by means of respiration), and so, being separated, it loses the power of memory that it formerly possessed. But when we wake up, our mind again peeps out through the sensory channels, as if they were windows, makes contact with what surrounds us, and is endowed with the power of reason. Just as cinders which are brought close to a fire undergo an alteration and start to glow, but are extinguished when they are separated, so the fraction of what surrounds us which is in exile in our bodies becomes more or less irrational in a state of separation, but in a state of union, which is achieved through the numerous sensory channels, it is restored to a condition of similarity to the whole. (Sextus Empiricus, *Against the Professors* 7.129–130 Bury)

T10 (DK 22B136; KRS 237; M 96) From Heraclitus: Souls slain in war are more pure than those which die through illness.* (Bodleian scholiast on Epictetus, Schenkl p. 71)

F50 (DK 22B29; KRS 251; W 85; M 95; K 97) The best choose one thing instead of everything, everlasting fame among mortals; but the masses stuff themselves like cattle. (Clement, *Miscellanies* 5.59.5.1–2 Stählin/Früchtel)

F51 (DK 22B25; KRS 235; W 70; M 97; K 96) The better the death, the better the portion.* (Clement, *Miscellanies* 4.49.3 Stählin/Früchtel)

F52 (DK 22B27; W 67; M 74; K 84) What awaits men after death cannot be anticipated or imagined. (Clement, *Miscellanies* 4.144.3.3–4 Stählin/Früchtel)

F53 (DK 22B44; KRS 249; W 82; M 103; K 65) The people must fight in defence of the law as they would for their city wall. (Diogenes Laertius, *Lives of Eminent Philosophers* 9.2.2–3 Long)

F54 (DK 22B33; W 83; M 104; K 66) It is also law to follow the plan of the one. (Clement, *Miscellanies* 5.115.2 Stählin/Früchtel)

F55 (DK 22B49; W 84; M 98; K 63) One man is worth ten thousand, as far as I am concerned, if he is outstanding. (Theodorus Prodromus, *Letters* 1240a1–2 Migne)

F56 (DK 22B121; W 95; M 105; K 64) For banishing Hermodorus, who was the best man among them, the Ephesians deserve to be hanged, every last one of them, and to leave the city to boys. They said, 'Let no single one of us be best, or else let him be so elsewhere, among others.' (Strabo, *Geography* 14.25.3–6 Meineke)

F57 (DK 22B125a; W 96; M 106) May your wealth never fail you, men of Ephesus, so that your baseness may be exposed! (John Tzetzes, *Notes on Aristophanes' 'Wealth'* 90a, Positano *et al.* p. 31)

F58 (DK 22B43; KRS 248; W 88; M 102; K 104) It is more important to quench insolence than a conflagration. (Diogenes Laertius, *Lives of Eminent Philosophers* 9.2.1–2 Long)

F59 (DK 22B11; W 41; M 80; K 76) It takes a blow to drive any animal to pasture. (Ps.-Aristotle, *On the World* 401ᵃ10–11 Bekker)

F60 (DK 22B119; KRS 247; W 69; M 94; K 114) Man's character is his guardian spirit. (John of Stobi, *Anthology* 4.40.23 Wachsmuth/ Hense)

F61 (DK 22B5; KRS 241; W 75, 78; M 86; K 117) They vainly† purify themselves with blood when they are defiled with it, which is like someone who has stepped into mud using mud to wash himself. Anyone who observed a person doing this would think him mad. And in their ignorance of the true nature of gods and heroes they pray to these statues, which is like someone chatting to a house.* (*Theosophia Tubigensis* 68 Erbse)

F62 (DK 22B14; KRS 242; W 76; M 87; K 115) They are initiated in an unholy manner into the mystery-rites followed by men. (Clement, *Protrepticus* 22.2.4–5 Montdésert)

F63 (DK 22B15; KRS 243; W 77; M 50; K 116) If the procession they perform, and the hymn they chant in honour of the phallus, were not undertaken for Dionysus, there would be nothing more disgraceful. But in fact Dionysus, for whom they rave and celebrate the Lenaea, is the same as Hades.* (Clement, *Protrepticus* 34.5.2–5 Montdésert)

F64 (DK 22B96; W 60; M 76; K 88) Corpses should be disposed of more readily than dung. (Strabo, *Geography* 16.26.26–7 Meineke)

T11 (DK 22B92; KRS 245; W 79; M 75; K 34) According to Heraclitus, the Sibyl, with raving mouth, utters things without humour, without adornment, without perfume, and yet, thanks to the god, she reaches down a thousand years with her voice.* (Plutarch, *On the Failure of the Oracles at Delphi These Days to Use Verse* 397a8–11 Babbit)

M. Adoménas, 'Heraclitus on Religion', *Phronesis*, 44 (1999), 87–113.
R. Bolton, 'Nature and Human Good in Heraclitus', in [24], 49–57.

C. J. Emlyn-Jones, 'Heraclitus and the Identity of Opposites', *Phronesis*, 21 (1976), 89–114.

A. Finkelberg, 'On Cosmogony and Ecpyrosis in Heraclitus', *American Journal of Philology*, 119 (1998), 195–222.

H. Fränkel, 'Heraclitus on God and the Phenomenal World', *Transactions of the American Philological Association*, 69 (1938), 230–44.

—— 'A Thought Pattern in Heraclitus', *American Journal of Philology*, 59 (1938), 309–37.

D. Gallop, 'The Riddles of Heraclitus', in [24], 123–35.

D. W. Graham, 'Heraclitus' Criticism of Ionian Philosophy', *Oxford Studies in Ancient Philosophy*, 15 (1997), 1–50.

U. Hölscher, 'Paradox, Simile, and Gnomic Utterance in Heraclitus', in [30], 229–38.

J. Hospers (ed.), *Heraclitus*, special issue of *The Monist* 74.4 (1991) (esp. the essays by T. M. Robinson, E. Hussey, P. K. Curd, and J. M. E. Moravcsik).

E. Hussey, 'Epistemology and Meaning in Heraclitus', in M. Schofield and M. Nussbaum (eds.), *Language and Logos* (Cambridge: Cambridge University Press, 1982), 33–59.

C. H. Kahn, 'A New Look at Heraclitus', *American Philosophical Quarterly*, 1 (1964), 189–203.

—— *The Art and Thought of Heraclitus* (Cambridge: Cambridge University Press, 1979).

—— 'Philosophy and the Written Word: Some Thoughts on Heraclitus and the Early Uses of Prose', in [31], 110–24.

G. S. Kirk, *Heraclitus: The Cosmic Fragments* (Cambridge: Cambridge University Press, 1954).

J. H. Lesher, 'Heraclitus' Epistemological Vocabulary', *Hermes*, 111 (1983), 155–70.

M. M. Mackenzie, 'Heraclitus and the Art of Paradox', *Oxford Studies in Ancient Philosophy*, 6 (1988), 1–37.

J. Mansfeld, 'Heraclitus on the Psychology and Physiology of Sleep and on Rivers', *Mnemosyne*, 20 (1967), 1–29.

M. Marcovich, *Heraclitus* (Merida: Los Andes University Press, 1967).

—— 'Heraclitus: Some Characteristics', *Illinois Classical Studies*, 7 (1982), 171–88.

J. M. E. Moravcsik, 'Heraclitean Concepts and Explanations', in [31], 134–52.

—— 'Heraclitus at the Crossroads of Presocratic Thought', in [24], 256–69.

A. P. D. Mourelatos, 'Heraclitus, Parmenides, and the Naive Metaphysics of Things', in [28], 16–48.

M. Nussbaum, 'ψυχή in Heraclitus', *Phronesis*, 17 (1972), 1–16, 153–70.

R. A. Prier, 'Symbol and Structure in Heraclitus', *Apeiron*, 7.2 (1973), 23–37.

C. D. C. Reeve, 'Ἐκπύρωσις and the Priority of Fire in Heraclitus', *Phronesis*, 27 (1982), 299–305.

T. M. Robinson, 'Heraclitus on Soul', *The Monist*, 69 (1986), 305–14.

—— *Heraclitus: Fragments* (Toronto: University of Toronto Press, 1987).

M. Schofield, 'Heraclitus' Theory of Soul and Its Antecedents', in S. Everson (ed.), *Companions to Ancient Thought*, vol. ii: *Psychology* (Cambridge: Cambridge University Press, 1991), 13–34.

D. Sider, 'Heraclitus in the Derveni Papyrus', in [44], 129–48.

G. Vlastos, 'On Heraclitus', in [33], 127–50 (first pub. *American Journal of Philology*, 76 (1955)).

P. Wheelwright, *Heraclitus* (Princeton: Princeton University Press, 1959).

D. Wiggins, 'Heraclitus' Conceptions of Flux, Fire and Material Persistence', in M. Schofield and M. Nussbaum (eds.), *Language and Logos* (Cambridge: Cambridge University Press, 1982), 1–32.

J. Wilcox, 'On the Distinction between Thought and Perception in Heraclitus', *Apeiron*, 26 (1993), 1–18.

PARMENIDES OF ELEA

Parmenides of Elea is the first Presocratic philosopher of whose work we have substantial fragments, which allow us not just to know some of his conclusions, but also, and importantly, to see that he *argued* for these conclusions (see **T1**), and how he did so.[1] However, there are still severe limitations on the evidence. For reasons that will become obvious, scholars divide his poem, after the prologue (which we have in its entirety) into the 'Way of Truth' (more accurately this should be the way to truth, or to reality) and the 'Way of Appearance'. Although we have a considerable amount of the Way of Truth, we have little of the Way of Appearance, and are again reduced to relying on a few late testimonia. A critical question, the relation between the two halves of the poem, thus remains almost entirely a matter of speculation. A second difficulty is that there are a few serious textual problems. And thirdly, there is the obscurity of Parmenides' thought. Nevertheless, he remains probably the single most important Presocratic thinker and one of the most interesting philosophers of the Western world. After Parmenides, Presocratic thought could not remain the same, since subsequent thinkers felt they had to respond to the challenge he offered to all scientific thought; and the resolution of certain logical difficulties he raised sharpened the thought of both Plato and Aristotle. And all this from a man who wrote poetry of a Homeric kind and saw himself, as the prologue (**F1**) clearly shows, as much a shaman or a mystic as a philosopher, making a spiritual and philosophical journey just as Homer's Odysseus had travelled the known world. For many people nowadays, the categories of rational and extra-rational thought are distinct, but this was clearly not the case for Parmenides (or Empedocles).

The prologue (**F1**) is clearly designed to set Parmenides apart from the majority of the human race, as a man of knowledge. Since ancient times it has often been interpreted as a journey into the clear light of knowledge, to enlightenment, but closer attention reveals that Parmenides starts in the upper world and is taken to the underworld, which was traditionally the place of the roots of night and day, and of the daily birthplace of the sun. Thus his maiden charioteers, the daughters of the Sun, have left a place of darkness and come up to the light to fetch Parmenides, and to

---

[1] Note, however, that in the case of Parmenides and his successors, I shall scarcely, if ever, be concerned to assess the validity of the arguments, only to display what I think they were.

take him back to their abode to meet an unnamed goddess;[2] so too the goddess hastens to tell Parmenides that it is no 'ill fate' (**F1** l. 26) that has brought him to her domain, where 'ill fate' is a common phrase for 'death'. This is what entitles us to think of him as a shaman of some kind. However, a number of scholars prefer to see the prologue as a mere literary device.

In devilishly obscure terms, and prosaic and somewhat tortured verse, **F3–7** lay out the heart of Parmenides' extraordinary philosophy. In **F3** the goddess offers a choice between two 'ways'. Since one is immediately called impossible and unthinkable, we are obviously supposed to approve and follow the other: '*that* (or *how*) *it is and it cannot not be*'. Parmenides does not describe the way as 'the way that states that it is': *that it is* is the name of the way (hence my use of italics, to attempt to communicate this identity), and it leads to truth or reality. It is, literally, a 'way of thinking' about the world, and there are two such ways of thinking, only one of which is possible and truly informative. Only if we assume *that it is* will we understand reality.

What is this 'it'? No subject is ever specified, except simply 'what can be spoken and thought of' (**F4**, **F5** l. 1), so it is safest to assume that the subject is anything at all: anything we care to think about either is or is not, and we are encouraged to think that it is, since what-is-not is nothing. What does it mean to say that it 'is'? It could mean that it exists, or that it is really the case, or that it is something—that we can predicate things of it. Parmenides makes no distinction between these various senses of 'is', and it is not clear that we should either. Perhaps he meant all of them, or as many of them as are appropriate in any given context. So, for instance, in **F5** and at **F8** ll. 5–21 the existential meaning is generally predominant; but in certain contexts one might think that the predicative sense of 'is' is uppermost, according to which to say 'it is' is to say 'it is . . . ' where the ellipsis is filled with a predicate or predicates.[3] The predicative sense in its turn shades into what is known as the 'veridical' sense, because surely it is only if X is F (if some attribute F can be predicated of X) that we can identify X as something real. Note that we need not necessarily conclude that Parmenides was confused about all these possible meanings of 'is': he may, as I suggested, unpack 'is' in different ways in different contexts.

[2] The goddess may be Necessity, mentioned in **T8**. Given the tight logical structure of Parmenides' argumentation, she would make an appropriate spokeswoman. On the other hand, since she is the goddess of the underworld, the Greeks would automatically think of Persephone, and the third-person reference to Necessity at **F8** l. 30 is perhaps unlikely in the mouth of Necessity.

[3] Mourelatos (see all his entries in bibliography below) and Curd [16] argue, in different ways that Parmenides means a special predicative sense of 'is', which answers the question 'What is it?' in such a way that the true nature of the object is pinpointed.

The end of **F3**, **F4** (which in fact fits metrically immediately after the end of **F3**, and almost certainly belongs there), the beginning of **F5**, and **F6** all tie together 'being' and 'being thought of' (or perhaps 'being ascertained'). Parmenides cannot mean, literally, that thinking and being are identical, but that they are co-extensive: thinking is thinking of a thing as it is. Here 'being' cannot be existential, because we can easily think of things that do not exist, such as unicorns and the King of Australia. But it is true that we can know something and think of it only if it has some attribute or attributes. And, on the veridical sense of being, we can only ever know something that is the case. The Greek word Parmenides used for 'thinking' carries connotations of 'recognition', with the consequent implication that what you think of is something out there to be recognized, not a fanciful object such as a unicorn or the King of Australia. Parmenides was a dialectician, leading his audience on to further conclusions: having gained our acceptance to the obvious fact that we cannot think of or know an attributeless entity, on the basis of this agreement, gained on one sense of 'being', he will go on, in **F7** and **F8** to try to force our agreement to other conclusions, gained on the existential sense of 'being'.

In various ways, **F3**, **F5**, and **F7** make further claims about the prohibited way of enquiry,[4] showing how completely unacceptable and impossible it is by outlining the difficulties encountered by those who attempt *per impossibile* to take it. The most thorough such description is that of **F5**, where the way is said to be that of 'two-headed mortals' and to 'turn back on itself'. Interpretations of what Parmenides means us to understand by this way differ, of course; but if we assume, as seems reasonable, that the mortals of this way are the same as the mortals whose opinions are reflected in the 'Way of Appearance', the second half of the poem, then the problem with the way is one of polar thinking, of seeing things in terms of opposites, as 'F and not-F'. So mortals are 'two-headed', Janus-like figures, looking both forward and backwards, because although they appear to be saying 'is' about something, it turns out that what they are saying about it might just as well be 'is not'. Puzzlingly, people on this way are described as both identifying and not identifying being and not being. Perhaps what is meant is that they identify being and not being, because, on the evidence of the senses, they say both 'X is . . . ' and 'X is not . . . ', where the ellipses are filled with different predicates; and they do not identify being and not-being precisely because the predicates with which they fill the ellipses are different. It is the way of mortals—the way

---

[4] Readers of the secondary literature will often find discussion of *three* ways in Parmenides, two of which are prohibited, but on the text and interpretation adopted here, there are only the two ways Parmenides announces programmatically in **F3**.

of most of us—because it unthinkingly relies on the senses and accepts as real phenomena such as birth and perishing, which imply both that a thing is and that it is not, as Parmenides will shortly argue.

The opening line of F7 is radically ambiguous. On the one hand, it could be taken to outlaw sentences of the form 'X is not F' in favour of those of the form 'X is F'. But this is unlikely, and not least because Parmenides himself constantly makes use of sentences of this form, saying that what-is is not born, not divisible, and so on. On the other hand, then, it could more plausibly be taken to be a corollary of the denial of generation that is about to be argued in F8 ll. 5–21, where Parmenides denies that anything can come into existence from something that does not exist.[5] Given a state of non-existence, we cannot explain a state of existence, since we have no way of moving from the one to the other. Since, by definition, what-is-not has no properties, it has no properties that could be taken to explain the generation of what-is. This, I suppose, is why at the beginning of F5 Parmenides appears (astonishingly) to deduce 'what-is must be' from 'what-is can be'; in fact, for him, the two propositions are more or less identical, since there could not possibly be anything other than what can be.

In the opening lines of F8 (which followed immediately on from F7), the goddess claims to be able to prove that what-is is 'unborn and imperishable, | Entire, alone of its kind [i.e. unique], unshaken, and complete [or perfect]'. This programme is then carried out very systematically in what follows: F8 ll. 5–21 argue that what-is is unborn and imperishable; ll. 22–5 argue that it is indivisible (i.e. entire and unique); ll. 26–31 argue that it is unchanging ('unshaken'); and ll. 32–49 that it is complete. Although at the start of the philosophical section of the poem it seemed as though the subject of 'is' was unrestricted, anything we could think about, by the end of F8 Parmenides has argued that following through the logic of just 'it is' reduces everything to an unchanging singularity, so that the only possible subject of 'is' is just this singularity, and nothing else.[6] Thus,

[5] This appears to confuse the possibility of something's coming to exist where it did not exist before—e.g. something turning pale instead of dark—with the (admittedly impossible) production of something by nothing.

[6] This attribution of what might be called 'numerical monism' has been challenged, but it seems indisputable on the basis of the text of F8 l. 4 read here, and because of Plato's and Aristotle's understanding of Parmenides as a numerical monist. The main challenge comes from an important and well-argued series of articles by Curd, later developed into a book [16]. She argues that nothing commits Parmenides to a single singularity, rather than a plurality of them (and that this explains the subsequent pluralist and atomist response to his work). So far from banishing cosmology, according to Curd, Parmenides is trying to establish the criteria for a coherent and meaningful cosmology.

at a stroke, Parmenides repudiated all the attempts of his predecessors to explain phenomena such as creation and change, and set up a severe challenge to those scientist-philosophers who came after him. As Colotes appears to have claimed (see **T2**), Parmenides seems to have argued away the real existence of the phenomenal world altogether. The typical pattern of the argument of these sections of **F8** is that Parmenides starts with his conclusion, and then proceeds to support the conclusion in a series of premisses linked by 'for'. His arguments are startling and brilliant in their boldness, but scholars still argue in minute detail about every single line and word within them.

First, creation must take place either from what-is or from what-is-not. In a 'neither . . . nor' dilemma, **F8** ll. 7–11 eliminate the latter possibility (on the grounds that there is no such thing as what-is-not, and that change from what-is-not is absurd),[7] and then ll. 12–13 eliminate the former possibility (on the ground that there can be no extra 'what-is' for 'what-is' to be created from). What-is exists in an unbroken continuum, from the infinite past and into the infinite future (ll. 5–6),[8] and so there can be no creation in the past or future. Parmenides does not argue for what-is being imperishable, but allows us to infer that, *mutatis mutandis*, the same arguments eliminate perishing too.

F8 ll. 22–5 then argue that what-is must be a singularity, continuous in both space and time (see also **F6**.1–2): there are no gaps of not being in what-is. **F8** ll. 26–31 argue that it is unchanging. Although Parmenides' words here make it sound as though physical change is his primary target, a more generous view would regard the 'limits' which constrain what-is not as spatial limits (an awkward concept for Parmenides, for what would lie beyond the limits?), but as limits of possibility, such that what-is cannot be other than what it is, in space, time, or intensity. Thus all kinds of change are eliminated—both local motion and qualitative change.

---

[7] In **F8** ll. 9–10 Parmenides argues: 'What need could have impelled it | To arise later or sooner, if it sprang from an origin in nothing?' By the principle of sufficient reason, it *could* not have been born at a given moment unless there was a sufficient reason for its having done so; but since it is being supposed to have been born from nothing, or what-is-not, then no such reason can be found.

[8] Some translate these lines (admittedly with good plausibility) as 'It never was nor will be, etc.', and argue that Parmenides (like Plato later, at *Timaeus* 37d–38a and *Parmenides* 140e–141d) had a concept of the 'timeless present'. Strictly, of course, having denied the reality of change, Parmenides could well also have denied the reality of time; but attention to the context of these lines makes it look as though all he is doing is, with the aim of disproving the reality of generation and perishing, prefacing his argument with the claim that what-is is not something that merely existed once in the past, or that merely will exist some time in the future. Moreover, infinite duration rather than timelessness is how Melissus understood Parmenides (see Melissus **F2** on p. 84).

F8 ll. 32–49 (with a recapitulatory digression at ll. 35–41) argue that, since what-is is unchanging in space and time, it is complete and perfect. At ll. 42–4 Parmenides could be taken to be saying that what-is is spherical. This cannot be his meaning, since it would naturally lead to the question: 'What, then, lies outside the sphere?'[9] In short, he likens what-is to a sphere in order to communicate the idea of its self-identity—its equiformity and equally dispersed intensity. A sphere is the only body that is the same from whatever direction you look at it, inside or outside.[10] Meanwhile, the digression at ll. 35–41 argues that, if there is only a singularity, there is no reality to all the different names we give things, since there is in reality no plurality of things.

After this astonishing *tour de force* it is strange, and even somewhat disappointing, to be taken abruptly into the domain of Presocratic cosmogony, presented as an abstract analysis of what 'mortals' already believe. **F5** forbade effectively the kind of thinking the goddess now goes on to explicate. The reason the goddess gives for going on to explain cosmology and cosmogony is to prevent Parmenides ever being outdone by other thinkers; he must have at his grasp the best cosmology, but armed with the Way of Truth he will also be able to see through this and any cosmology. It is the best cosmology to deal with the illusory world of change, if one were to take it as real (see also the difficult and obscure **F1** ll. 31–2), but in reality there are no such things—or at any rate, no such *knowable* things—as change, creation, destruction, and so on. The cosmology is an accurate description of things as they appear to be, but it is deceptive because it purports to be a description of reality. As **F12** suggests, things such as creation and destruction are all just conventional names, and when we stop 'nourishing' them—that is, giving them the force of currency—they will die out. In the mean time, perhaps, the validity of the cosmology of the Way of Appearance should be tested, sceptically, by examining it (and any other attempt at cosmology) against the truths of the Way of Truth.

When the goddess tells us that what is true is that there is just the singularity, we should perhaps not think so much that this is an *ontological* truth—that the singularity is all that exists—as an *epistemological* truth: there is only one true way to understand the world. After all, the prologue

---

[9] At any rate, about 100 years later than Parmenides the philosopher Archytas of Tarentum posed the following famous dilemma: 'If I were to reach the edge, the part of the skies where the fixed stars are, could I stretch my hand or my stick outside or not?' (DK 47A24).

[10] However, there are scholars who believe that Parmenides did think of what-is as a sphere; and it is interesting to note that in ancient Egyptian religion the phrase 'to know what-is-not' meant to have transgressed the cosmic order, to have gone beyond the limits of the created order of things. At any rate, it would certainly be right to see the provenance of what Parmenides is saying here in Anaximander **T15** (p. 14).

to the whole poem establishes Parmenides' quest as an epistemological one. The mistake 'mortals' make is to think they can know the world of the senses. Somehow, underlying the world of the senses (whose evidence Parmenides of course altogether distrusts), there is the real world of unchanging singularity. The singularity is the physical world viewed by reason rather than the senses (as Aristotle saw, **T5**). This distinction between two worlds, or between a right and a wrong way of viewing the one world, was to prove very influential on Plato. However, as **T3** suggests, Aristotle saw no such radical split between two worlds, and found Parmenides' two ways perfectly reconcilable: somehow the cosmogony of light and night was to explain the creation of the singularity. So elsewhere (**T5**) Aristotle suggests that Parmenides identified fire/light with what-is, and night/dark with what-is-not.[11] In this context it is crucial to look back to the prologue (**F1**), where Parmenides' vision of unity and singularity was granted to him in a realm that transcends the polarity of light and dark, symbolized by his passing through the gates of day and night.

The details of Parmenides' cosmogony are somewhat obscure, though our main evidence (**T8**, **F13**) is coherent enough if taken at face value. Even by Plato's time, however, as **T6** shows, Parmenides was famous as the spokesman for singularity, and the second half of his poem was overlooked. At any rate, it seems that there are two factors or stuffs, called light (or fire, or flame) and darkness (or earth, or night), which are complete opposites, with opposite characteristics (hot/cold, rare/dense, light/heavy) (**F8** ll. 50–9; **T4**). In contrast to the singularity of the first part of **F8**, light and darkness exist only relative to each other. Light and darkness are very close to being true elements; they form the whole world, perhaps by means of the processes of separation and combination (**T2**, **T7**), and were used to explain all celestial phenomena (**F9–11**). The sun, moon, and other heavenly bodies occupied 'rings' surrounding the earth (like those of Anaximander?), which presumably carried them round at different rates.[12] But more than this we cannot say, except that, as **F15** and **F16** show, Parmenides recognized that the moon derived its light from the sun. Later sources also say that he was the first to recognize the identity of the morning and evening star, but they do not say whether he recognized it as a planet (**T9**). Even these discoveries are remarkable from a thinker whose chief intention was utterly to repudiate the world of the senses. **T10** attributes another remarkable innovation to Parmenides, but we need not

---

[11] A number of modern scholars have followed Aristotle in this ascription. I cannot see how to reconcile it with **F11**, which clearly states a fully fledged duality of being (as far as mortals are concerned).

[12] Compare Plato, *Republic* 616d–e, describing a similar arrangement of concentric rings to explain the movement of the heavenly bodies.

think that Parmenides based the division of the earth into zones on precise astronomical measurement, rather than on his usual foundation of hot and cold.

There is some evidence (**F14**) that Parmenides postulated a goddess, Love, as the prime force of cosmic creation,[13] as well as of animal procreation (**F13** ll. 3–6; see also, perhaps, **T8**); but as **F14** shows, there was already a prior female deity of some kind (on whom see n. 2 above). Parmenides went into procreation to a certain extent (**F17**, **T11**), claiming that male embryos lay on the warmer right of the uterus, females on the colder left; and may also have discussed other physiological issues. Note the consistency with which he makes use of his two primary factors, light and night. Finally, **F18** is a fascinating and tantalizing glimpse of a theory of mind–body interaction (or perhaps of a materialist theory of mind),[14] more fully spelled out by Theophrastus who preserves the fragment in a discussion of Parmenides' views about sense-perception and related phenomena. Theophrastus seems to deduce from Parmenides' obscure lines the notion (somewhat in anticipation of Empedocles' theory of perception) that of the two elements in the body, hot and cold, the hot perceives the hot in the world, and the cold perceives the cold.

––––––––

T1 (DK 28A28; C t36) For Parmenides would not agree with anything unless it seemed necessary, whereas his predecessors used to come up with unsubstantiated assertions.   (Eudemus [fr. 11 Wehrli] in Simplicius, *Commentary on Aristotle's 'Physics'*, CAG IX, 116.2–4 Diels)

F1 (DK 28B1; KRS 288, 301; C 1)

My carriage was drawn by the mares which carry me to the limits
Of my heart's desire; they took me and set me on the renowned way
Of the deity,† which takes a man of knowledge unharmed† through
    all.
There I rode, for there the much-prompted mares were carrying
    me,
Straining at the carriage, and maidens were guiding my way.   5
The axle in its naves screeched like a pipe and glowed red-hot,
For the two wheels on either side were whirling and urging it on,

[13] On somewhat slender evidence, Finkelberg 1986 attributes to Parmenides a force for destruction, equivalent in power to Love; this turns Parmenides into a proto-Empedocles.

[14] Empedocles in DK 31B108 says something very similar to Parmenides in **F18**. For an explanation of Presocratic theories of the mind in materialist terms, see Wright [73].

Thanks to the haste with which the maiden daughters of the Sun
Drove the carriage, having left the abode of night and entered the
   light.
They pushed the veils off their heads with their hands.*   10
There stand the gates of the paths of night and day,
And a lintel and threshold of stone enclose them round about.
The gates are of aither and they fill the huge frame of the gate,
And vengeful Justice controls the alternating locks.*
The maidens spoke soft and beguiling words to Lady Justice,   15
And cunningly persuaded her to take the pin quickly out of the lock
And pull it away from the gates for them; the gates opened wide,
Creating a yawning gap through the frame, as one and then the other
Turned in their sockets the bronze pivots which were fastened to
   them
With nails and rivets. Then the maidens steered the carriage   20
And the horses straight through the gates and down the road.
The goddess received me kindly. Taking in her hand my right hand
She spoke and addressed me with these words: 'Young man,
You have reached my abode as the companion of immortal
   charioteers
And of the mares which carry you.† You are welcome.   25
It was no ill fate that prompted you to travel this way,
Which is indeed far from mortal men, beyond their beaten paths;
No, it was Right and Justice. You must learn everything—
Both the steady heart of well-rounded truth,
And the beliefs of mortals, in which there is no true trust.   30
Still, you shall learn them too, and come to see how beliefs
Must exist in an acceptable form, all-pervasive as they altogether
   are.'*

(pieced together from: Sextus Empiricus, *Against the Professors*
7.111 Bury; and Simplicius, *Commentary on Aristotle's 'On the
Heavens'*, CAG VII, 557.25–558.2 Heiberg)

F2 (DK 28B5; KRS 289; C 2)

'The point from which I start
Is common; for there shall I return again.'

(Proclus, *Commentary on Plato's
'Parmenides'* 708.15–16 Cousin)

F3 (DK 28B2; KRS 291; C 3)

'Come then, I will tell you[†]—and do you for your part listen to
    my tale
And pass it on—of those ways of seeking which alone can be
    thought of.
There is the way *that it is and it cannot not be*:
This is the path of Trust, for Truth attends it.[†]
Then there is the way *that it is not and that it must not be*:   5
This, as I show you, is an altogether misguided route.
For you may not know what-is-not—there is no end to it*—
Nor may you tell of it.'

(pieced together from: Proclus, *Commentary on Plato's
'Timaeus'* 1.345 Diehl; and Simplicius, *Commentary on
Aristotle's 'Physics'*, CAG IX, 116.28–117.1 Diels)

F4 (DK 28B3; KRS 292; C 4)

'For the same thing both can be thought and can be.'*

(Clement, *Miscellanies* 6.23.3 Stählin/Früchtel)

F5 (DK 28B6: KRS 293; C 5)

'It must be that what can be spoken and thought is, for it is there for
    being
And there is no such thing as nothing. These are the guidelines I
    suggest for you.
For I shall start my exposition to you first with this way of seeking,[†]
And then go on to the one on which mortals, knowing nothing,
Stray[†] two-headed; for confusion in their breasts   5
Leads astray their thinking. On this way they journey
Deaf and blind, bewildered, indecisive herds,
In whose thinking being and not being are the same
And yet not the same. For all of them the path turns back on itself.'*

(pieced together from Simplicius, *Commentary on Aristotle's
'Physics'*, CAG IX, 86.27–8 and 117.4–13 Diels)

F6 (DK 28B4; KRS 313; C 6)

'By thinking gaze unshaken on things which, though absent, are
    present,*
For thinking will not sever what-is from clinging to what-is,

Whether it is scattered at random everywhere throughout my
   composition,
Or whether it comes together.'*

   (Clement, *Miscellanies* 5.15.5 Stählin/Früchtel)

F7 (DK 28B7; KRS 294; C 7)

'For never shall this be overcome, so that things-that-are-not are;
You should restrain your thinking from this way of seeking.
And do not let habit compel you, along this well-tried path,
To wield the aimless eye and noise-filled ear and tongue,
But use reason to come to a decision on the contentious test   5
I have announced.'

   (pieced together from: Plato, *Sophist* 237a8–9 Duke *et al.*; and
      Sextus Empiricus, *Against the Professors* 7.114.37–41 Bury)

F8 (DK 28B8; KRS 295, 296, 297, 298, 299, 300, 302; C 8)

                              'Now only the one tale remains
Of the way *that it is*. On this way† there are very many signs
Indicating that what-is is unborn and imperishable,
Entire, alone of its kind,† unshaken, and complete.†
It was not once nor will it be, since it is now, all together,   5
Single, and continuous. For what birth could you seek for it?
How and from what did it grow? Neither† will I allow you to say
Or to think that it grew from what-is-not, for *that it is not*
Cannot be spoken or thought. Also, what need could have impelled it
To arise later or sooner, if it sprang from an origin in nothing?   10
And so it should either entirely be, or not be at all.
Nor ever will the power of trust allow that from what-is†
It becomes something other than itself. That is why Justice has not
   freed it,
Relaxing the grip of her fetters, either to be born or to perish;
No, she holds it fast. The decision on these matters depends on
   this: 15
It is or *it is not*. And it has been decided, as was necessary,
To leave the one way unthought and nameless, as no real way,
And that the other truly is a way and is truth-bearing.
And how could what-is be hereafter?† How could it have been?
If it came to be, it is not, and likewise if it will be some time in the
   future.   20

Thus birth has been extinguished and perishing made inconceivable.
Nor can it be divided, since all alike it is.† Nor is there
More of it here and an inferior amount of it elsewhere,
Which would restrain it from cohering, but it is all full of what–is.
And so it is all coherent, for what–is is in contact with what–is.*   25
Now, changeless within the limits of great bonds,
It is without beginning and without end, since birth and perishing
Have been driven far off, and true trust has cast them away.
It stays in the same state and in the same place, lying by itself,
And so it stays firmly as it is, for mighty Necessity   30
Holds it in the bonds of a limit which restrains it all about,
Because it is not lawful for what–is to be incomplete.
For there is no lack in it; if there were, it would lack everything.
The same thing both can be thought and is that which enables
    thinking.
For you will not find thinking apart from what–is, on which it
    depends   35
For its expression. For apart from what–is nothing else
Either is or will be, since what–is is what Fate bound
To be entire and changeless. Therefore all those things which mortal
    men,
Trusting in their true reality, have proposed, are no more than
    names –
Both birth and perishing, both being and not being,   40
Change of place, and alteration of bright colouring.
Now, since there is a last limit, what–is is complete,
From every side like the body of a well–rounded sphere,
Everywhere of equal intensity from the centre. For it must not be
Somewhat greater in one part and somewhat smaller in another.   45
For, first, there is no such thing as what–is–not, to stop what–is
From joining up with itself; and, second, it is impossible for what–is
To be more here and less there than what–is, since it all inviolably is.
For from every direction it is equal to itself, and meets with limits.
Here I end what I have to tell you of trustworthy arguments   50
And thinking about reality. From this point onward, learn
Mortal beliefs, listening to words which, though composed, will be
    lies.*
For they proposed in their minds to name two forms,
One of which should not be named;* this is where they went wrong.

They selected things† oppositely configured and attributed to them
    features   55
Distinct from one another—to the one form the bright fire of flame,
Which is gentle, very light, and in every way the same as itself,
But not the same as the other. This too is self-consistent
In the opposite manner, as impenetrable night, a dense and heavy
    body.
I tell you this way of composing things in all its plausibility,   60
So that never shall any mortal man outstrip you in judgement.'†

    (pieced together from Simplicius, *Commentary on Aristotle's
    'Physics'*, CAG IX, 145.1–146.25 and 38.30–39.9 Diels)

T2 (DK 28B10; KRS 304; C T113) Actually, Parmenides has not done
away with fire and water and crags and the settlements of Europe
and Asia, as Colotes says, because he has composed a cosmology as
well, and he produces the whole phenomenal world out of and as a
result of the combination of his elements, the bright and the dark.
He has a great deal to say about the earth, the heavens, the sun,
moon, and heavenly bodies; he has an account of the creation of the
human race; and in the true fashion of a scientist of old who is
developing his own theory, rather than criticizing someone else's, he
covers every issue of importance. (Plutarch, *Against Colotes*
1114b7–c5 Einarson/de Lacy)

T3 (DK 28A25; C T20) Some of them [*earlier philosophers*] did away
with generation and destruction altogether, on the grounds that
nothing that *is* is generated or destroyed, but only seems to us to be
generated or destroyed. This is the view of Melissus, Parmenides,
and so on. Even if basically they argue well, we have to regard their
arguments as not relevant to science as such, since the existence of
things which are not liable to generation or to change in general is
more properly a question dealt with by a different discipline, not
natural science, but a prior form of study. However, because they
assumed the existence of nothing other than what is accessible to the
senses, and because they were the first to appreciate that there must
be unchanging entities, if recognition and knowledge are to exist,
they transferred arguments proper to the higher form of study from
there on to sensible things. (Aristotle, *On the Heavens* 298b14–24
Allan)

T4 (C T22) That the opposites are principles is agreed by everyone, including those who say that the universe is single and unchanging: even Parmenides regards hot and cold—or fire and earth, as he calls them—as principles.   (Aristotle, *Physics* 188ª19–22 Ross)

T5 (DK 28A24; C T26) Parmenides seems to speak with somewhat more insight [*than Xenophanes and Melissus*] in arguing that what-is-not is nothing—that there is nothing apart from what-is; he necessarily thinks, then, that being is single and that nothing else exists; I have gone into this in more detail in my *Physics*. But since he is forced to be guided by appearances, he assumes that the one exists from the viewpoint of reason, but that a plurality exists from the viewpoint of the senses, and therefore, in a volte-face, posits two causes and two first principles, hot and cold, by which he means, for example, fire and earth. Of these he ranks the hot with what-is and the other with what-is-not.   (Aristotle, *Metaphysics* 986ᵇ27–987ª2 Ross)

T6 (DK 28B8; C T6) [*Socrates speaking*] But I was in danger of forgetting the other side to the controversy, Theodorus, the assertion that 'Unique† and unchanging is that for which, as a whole, there is the name "to be" ',* and all the other propositions which people like Melissus and Parmenides maintain and which contradict the former theory [*of perpetual flux and change*]—that all is one, and that this oneness is fixed within itself, having no space in which to change or move.   (Plato, *Theaetetus* 180d7–e4 Duke *et al.*)

T7 (DK 28A35; C T33) Since, they say,* it is the nature of the hot to separate and of the cold to combine, and since it is the nature of each of the other bodies to act and be acted upon, they say that everything else is both generated and destroyed out of and because of these factors.   (Aristotle, *On Generation and Destruction* 336ª3–6 Joachim)

F9 (DK 28B10; KRS 305; C 9)

'You shall know the nature of the aither, and all the signs in the
    aither;*
You shall know the baneful deeds of the immaculate torch
That is the brilliant sun; and you shall know the origins of all these
    things.

You will come to understand the wanderings of the round-faced
  moon
And her nature; you will comprehend also the enclosing heaven,   5
And know from where it came and how necessity bound it
To hold the limits of the stars.'

>   (Clement, *Miscellanies* 5.138.1 Stählin/Früchtel)

F10 (DK 28B11; C 10)

>   'How earth and sun and moon,
How the aither, shared by all, the Milky Way, the outermost heaven,
And the hot force of the stars, all strove to come into existence.'

>   (Simplicius, *Commentary on Aristotle's 'On the Heavens'*,
>   CAG VII, 559.22–5 Heiberg)

F11 (DK 28B9; KRS 303; C 11)

'Now, since light and night have been given all names
And been predicated of this and that in accordance with their powers,
Everything is full of light and dark night at once,
And of both equally, since neither of them contains what-is-not.'

>   (Simplicius, *Commentary on Aristotle's 'Physics'*,
>   CAG IX, 180.9–12 Diels)

F12 (DK 28B19; KRS 312; C 20)

'And so these things came into being thanks to belief, and are now,
And in time to come will end when their nourishment is complete.
Men proposed names for each thing, to distinguish them.'

>   (Simplicius, *Commentary on Aristotle's 'On the Heavens'*,
>   CAG VII, 558.9–11 Heiberg)

F13 (DK 28B12; KRS 306; C 12)

'The narrower ones* became filled with unadulterated fire,
And subsequent ones with night, and a portion of flame permeates
  them;
Between these is the goddess who controls all things,
Since for all things† she initiated vile intercourse and childbirth,
Sending female to join with male and again conversely   5
Male with female.'

>   (pieced together from Simplicius, *Commentary on Aristotle's
>   'Physics'*, CAG IX, 31.13–17 and 39.14–16 Diels)

F14 (DK 28B13; C 13)

'The very first of all the gods she devised was Love.'

(Plato, *Symposium* 178b11 Burnet)

T8 (DK 28A37; KRS 307; C t61) Parmenides said that there are rings wound round each other, one made out of the rare and one out of the dense, and that there are other rings between the rare and the dense ones which are a mixture of light and dark.* He said that what surrounds them all is solid, like a wall, and that under it is a fiery ring; and also that what lies in the centre of them all is also solid, and that around it is another fiery ring. Of the mixed rings, the one that lies closest to the centre is the principle and cause of movement and generation for them all, and he called it the divine helmswoman and the key-holder, Justice and Necessity. And he said that air is a secretion from the earth which is emitted as vapour as a result of the earth's more powerful felting.* He said that the sun is an exhalation of fire, and so is the circle of the Milky Way; that the moon is a mixture of both air and fire; that the aither is the outermost region, surrounding everything, that under it is located the fiery region we call heaven, and that under this finally are located the regions that surround the earth.   (Aëtius, *Opinions* 2.7.1 Diels)

F15 (DK 28B14; KRS 308; C 14)

'An alien light wandering around the earth, shining in the night.'

(Plutarch, *Against Colotes* 1116a6 Einarson/de Lacy)

F16 (DK 28B15; C 15)

'With gaze always fixed on the rays of the sun.'

(Plutarch, *On the Face on the Moon*
929b1 Cherniss)

T9 (DK 28A40a; C t65) Parmenides was the first to locate the Morning Star (which was considered by him to be identical to the Evening Star) in the heavenly fire, after which came the sun, according to him. Under the sun came the heavenly bodies in the fiery region, which is what he calls the heaven.   (Aëtius, *Opinions* 2.25.7 Diels)

T10 (C t99) Posidonius says that Parmenides was the originator of the division into five zones, but that he had made the breadth of the torrid zone almost double its correct size, until the area between the tropics extended beyond both tropics and ended near the temperate zones.   (Posidonius [fr. 49 Edelstein/Kidd] in Strabo, *Geography* 2.2.2.1–5 Meineke)

F17 (DK 28B17; KRS 309; C 18, t125) But others too among the ancients claimed that a male embryo is conceived in the right part of the womb. So, for instance, Parmenides says: 'Boys on the right, girls on the left.'   (Galen, *Commentary on Hippocrates' 'Epidemics'* 2.46.19–22 Wenkebach/Pfaff)

T11 (DK 28A52; C t34) Parmenides and a few others, for instance, claim that women are warmer than men, and say that it is because of their warmth and the abundance of their blood that menstruation occurs.   (Aristotle, *On the Parts of Animals* 648ᵃ29–31 Bekker)

F18 (DK 28A46, B16; KRS 311; C 17, t45) Broadly speaking, there are two schools of thought concerning sense perception: some attribute it to similarity, others to opposition.† Parmenides, Empedocles, and Plato attribute it to similarity, Anaxagoras and Heraclitus to opposition . . . On the whole, Parmenides did not go into this [*the operation of each of the five senses*] with any clarity, but only said that there were two elements and that knowledge is due to one of them being in excess of the other. For our thinking, he says, becomes different depending on whether the hot or the cold is predominant. Moreover, he claims that the kind of thinking that is caused by the hot is better and more pure. However, even this kind of thinking needs a certain adaptation, as he says:

'For thinking comes† to men according to the condition which the blend†
Of the much-straying body is in at any moment. For it is the same thing
That the constitution of the human body thinks,
In each and every man. For the full is what is thought.'

For he treats perception and intellectual activity as the same, and that is why he says that remembering and forgetting are also due to the same factors and occur as a result of the physical blend in us. But he fails to explain whether, if they were equally mixed, intellectual activity would or would not occur, or what the general condition of the person would be like. And that he also attributes perception to opposition in itself is clear when he says that because of its lack of fire a corpse does not perceive light and warmth and sound, but does perceive their opposites, such as cold and silence. And at the general level he says that everything that exists has knowledge to a certain extent. (Theophrastus, *On the Senses* 1.1–4.9 Stratton)

S. Austin, 'Genesis and Motion in Parmenides: B8.12–13', *Harvard Studies in Classical Philology*, 87 (1983), 151–68.

—— *Parmenides: Being, Bounds, and Logic* (New Haven: Yale University Press, 1986).

J. Barnes, 'Parmenides and the Eleatic One', *Archiv für Geschichte der Philosophie*, 61 (1979), 1–21.

P. J. Bicknell, 'A New Arrangement of Some Parmenidean Verses', *Symbolae Osloenses*, 42 (1968), 44–50.

D. Blank, 'Faith and Persuasion in Parmenides', *Classical Antiquity*, 1 (1982), 167–77.

C. M. Bowra, 'The Proem of Parmenides', *Classical Philology*, 32 (1937), 97–112.

W. R. Chalmers, 'Parmenides and the Beliefs of Mortals', *Phronesis*, 5 (1960), 5–22.

R. J. Clark, 'Parmenides and Sense-perception', *Revue des études grecques*, 82 (1969), 14–32.

F. M. Cornford, 'A New Fragment of Parmenides', *Classical Review*, 49 (1935), 122–3.

A. H. Coxon, *The Fragments of Parmenides* (Assen: Van Gorcum, 1986 = *Phronesis*, suppl. vol. 3).

P. K. Curd, 'Eleatic Arguments', in J. Gentzler (ed.), *Method in Ancient Philosophy* (Oxford: Oxford University Press, 1997), 1–28.

A. Finkelberg, 'The Cosmology of Parmenides', *American Journal of Philology*, 107 (1986), 303–17.

—— 'Parmenides: Between Material and Logical Monism', *Archiv für Geschichte der Philosophie*, 70 (1988), 1–14.

—— 'Parmenides' Foundation of the Way of Truth', *Oxford Studies in Ancient Philosophy*, 6 (1988), 39–67.

—— 'Xenophanes' Physis, Parmenides' Doxa, and Empedocles' Theory of Cosmogonical Mixture', *Hermes*, 125 (1997), 1–16.

H. Fränkel, 'Studies in Parmenides', in [26], ii. 1–47.

D. J. Furley, 'Notes on Parmenides', in [28], 1–15.

M. Furth, 'Elements of Eleatic Ontology', in [30], 241–70 (first pub. *Journal of the History of Philosophy*, 6 (1968)).

D. Gallop, *Parmenides of Elea: Fragments* (Toronto: University of Toronto Press, 1984).

O. Goldin, 'Parmenides on Possibility and Thought', *Apeiron*, 26 (1993), 19–35.

L. Groarke, 'Parmenides' Timeless Universe', *Dialogue*, 24 (1985), 535–41.

E. A. Havelock, 'Parmenides and Odysseus', *Harvard Studies in Classical Philology*, 63 (1958), 133–43.

J. Hintikka, 'Parmenides' Cogito Argument', *Ancient Philosophy*, 1 (1980/1), 5–16.

G. Jameson, ' "Well-rounded Truth" and Circular Thought in Parmenides', *Phronesis*, 3 (1958), 15–30.

C. H. Kahn, 'The Thesis of Parmenides', *Review of Metaphysics*, 22 (1968–9), 700–24.

—— *The Verb 'Be' in Ancient Greek* (Dordrecht: D. Reidel, 1973).

—— 'Being in Parmenides and Plato', *La parola del passato*, 43 (1988), 237–61.

R. J. Ketchum, 'Parmenides on What There is', *Canadian Journal of Philosophy*, 20 (1990), 167–90.

P. Kingsley, *In the Dark Places of Wisdom* (Inverness, Calif.: Golden Sufi Center Publishing, 1999).

A. Laks, ' "The More" and "The Full": On the Reconstruction of Parmenides' Theory of Sensation in Theophrastus, *De Sensibus*, 3–4', *Oxford Studies in Ancient Philosophy*, 8 (1990), 1–18.

J. H. Lesher, 'Parmenides' Critique of Thinking: The *Poluderis Elenchos* of Fragment 7', *Oxford Studies in Ancient Philosophy*, 2 (1984), 1–30.

A. A. Long, 'The Principles of Parmenides' Cosmogony', in [26], ii. 82–101 (first pub. *Phronesis*, 8 (1963)).

—— 'Parmenides on Thinking Being', *Proceedings of the Boston Area Colloquium in Ancient Philosophy*, 12 (1996), 125–51.

M. M. Mackenzie, 'Parmenides' Dilemma', *Phronesis*, 27 (1982), 1–12.

J. Malcolm, 'On Avoiding the Void', *Oxford Studies in Ancient Philosophy*, 9 (1991), 75–94.

R. Mason, 'Parmenides and Language', *Ancient Philosophy*, 8 (1988), 149–56.

W. I. Matson, 'Parmenides Unbound', *Philosophical Inquiry*, 2 (1980), 345–60.

F. D. Miller, 'Parmenides on Mortal Belief', *Journal of the History of Philosophy*, 15 (1977), 253–65.

M. H. Miller, 'Parmenides and the Disclosure of Being', *Apeiron*, 13 (1979), 12–35.

J. S. Morrison, 'Parmenides and Er', *Journal of Hellenic Studies*, 75 (1955), 59–68.

A. P. D. Mourelatos, *The Route of Parmenides: A Study of Word, Image, and Argument in the Fragments* (New Haven: Yale University Press, 1970).

A. P. D. Mourelatos, 'Heraclitus, Parmenides, and the Naive Metaphysics of Things', in [28], 16–48.

—— 'Determinacy and Indeterminacy, Being and Non-being in the Fragments of Parmenides', in [32], 45–60.

A. Nehamas, 'On Parmenides' Three Ways of Inquiry', *Deucalion*, 33/34 (1981), 97–111.

M. Nussbaum, 'Eleatic Conventionalism and Philolaus on the Conditions of Thought', *Harvard Studies in Classical Philology*, 83 (1979), 63–108.

G. E. L. Owen, 'Eleatic Questions', in [26], ii. 48–81 (first pub. *Classical Quarterly*, 10 (1960)).

—— 'Plato and Parmenides on the Timeless Present', in [30], 271–92 (first pub. *The Monist*, 50 (1966)).

J. Owens, 'The Physical World of Parmenides', in J. R. O'Donnell (ed.), *Essays in Honour of Anton Charles Pegis* (Toronto: Pontifical Institute of Medieval Studies, 1974), 378–95.

—— (ed.), *Parmenides Studies Today*, special issue of *The Monist*, 62.1 (1979) (esp. the essays by A. P. D. Mourelatos, L. Tarán, T. M. Robinson, and D. Gallop).

M. E. Pellikaan-Engel, *Hesiod and Parmenides: A New View on Their Cosmologies and on Parmenides' Proem* (Amsterdam: Hakkert, 1974).

B. M. Perry, 'On the Cornford-Fragment (28B8.38*)', *Archiv für Geschichte der Philosophie*, 71 (1989), 1–9.

K. Reinhardt, 'The Relation Between the Two Parts of Parmenides' Poem', in [30], 293–311.

L. M. de Rijk, 'Did Parmenides Reject the Sensible World?', in L. P. Gerson (ed.), *Graceful Reason: Essays in Ancient and Medieval Philosophy* (Toronto: Pontifical Institute of Medieval Studies, 1983), 29–53.

T. M. Robinson, 'Parmenides on Ascertainment of the Real', *Canadian Journal of Philosophy*, 4 (1975), 623–33.

M. Schofield, 'Did Parmenides Discover Eternity?', *Archiv für Geschichte der Philosophie*, 52 (1970), 113–35.

D. Stewart, 'Contradiction and the Ways of Truth and Seeming', *Apeiron*, 14 (1980), 1–14.

L. Tarán, *Parmenides* (Princeton: Princeton University Press, 1965).

S. Tugwell, 'The Way of Truth', *Classical Quarterly*, 14 (1964), 36–41.

W. J. Verdenius, *Parmenides: Some Comments on his Poem* (Groningen: Walters, 1942; repr. with new preface, 1964).

—— 'Parmenides' Conception of Light', *Mnemosyne*, 2 (1949), 116–31.

G. Vlastos, 'Parmenides' Theory of Knowledge', in [33], 153–63 (first pub. *Transactions of the American Philological Association*, 77 (1946)).

L. Woodbury, 'Parmenides on Names', in [21], 145–62 (first pub. *Harvard Studies in Classical Philology*, 63 (1958)).

ZENO OF ELEA

T1 gives us both a summary of one of Zeno's arguments (on similarity and dissimilarity) and an influential account of their purpose. There were said (by Proclus, *Commentary on Plato's 'Parmenides'* 694.23–4 Cousin) to be forty arguments in his original treatise, all with the same purpose—to defend Parmenides' thesis that all is one, by demonstrating the absurdity of the consequences of the assumption that there is a plurality. What we have extant are the reports of a number of arguments which, by and large, pursue this aim. They do not necessarily pursue this aim directly, but if Parmenides' monism outraged common sense, then Zeno's paradoxes constitute an assault on common sense, and so offer at least indirect support for Parmenides. The surviving arguments fall into several categories: there are arguments against the possibility of plurality, motion, and place; and one miscellaneous argument whose original purpose is unclear. However, the original forty also contained, for instance, an argument aiming to prove that if there is a plurality, every member of that plurality is both similar and dissimilar (Plato, *Phaedrus* 261d).

The most famous are the arguments against the possibility of motion,[1] in which he claims to show that the assumption of motion leads to paradoxical consequences, and so that there can be no such thing (compare Parmenides F8. ll. 26–33 on p. 60). These arguments are summarized and criticized by Aristotle in **T2** and **T3**. Aristotle's paraphrases are for the most part perfectly clear. There are four arguments, known respectively as the Dichotomy, the Achilles, the Arrow, and the Stadium (or the Moving Rows). The Dichotomy states that in order to complete any process of motion, the moving object first has to cross half of the space on the way to its goal; it then has to cross half the remaining space, and then again half the remaining space, and so on *ad infinitum*. So it has an infinite number of tasks to perform in a finite time (see **T2**); but this is absurd, and so the whole notion of motion is absurd. The solution, according to Aristotle in **T2**, is to appreciate that time is just as liable to infinite division as space. It has been objected that Zeno was perfectly well aware of the notion of infinite divisibility, but it is hard to find it in the extant evidence (above all when Zeno talks of the possibility of dividing something down into nothing), and I think Aristotle's criticism is fair here, as far as it goes.[2]

---

[1] However, the thesis of Matson (see bibliography below) and others that all these arguments are actually directed against plurality, not motion, is worth considering.

[2] Aristotle himself was probably the discoverer of the infinite divisibility of space and time.

As Aristotle himself admits at *Physics* 263ᵃ⁻ᵇ, this reply is effective against the paradox as formulated by Zeno, but does not address the potential importance and interest of Zeno's argument.[3] It would perhaps have been more relevant, then, for Aristotle to have argued against Zeno's assumption that an infinite series of tasks has to be performed. For while it is true that an infinite series of tasks would have to be performed were the runner to mark every successive half-way point that he reaches, the conditional form of this sentence is important: it is true, logically, that it is always possible for another mark to be made, however many marks have already been made, but it is not true that any runner need make an infinite series of marks.

The Achilles is probably the best-known of Zeno's paradoxes. As Aristotle says, it depends on the same fallacy as the Dichotomy, and therefore its solution is the same. The puzzle states that in a race in which Achilles has a handicap and starts behind a slower runner (e.g. a tortoise), in order to overtake the tortoise he has first to reach the place where the tortoise started from; but by then the tortoise has moved on, so Achilles has next to cross the (shorter) distance to where the tortoise is now; but by the time he gets there the tortoise has moved on ... and so on *ad infinitum*. As Aristotle protests, Zeno must grant the evidence of his senses, that Achilles does catch up with and overtake the tortoise—that a finite distance can be traversed. One can complete an infinite series of tasks, provided it is understood that the infinitude comes in this case from infinite divisibility, not infinite extension. No one doubts that Achilles cannot mark his traversal of an infinite series of decreasing distances, but equally, Aristotle says, no one doubts that Achilles can traverse an infinitely divisible distance. Zeno needs, then, to distinguish which kinds of infinite tasks are not completable, and which are.

The third paradox of motion is the Arrow. This states that at any given moment an arrow in flight is occupying a space equal to its own size. But this is by definition what it is to be at rest: it is to be occupying a space which is, as one might put it, opposite another space of equal size. Therefore an arrow cannot move, since at every given moment it is at rest. Aristotle's solution is to suggest that time is more fluid than Zeno supposes: it does not consist (cinematographically, so to speak) of a series of discrete units of time,[4] and from the fact that an arrow is not moving at

---

[3] This can be taken as a paradigm of how Zeno has been treated through the ages; his paradoxes have the ability to engage each generation of thinkers as they build interesting problems on the foundations of the original paradoxes.

[4] I say this, trying not to beg the question of what Aristotle, or Zeno, might have meant by a 'unit of time'. Aristotle says that Zeno's false assumption is that time consists of 'indivisible nows'. This is technical Aristotelian terminology, and scholars

any given instant, it does not follow that it does not move in the overall stretch of time involved. In any case, the concepts of motion and being at rest implicitly import the concept of a stretch of time: motion entails speed, and speed is a measure of distance covered at a certain time; by the same token we call a thing at rest if it does not cover any distance in a given period of time. Therefore, Aristotle implies, Zeno was wrong to talk of motion and being at rest in an instant (see *Physics* 234ᵃ24–ᵇ9).

The fourth paradox, the Stadium, is the most controversial. It will help to have a diagrammatic representation of the puzzle. The starting-point is this:

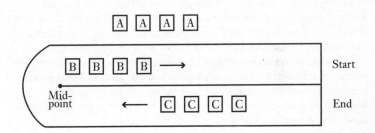

Now, apparently Zeno's 'paradox' is simply that by the time the Bs have reached the end of the As, having traversed two As, they have also reached the end of the Cs, having traversed four Cs. How can the Bs traverse two As and four Cs in the same time, when the As and the Cs are the same size? As Aristotle remarks, the solution is simple: it takes longer to pass a stationary body than it does to pass a body which is coming towards you.

It may well be that this was all the Stadium stated, and that it was that straightforward. There are signs of equal 'naïvety' in others of Zeno's arguments. It is just as likely that Zeno supported Parmenides' monism by sheer weight of the number of his arguments, as that he made each and every argument a deep paradox. However, many scholars think that Zeno could not have been so naïve, and so that Aristotle misunderstood his

---

are divided over what precisely a 'now' was for Aristotle. Since Aristotle plainly did not believe in the existence of atomic units of time (*Physics* 231ᵇ–233ᵇ), and since he describes a now as the 'limit of the past and the future' (233ᵇ33–234ᵃ5), it must be a durationless instant, if that is not an oxymoron. Aristotle's criticism of Zeno, then, is that his paradox had frozen the arrow in a durationless instant, but time does not consist of durationless instants. Whether this accurately represents Zeno's original thinking may be doubted. It is more likely that he was thinking of present instants of some minimal duration (though not quite atomic instants).

argument. They generate a more profound argument out of the elements given by Aristotle. Suppose that each of the blocks of As, Bs, and Cs is an atomic unit of space, and suppose that it takes one atomic unit of time (let's call it a 'click') for one atomic unit of space to pass another atomic unit of space. In one click, then, the leading B has moved from being opposite the second A to being opposite the third A. But in the same click it has moved from being opposite none of the Cs, to being opposite the second C. When, then, was it opposite the first C? It looks as though the click, which is by definition atomic (that is, indivisible), has to be sub-divided, and by the same token so do the supposedly atomic blocks. (The solution, I suppose, is to insist that there was no time when the first B-block was opposite the first C-block.) The advantage of this interpretation is that it gives Zeno a more interesting argument; the main problems with it are that it departs from what Aristotle says, and there is no evidence that in Zeno's time there was a theory of atomic units of space and time.

In a somewhat roundabout way, F1 gives us the bare bones of a series of Zenonian arguments against the possibility of plurality. If we need to find a particular target for these arguments, the theories of Anaxagoras are the best bet. Restoring its parts to their natural order, the argument would have gone somewhat as follows:

1. If there are many things, each of them is both infinitely small (i.e. non-existent) and infinitely large. Any thing, X, is the same as itself; if anything were added to it, it would not be X, but X + Y. But everything is divisible into parts (this is as close as Zeno comes to the notion of infinite divisibility). Everything has magnitude, which is to say that there is distance between one part of it and another; wherever you divide it there will always be an extra, protruding part yet to be divided. The possession of magnitude is an essential property of existence, because if something had no magnitude, it would make no difference were it to be added to or subtracted from something, which is to say that it would have no existence. But if the possession of magnitude is an essential property of existence, and if every magnitude is divisible into parts, then every existing thing is X+ Y, and if anything were just X it would not exist. Therefore, if there are many things, they are either self-identical, which is to say that they have no parts, which is to say that they are infinitely small, which is to say that they do not exist; or they are infinitely large, because they are divisible into infinite parts, and infinite parts do not add up to anything of merely finite size.

2. If every existing thing is infinitely divisible into parts, then either nothing exists or everything is one. For either division ends at an infinite number of atomic minimal parts (but anything made up of infinite parts has infinite magnitude), or it ends when the division of the last two parts

leaves nothing (but this is inconceivable). But the concept of a plurality of existing things stands or falls with the concept of infinite divisibility into parts. Therefore, since the concept of infinite divisibility into parts is absurd, there is no plurality, only unity.

3. If there are many things they are both infinite and finite in number. They are either just as many as they are, in which case they are finite in number, or, given infinite divisibility into parts, they are infinite in number. But this is absurd, and so there cannot be many things, only unity.

This must have seemed a pretty devastating series of arguments to Zeno's contemporaries. The arguments are flawed, of course: Zeno appears to assume, for instance, that anything made up of infinite parts must be infinitely huge. But the solution to the puzzles requires some fairly complex thinking about infinity, and in particular the recognition of the possibility of infinite division: this is effectively the challenge Zeno set his successors.

It must also be noticed that in arguing that anything without magnitude does not exist, Zeno is arguing against the existence of Parmenides' 'what-is', just as much as he is arguing against common sense.[5] What, then, of Plato's statement, in **T1**, that Zeno's purpose was to defend Parmenidean monism? On the whole, this seems to fit Zeno's arguments well, but for someone like Zeno there are no sacred cows. He demands that we think about all our assumptions, whether they are derived from common sense or from the authority of Parmenides; and he delights in the argumentative methods he polished: the infinite regress, the *reductio ad absurdum*.

T4 is a good example of an infinite regress, by which Zeno attempted to reduce to absurdity the idea of place. Since pluralism requires the existence of places, the argument can again be seen as supportive of Parmenidean monism; also, if existence is conceived of as corporeal, and corporeality as requiring space or place, then Zeno may be seen as attacking the notion that all existence is corporeal. Aristotle's solution in **T5** is to point out that 'in' can mean different things. There need be no infinite series of containing places, because you can say that one thing is 'in' another without meaning that it is 'in a place'. This is a good argument as far as it goes, but it is still not clear how it stops the regress, rather than simply providing a different perspective on how to describe any member of the regress. Perhaps Aristotle means that we can say that the duvet is 'in' the cover, in the sense that the cover is the place of the duvet; but in saying this we are not attaching the property of 'being in a place' to the

---

[5] This was appreciated even in ancient times. In his *Commentary on Aristotle's Physics*, at 138.29 ff. (see also 97.12 f. and 99.7 ff.), Simplicius says that both Eudemus (who was Aristotle's pupil) and, following him, Alexander of Aphrodisias, noticed the implication.

duvet, so much as attaching the property of 'being a place' to the cover. This would stop the regress immediately, because it would take a fresh argument to claim that the cover itself was in a place. Alternatively, one might argue that the place of the place of anything was just the place of that thing; this too effectively stops the regress.

Zeno's argument in **T6** is perfectly clear and straightforward. It is not clear how it serves his overall purpose of defending Parmenidean monism (or at least assaulting common sense), but one can see how it might fit in with his general concerns to argue that the smallest part of anything (here each individual seed in a bushel of millet seeds) has magnitude. Alternatively, it may simply have been an argument against reliance on the senses: the senses tell us that a single seed makes no sound as it falls, but reason, more reliably, informs us that it must, otherwise the whole bushel would not make a sound.

Aristotle, so important in preserving accounts of Zeno's arguments, may have the last word. In **T7** he describes Zeno as the founder of dialectic. In this context, 'dialectic' means a polemical method of arguing which shows the falsity of an opponent's premises and assumptions. This is how Zeno earns his place in the history of philosophy, for a similar argumentative method was to flourish in Plato's dialogues and give rise to the origins of logic in Aristotle.

T1 (DK 29A12; KRS 314, 327) [*Part of a discussion between Socrates, Parmenides, and Zeno*] After Socrates had listened to Zeno reading his treatise, he asked him to repeat the first hypothesis of the first argument. After it had been read through he said, 'What do you mean by this, Zeno? If there are many things, they must be both like and unlike one another, and this is impossible, because dissimilar things cannot be similar and similar things cannot be dissimilar. Is that what you mean?'*

'Yes,' said Zeno.

'So if it is impossible for dissimilars to be similar and similars to be dissimilar, it is also impossible for there to be a plurality of things, because if there were a plurality of things, they would be liable to impossibilities. Is this the point of your arguments? Isn't it precisely to insist, contrary to everything that is said, that there is no plurality? And don't you think that each of your arguments proves just this same point, with the result that you think that you have come up with as many proofs that there is no plurality as you have written arguments? Is this what you mean, or have I misunderstood you?'

'No,' said Zeno. 'You have an excellent grasp of the point of the whole treatise.'

'Parmenides,' Socrates said, 'I see that Zeno's treatise is another means he uses, along with his general friendship, to get close to you. In a sense his work is the same as yours, but he has made it look different as a way of trying to fool us into thinking that he is saying something different. I mean, in your poem you say that everything is one, and you come up with excellent arguments to demonstrate this, while he says that there is no plurality, and again comes up with a huge number of arguments to prove this at enormous length. So, with the one of you saying "One" and the other saying "Not many", and with each of you speaking in such a way as to make it seem as though there is nothing remotely the same in what you're saying, although in fact what you're saying is more or less identical, it looks as though the rest of us have missed the point of what you've been saying.'

'Yes, Socrates,' said Zeno, 'but in certain respects the true facts about my treatise have escaped your notice . . . The truth is that it is a kind of reinforcement of Parmenides' argument against those who try to mock it by arguing that, if there is only unity, the argument entails many absurd and even self-contradictory consequences. My treatise, then, responds to those who argue in favour of a plurality, paying them back what is due to them and then more besides. My intention is to demonstrate that their assumption of plurality, when followed through far enough, is even more absurd than the assumption of unity.' (Plato, *Parmenides* 127d6–128d6 Burnet)

T2 (DK 29A25; KRS 320; L 19) That is why Zeno's argument makes a false assumption, that it is impossible to traverse what is infinite or make contact with infinitely many things one by one in a finite time. For there are two ways in which distance and time (and, in general, any continuum) are described as infinite: they can be infinitely divisible or infinite in extent. So although it is impossible to make contact in a finite time with things that are infinite in quantity, it is possible to do so with things that are infinitely divisible, since the time itself is also infinite in this way. And so the upshot is that it takes an infinite rather than a finite time to traverse an infinite distance, and it takes infinitely many rather than finitely many nows to make contact with infinitely many things. (Aristotle, *Physics* 233ᵃ21–31 Ross)

T3 (DK 29A25–8; KRS 317, 318, 322, 323, 325; L 19, 26, 28, 29, 35) Zeno's reasoning is invalid. He claims that if it is always true that a thing is at rest[†] when it is opposite to something equal to itself, and if a moving object is always in the now, then a moving arrow is motionless. But this is false, because time is not composed of indivisible nows, and neither is any other magnitude.

Zeno came up with four arguments about motion which have proved troublesome for people to solve. The first is the one about a moving object not moving because of its having to reach the half-way point before it reaches the end. We have discussed this argument earlier [T2].

The second is the so-called Achilles. This claims that the slowest runner will never be caught by the fastest runner, because the one behind has first to reach the point from which the one in front started, and so the slower one is bound always to be in front. This is in fact the same argument as the Dichotomy, with the difference that the magnitude remaining is not divided in half. Now, we have seen that the argument entails that the slower runner is not caught, but this depends on the same point as the Dichotomy; in both cases the conclusion that it is impossible to reach a limit is a result of dividing the magnitude in a certain way. (However, the present argument includes the extra feature that not even that which is, in the story, the fastest thing in the world can succeed in its pursuit of the slowest thing in the world.*) The solution, then, must be the same in both cases. It is the claim that the one in front cannot be caught that is false. It is not caught as long as it is in front, but it still is caught if Zeno grants that a moving object can traverse a finite distance.

So much for two of his arguments. The third is the one I mentioned a short while ago, which claims that a moving arrow is still. Here the conclusion depends on assuming that time is composed of nows; if this assumption is not granted, the argument fails.

His fourth argument is the one about equal bodies in a stadium moving from opposite directions past one another; one set starts from the end of the stadium, another (moving at the same speed) from the middle. The result, according to Zeno, is that half a given time is equal to double that time. The mistake in his reasoning lies in supposing that it takes the same time for one moving body to move past a body in motion as it does for another to move past a body at rest, where both are the same size as each other and are moving at the same speed. This is false. For example, let AA . . . be the stationary bodies, all the same size as one another; let BB . . . be the bodies, equal in number and in size to AA . . . , which move from the middle of the stadium; and let CC . . . be the bodies, equal in number and in size to the others, which start from the end of the stadium and move at the same speed as BB . . . Now, it follows that the first B and the first C, as the two rows move past each other, will reach the end of each other's rows at the same time. And from this it follows that although the first C has passed all the Bs, the first B has passed half the number of As; and so (he claims) the time taken by the first B is half the time taken by the first C, because in each case we have equal bodies passing equal bodies. And it also follows that the first B has passed all the Cs, because the first C and the first B will be at opposite ends of the As at the same time, since (according to Zeno) the first C spends the same amount of time alongside each B as it does alongside each A,[†] because both the Cs and the Bs spend the same amount of time passing the As. Anyway, that is Zeno's argument, but his conclusion depends on the fallacy I mentioned. (Aristotle, *Physics* 239[b]5–240[a]18 Ross)

F1 (DK 29B1–3; KRS 315, 316; L 2, 9–12) In his treatise, however, which contains many arguments, he shows in each case the contradictory consequences of the assertion that there is a plurality. One of these arguments is the one in which he demonstrates that if there are many things they are both large and small—large enough to be infinite in magnitude, and small enough to have no magnitude at all.

In the following argument he demonstrates that anything which has no magnitude, solidity, or bulk does not exist. After all, he says, 'If such a thing were added to anything else, it would not make it larger; for if (despite the fact that it has no magnitude) it is added, no increase with respect to magnitude can take place. And therefore the thing which is added is bound to be nothing. If when it is subtracted the other item becomes no smaller and when it is added the other item does not increase, obviously what was added or subtracted is nothing.' Now, the point of this argument of Zeno's is not to reject singularity,* but to claim that each member of a plurality has magnitude—and so that the many are infinitely many, by virtue of the fact that, on account of infinite divisibility, there is always something in front of any given thing. But his demonstration of this point is preceded by his demonstration that no member of the plurality has magnitude because each member of the plurality is the same as itself and is one . . .

Porphyry believes that it was Parmenides who made use of the argument from dichotomy, in an attempt to show that what exists is one. Porphyry writes as follows: 'Parmenides had another argument which used dichotomy to prove, apparently, that what-is is only one, and that it has no parts and is indivisible. For supposing it to be divisible, he says, let it be divided into two, and then let each of the parts be further divided into two. Once this has gone on and on happening, it is obvious, he says, that either there will remain certain ultimate magnitudes, which are minima and are indivisible, but infinite in number, in which case the whole will be composed of numerically infinite minima; or else it will vanish and be dissolved into nothing, in which case it will be composed of nothing. Both of these outcomes are absurd, and therefore it is indivisible, and remains one. Or again, since it is everywhere alike, then if it is divisible, it will be equally divisible everywhere, rather than being divisible in one place but not in another. So let it be divided everywhere. Again, it is obvious that nothing will remain and that the whole will vanish, and that (supposing it to be a compound) it is composed of nothing. For as long as anything remains, it will not yet have been divided everywhere. And the upshot of these considerations is, he says, that what-is will be indivisible, without parts, and one.' [*Simplicius goes on to argue, rightly, that the attribution of this argument to Parmenides is incorrect, and that the argument stems from Zeno*] . . .

Then again, in demonstrating that if there is a plurality, the same things are both finite and infinite, Zeno writes as follows (I quote his exact words): 'If there are many things, they are bound to be as many as they are, neither more nor less; but if they are as many as they are, they are finite in number. If there are many things, there are infinitely many things, since there are always other things between any two given things, and others again between any two of those, and so things are infinite in number.'

As for infinity with respect to magnitude, he demonstrated that earlier in his book by the same kind of argument. He first demon-strates that anything without magnitude does not exist, and then he goes on: 'But if there is a plurality,[†] it is necessary for each thing to have a certain magnitude and solidity, and for there to be distance between one part of it and another. And the same goes for the part of it that protrudes: it too will have magnitude and some part of it will protrude. And it makes no difference whether one says this once or goes on and on saying it, since the item will have no such thing as a last part, and there will not be a part that does not stand in relation to another part. And so, if there are many things, they are bound to be both small and large—small enough to have no magnitude and large enough to be infinite.' (Simplicius, *Commentary on Aristotle's 'Physics'*, CAG IX, 139.5–141.8 Diels)

T4 (DK 29A24; L 15) Zeno's argument seemed to do away with the existence of place. It raised the following puzzle: If there is a place, it will be in something, because everything that exists is in something. But what is in something is in a place. Therefore the place will be in a place, and so on *ad infinitum*. Therefore, there is no such thing as place. (Simplicius, *Commentary on Aristotle's 'Physics'*, CAG IX, 562.3–6 Diels)

T5 (DK 29A24; L 14) We can see, then, that it is impossible for something to be in itself in the primary sense of the expression. Nor is it difficult to find a solution to Zeno's puzzle that if there is such a thing as place, it must be in something. For it is perfectly plausible for the immediate place to be in something else, as long as 'in' is not understood as implying location within a place, but is taken in the sense in which health is 'in' hot things (because it is a state of hot things) and in which heat is 'in' the body (because it is an affection of the body). This avoids the infinite regress. (Aristotle, *Physics* 210^{b}21–7 Ross)

T6 (DK 29A29; L 37) The fact that a given power as a whole has moved an object such-and-such a distance does not mean that half the power will move it any distance in any amount of time. If it did, one man could move a ship, since the power of the haulers and the distance which they all moved the ship together are divisible by the number of haulers. That is why Zeno is wrong in arguing that the tiniest fragment of millet makes a sound; there is no reason why the fragment should be able to move in any amount of time the air which the whole bushel moved as it fell. (Aristotle, *Physics* 250ª16–22 Ross)

T7 (DK 29A10; KRS 328) In his *Sophist* Aristotle describes Emped-ocles as the discoverer of rhetoric and Zeno as the discoverer of dialectic. (Aristotle [fr. 65 Rose] in Diogenes Laertius, *Lives of Eminent Philosophers* 8.57.1–2 Long)

W. E. Abraham, 'The Nature of Zeno's Arguments against Plurality in DK 29B1', *Phronesis*, 17 (1972), 40–52.

P. J. Bicknell, 'Zeno's Arguments on Motion', *Acta Classica*, 6 (1963), 81–105.

N. B. Booth, 'Zeno's Paradoxes', *Journal of Hellenic Studies*, 77 (1957), 189–201.

D. Bostock, 'Aristotle, Zeno and the Potential Infinite', *Proceedings of the Aristotelian Society*, 73 (1972/3), 37–53.

F. Cajori, 'The Purpose of Zeno's Arguments on Motion', *Isis*, 3 (1920/1), 7–20.

J. A. Faris, *The Paradoxes of Zeno* (Aldershot: Avebury, 1996).

H. Fränkel, 'Zeno of Elea's Attacks on Plurality', in [26], ii. 102–42.

D. J. Furley, 'Zeno and Indivisible Magnitudes', in [30], 353–67.

A. Grünbaum, *Modern Science and Zeno's Paradoxes* (London: George Allen & Unwin, 1968).

J. Lear, 'A Note on Zeno's Arrow', *Phronesis*, 26 (1981), 91–104.

H. D. P. Lee, *Zeno of Elea* (Cambridge: Cambridge University Press, 1936).

J. Mansfeld, 'Digging up a Paradox: A Philological Note on Zeno's Stadium', in [29], 319–42 (first pub. *Rheinisches Museum für Klassische Philologie*, 125 (1982)).

W. Matson, 'The Zeno of Plato and Tannery Vindicated', *La parola del passato*, 43 (1988), 312–36.

G. E. L. Owen, 'Zeno and the Mathematicians', in [26], ii. 143–65 (first pub. *Proceedings of the Aristotelian Society*, 58 (1957/8)).

F. R. Pickering, 'Aristotle on Zeno and the Now', *Phronesis*, 23 (1978), 253–7.

W. J. Prior, 'Zeno's First Argument Concerning Plurality', *Archiv für Geschichte der Philosophie*, 60 (1978), 247–56.

S. Quan, 'The Solution of Zeno's First Paradox', *Mind*, 77 (1968), 206–21.

W. D. Ross, *Aristotle's Physics* (London: Oxford University Press, 1936), 71–85, 655–66.

B. Russell, 'The Problem of Infinity Considered Historically', in id., *Our Knowledge of the External World* (London: Open Court, 1914), 159–88.

G. Ryle, 'Achilles and the Tortoise', in id., *Dilemmas* (Cambridge: Cambridge University Press, 1954), 36–53.

W. C. Salmon, *Zeno's Paradoxes* (Indianapolis: Bobbs-Merrill, 1970).

F. A. Shamsi, 'A Note on Aristotle, *Physics* 239b5–7: What Exactly Was Zeno's Argument of the Arrow?', *Ancient Philosophy*, 14 (1994), 51–72.

F. Solmsen, 'The Tradition About Zeno of Elea Re-examined', in [30], 368–93 (first pub. *Phronesis*, 16 (1971)).

O. Testudo [= J. Barnes], 'Space for Zeno', *Deucalion*, 33/34 (1981), 131–45.

G. Vlastos, 'Zeno's Race Course: With an Appendix on the Achilles', in [26], ii. 201–20, and in [33], 189–204 (first pub. *Journal of the History of Philosophy*, 4 (1966)).

—— 'A Note on Zeno's Arrow', in [26], ii. 184–200, and in [33], 205–18 (first pub. *Phronesis*, 11 (1966)).

—— 'A Zenonian Argument against Plurality', in [21], 119–44, and in [33], 219–40.

—— 'Plato's Testimony Concerning Zeno of Elea', in [33], 264–300 (first pub. *Journal of Hellenic Studies*, 95 (1975)).

MELISSUS OF SAMOS

Melissus is something of an oddity in the history of philosophy. A convinced Eleatic, who came up with some powerful arguments in defence of Parmenidean monism, he also served as the military commander of his island home, Samos, in which capacity he even managed to defeat the great Athenian leader Pericles in a battle in 441. One cannot help thinking that he must have temporarily shelved the changelessness of the Parmenidean 'what-is' in order to engage in politics and warfare, and so that by his very life he demonstrates that Parmenidean monism was epistemological—a state of mind, rather than an ontological statement about the world.

In his short treatise, Melissus started with the assumption that there is something that exists (**F1**), and then deduced the consequences of this assumption in a rigorous fashion. The deductive nature of his work enables us to order the few fragments we possess with some confidence. From the premiss that there is something that exists, he deduced, in order, that this existent thing is not liable to generation and destruction (**F2**), is of unlimited magnitude (**F3**), eternal (**F4**), single (**F5**), homogeneous (though the text where he proved this is missing), unchanging, and motionless (**F6**). It is tempting to see the assertion that it is of unlimited magnitude as a response to Zeno's argument that anything of no magnitude cannot exist.

Melissus reached substantially the same position as Parmenides, but by a somewhat different route. Despite the raft of properties of what-is in respect of which Melissus straightforwardly agrees with Parmenides— that it is eternal, single, homogeneous, ungenerated and unperishing, changeless, and motionless—there is arguably some disagreement between them. Consider his denial of void: not only can there be no internal void, and so no change, there can be no emptiness beyond what-is either. Whereas Parmenides had said (**F8** ll. 26–33, 49 on p. 60) that what-is was constrained within limits, for Melissus what-is has no limits. Not only is it everlasting in time, but it is of unlimited magnitude (**F3**). It is beginning to look as though, on Melissus' version (whatever we are to make of Parmenides in this respect), what-is is corporeal; and this seems to be confirmed by the idea that what-is is full, and can have no emptiness in it. In other words, it is apparently a solid body. But what, then, are we to make of **F7**, which plainly says that what-is is incorporeal? Many scholars are inclined to think that in this case Simplicius (who preserves all these fragments of Melissus) has made a mistake and attributed some words to him that were not his. However, (1) when Melissus talks of the 'fullness' of what-is, he is using a metaphor (much as Parmenides had talked of what-is being like a sphere) to express its homogeneous intensity. Similarly, the idea (even though denied by Melissus) that what-is could feel pain and suffer loss (**F6**) is clearly a metaphor to express its endurance (since anything in pain is not as strong as something healthy) and lack of parts. (2) In Melissus' day, something could be called 'incorporeal' or 'bodiless' simply because it lacked a body in the sense of lacking definite boundaries and of being inaccessible to the senses. In other words, in calling what-is 'incorporeal' Melissus may have meant, again, that it is boundless.

There is no difficulty, then, in thinking that for Melissus what-is is both full and 'incorporeal'. However, in **F6** he uses the lack of emptiness of what-is to explain its motionlessness: there is no void or empty space for any part of it to move into. This is clearly not a metaphor, but a straightforward argument, and one which presupposes the physicality of what-is. But it only presupposes the corporeality of what-is in a counterfactual fashion. The only way to explain movement, Melissus is saying, is to assume the existence of void and matter to move into the void; but in fact there is no such thing as void, nor as movement, and so we have no need to think of what-is as corporeal.

In **F8** Melissus comes up with an interesting argument designed to undermine our naïve reliance on the senses. In effect, he offers us a dilemma: either we believe the argument he has provided that what is real or true is unchanging, or we go along with the evidence of our senses that things change. If we were to see anything as it really is, we would see that it is unchanging; but our senses show us change; therefore our senses are not reliable. Either there is no reality to the changing things of this world, and what-is is one, unchanging, etc., or there is no validity to Melissus' reasoning. The polar opposition between reason and the senses, implicit in Zeno and Parmenides, is here brought out into the open. And we can again see why the denial of the corporeality of what-is is central to Melissus' thought, and should not be eliminated as a mistake by Simplicius: corporeality is what our senses perceive; what-is, on the other hand, has no sensible qualities. It has no shape, because it is of unlimited magnitude in all directions; it has no colour, taste, etc., because all these things change, and there can be no change in what-is.

Melissus' strengths lie not so much in original thinking as in (usually) clear arguing—at least, the intention of his arguments is clear, even if their logical validity is often doubtful or worse. Given the obscurity of a great deal of Parmenides' own words, it was invariably to Melissus that later thinkers turned for clarity about the Eleatic position. But his main contribution was in formulating (apparently for the first time) the notion that movement requires the existence of matter and void. This idea was to flourish in atomist thought, and then for many centuries afterwards.

———————

F1 (DK 30B1; KRS 525) It always was what it was and always will be. For if it had come into existence, there was necessarily nothing before it came into existence. Now, if there was nothing, there is no way that anything could have come into existence from nothing. (Simplicius, *Commentary on Aristotle's 'Physics'*, CAG IX, 162.24–6 Diels)

F2 (DK 30B2; KRS 526) Now, since it did not come into existence, it not only is, but always was and always will be, and it has no beginning and no end, but is without limits. For if it had come into existence, it would have had a beginning (since its coming-into-existence would have begun at some time) and it would have had an end (since its coming-into-existence would have ended at some time). But since it had no beginning and no end, it always was and always will be and has no beginning nor end, since anything that is not complete cannot always exist. (Simplicius, *Commentary on Aristotle's 'Physics'*, CAG IX, 109.20–5 Diels)

F3 (DK 30B3; KRS 527) But as it always exists, so too it must always be unlimited in magnitude. (Simplicius, *Commentary on Aristotle's 'Physics'*, CAG IX, 109.31–2 Diels)

F4 (DK 30B4; KRS 528) Nothing with a beginning and an end is either eternal or unlimited. (Simplicius, *Commentary on Aristotle's 'Physics'*, CAG IX, 110.3–4 Diels)

F5 (DK 30B6; KRS 531) If it is unlimited, only one thing can exist; for if there were two things, they could not be unlimited, but would have limits in relation to each other. (Simplicius, *Commentary on Aristotle's 'On the Heavens'*, CAG VII, 557.16–17 Heiberg)

F6 (DK 30B7; KRS 533, 534) And so it is eternal, unlimited, single, and homogeneous. And it can neither be destroyed, nor become larger, nor change in organization, nor feel pain, nor suffer loss, because if it were susceptible to any of these things it would no longer be one. If it were to alter, what-is would necessarily not be homogeneous, but what-was-before would perish and what-was-not would come into existence. So if it were to alter by a single hair in 10,000 years, it would perish utterly in time as a whole.

Nor can its organization be changed, because the organization that existed before does not perish, nor does an organization that did not exist come into existence. And since nothing is either added or destroyed or altered, how can anything that exists have its organization changed? For if it underwent alteration in any respect it would thereby have had its organization changed as well.

Nor does it feel pain, because it it were in pain it would not be complete. After all, something in pain could not always exist, nor is it as strong as something healthy, nor would it be homogeneous, if were in pain, because the pain it was feeling would be a result of something being taken away or something being added, so that it would no longer be homogeneous. Nor could what is healthy feel pain, since the health—that is, what existed—would perish and what did not exist would come into existence. The same argument holds for its suffering loss as for its feeling pain.

Nor is it empty in any respect, for emptiness is nothing, and what is nothing cannot exist. Nor does it move, because, since it is full, there is nowhere for it to give way. If there were emptiness, it would give way into the emptiness, but since it is not empty there is nowhere for it to give way. It cannot be dense and rare, because anything that is rare cannot be as full as something that is dense; anything that is rare is thereby emptier than something that is dense. The way to come to a verdict about what is full or not full must be as follows: if it gives way at all or is receptive, it is not full; if it does not give way and is not receptive, it is full. Now, if it is not empty, it is bound to be full; and if it is full, it does not move.   (Simplicius, *Commentary on Aristotle's 'Physics'*, CAG IX, 111.19–112.15 Diels)

F7 (DK 30B9; KRS 538) So if it exists, it must be one; and being one it must be incorporeal; but if it had solidity, it would have parts, and then it would no longer be one.   (pieced together from Simplicius, *Commentary on Aristotle's 'Physics'*, CAG IX, 110.1–2 and 87.6–7 Diels)

F8 (DK 30B8; KRS 537) The greatest indication that there is only one thing is this argument, but there are the following indications too. If there were many things, they would have to be no different from how I am describing the one thing to be. For if there were earth, water, air, fire, iron, and gold; if one thing is alive while another is dead; if there is blackness and whiteness and all the other things that people take to be true; if this is so, and we see things and hear things correctly, then each thing has to be just as it first appeared to us: things cannot change or alter, but must be for ever as they are. In fact, though, we say we see and hear and grasp things correctly, but it seems to us that something warm becomes cold and something cold becomes warm; that something hard becomes soft and something soft becomes hard; that something alive dies and comes into existence from a state of not being alive. In other words, it seems to us that all these things alter, and that what was the case and what is now the case are quite different. It seems to us that iron, which is hard, is rubbed away by contact with our fingers, and that the same goes for gold and stone and everything else that we take to be strong, and that earth and stone are made up of water.[†] Now, there is inconsistency here, because although we are saying that there are many things which are eternal and have particular characteristics and endurance, we also think that they all alter and change from what we see on any given occasion. Clearly, then, we did not see things correctly and we are wrong in taking these many things to exist. If they were true, things would not change, but everything would be just as we take it to be; for there is nothing stronger than something which is true. But if something has changed, what-is has perished and what-was-not has come into existence. And so, if there were many things, they would have to be just like the one.   (Simplicius, *Commentary on Aristotle's 'On the Heavens'*, CAG VII, 558.21–559.12 Heiberg)

N. B. Booth, 'Did Melissus Believe in Incorporeal Being?', *American Journal of Philology*, 79 (1958), 61–5.

D. J. Furley, 'Melissus of Samos', in [24], 114–22.

F. Solmsen, 'The "Eleatic One" in Melissus', *Mededelingen der Koninklijke Nederlandse Akademie van Wetenschappen*, 32.8 (1969), 221–33.

PYTHAGORAS AND FIFTH-CENTURY PYTHAGOREANISM

(PYTHAGORAS OF SAMOS, PHILOLAUS OF CROTON, PETRON OF HIMERA, EURYTUS OF CROTON)

We have no extant fragments of Pythagoras himself—he probably wrote nothing—and the historical record is indelibly confused by his great fame, since this meant that later generations attributed all kinds of ideas and mathematical theorems to their illustrious founder, with no regard for the modern concept of historical truth. The difficulty of recovering pre-Platonic Pythagorean thought is increased by the fact that many of Plato's ideas are Pythagorean in inspiration, and he was such a famous philosopher that subsequent writings about Pythagoreanism are tainted, as some scholars see it, with Platonic views. There is a large number of such writings, and they need judicious mining for nuggets of genuine early Pythagorean thought. However, others regard Pythagoreanism more as a continuing and stable tradition, from which Plato borrowed; if this is the case, post-Platonic evidence about Pythagoreanism may be just as informative about the tradition as any other.

Pythagoras soon became well known as a sage: he lived around the end of the sixth century, and T1–5 were all written within about fifty years of his death. Heraclitus grumpily accuses Pythagoras of plagiarism (probably from Orphic texts) and lack of insight, but Herodotus, Ion, and Empedocles see him as a great teacher. Since later tradition credits Pythagoras with teaching reincarnation,[1] it is likely that T6, along with Xenophanes F20 (p. 30), are also early references to Pythagoras. T7 (from Aristotle) and T8 (from a contemporary of Aristotle) confirm that metempsychosis was central to early Pythagorean thought.[2] The religious

---

[1] The doctrine of metempsychosis or transmigration of souls was not original to Pythagoras: in Greece the idea first occurs in Pherecydes of Syros, who for this reason is sometimes called the teacher of Pythagoras. Pherecydes lived in the 6th cent. and was described by Aristotle as half philosopher, half mythologer (*Metaphysics* 1091[b]). There are only two certain fragments (one fortunately preserved on papyrus), but a number of testimonia allow us to reconstruct the outline of his thought in surprising detail. There is an excellent monograph on Pherecydes by Schibli [48], whose only failing is a certain insensitivity to the symbolical aspects of Pherecydes' thinking. As well as Schibli, see West [72] and Kirk/Raven/Schofield [2].

[2] It is not clear, however, that early Pythagoreans came up with *arguments* for metempsychosis. But the Pythagorizing physician, Alcmaeon of Croton, who lived early in the 5th cent., did. On Alcmaeon, see Barnes [15] i. 114–20.

flavour of early Pythagoreanism is also clear in **T9–11** (certain practices were forbidden to members of the sect), **T12** (miracles were ascribed to Pythagoras), and **T14** and **T18** (some Pythagoreans took a vow of silence). The connection between Pythagoreanism and the Orphic religion (hinted at in **T9**) is hard to unravel, but the following elements of Orphism are almost certainly relevant: the soul is imprisoned in the body until it has paid the penalty for past misdeeds; a life of ritual purity is required to cleanse our souls; ascetic prescriptions for purity include abstention from blood sacrifice, and from eating meat and most fish. For the Pythagoreans, vegetarianism was a natural consequence of their belief in the transmigration of the soul: today's dinner may be your dead grandmother. But since they also believed that plants had souls of a kind, it is not known how far down the food chain they took their proscription, or even whether only certain kinds of meat were prohibited, rather than all meat. Moreover, since other testimonia commend sacrifice (see **T15**, **T18**, **T22**), it is not clear to what extent, if at all, they undertook the radical step of abstaining from sacrifice. On the imprisonment of the soul, see the fragment **F1** of the fifth-century Pythagorean Philolaus, a contemporary of Socrates. The idea that the soul is independent of the body, and in some sense represents one's true self, has of course been of immense significance in Western thought. Boosted by Plato and Christianity, until recently it was taken more or less for granted.

The meaning of many of the Pythagorean prohibitions, such as those listed in **T10** and **T11**, is obscure. They were a particularly famous feature of the Pythagorean way of life, and were known as *akousmata* ('things heard', or passed down by word of mouth) or *sumbola* ('tokens' or 'passwords'). At any rate, it is clear that anyone attempting to obey these injunctions would have to remain alert, rather than succumbing to the semi-sleep state that constitutes normal consciousness. **T13**, although late testimony, is probably based on the fourth-century writer Aristoxenus, and well sums up the mystical thrust of Pythagorean practices, one of the consequences of which, given by Plato at *Phaedo* 61e–62c, is a prohibition of suicide; if I am the gods' subordinate, I do not have the right to take my own life. Even their mathematical teaching was subordinate to the aim of harmonizing one's life with god's wishes. In short, it is likely that Pythagoras was a teacher of perennial wisdom, rather than a Presocratic philosopher in the Milesian mould. Some of his followers later developed his views into a more scientific form (or, just possibly, revealed them where they had previously been considered secret). We hear of many individual Pythagoreans (over 200), but few of them are more than just a name: we rarely know enough to be able to attribute particular doctrines to them. And all we can safely say about the doctrines of Pythagoras himself is summed up in **T14** (which probably stems from Dicaearchus), with the possible addition of **T15–16**.

The biographical tradition concerning Pythagoras is often contradictory, but it is reasonably safe to say that though he was born on the eastern Greek island of Samos, at the time of its greatest prosperity, he fled from there during the reign of the tyrant Polycrates (535–522) and settled in southern Italy, first in Croton, and then later in Metapontum, where he died. The move to Metapontum may have been made necessary by hostility towards Pythagorean political influence in Croton; there were two waves of attacks on Pythagoreans in southern Italy, one *c.*510 and the other *c.*450. Pythagoras' activities in southern Italy included setting up communes (**T17**), run on religious and mystical principles (**T13**), which also gained political power in a number of communities in southern Italy (**T19**). For the first time, women were admitted into these schools. Others, however, downplay the religious side of these communes and try to see them purely as political pressure groups.

Plato's view of the Pythagoreans covers both their quasi-monastic way of life and their interest in mathematics and science (**T20–1**); the idea that astronomy and harmonics are sister sciences was probably traditionally Pythagorean, but was certainly expressed by Plato's contemporary, Archytas of Tarentum. These are Plato's only two explicit references to Pythagoras or Pythagoreans, but they do not reveal the extent of his debt to them in certain passages of *Gorgias*, *Phaedo*, and *Republic*, in *Philebus* and *Timaeus* as a whole, and in his famous 'unwritten doctrines'. Not all *akousmata* were commandments, and the essence of Pythagorean arithmology is expressed in the centrality of the *tetraktys* to their system (**T22**, **T23**). The *tetraktys* is the decad considered as the sum of the first four numbers, and is usually portrayed as a triangular number:

It could be, and was, used to express the arithmetical, geometric, and harmonic relations between the first ten numbers, in a number of complex ways.[3] Some Pythagorean arithmology has survived today, although we may have shed the geometrical conception of mathematics the Pythagoreans perpetuated in favour of abstract notation; they were the first to define different kinds of numbers as, for instance, odd and even, square and cube, prime and composite; and we are still impressed by the fact that, for instance, successive odd numbers always add up to successive square numbers. **T23** is only the tip of the iceberg of uses to which the Pythagoreans put the *tetraktys*. The musical use, prominent in Sextus, is certainly early (as **T24** shows), and many would attribute the discovery of the mathematics of the primary musical intervals to Pythagoras himself (e.g. **T16**, also an early piece of evidence). But how much further the first Pythagoreans went in mathematical musicology is complex and unclear; in **T21** Plato complains that they did not pay enough attention to pure mathematics.

But, if **T25–8** are to be trusted, the connection the Pythagoreans saw between number and the universe lay not just in the kinds of correspondences the *tetraktys* could display. Aristotle tells us that they saw number as somehow the principle of all things. This view is likely to be confusing, until we appreciate that the Pythagoreans were not Milesians: they were not interested in the material nature of things so much as their organization. Thus as **T25** suggests, and **T29** and **T30** show at greater length, even abstract concepts such as justice could be accommodated. Note also that the Pythagorean attribution of properties to numbers was not stable; **T29** calls either 4 or 9 'justice', while **T30** is an extended reflection on how 5 (the pentad) can be seen as justice. It is clear that Aristotle talks correctly of numbers being 'analogues' or 'resemblances' of things (**T25**); so when elsewhere he talks as if the Pythagoreans identified things with numbers (**T26–8**, and see also Alexander at the end of **T29**) and suggested that things were literally made out of numbers, he is trying too hard to incorporate Pythagorean views into his own theory of the material cause. At any rate, on Aristotle's evidence, according to the Pythagoreans things are numbers,[4] things are like numbers, and the elements of number, the limit and the unlimited, or the even and the odd, are the elements of all things.

The famous table of opposites with which Aristotle concludes **T25** is

---

[3] Although it is a late text, *The Theology of Arithmetic*, preserved in the corpus of works ascribed to Iamblichus, gives a good impression of this aspect of the Pythagorean tradition.

[4] 'Things are numbers, or, if you like, the basis of nature is numerical, because solid bodies are built up of surfaces, surfaces of planes, planes of lines and lines of points, and in their geometric view of number the Pythagoreans saw no difference between points and units' (Guthrie [10], i. 259).

puzzling, because it seems to combine different kinds of opposites. However, in each of the ten pairs, the first one should be seen as a limiter and the second as something unlimited (see Philolaus in **F3**, below). This begins to suggest a way in which limit and the unlimited are the elements of things, or account in some way for the properties of things. Every property of every object can be seen to be either a limiter or unlimited. What is particularly important about this is that (at any rate, by the later fifth century) the Pythagoreans had clearly moved beyond the Milesian conception of the opposites as concrete stuffs to the realization that they were abstract qualities. But in any case, although the primary pairs, limit–unlimited and odd–even, are early the full table of opposites may stem from fourth-century Pythagoreanism, later than the time-frame of this book. With the words 'Other members of the same school', Aristotle distinguishes its authors from the fifth-century Pythagoreans he had previously been discussing.

Pythagorean interest in number led them to investigate its properties widely, and there is no doubt that they made significant advances in mathematics (though nowhere near as many as later tradition credits them with), as well as in the pseudo-science of arithmology. Here it is especially hard to know which, if any, of the theorems derive from Pythagoras himself. **T31–5** give a few important theorems which we may date with some but not total confidence to early in the history of Pythagorean mathematics (see also **T15** on 'Pythagoras' theorem'—but that, in any case, may have been learnt from Babylon, where knowledge of the Pythagorean triangle goes back to about 1700 BCE). **T36** shows that mathematics (or arithmology) was considered esoteric. But **T37** suggests that the arithmologists, representing the mystical side of Pythagoreanism, considered themselves the only true Pythagoreans; and it is true that our sources do show a tendency to label any mathematician a 'Pythagorean', solely because he worked on mathematics.

The Pythagoreans (and especially Philolaus and Archytas) greatly enhanced our knowledge of astronomy. Although it is probably going too far to suggest that **T38** shows that they saw the earth as simply one of the planets (since they had no conception of a heliocentric universe), and although it is not clear that they discovered the correct order of the planets, let alone explained the irregularities of their motions, they did distinguish the planets from the sun, moon, and fixed stars (**T39–40**), and they recognized that the heavenly bodies were of an enormous size (**T41**). **T42** is an ingenious accommodation of the fieriness of the sun with the teaching about heavenly fire contained in **T40**. Aristotle's notorious accusation in **T25** that the Pythagoreans invented heavenly bodies for arithmological purposes is clearly the last resort of an intellectual failing to understand a system constructed more for its resonance with the inner psyche of people than for its correspondence with observable facts. The mystical or mind-expanding aspect of Pythagoreanism is never far from the surface: **T41** introduces us to the famous Pythagorean doctrine of the Harmony of the Spheres, the beauty of which has cast a spell on all subsequent generations.[5] Anaximander's proportionate universe is here given majestic elaboration, but note that in its earliest manifestation, as reported here by Aristotle, it is not clear how many notes make up the harmony—that is, it is not clear that the early Pythagoreans distinguished the five visible planets and assigned them each a different sound. **T43**, sounding like something from H. G. Wells, again reminds us that we are in the domain of shamanistic visions, not science.

Pythagorean cosmogony is difficult to reconstruct, and our sources are full of obvious contradictions, or at least alternative views. As **T25** and **F2** show, the opposites, limit and the unlimited, are primary. The imposition of limit on the unlimited creates the universe, the One, which is both even and odd simultaneously. The other numbers, which are somehow identical with things, proceed from the One. Aristotle was severely critical of this view, both because it involved the generation of numbers (which he considered eternal: *Metaphysics* 1091a12–22) and because it constructed the material universe out of immaterial entities, numbers (*Metaphysics* 1090a30–35). It is clear (and Aristotle, *Physics* 203a confirms it) that the Pythagoreans thought of the universe as spherical and as being surrounded by 'the unlimited' (the same word as Anaximander's 'boundless'). Some kind of drawing in takes place, perhaps like an inbreath (**T44–5**); this introduces void, which distinguishes one thing, one number, from another. The first thing to be distinguished in this way is the central hearth of the universe (**F6**), and then the rest of the major features of the universe—the planets and so on (**F7**). It is legitimate to connect fragments of Philolaus with Aristotle's testimonia about 'the Pythagoreans', because it is likely that Philolaus is actually the Pythagorean Aristotle most commonly has in mind. But at the same time it is clear that to be a Pythagorean meant, primarily, to practise a certain way of life, not to adhere to a particular cosmology in all its details, and so we do hear of significant theoretical differences between thinkers classified as 'Pythagoreans'.

Philolaus' cosmogony is the most sophisticated extant. His thinking reflects the symmetry of Anaximander's universe, which balances up and

[5] After Plato, *Republic* 616b–617d, see especially 'The Dream of Scipio' at the end of the sixth book of Cicero's *On the Republic*, and Macrobius' commentary on this passage. Both are conveniently available in translation in a single volume: W. H. Stahl, *Macrobius: Commentary on the Dream of Scipio* (New York: Columbia University Press, 1952).

down in an era before knowledge of gravity (**F7**). He based his cosmogony entirely on a primary pair of opposites, limitation and unlimitedness (which are most profitably thought of as that which provides structure and that which becomes structured, or quasi-Aristotelian form and matter), thus continuing both the Milesian reduction of the first principles of the universe to as few as possible and their emphasis on opposites, but in response to Parmenides' strictures made the 'being' of these things eternal (**F5**). Since it was standard Pythagorean teaching that odd numbers limit, while even numbers are unlimited,[6] it is likely that he was an orthodox Pythagorean at least to the extent that his cosmogony was arithmological. Harmony, or mathematically conformable adjustment, relates the odd and even numbers, limiters and unlimiteds. The harmony or structure of the world is always uppermost in Philolaus' mind as the chief thing he needs to explain.

Also noteworthy are his comments—almost asides—on the limitations of human knowledge. The true essence of things is accessible only to the gods, or perhaps to a man with divine knowledge; and in the nature of things we cannot know the infinite (**F4**, **F5**). In part, Philolaus is here criticizing Milesian or similar attempts to divine an ultimate reality behind the things of this world. He is suggesting that this is impossible, and that the best one can do, instead, is to try to say what the necessary preconditions are for the world we are faced with to exist. Those necessary

---

[6] The reasons for this doctrine are complex. There was a Pythagorean way of portraying the sequences of odd and even numbers as follows.

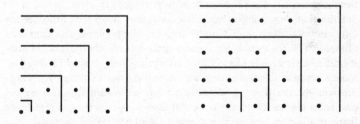

In these diagrams, the lines separating each successive odd or even numbers are called 'gnomons' (after a certain carpenter's tool). Now, the sequence of odd or masculine numbers produce only square numbers, whereas the sequence of even or female numbers produce an unlimited variety of different oblongs. Secondly, in current embryological theory, the male was supposed to give the form to the embryo, while the female was a kind of material receptacle. This still does not quite explain how the Pythagoreans took even numbers to underly the unlimitedness of things, or odd numbers the limitedness of things, but this is the recurrent problem in understanding ancient Pythagoreanism: the difficulty of understanding in what sense 'All is number'.

preconditions are, he suggests, the existence of things that limit and things that are unlimited, and of *harmonia* to bind them together; and he suggests that these are easily identifiable features of our world. One can, then, analyse any event or entity into something unlimited which has been limited in a harmonious fashion. As a Pythagorean, Philolaus would probably argue that ultimately the limiter and the unlimited are numerical, but in the first instance this is not necessary: this book, for instance, is simply unlimited vegetable matter which has been limited by something (human will?) in a harmonious fashion.

It is not clear in detail how Philolaus or other Pythagoreans explained the creation of the various minutiae of life on earth (**T46** is tantalizing, but its attribution to Philolaus is controversial), but they did speculate about the nature of the human soul (**T47** and **T48**). In **T48**, which is probably the theory of Philolaus, it is likely that Aristotle has been unduly influenced by Plato's elaboration of this theory in his dialogue *Phaedo* (especially 86b–c), and that originally Philolaus said that the soul was a numerical ratio rather than a blending of opposites. It is more likely to be authentically Pythagorean that the soul is or has its own harmony. Apart from anything else, if the soul is the harmony of the bodily elements, it is hard to see how the soul could survive the dissolution of the body, and yet transmigration of the soul was standard Pythagorean doctrine. As **T49** and **F8** show, Philolaus also speculated about the nature of the body. He might have added that warm bodies grow cold on death. As we have found with the Milesians, Philolaus here adumbrates an analogy between macrocosm and microcosm. Just as the universe is formed first out of central fire, and then draws in void from the unlimited (**T44–5**), so a new-born human is hot and draws in air from outside.

I conclude with almost all we know about two other fifth-century Pythagoreans, Eurytus of Croton (a pupil of Philolaus) and Petron of Himera.[7] **T50** shows how bizarre and amazing early Pythagorean cosmological speculation could be. The testimonia about Eurytus (**T51–2**) are more interesting: they demonstrate how, in Aristotle's terms, Pythagoreans could think that everything was made out of numbers. An unkind interpretation has Eurytus playing silly games—blocking out a pre-drawn figure of a human being with 250 pebbles and then saying, 'Eureka! 250 is the number of a human being!' More charitably, his reasoning was probably that if 3 is the minimum number required to define a triangle, and 4 a pyramid, then there may be a minimum number required to define the

---

[7] The only other testimony on Petron comes from Proclus (*Commentary on Plato's Timaeus* 138b), but this merely summarizes Plutarch's testimony, adding the guess that the worlds at the corners were somehow authoritative. Plutarch's testimony has been contaminated with Platonic talk of forms and essences.

specific form of a human being. On this view, Eurytus may be seen as moving towards the kind of science we have nowadays, which is based on mathematics.

————

T1 (DK 22B129; KRS 256) There was no more diligent investigator than Pythagoras the son of Mnesarchus; he made a selection from these writings and created a wisdom of his own, a thing of wide learning and fraudulent artifice.   (Heraclitus [fr. 129 Diels/Kranz] in Diogenes Laertius, *Lives of the Eminent Philosophers* 8.6.3–5 Long)

T2 (DK 22B40; KRS 255) Wide learning does not teach insight; otherwise it would have taught Hesiod and Pythagoras, not to mention Xenophanes and Hecataeus.   (Heraclitus [fr. 40 Diels/ Kranz] in Diogenes Laertius, *Lives of Eminent Philosophers* 9.1.5–7 Long)

T3 (DK 14A2; KRS 257) [*Herodotus records a story, which he himself does not believe, that the Thracian deity Salmoxis had once been a slave of Pythagoras, and duped the Thracian tribe, the Getae, into a belief in personal immortality by hiding away for three years and then reappearing. In the course of telling the story he says*:] Now, Salmoxis had experienced life in Ionia and was familiar with Ionian customs, which are more profound than those of the Thracians, who are an uncivilized and rather naïve people; after all, he had associated with Greeks, and in particular with Pythagoras, who was hardly the weakest intellect in Greece.   (Herodotus, *Histories* 4.95.2.4–7 Hude)

T4 (DK 36B4; KRS 258) Ion of Chios says about Pherecydes:

> Well furnished, then, with manly vigour and dignity,
> Even when dead he has a pleasant life for his soul,
> If Pythagoras really knew what he was talking about,[†]
> And he excelled in knowing and studying men's views.

> (Ion of Chios [fr. 5 Diehl] in Diogenes Laertius,
> *Lives of Eminent Philosophers* 1.120.5–8 Long)

T5 (DK 31B129; KRS 259) Empedocles too testifies to this when he says about Pythagoras:

> There was among them a certain man of rare knowledge,
> Master especially of all kinds of wise deeds,
> Who had acquired the greatest wealth of mind:†
> For whenever he reached out with his entire mind
> He easily saw each and every individual thing   5
> In ten and twenty lifetimes of men.

(Empedocles [fr. 129 Diels/Kranz] in Porphyry, *Life of Pythagoras* 30.7–14 Nauck)

T6 (DK 14A1; KRS 261) The Egyptians were also the first to claim that the soul of a human being is immortal, and that each time the body dies the soul enters another creature just as it is being born. They also say that when the soul has made the round of every creature on land, in the sea, and in the air, it once more clothes itself in the body of a human being just as it is being born, and that a complete cycle takes three thousand years. This theory has been adopted by certain Greeks too—some from a long time ago, some more recently—who presented it as if it were their own. I know their names, but I will not write them down.   (Herodotus, *Histories* 2.123.2–3 Hude)

T7 (DK 58B39) They [*Aristotle's predecessors*] try only to describe the soul, but they fail to go into any kind of detail about the body which is to receive the soul, as if it were possible (as it is in the Pythagorean tales) for just any old soul to be clothed in just any old body.   (Aristotle, *On the Soul* 407ᵇ20–3 Ross)

T8 (DK 14A8) Heraclides of Pontus says that Pythagoras used to say about himself that he had once been born as Aethalides and was regarded as a son of Hermes. Hermes told him that he could choose anything he wanted except immortality, and he asked to be able to retain, both alive and dead, the memory of things that had happened. He therefore remembered everything during his lifetimes, and when dead he still preserved the same memories. Later he entered into Euphorbus and was wounded by Menelaus. Euphorbus used to say that he had formerly been born as Aethalides and had received the gift from Hermes, and used to tell of the journeying of his soul and all its migrations, recount all the plants and creatures to which it had belonged, and describe everything he had experienced in Hades and the experiences undergone by the rest of the souls there. When Euphorbus died, his soul moved into Hermotimus, who also wanted to prove the point, so he went to Branchidae, entered the sanctuary of Apollo, and pointed out the shield which Menelaus had dedicated there . . . When Hermotimus died, he became Pyrrhus, the fisherman from Delos, and again remembered everything, how he had formerly been Aethalides, then Euphorbus, then Hermotimus, and then Pyrrhus. And when Pyrrhus died, he became Pythagoras and remembered everything that has just been mentioned.   (Heraclides of Pontus [fr. 89 Wehrli] in Diogenes Laertius, *Lives of Eminent Philosophers* 8.4–5 Long)

F1 (DK 44B14) The ancient theologians and prophets testify to the fact that the soul has been yoked to the body as a punishment of some kind and that it has been buried in the body as in a tomb. (Philolaus [fr. 14 Diels/Kranz] in Clement, *Miscellanies* 2.203.11 Stählin/Früchtel)

T9 (DK 14A1; KRS 263) It is against religious law for the Egyptians to take anything woollen into their sanctuaries or to be buried along with any woollen items. This custom of theirs accords with Orphic and Bacchic rites, as they are called (though they are actually Egyptian and Pythagorean), because no initiate of these rites either is allowed to be buried in woollen clothing.   (Herodotus, *Histories* 2.81.1–2 Hude)

T10 (DK 58C3; KRS 275) In *On the Pythagoreans* Aristotle explains the Pythagorean injunction *to abstain from beans* as being due either to the fact that they resemble the genitals in shape, or because they resemble the gates of Hades (since it is the only plant which has no joints), or because they ruin the constitution, or because they resemble the nature of the universe, or because they are oligarchic, in the sense that they are used in the election of magistrates by lot.* And the injunction *not to pick up things that have fallen* he explains as being an attempt to accustom them not to eat in immoderate quantities, or due to the fact that it signals someone's death . . . The injunction *not to touch a white cock* is due to the fact that the creature is sacred to the New Month and is a suppliant . . . The injunction *not to touch any sacred fish* is due to the fact that the same food should not be served to gods and men, just as free men and slaves should have different food too. The injunction *not to break a loaf* is due to the fact that in olden days friends used to meet over a single loaf.   (Aristotle [fr. 195 Rose] in Diogenes Laertius, *Lives of Eminent Philosophers* 8.34.1–35.2 Long)

T11 (DK 58C6; KRS 276) There was another kind of token, such as *do not step over a balance* (i.e. do not desire more than your share), and *do not poke a fire with a sword* (i.e. avoid irritating with sharp words anyone who is seething with anger), and *do not pluck leaves from a garland* (i.e. do not maltreat the laws, which are the garlands of communities). Then again there were other similar tokens, such as *do not eat heart* (i.e. do not upset yourself with regrets), and *do not sit on a bushel* (i.e. do not live an idle life), and *do not turn back from a journey* (i.e. do not cling to this life when you are dying), and *do not walk on the highways* (a recommendation not to follow the opinions of the many, but the views of those few people who are educated), and *do not let swallows in your house* (i.e. do not take in as lodgers chatterboxes with no control over their tongues) . . .   (Aristotle [fr. 197 Rose] in Porphyry, *Life of Pythagoras* 42.1–15 Nauck)

T12 (DK 14A7; KRS 273) He was once seen in Croton and Metapontum at the same time of the same day.   (Aristotle [fr. 191 Rose] in Apollonius, *Enquiry into Miracles* 6.2e Giannini)

T13 (DK 58D2; KRS 456) The aim of all the Pythagorean precision about what should and should not be done is association with the divine. This is their starting-point, and their way of life has been wholly organized with a view to following God. The thinking behind their philosophy is that people behave in an absurd fashion if they try to find any source for the good other than the gods . . . Since there is a god, since he has supreme authority, since it goes without saying that one should ask for the good from whoever has authority [*rather than from a subordinate*], and since everyone gives good things to those whom they love and who please them, and the opposite to those who do the opposite of pleasing them, it obviously follows that we should act in ways which please God.   (Iamblichus, *Pythagorean Life* 137 Deubner)

T14 (DK 14A8a; KRS 285) But no one can tell for certain what

Pythagoras used to say to his companions, because of the extraordinary silence they practised. However, certain of his teachings became particularly well known throughout the world: first, his claim that the soul is immortal; second, that it changes into other species of living things; third, that past events happen again in specific cycles, and that nothing is simply new; and fourth, that we should regard all ensouled creatures as akin.   (Porphyry, *Life of Pythagoras* 19.6–13 Nauck)

T15 (KRS 434) Anticleides says that Pythagoras was particularly interested in the arithmetical aspect of geometry, and discovered the properties of the monochord. Nor did he neglect medicine either. Apollodorus the mathematician says that Pythagoras sacrificed a hecatomb when he discovered that the square on the hypotenuse of the right-angled triangle is equal to the squares on the sides which encompass the right angle.   (Anticleides [fr. 1 Jacoby] in Diogenes Laertius, *Lives of Eminent Philosophers* 8.11.10–12.5 Long)

T16 In his *Introduction to Music* Heraclides says that, according to Xenocrates, it was Pythagoras who discovered that the musical intervals also come about inevitably because of number, in the sense that they consist in a comparison of one quantity with another, and that he also looked into the question of what makes the intervals concordant or discordant, and in general what factors are responsible for harmony and disharmony   (Xenocrates [fr. 9 Heinze] in Porphyry, *Commentary on Ptolemy's 'Harmonics'* 30.1–6 Düring]

T17 (KRS 271) At any rate, in his ninth book Timaeus says, 'When the younger men came to him and expressed their desire to associate with him, he did not immediately accede to their request, but said that their property would also have to be held in common with other members.'   (Timaeus [fr. 13a Jacoby] in a scholiast on Plato, *Phaedrus* 279c, Greene p. 88)

T18 (DK 14A4) Pythagoras of Samos visited Egypt and studied with the Egyptians. He was the first to import philosophy in general into Greece, and he was especially concerned, more conspicuously than anyone else, with sacrifice and ritual purification in sanctuaries, since he thought that even if, as a result of these practices, no advantage accrued to him from the gods, they would at least gain him a particularly fine reputation among men. And this is exactly what happened.

He became so much more famous than anyone else that all the young men wanted to become his disciples, while the older men preferred to see their sons associating with him than looking after their own affairs. And it is impossible to mistrust their opinion, because even now those who claim to be his followers are more impressive in their silence than those with the greatest reputation for eloquence. (Isocrates, *Busiris* 28.5–29.9 van Hook)

T19 (DK 14A16; KRS 267) Cylon of Croton was one of the leading men of his community, thanks to his birth, reputation, and wealth, but in other respects he was a cruel, brutal, disruptive, and tyrannical man. He expressed a heart-felt desire to join in the Pythagorean way of life and met with Pythagoras himself, who was then an old man, but was rejected because of the character flaws I have already mentioned. As a result of this he and his friends declared unrelenting war on Pythagoras and his companions . . . Nevertheless, for a while the true goodness of the Pythagoreans prevailed, along with the desire of the communities themselves to have their political affairs administered by them. But eventually the Cylonians' intrigues against the men reached such a pitch that when the Pythagoreans convened in Milo's house in Croton to discuss political business, the Cylonians set fire to the house and burnt to death all the men inside, except for the two youngest and strongest, Archippus and Lysis, who managed to break out. But the Italian communities ignored what had happened, and so the Pythagoreans abandoned their involvement in politics . . . The remaining Pythagoreans gathered in Rhegium and continued to associate with one another there, but as time went on and the political situation deteriorated they left Italy, with the exception of Archytas of Tarentum. (Aristoxenus [fr. 11 Müller] in Iamblichus, *Pythagorean Life* 248.8–251.3 Deubner)

T20 (DK 14A10; KRS 252) So there is no evidence of Homer's having been a public benefactor, but what about in private? Is there any evidence that, during his lifetime, he was a mentor to people, and that they used to value him for his teaching and then handed down to their successors a particular Homeric way of life? This is what happened to Pythagoras: he wasn't only held in extremely high regard for his teaching during his lifetime, but his successors even now call their way of life Pythagorean and somehow seem to stand out from all other people. (Plato, *Republic* 600a9–b5 Burnet)

T21 (DK 47B1; KRS 253) The eyes are made for astronomy, and by the same token the ears are presumably made for the type of movement that constitutes music. If so, these branches of knowledge are allied to each other. This is what the Pythagoreans claim, and we should agree, Glaucon, don't you think? Music is a difficult subject, so we'll consult the Pythagoreans to find out their views . . . [*Socrates and Glaucon go on to criticize the kind of musicologists who 'laboriously measure the interrelations between audible concords and sounds'*] But I wasn't thinking of those people, but the ones we were saying just now would explain music to us, because they act in the same way that astronomers do. They limit their research to the numbers they can find within audible concords, but they fail to come up with general matters for elucidation, such as which numbers form concords together and which don't, and why some do and some don't. (Plato, *Republic* 530d6–e2, 531b7–c4 Burnet)

T22 (DK 58C4; KRS 277) The philosophy of the acousmatics consists in unproved and unjustified *akousmata*, to the effect that one should act in such-and-such a way, and they try to preserve everything else which is said to stem from Pythagoras as divine dogma. They claim that they say nothing of their own accord and that it would be not be right for them to do so, and even go so far as to account those of their number the most advanced in terms of wisdom who have grasped the most *akousmata*. There are three categories of these so-called *akousmata*: some of them indicate what a thing is, some of them indicate superlatives, and some of them indicate what one should or should not do. For example, among those that indicate what a thing is are: *What are the Isles of the Blessed? The sun and moon.** Or again: *What is the Delphic oracle? The tetraktys, which is the harmony in which the Sirens sing.* Examples of those that indicate superlatives are: *What is most moral? To sacrifice.* Or: *What is wisest? Number.* (Iamblichus, *Pythagorean Life* 82.1–15 Deubner)

T23 (KRS 279) In order to indicate this [*the importance of number in things*] the Pythagoreans are accustomed on occasion to say that 'There is a resemblance to number in all things', and also on occasion to swear their most characteristic oath: 'No, by him who handed down to our company the *tetraktys*, the fount which holds the roots of ever-flowing nature.' By 'him who handed down' they mean Pythagoras, whom they regarded as divine, and by the '*tetraktys*' they mean a certain number which, being composed out of the first four numbers, produces the most perfect number—that is, ten (for $1 + 2 + 3 + 4 = 10$). This number is the first *tetraktys* and it is called 'the fount of ever-flowing nature' because it is their view that the whole universe is organized on harmonic principles, and harmony is a system of three concords (the fourth, the fifth, and the octave), and the ratios of these three concords are found in the four numbers I have already mentioned—that is, in 1, 2, 3, and 4. For the fourth is constituted by $4:3$, the fifth by $3:2$, and the octave by $2:1$.   (Sextus Empiricus, *Against the Professors* 7.94–6 Bury)

T24 (DK 18A12) A certain Hippasus prepared four bronze discs in such a way that, although their diameters were equal, the thickness of the first was in the ratio $4:3$ to that of the second, in the ratio $3:2$ of that to the third, and in the ratio $2:1$ to that of the fourth. When struck, they produced a concord.   (Aristoxenus [fr. 77 Müller] in a scholiast on Plato, *Phaedo* 108d, Greene p. 15)

T25 (DK 58B4, B5; KRS 430) At the same time [*as Leucippus and Democritus*] and earlier than them were the so-called Pythagoreans, who were interested in mathematics. They were the first to make mathematics prominent, and because this discipline constituted their education they thought that its principles were the principles of all things. Now, in the nature of things, numbers are the primary mathematical principles; they also imagined that they could perceive in numbers many analogues to things that are and that come into being (more analogues than fire and earth and water reveal)—such-and-such an attribute of numbers being justice, such-and-such an attribute being soul and mind, due season another, and so on for pretty well everything else; moreover, they saw that the attributes and ratios of harmonies depend on numbers. Since, then, the whole natural world seemed basically to be an analogue of numbers, and numbers seemed to be the primary facet of the natural world, they concluded that the elements of numbers are the elements of all things, and that the whole universe is harmony and number. They collected together all the properties of numbers and harmonies which were arguably conformable to the attributes and parts of the universe, and to its organization as a whole, and fitted them into place; and the existence of any gaps only made them long for the whole thing to form a connected system. Here is an example of what

I mean: ten was, to their way of thinking, a perfect number, and one which encompassed the nature of numbers in general, and they said that there were ten bodies moving through the heavens; but since there are only nine visible heavenly bodies, they came up with a tenth, the counter-earth . . .

They hold that the elements of number are the even and the odd, of which the even is unlimited and the odd limited; one is formed from both even and odd, since it is both even and odd; number is formed from one and, as I have said, numbers constitute the whole universe. Other members of the same school say that there are ten principles, which they arrange in co-ordinate pairs: limit and unlimited; odd and even; unity and multiplicity; right and left; male and female; still and moving; straight and bent; light and darkness; good and bad; square and oblong. (Aristotle, *Metaphysics* 985^{b}23–986^{a}26 Ross)

T26 (DK 58A8) The Pythagoreans spoke of two causes in the same way, but added, as an idiosyncratic feature, that the limited and the unlimited and the one were not separate natures, on a par with fire or earth or something, but the unlimited itself and the one itself were taken to be the substance of the things of which they are predicated. This is why they said that number was the substance of everything. (Aristotle, *Metaphysics* 987^{a}13–19 Ross)

T27 The Pythagoreans, as a result of observing that many properties of numbers exist in perceptible bodies, came up with the idea that existing things *are* numbers, but not separate numbers: they said that existing things consist of numbers. Why? Because the properties of numbers exist in musical harmony, in the heavens, and in many other cases. (Aristotle, *Metaphysics* 1090^{a}20–5 Ross)

T28 (DK 58B9; KRS 431) The Pythagoreans recognize only one kind of number, mathematical number, but they say that it is not separate, but that perceptible things are made up of it. For they construct the whole universe out of numbers—and not numbers made up of abstract units, but they take their numerical units to have spatial magnitude. But they apparently have no way to explain how the first spatially extended unit was put together. (Aristotle, *Metaphysics* 1080^{b}16–21 Ross)

T29 Aristotle has shown the kinds of analogues the Pythagoreans said existed between numbers and the things that are and that come into being. On the assumption that reciprocity or equality is a property of justice, and finding that equality is also a property of numbers, they said that justice is the first square number, on the grounds that the first of a series of things with the same definition is, in each case, most truly what it is said to be. Some said that the number of justice was 4, because, being the first square number, it is divided into equal parts and is itself equal (since it is 2 × 2), but others said that it was 9, since it is the first square number produced by multiplying an odd number—3—by itself. Again, they said that 7 was due season, since natural things seem to have their perfect seasons of birth and completion in terms of sevens . . . Since the sun is responsible for the seasons, they thought, according to Aristotle, that it was located in the place of the seventh number, which they call 'due season'; for the sun, they said, occupied the seventh rank among the ten bodies which move around the centre and the hearth. First come the sphere of the fixed stars and the five spheres of the planets, and then the sun; after the sun, the moon occupies the eighth place, the earth the ninth, and then the counter-earth.* Since 7 neither generates any other number within the decad nor is generated by any of them, they called it 'Athena' . . . Marriage, they said, was 5, because it is the union of male and female and they thought that the odd was male and the even female; and 5 is the first number formed from the first even number, 2, and the first odd number, 3; for, as I said, they thought that the odd was male and the even female. Reason (which was what they called soul) and substance they identified with 1. Because it is unchanging, everywhere alike, and a ruling principle, they called reason a monad, or 1; but they also applied these names to substance, because it is primary. Opinion they identified with 2 because it can move in two directions; they also called it movement and addition. Picking out such analogues between things and numbers, they assumed numbers to be the first principles of things, and said that all things are made up of numbers.   (Aristotle [fr. 203 Rose] in Alexander of Aphrodisias, *Commentary on Aristotle's 'Metaphysics'*, CAG I, 38.8–39.19 Hayduck)

T30[†] In the first place, we must set out in a row the sequence of numbers from the monad up to nine: 1, 2, 3, 4, 5, 6, 7, 8, 9. Then we must add up the amount of all of them together, and since the row contains nine terms, we must look for the ninth part of the total, to see if it is already naturally present among the numbers in the row; and we will find that the property of being the ninth belongs only to the mean itself. So the pentad is another thing which has neither excess nor defectiveness in it, and it will turn out to provide this property for the rest of the numbers, so that it is a kind of justice, on the analogy of a weighing instrument. For if we suppose that the row of numbers is some such weighing instrument, and the mean number 5 is the hole of the balance, then all the parts towards the ennead, starting with the hexad, will sink down because of their quantity, and those towards the monad, starting with the tetrad, will rise up because of their fewness, and the ones which have the advantage will altogether be triple the total of the ones over which they have the advantage, but 5 itself, as the hole in the beam, partakes of neither advantage nor disadvantage, but it alone has equality and sameness.

The parts adjacent to it gradually decrease in advantage or disadvantage the closer they get to it, just like the parts which move away little by little from the scales on the beam towards the balance. The ennead and the monad are at the furthest distance, whence the ennead has the greatest advantage, the monad the greatest disadvantage, each by a full tetrad. A little further in from these are the ogdoad and the dyad, whence the ogdoad has a little less excess, the dyad a little less defectiveness; in each case the excess or defectiveness is a triad. Then, next to these, are the hebdomad and the triad, whence the triad is defective and the hebdomad excessive by the next amount—they are a dyad away from the centre. Further in from these and next to the pentad, as it were to the balance, are the tetrad and the hexad, which has the least excess, for no smaller number than this can be thought of.

When the beam is suspended, the parts with excess make excessive both the angle at the scales and the angle at the balance, while the parts with defectiveness make the angle defective in both cases, and the obtuse angle is the excessive one, since a right angle has the principle of maximum equality.

Since in a case of injustice those who are wronged and those who do wrong are equivalent, just as in a case of inequality the greater and the lesser parts are equivalent, but nevertheless those who do wrong are more unjust than those who suffer wrong (for the one group requires punishment, the other compensation and help), therefore the parts which are at a distance on the side of the obtuse angle, where the weighing instrument is concerned and in the terms of our mathematical illustration (i.e. the parts with advantage), are progressively further away from the mean, which is justice; but the parts on the side of the acute angle will increasingly approach and come near, and as it were through continually suffering wrong in being at a disadvantage, while the others will travel downwards and into corruption and immersion in evil, they will rise up and take refuge in God through their need for retribution and compensation.

At any rate, if it is necessary, taking the beam as a whole, for equality to be in this mathematical illustration, then again such a thing will be contrived thanks to the pentad's participation as it were in a kind of justice. For one possibility is that if all the parts which are arranged at a fifth remove from the excessive parts are subtracted from them and added to the disadvantaged parts, then what is being sought will be the result.* Alternatively, thanks to the pentad's being a point of distinction and reciprocal separation, if the disadvantaged one which is closest to the balance on that side is subtracted from the one which is furthest from the balance on the excessive side and added to the one which is furthest from the balance on the other side (i.e. 1)—if, to effect equalization, 4 is subtracted from 9 and added to 1; and from 8, 3 is subtracted, which will be the addition to 2; and from 7, 2 is subtracted, and added to 3; and from 6, 1 is subtracted, which is the addition to 4 to effect equalization, then all of them equally, both the ones which have been punished, as excessive, and the ones which have been set right, as wronged, will be assimilated to the mean of justice. For all of them will be 5 each, and 5 alone remains unsubtracted and unadded, so that it is neither more nor less, but it alone encompasses by nature what is fitting and appropriate. (Ps.-Iamblichus, *The Theology of Arithmetic* 37.4– 39.24 de Falco)

T31 (DK 18A15) In the old days, in the time of Pythagoras and the mathematicians of his ilk, there were only three means, the arithmetic, the geometric, and the third in the list, the one which used to be called the subcontrary mean, but which was renamed the harmonic by the circle of Archytas and Hippasus, because it seemed to encompass the ratios relevant to what is harmonized and tuneful. (Iamblichus, *Commentary on Nicomachus' 'Introduction to Arithmetic'* 100.19–25 Pistelli)

T32 (DK 58B21; KRS 436) Eudemus the Peripatetic attributes to the Pythagoreans the discovery of the theorem that the internal angles of every triangle are equal to two right angles. He says that they proved the theorem in question as follows.

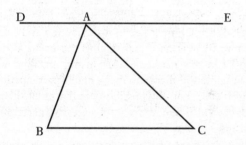

Let ABC be a triangle, and through A let the line DE be drawn parallel to BC. Since BC and DE are parallel, and the alternate angles are equal, then the angle DAB is equal to the angle ABC, and EAC is equal to ACB. Let BAC be added to both. Then the angles DAB, BAC, and CAE, that is, the angles DAB and BAE, that is, two right angles, are equal to the three angles of the triangle. Therefore the three angles of the triangle are equal to two right angles. (Eudemus [fr. 88 Spengel] in Proclus, *Commentary on Euclid* 379.2–16 Friedlein)

T33 (DK 58B20; KRS 435) These things are ancient, according to Eudemus, and are discoveries of the Muse of the Pythagoreans—I mean, the application of areas, and their exceeding and falling short.* (Eudemus [fr. 89 Spengel] in Proclus, *Commentary on Euclid* 419.15–17 Friedlein)

T34 (DK 58B1) Pythagoras ... discovered the construction of the cosmic figures.* (Proclus, *Commentary on Euclid* 65.19 Friedlein)

T35 The Pythagoreans proposed the following elegant theorem about diameter and side numbers. When to a diameter there is added the side of which it is the diameter, it becomes a side, while the side, when added to itself and receiving its own diameter in addition as well, becomes a diameter. This is proved with the aid of a diagram by Euclid in the second book of the *Elements*. If a straight line is bisected and a straight line is added to it, the square on the whole line (that is, including the added line) plus the square on the added line by itself are together double the square on the half and of the square on the straight line made up of the half and the added line.*   (Proclus, *Commentary on Plato's 'Republic'* 2.27.11–22 Kroll)

T36 (DK 18A4) Concerning Hippasus, they say that he was a Pythagorean, and that because he was the first to publish and construct the sphere of twelve pentagons [*the dodecahedron*], he died at sea for this act of impiety.* They add that although he gained the reputation for this discovery, it really belongs, as does everything else, to 'the master'. This is how they refer to Pythagoras, since they never call him by name.   (Iamblichus, *Pythagorean Life* 88.13–19 Deubner)

T37 (KRS 280) Of those who practised Pythagorean philosophy, the acousmatics are admitted to be Pythagoreans by the others, but they withhold the title from the mathematicians, saying that their branch of study stems from Hippasus rather than Pythagoras . . . Those of the Pythagoreans who are concerned with mathematics, however, recognize the others as Pythagoreans, but claim that they are more deserving of the title.   (Iamblichus, *On General Mathematical Knowledge* 76.19–77.2 Festa)

T38 (DK 58B37; KRS 446) Most of those who maintain that the universe is finite say that the earth lies at the centre, but with this the Pythagoreans, as they are known, from Italy, disagree. They say that there is fire in the centre, that the earth is one of the heavenly bodies, and that it is its motion around the centre that creates night and day. Moreover, they invent another earth, opposite to ours, which they call the 'counter-earth'.   (Aristotle, *On the Heavens* 293ª18–24 Allan)

T39 Those who deny that the earth lies at the centre claim that it moves in a circle around the centre, and that it is not just the earth that does this, but also the counter-earth, as I have already mentioned. Some even think that there might be several such bodies in motion around the centre, which are invisible to us because the earth is in the way. This allows them to explain the greater frequency of lunar over solar eclipses: they say that each of these invisible bodies, and not just the earth, blocks the moon.   (Aristotle, *On the Heavens* 293ᵇ18–25 Allan)

T40 (DK 44A16; KRS 447) Philolaus says that there is fire in the middle, around the centre, and he calls it the 'hearth of the universe' and the 'house of Zeus', 'mother of the gods', 'altar, bond, and measure of nature'. Then again, he says, there is another fire surrounding the universe at the periphery. But he says that the centre is naturally primary, and that around the centre dance ten divine bodies—heaven, planets,† and then the sun, and then under the sun the moon, and then under the moon the earth, and then under the earth the counter-earth, and last in this whole sequence the hearth-fire which is located around the centre.   (Aëtius, *Opinions* 2.7.7 Diels)

T41 (DK 58B35; KRS 449) It is clear from what has been said that the notion that the movement of the heavenly bodies produces a harmony, because the sounds they make are concordant, is untrue, despite having been ingeniously and brilliantly expressed by its authors. The idea was that bodies that are large are bound to make a sound, since here on earth bodies far inferior in size and speed of movement make sounds. So given that the sun and moon and stars, in all their quantity and enormity of size, are moving at such a great speed, it is impossible, they claimed, for them not to produce an incredibly loud noise. Having made this assumption, and having also supposed that the speeds of the heavenly bodies, as judged by their distances, are in the same ratios as musical concordances, they claim that the sound produced by the circular motion of the heavenly bodies is harmonic. And they explain the apparent absurdity of our inability to hear this sound by claiming that the sound is present to us right from the moment of our birth, with the result that it is never distinguished by comparison with a contrasting silence.   (Aristotle, *On the Heavens* 290ᵇ12–27 Allan)

T42 (DK 44A19; KRS 448) Philolaus the Pythagorean says that the sun is glass-like, so that it receives the direct light of the fire in the universe and filters its light and heat to us.* This means that in a sense there are two suns, the fiery one in the heavens and the one which is dependent on it and is fiery in a mirror-like way—unless one were to say that there is also a third, which is the light that is spread from the mirror to us by reflection. For this light too we call a sun, and it is, so to speak, the image of an image.   (Aëtius, *Opinions* 2.20.12 Diels)

T43 (DK 44A20) Some of the Pythagoreans, including Philolaus, say that the moon looks like the earth because it is inhabited, just like our earth, but by creatures and plants which are taller and more beautiful; for creatures there are fifteen times as strong as those here, and never excrete anything, and their day is fifteen times longer than ours here.   (Aëtius, *Opinions* 2.30.1 Diels)

T44 (DK 58B30; KRS 443) The Pythagoreans also claim that there is such a thing as void. According to them, it enters the universe from the infinite breath because the universe breathes in void as well as breath. What void does, they say, is differentiate things; they think of void as being a kind of separation and distinction when one thing comes after another. This happens first among the numbers, because on their view it is the void that distinguishes one number from another.*   (Aristotle, *Physics* 213^{b}22–7 Ross)

T45 (DK 58B30; KRS 444) In the first book of his work on Pythagorean philosophy Aristotle writes that the universe is one, and that time and breath and the void, which differentiates the places of all individual things, are drawn into the universe from the unlimited. (Aristotle [fr. 201 Rose] in John of Stobi, *Anthology* 1.18.1c Wachsmuth/Hense)

F2 (DK 44B1; KRS 424)   Nature in the universe was harmonized out of both things which are unlimited and things which limit; this applies to the universe as a whole and to all its components. (Philolaus [fr. 1 Diels/Kranz] in Diogenes Laertius, *Lives of Eminent Philosophers* 8.85.13–14 Long)

F3 (DK 44B2; KRS 425) All the things that exist must be either limiting or unlimited, or both limiting and unlimited. But they cannot be only unlimited. So since they evidently arise neither from things that are all limiters nor from things that are all unlimited, it clearly follows that the universe and its components were harmonized out of both things which limit and things which are unlimited. And the facts of things also make this clear, since some things arise from limiters and are limiters, while others arise from both limiters and unlimiteds and both limit and fail to impose limit, and others arise from unlimiteds and are plainly unlimited.* (Philolaus [fr. 2 Diels/Kranz] in John of Stobi, *Anthology* 1.21.7a Wachsmuth/ Hense)

F4 (DK 44B4; KRS 427) And everything which is known has number, because otherwise it is impossible for anything to be the object of thought or knowledge. (Philolaus [fr. 4 Diels/Kranz] in John of Stobi, *Anthology* 1.21.7b Wachsmuth/Hense)

F5 (DK 44B6; KRS 429) On the subject of nature and harmony, this is how things stand: the being of things, *qua* eternal, and nature itself are accessible only to divine and not human knowledge— except that it is impossible for any of the things that exist and are known by us to have arisen without the prior existence of the being of the things out of which the universe is composed, namely limiters and unlimiteds. Now, since these sources existed in all their dis-similarity and incompatibility, it would have been impossible for them to have been made into an orderly universe unless harmony had been present in some form or other. Things that were similar and compatible had no need of harmony, but things that were dis-similar and incompatible and incommensurate had to be connected by this kind of harmony, if they are to persist in an ordered uni-verse. (Philolaus [fr. 6 Diels/Kranz] in John of Stobi, *Anthology* 1.21.7d Wachsmuth/Hense)

F6 (DK 44B7; KRS 441) The first thing to be harmonized, the one, in the centre of the sphere, is called the hearth. (Philolaus [fr. 7 Diels/Kranz] in John of Stobi, *Anthology* 1.21.8 Wachsmuth/Hense)

F7 (DK 44B17) The universe is single. It originally arose from the centre, and from the centre upwards and downwards in the same way. For what is above the centre is the opposite in disposition to what is below, in the sense that to lower things the lowest part is like the highest part,† and the same goes for the upper things too. For the relation to the centre is the same in either case, except that their positions are reversed.* (Philolaus [fr. 17 Diels/Kranz] in John of Stobi, *Anthology* 1.15.7 Wachsmuth/Hense)

T46 (DK 44A12) Philolaus says that after mathematical magnitude has become three-dimensional thanks to the tetrad [*i.e. has progressed to solidity from the primary point (1), line (2), and plane figure (triangle, 3)*], there is the quality and 'colour' of visible nature in the pentad, and ensoulment in the hexad, and intelligence and health and what he calls 'light' in the hebdomad, and then next, with the ogdoad, things come by love and friendship and wisdom and creative thought.   (Ps.-Iamblichus, *The Theology of Arithmetic* 74.10–15 de Falco)

T47 (DK 58B40; KRS 450) The doctrine handed down by the Pythagoreans seems to have the same purport [*that respiration is the prerequisite for life*], since some of them identified the soul with the motes in the air, while others said that the soul was what caused these motes to move. The reason for the importance of these motes in their theory is that they are apparently in continuous motion, even when there is not the slightest breath of wind.   (Aristotle, *On the Soul* 404^{a}16–20 Ross)

T48 (DK 44A23; KRS 451) There is another theory about the soul that has come down to us, which many people find the most plausible one around . . . They say that the soul is a kind of attunement (*harmonia*), on the grounds that attunement is a mixture and compound of opposites, and the body is made up of opposites. (Aristotle, *On the Soul* 407^{b}27–32 Ross)

T49 (DK 44A27; KRS 445)   Philolaus of Croton says that our bodies are composed of heat and have no share in cold. The evidence he adduces for this is as follows. Semen is warm, and it is semen that is constitutive of a living creature; and the place where semen is deposited—that is, the womb—is warmer. The womb resembles semen, and anything that is like anything else has the same property as that which it resembles. Since the constitutive agent has no share in cold and the place where it is deposited has no share in cold, it obviously follows that the living creature which is constituted will be of the same kind. With regard to its constitution he refers to the following facts. Immediately after birth a living creature inhales the external air, which is cold, and then expels it again, as if it were discharging a debt. Also, the reason why it has an instinctive appetite for the external air is to enable our bodies, which are too hot, by drawing in the air from outside, to be cooled by it. This is the way in which he describes the composition of our bodies.

As for diseases, he says that they arise as a result of bile, blood and phlegm, which are the sources of diseases. He says that blood is thickened when the flesh is compressed internally, and thinned when the vessels in the flesh are dilated. He says that phlegm is composed of the waters of the body. He says that bile is a discharge from flesh . . . While most people claim that phlegm is cold, he supposes that it is hot by nature, and derives the word 'phlegm' from *phlegein*, to burn. So, he says, it is because they have a share in phlegm that inflammatory agents cause inflammation. These are the sources of diseases, according to him. Secondary causes, he says, are either excess or lack of warmth, food, cold, and so on. (Meno in *Anonymus Londinensis*, 18.20–19.21 Jones)

F8 (DK 44B13) There are four sources of a rational creature (as Philolaus also says in *On Nature*)—brain, heart, navel, and genitals: 'Head for thought, heart for soul and for feeling, navel for the embryo to take root and to grow, genitals for the emission of seed and for birth. The brain provides the source for man, the heart for animals, the navel for plants, the genitals for them all; for they all both sprout and grow from seed.' (Philolaus [fr. 13 Diels/Kranz] in Ps.-Iamblichus, *The Theology of Arithmetic* 25.17–26.3 de Falco)

T50 (DK 16A1) He [*a non-Greek sage met by Cleombrotus, one of the participants in this dialogue of Plutarch*] said that the number of worlds is not infinite, nor one, nor five, but 183, arranged in a triangle of which each side has sixty worlds. Each of the three remaining worlds is situated at an angle. The worlds that are next to one another are contiguous and revolve gently, as in a dance. The interior of the triangle is the common hearth of all the worlds, and is called the plain of truth, in which lie unchanging the essences, forms, and patterns of things past and future. Around them time is communicated to the worlds like an effluence from eternity. Human souls may see and contemplate these things once in 10,000 years, provided they have lived well. The best mystery rites on earth are only a shadow of that initiation and rite. If our philosophical discussions are not conducted with a view to recollecting the beauties there, they are in vain . . . But he is convicted by the number of his worlds, which is not Egyptian or Indian, but Dorian, from Sicily, the idea of a man from Himera called Petron. Now, I have not read his work and I do not know if it has been preserved, but Hippys of Rhegium, according to

Phanias of Eresus, reports that this was the opinion and teaching of Petron, that there are 183 worlds in contact with one another according to element. But what 'contact according to element' means he does not make clear, nor does he add any proof.   (Plutarch, *On the Decline of Oracles* 422b3–e6 Babbit)

T51 (DK 45A3; KRS 433) Nothing at all clear has been said about how numbers are the causes of substantial things and of being. Is it that they are limits, as points are the limits of magnitudes? This is how Eurytus used to arrange things, to see what was the number of what—that such-and-such is the number of a human being, and such-and-such the number of a horse. In the way that people adduce numbers to explain the shapes of a triangle or a square, he used to make likenesses of the forms of creatures and plants with his pebbles.   (Aristotle, *Metaphysics* 1092^{b}8–13 Ross)

T52 (DK 45A3) Suppose, for the sake of argument, that 250 is the definition of a human being and 360 of a plant. On this assumption he used to take 250 pebbles (green, black, red, and all sorts of colours), smear the wall with plaster, draw an outline of a man (or a plant), and then fix some of the pebbles on the outline of the face, others on the hands, others elsewhere, and he would fill in the outline of the whole imitation human being with pebbles equal in number to the units which he said defined a human being.   (Ps.-Alexander, *Commentary on Aristotle's 'Metaphysics'*, CAG I, 827.9–17 Hayduck)

K. J. Boudouris (ed.), *Pythagorean Philosophy* (Athens: International Center for Greek Philosophy and Culture, 1992).

R. S. Brumbaugh and J. Schwartz, 'Pythagoras and Beans: A Medical Explanation', *Classical World*, 73 (1980), 421–3.

W. Burkert, *Lore and Science in Ancient Pythagoreanism* (Cambridge, Mass.: Harvard University Press, 1972).

A. Burns, 'The Fragments of Philolaus and Aristotle's Account of Pythagorean Theories in *Metaphysics* A', *Classica et Mediaevalia*, 25 (1964), 93–128.

I. Bywater, 'On the Fragments Attributed to Philolaus the Pythagorean', *Journal of Philology*, 1 (1868), 21–53.

F. M. Cornford, 'Mysticism and Science in the Pythagorean Tradition', in [30], 135–60 (first pub. *Classical Quarterly*, 16 (1922) and 17 (1923)).

K. von Fritz, *Pythagorean Politics in Southern Italy: An Analysis of the Sources* (New York: Columbia University Press, 1940).

—— 'The Discovery of Incommensurability by Hippasus of Metapontum', in [26], i. 382–412 (first pub. *Annals of Mathematics*, 46 (1945)).

K. S. Guthrie, *The Pythagorean Sourcebook and Library* (1920; Grand Rapids, Mich.: Phanes Press, 1987).

T. Heath, *A History of Greek Mathematics*, vol. i: *From Thales to Euclid* (Oxford: Oxford University Press, 1921).

W. A. Heidel, 'The Pythagoreans and Greek Mathematics', in [26], i. 350–81 (first pub. *American Journal of Philology*, 61 (1940)).

C. Huffman, *Philolaus of Croton: Pythagorean and Presocratic* (Cambridge: Cambridge University Press, 1993).

C. H. Kahn, 'Pythagorean Philosophy Before Plato', in [30], 161–85.

I. L. Minar, *Early Pythagorean Politics in Practice and Theory* (Baltimore: Waverly, 1942).

J. S. Morrison, 'Pythagoras of Samos', *Classical Quarterly*, 6 (1956), 133–56.

M. Nussbaum, 'Eleatic Conventionalism and Philolaus on the Conditions of Thought', *Harvard Studies in Classical Philology* 83, (1979), 63–108.

E. N. Ostenfeld, 'Early Pythagorean Principles: Peras and Apeiron', in [24], 304–11.

J. A. Philip, *Pythagoras and Early Pythagoreanism* (Toronto: University of Toronto Press, 1966).

H. S. Schibli, 'On "the One" in Philolaus, Fragment 7', *Classical Quarterly*, 46 (1996), 114–30.

L. P. Schrenk, 'World as Structure: The Ontology of Philolaus of Croton', *Apeiron*, 27 (1994), 171–90.

I. Thomas, *Greek Mathematical Works*, vol. i: *Thales to Euclid* (Cambridge, Mass.: Harvard University Press, 1939).

C. J. de Vogel, *Pythagoras and Early Pythagoreanism* (Assen: Van Gorcum, 1966).

R. A. H. Waterfield, *The Theology of Arithmetic* (Grand Rapids, Mich.: Phanes Press, 1988).

L. J. A. Zhmud', ' "All is Number?" ', *Phronesis*, 34 (1989), 270–92.

ANAXAGORAS OF CLAZOMENAE

As a prominent figure in intellectual circles in Athens in the middle of the fifth century, and a close friend of the great statesman Pericles, Anaxagoras attracted a great deal of rumour and suspicion. He became something of an archetypal wise man (calm in the face of the death of his son), and also an atheistic scientist figure (calm in the face of a solar eclipse)—and indeed there is some truth to this picture, since mechanical causes play a great part in his system, and he seems less inclined than some of his predecessors to describe even his cosmogonic mind as 'god'. He may even have been put on trial for impiety, though, if so, the trial is likely to have been motivated by the political desire to hurt one of Pericles' friends.

Anaxagoras' book, written in ponderous and almost incantatory prose, followed a straightforward cosmogonical course, from the original state of affairs to the finished world. In **F1** he sketches his picture of the original state: all the things that would later make up the finished world were mixed together in infinitely minute quantities—so small that nothing was distinct and the whole mixture was uniform (we shall return to the problem of air and aither in this fragment below). This original mixture seems to be envisaged as occupying the infinite region beyond the reaches of the spherical universe, and from this 'vault' air and aither were separated off in the beginning, as they still are now (**F2**). The infinitude of the original mixture is stressed in both **F2** and **F3**: it is an inexhaustible source.

Next Anaxagoras immediately went on (**F4** and **F5**[1]) to state his two most startling theses—that all things, including humans, are aggregates of the stuffs that were present in the original mixture, so that all physical change is no more than the manifestation of what was previously latent; and that there is no reason not to think that more worlds than our own might have been separated out from the original mixture. Quite how he envisaged these parallel universes is not clear (and indeed the whole idea might be some kind of thought-experiment), but, however extraordinary it might seem, the most likely explanation is that Anaxagoras considered the possibility that the original mixture could generate not only large structures such as our world, but also extremely small ones. As **F7** stresses, there is equivalence between large structures and small structures, so why might there not be infinitely small universes? Also, if these infinitely small universes were contained within our familiar universe,

---

[1] The way in which Simplicius cites **F5** strongly suggests that it did not follow immediately after **F4**, but that a clause or two has been omitted in between.

this would explain the otherwise puzzling insistence in the doxographic tradition that Anaxagoras did not believe in a plurality of universes (**T1**; see also **F6**).[2] But what is important to note is that Anaxagoras imagines all possible worlds to be identical in all respects except for size; in other words, he feels that the ingredients and factors and laws he will specify in his book guarantee only one kind of world. The seeds within the original mixture are seeds that can give rise only to certain kinds of things, just as in modern physics the nature of our universe is dictated by the set of laws that govern it, while a different set of laws would create a different universe.

Anaxagoras has stressed the uniformity of the original mixture, so it is odd to find him also asserting that there were 'seeds' present in it (**F4**), and then to read in **F5** that these seeds are 'dissimilar to one another' and have shape, colour, and flavour. But some of the confusion is dispelled by attending to an important difference between **F4** and **F5**: although one of the qualities the seeds have is said to be colour, it is also stressed that the original mixture does not have colour. In other words, talk of 'seeds' occurs at two stages of Anaxagoras' cosmogony: in the finished things of the world there are seeds with determinate qualities, infinite in quantity but only 'numerous' in quality, but in the original mixture there are seeds with no qualities. If we are to preserve Anaxagoras' emphatic talk of uniformity, we need to understand the seeds of the original mixture metaphorically. Although to us a 'seed' sounds like a discrete parcel of matter, it is more likely that Anaxagoras was merely trying to express, by a biological metaphor, the idea that the original mixture contained all things in potential. Though uniform and homogeneous, it contained the potential for aggregation in different proportions—which is just another way of saying that it contained in potential all the finished things of the universe, because anything and everything is no more than an aggregate of stuffs in a different proportion (**F10**). In this sense, the seeds are the true originative substances of the worlds.

It is axiomatic for Anaxagoras that, apart from mind, which is pure, everything contains a portion of everything else (**F8–10**); hence too he insists that even opposites are not entirely separate from each other (**F5** and **F6**), and that just as there were seeds in the original mixture, so there are seeds in the finished things of this world.[3] He found it as impossible as Parmenides had to imagine that anything could come into existence from

---

[2] However, it is to be noted that Simplicius contradicts himself on this issue, attributing only the one universe to Anaxagoras at *Commentary on Aristotle's 'Physics'* 178.25, and a plurality of universes at *Commentary on Aristotle's 'Physics'* 27.17.

[3] Contrary to a number of scholars, I do not believe that the opposites have special status in Anaxagoras' thought.

something that did not already exist. Hence, in a cosmogonic context, the idea that the things of this world were preceded by seeds, and in the finished world the idea that the things of this world contain the seeds of everything else. But the seeds themselves, as well as their offspring, also consist of minute portions of everything else. Everything is present in every seed and in every item of the universe, but in different proportions. The difference in proportion explains the different qualities things have (**F10**, **T5**), while the fact that everything consists of the same ingredients explains how things can interact, and explains phenomena such as growth by nutrition and reproduction (**T2**, **T3**): our flesh can be nourished by eating bread because the bread already contains flesh in it (or the qualities that characterize flesh), and a child can come from a sperm because the sperm already contains the ingredients of the child's body.[4] A thing of finite size can contain an infinite number of ingredients, because of Anaxagoras' principle of infinite smallness (**F1**, **F7**).

But can we further specify what these basic ingredients actually were in Anaxagoras' system? Occasionally, in describing Anaxagoras' ideas, the doxographic tradition makes use of the convenient Aristotelian term 'homoeomeries'. For Aristotle, a homoeomerous substance was one which, as the name implies, is the same throughout: however far it is divided, it is the same substance. His prime examples are natural substances such as flesh and bone, wood and metal, and the four elements. There seems to be no reason not to accept this as an accurate paraphrase of Anaxagoras' ideas, with the qualification added by **T4** that Anaxagoras regarded the elements as compounds of his homoeomeries. The original mixture consisted of homoeomerous substances, fused into a uniform blend (with the 'seeds' of potential future growth), or compounded as air and aither; the finished products of this or any other world are made up of everything—all the seeds or homoeomerous substances—in different proportions.[5] The proportion of the homoeomerous substances that make up flesh, say, remains constant throughout any bit of flesh. Of course, there are more than just homoeomeries in this world, but they can be broken down into homoeomeries; human beings are not homoeomerous in themselves, but their parts (flesh, bone, hair, etc.) are. Gold is homoe-

---

[4] Then why aren't we nourished by eating stones? Because stones do not have enough flesh etc. in them (see the last words of **F10** for the notion that things contain all other things, but in different proportions).

[5] Of course, this entails a regress: if we call gold 'gold' because its predominant ingredient is gold (though it has all the other homoeomeries in it too), we also call that predominant ingredient 'gold' because its predominant ingredient is gold . . . and so on *ad infinitum*. I do not think this would have worried Anaxagoras; it is enough that he has given an explanation of things at the macroscopic level. But Strang (see bibliography below) comes up with an ingenious way of stopping the regress.

omerous, but an alloy is not; clay is, not cement; wheat, but not bread. But how can Anaxagoras simultaneously hold that some things are homoe-omerous, and that 'in everything there is a portion of everything'? Are these two ideas not contradictory, in the sense that a homoeomerous sub-stance should consist only of parts that are identical in nature to the whole? No, they are not: even if, however far I divide a homoeomerous substance such as gold, I still get gold, that does not mean that what we call 'gold' does not contain minute portions of everything else, every other basic ingredient.

F7 and F8 closely connect the notion that everything contains a portion of everything with the idea of infinite smallness, and with the idea that the large and the small are numerically equal 'since each thing is both large and small in relation to itself'. F8 goes so far as to say, 'Since there are numerically equal portions of the great and the small, it follows that everything is in everything.' How does this follow? Perhaps Anaxagoras means that however many large (i.e. manifest) things there are, there are just as many small (i.e. unmanifest) things still latent in the mixture, and that this not only applies as a generalization relevant to the sum totality of all things, but is also true of any particular stuff. If there was not as much stuff latent in the mixture as there was manifest in the world, and if this was not true at any given time, then stuffs would begin to fail. From this it follows that everything is in everything.

Moreover, if it were not the case that in everything there was a portion of everything, we would be able to divide something down to its final component, which would be a particle of just one type of stuff, not a blend of all stuffs. This may be seen as an Anaxagorean response to Empedocles and Parmenides (except that it is not clear that his philosophical activity post-dated that of Empedocles): if a piece of copper, say, were not infin-itely divisible, then it would be destroyed once it was divided down to its ultimate elements; but Parmenides had outlawed such destruction. Here, then, Anaxagoras sets his face against the idea of infinite divisibility, because it implies a particulate theory of matter, whereas on his theory there are no such particles.

The idea that there is no limit to smallness is also Anaxagoras' solution to another potential difficulty, one generated from within his own system. He has posited an infinite number of stuffs, but it is also axiomatic for him that in everything there is a portion of everything. Everything contains infinite stuffs, then—but how is that possible without things being infin-itely large? If every stuff in the mixture has finite size, then the object in question would be infinitely large. Anaxagoras' solution is to deny that every stuff in the mixture has to have finite size. In fact this again dis-proves the idea (although it is a common interpretation of Anaxagorean physics) that when Anaxagoras says that everything is in everything, he means to imply a particulate theory of matter. If there were infinite particles in anything, it would be infinitely large. When Anaxagoras says that everything is in everything, he means to imply a smooth blend; 'portions' are not 'pieces'. Everything is blended smoothly, but different things have different proportions of the homoeomeries in them.

Mind has a unique role in Anaxagoras' thought. Not only is it the only thing that is pure, without a portion of every other basic stuff, but it is the only thing that is not necessarily present in everything to some degree (F9, F10). Thus it is present in humans and horses and herbs, but not in stones and rivers. Moreover, it has a unique cosmogonic role to play, since it started the initial rotation which began to separate things out of the primordial mixture, which was originally at rest (F10).[6] As a consequence of the heavy baggage mind carries in Anaxagoras' philosophy, there is considerable ambiguity within the fragments between whether at any point he is talking about Mind with a capital M, almost equivalent to God, or mind—your mind and my mind. Obviously a mind may be regarded as a splinter of the Mind, but it is not clear whether a mind has all the attributes—e.g. omniscience—of Mind, or just the principle of movement.

The rotation (which is super-fast, F11) began in a small area and is still spreading outwards. It is probably to be thought of as a vortex, since it separates denser material from lighter material (F12). Although mind comes in for a great deal of praise for its work (F10), and is said to pervade everything (F13), it is not clear that it plays a part in the finished universe except in animate creatures. In a vortex, heavier material tends towards the centre, and at the same time Anaxagoras seems to have invoked another physical law—the attraction of like to like (T7). The action of these two laws sets up broad features of the universe as we know it (F16).

T5 and T6 are useful Aristotelian paraphrases of important features of Anaxagoras' system, with good guesses as to his underlying thinking. In T4 Aristotle seems to suggest that air and aither, specified in F1 as somehow distinguishable within the original mixture, play an important cosmogonic role (see now F2 in this light). In fact, he implies that air and aither are the first principles of everything else, and so that the cosmogonic process goes, by stages, from the original mixture to the separation out of air and aither to the generation of the world as we know it. Assuming that Aristotle is correct in identifying Anaxagoras' aither with fire,

---

[6] The idea that a vortex or rotation is the principal cosmogonic motion is an important innovation (which some attribute to Empedocles on the basis of the ambiguous F21 on p. 149). Earlier cosmogonies had of course paid attention to the apparent rotatory motion of the universe, but had not suggested that the universe was a *result* of such motion.

then in air and aither we have oppositely qualified substances: moist, dark, cloudy air, and light, bright, fiery aither. It cannot be a coincidence that these are precisely the sets of opposites that Anaxagoras specifies in **F12** as vital within the cosmogonic process. It seems most likely, then, that 'air' and 'aither' are collective names for, respectively, seeds which are cold and moist, and seeds which are light, dry, and fiery (just as, in general, the only role the opposites seem to play in Anaxagoras' thought is to specify the characteristics of seeds). In the original mixture, air and aither are not actually distinct, though since they represent the most primitive forms of matter, you could say that the original mixture contains limitless air and aither (**F1**), just as you can say that it contains seeds. Then in the early stages of the cosmogonic process these two masses were separated out, and then the action of the vortex and the attraction of like to like continued the creation of the world. The 'air' seeds are condensed into the things of this world (**F16**), while the 'aither' seeds form the outer heavens and the heavenly bodies. However, since 'in everything there is a portion of everything', there will be some aither inside the earth; although normally this has free passage to its natural upper region, under certain circumstances it can become trapped and cause earthquakes (**T8**). Because it is always the case that in everything there is a portion of everything, this and other natural processes will never fail. It is clear from **F17** and **F18**, as well as **T9–11**, that Anaxagoras also found explanations for other familiar meteorological and astronomical phenomena. **T12–15** remind us that he spread his scientific net wide, not only into botany and embryology, but also comparative anatomy and other areas; he even entered the fifth-century debate on why the Nile floods in summer (due to the melting of snow in the mountains of Ethiopia, he not unreasonably held). And, given his construction of the world out of seeds containing portions of everything within them, it is hardly surprising to find him disparaging the reliability of the senses as guides to the truth (**F20**; see also **T3** and **T5** in this context): we cannot see or taste the bitter ingredients of figs, fortunately. **T16** is a cursory report of Anaxagoras' views on the various senses, in which it is noticeable how consistently he makes use of the principle of similars and dissimilars.

Anaxagoras' reaction to Parmenides is noticeable right from the start of his book, with its emphatic denial of singularity. Parmenides had forbidden the generation of plurality out of singularity, so Anaxagoras generated plurality out of plurality. However, although like his pluralist peers, Empedocles and the atomists, he simply affirmed plurality, he did (again like his peers) address the problem of change, generation, and destruction within a Parmenidean framework (**F19**). His awareness of Parmenides' poem is reflected in a number of Parmenidean phrases and echoes throughout the extant fragments, and in fact he adopts a particularly strong form of Eleaticism, maintaining not only that what-is cannot not be, but that since what-is cannot come from what-is-not it must already have existed.

———

F1 (DK 59B1; KRS 467) All things were together, with no limits set on either number or smallness; for there were in fact no limits set on smallness. And while everything was together the smallness of things meant that nothing was distinct. For air and aither prevailed over everything, since these two are limitless.[†] (Simplicius, *Commentary on Aristotle's 'Physics'*, CAG IX, 155.26–9 Diels)

F2 (DK 59B2; KRS 488) For in fact air and aither are being separated off from the vault[†] of the surrounding matter, which is limitless in amount. (Simplicius, *Commentary on Aristotle's 'Physics'*, CAG IX, 155.31–156.1 Diels)

F3 (DK 59B7) And the upshot is that it is impossible to know, in theory or in practice, the number of things that are being separated out. (Simplicius, *Commentary on Aristotle's 'On the Heavens'*, CAG VII, 608.26 Heiberg)

F4 (DK 59B4a; KRS 483, 498, 468) Since this is how things are, one is bound to think that in all things, which are compounds, there are many diverse stuffs—that is, that there are present in them the seeds of all things, possessed of all kinds of shapes, colours, and flavours. And one is bound also to think that human beings and every other kind of animate creature have been constructed. (Simplicius, *Commentary on Aristotle's 'Physics'*, CAG IX, 34.29–35.4 Diels)

F5 (DK 59B4b; KRS 498, 468) One is also bound to think that these human beings possess inhabited communities and manufactured objects, just as we do; that they have sun and moon and so on, just as we do; and that the earth yields all kinds of products for them, the most beneficial of which they gather into their homes and make use of. This is what I am saying about the separation—that separation would have taken place not only here with us, but also elsewhere. Before there was separation,[†] while all things were together, not even any colour was distinct, because the mixture of all things made that impossible—the mixture of the moist and the dry, the warm and the cold, the bright and the dark,* with a great deal of earth among them, and an infinite number of seeds quite dissimilar to one another.* For in fact none of all the seeds is like any of the others. Since this is how things are, we are bound to think that all things were present in the totality. (pieced together from Simplicius, *Commentary on Aristotle's 'Physics'*, CAG IX, 35.4–9 and 34.21–6 Diels)

T1 (DK 59A63) Thales, Anaxagoras, Plato, Aristotle, and Zeno say that there is only one universe. (Aëtius 2.1.2 Diels)

F6 (DK 59B8; KRS 486) The items of the universe, which is one, are not separate from one another nor cut off from one another with an axe, neither the warm from the cold nor the cold from the warm. (Simplicius, *Commentary on Aristotle's 'Physics'*, CAG IX, 175.11–14 Diels)

T2 (DK 59B10; KRS 484) Anaxagoras, having come across an old theory that nothing comes from nothing, did away with creation and introduced dispersal instead. In his foolishness he claimed that everything was mixed with everything else and that everything grew as it was dispersed. He claimed that one and the same sperm contained hair, nails, veins, arteries, sinews, and bones, and that these were too minute to be perceived, but gradually grew as they were dispersed. For how, he says, could hair come from not-hair or flesh from not-flesh?* (Elias of Crete, *Commentary on the Speeches of Gregory of Nazianzus* 36.911 Migne)

T3 (DK 59A46; KRS 496) Anaxagoras of Clazomenae, the son of Hegesibulus, said that the first principles of things were the homoeomeries. For he found it completely impossible for anything to be generated out of non-being or to perish into non-being. So, for instance, he said that the plain, simple food we take in, such as bread and water, nourishes hair, veins, arteries, flesh, sinews, bones, and all the other parts of the body. Since this is so, he said, we have to admit that the food we eat contains all things, and that everything grows as a result of things that already exist. So in our food there must be parts that are productive of blood, sinews, bones, and so on. But these parts can be appreciated only by the rational mind, because there is no point in asking the senses to cope with everything, such as the fact that bread and water produce these things; no, in bread and water there are parts which only the rational mind can appreciate. Because these parts in our food are similar to the things that are generated by them, he called them 'homoeomeries' and declared that they are the first principles of things. He held that the homoeomeries were the matter, while the effective cause was mind, which organizes the universe.   (Aëtius, *Opinions* 1.3.5 Diels)

T4 (DK 59A43; KRS 494) The views of Anaxagoras and Empedocles on the elements are opposed. While Empedocles says that fire and the others in the standard list are the elements of bodies and that everything is composed of them, Anaxagoras says, on the contrary, that the homoeomeries are the elements—e.g. flesh, bone, and so on—and that air and fire are blends of these and all the other seeds; for he says that air and fire are aggregates of all the invisible homoeomeries. That is why everything is generated out of air and fire ('fire' and 'aither' being the same in his terminology).   (Aristotle, *On the Heavens* 302ª28–ᵇ4 Allan)

F7 (DK 59B3; KRS 472) For there is no smallest part of the small, but there is always a smaller part (for it is impossible for division† to make what-is not be); and by the same token there is always a larger part than what is large. And what is large is numerically equal to what is small, since each thing is both large and small in relation to itself.   (Simplicius, *Commentary on Aristotle's 'Physics'*, CAG IX, 164.17–20 Diels)

F8 (DK 59B6; KRS 481) Since there are numerically equal portions of the great and the small, it follows that everything is in everything. It is impossible for there to be isolation, but everything has a portion of everything. Since there is no smallest part, it is impossible for there to be isolation, nor is it possible for anything to exist by itself; the original state of things still persists, and all things are together now as well. For there is a plurality of things present in everything, and in everything that is being separated off, however large or small it may be, there are equal portions.   (Simplicius, *Commentary on Aristotle's 'Physics'*, CAG IX, 164.25–165.1 Diels)

F9 (DK 59B11; KRS 482) In everything there is a portion of everything except of mind, and there are some things in which mind is present too.*   (Simplicius, *Commentary on Aristotle's 'Physics'*, CAG IX, 164.23–4 Diels)

F10 (DK 59B12; KRS 476) Everything else has a portion of everything, but mind is limitless* and independent; it is mixed with nothing, but is on its own and by itself. If it were not by itself, but were mixed with anything else, it would have a share of everything: all it would take is for it to be mixed with anything, since in everything there is a portion of everything, as I have already said. Moreover, the things mixed with it would stop it ruling anything in the way it does by being on its own and by itself. For it is the most refined and pure of all things, it forms every decision about everything, and there is nothing with more power than it. So, for instance, mind rules every animate creature, however large or small. Mind also controlled the whole rotation, in the sense that it was responsible for initiating the rotation.* At first it began to rotate out from a small area, but now it is rotating over a wider area, and it will rotate over a wider area still.* Mind decided about the combining, the separation, and the dispersal of all things. Mind ordered all the things that were to be (the things that formerly existed but do not now, the things that are now, and the things that will be in the future), including the present rotation in which the heavenly bodies, sun, moon, air, and aither are now rotating and being separated off (their separating off being a product of this rotation). And the dense is separated off from the rare, the warm from the cold, the bright from the dark, the dry from the moist. But there are numerous portions of a large number of things, and nothing except mind is completely separated off or dispersed from another thing. Wherever it is found, in larger or smaller amounts, mind is always identical, whereas nothing else has this kind of identity:† each item is and was most distinctly those ingredients which predominate in its mixture.   (pieced together from Simplicius, *Commentary on Aristotle's 'Physics'*, CAG IX, 164.24 and 156.13–157.4 Diels)

T5 (DK 59A52; KRS 485) The differences between Empedocles and Anaxagoras are that according to Empedocles mixture and separation occur in cycles, while according to Anaxagoras the separation was a unique event, and that Anaxagoras separates out an infinite number of things—the homoeomerous substances and the opposites—while Empedocles separates out only the familiar elements. It seems likely that Anaxagoras posited an infinite number of things in this way because he assumed the truth of the view held by all the natural scientists that nothing comes into being from non-being. That is why they make statements like 'Everything was originally mixed together', and 'This is the kind of thing that coming into being is—alteration', though others talk in this context of combination and separation. They also thought that since the opposites come from each other, they must have been present in each other. They reasoned as follows: necessarily, everything which comes into being comes either from things with being or from things without being; but it is impossible for anything to come into being from non-being (all the natural scientists are unanimous on this point); therefore, the only remaining possible conclusion, they thought, was that anything which comes into being comes from things with being, which are already present in the source, but which are too small for us to detect with our senses. So the reason they say that everything is mixed in everything is because, in their view, everything comes from everything; and they explain the fact that although everything is a mixture consisting of an infinite number of ingredients, things still look different from one another and are called one thing rather than another, by saying that this depends on which ingredient is numerically predominant within the mixture. There is nothing, they say, which is wholly and purely pale or dark or sweet or flesh or bone; people assess the nature of an object according to whichever ingredient there is most of within that object.   (Aristotle, *Physics* 187ª23–ᵇ7 Ross)

T6 (DK 59A45) Anaxagoras said that every part is just as much a mixture as the whole universe is; he based this view on the observation that anything can come from anything. That is also probably why he said that all things were once mixed together. His reasoning was probably as follows: this flesh and this bone are like that, and so is anything else, so everything must be like that, and must have been like that at one and the same time, because not only is there a beginning of the separating process from which each individual arises, but there must also be a beginning for the universe as a whole. Why? Because anything which comes into being comes from that kind of body, and everything does in fact come into being (although not at the same time), and this process of coming to be must have a source.

Moreover, this source must be a single principle, of the kind which Anaxagoras calls 'mind', and there is always a starting-point at which our minds stop thinking and set to work. And the upshot of all this is that everything must once have been mixed together and must have started changing at some point in time. (Aristotle, *Physics* 203ᵃ16–33 Ross)

F11 (DK 59B9; KRS 478) So these things are rotating in this way and are being separated off by force and speed (force being a product of speed). Their speed is unlike the speed of anything that now exists on earth, but is altogether many times as fast. (Simplicius, *Commentary on Aristotle's 'Physics'*, CAG IX, 35.14–18 Diels)

F12 (DK 59B15; KRS 489) The dense, the moist, the cold, and the dark† came together here, where the earth is now, while the fine, the warm, the dry, and the bright† departed into the further reaches of the aither. (Simplicius, *Commentary on Aristotle's 'Physics'*, CAG IX, 179.3–6 Diels)

F13 (DK 59B14; KRS 479) Mind controlled all that is,† and mind is now where everything else is: it is in that which surrounds the plurality,† in the aggregates that have been formed, and in the things that have been separated off. (Simplicius, *Commentary on Aristotle's 'Physics'*, CAG IX, 157.7–9 Diels)

F14 (DK 59B13; KRS 477) And when mind had initiated motion, separation began from everything that was in motion,* and all that mind set in motion was dispersed. And as things were moving and being dispersed, the rotation greatly accelerated the process of dispersal. (Simplicius, *Commentary on Aristotle's 'Physics'*, CAG IX, 300.31–301.1 Diels)

F15 (DK 59B5; KRS 473) One has to appreciate that this dispersal of these things did not either add to or subtract from the sum total of all things. It is impossible for there to be more things than all the things there are; no, all things are always equal in number. (Simplicius, *Commentary on Aristotle's 'Physics'*, CAG IX, 156.10–12 Diels)

F16 (DK 59B16; KRS 490) Earth is made out of these things* during the process of separation; for water is separated off from clouds and earth from water; stones are formed from earth by cold, and stones tend outwards more than water.* (pieced together from Simplicius, *Commentary on Aristotle's 'Physics'*, CAG IX, 179.8–10 and 155.21–3 Diels)

T7 (DK 59A41; KRS 492) Theophrastus says that Anaximander and Anaxagoras are very close on this issue; for Anaxagoras says that in the course of the dispersal of the boundless, like things are attracted to one another, and that what was gold in the original totality becomes gold, while what was earth becomes earth. (Theophrastus [fr. 228a Fortenbaugh *et al.*] in Simplicius, *Commentary on Aristotle's 'Physics'*, CAG IX, 27.11–14 Diels)

F17 (DK 59B18; KRS 500) The sun instils the moon with brightness. (Plutarch, *On the Face on the Moon* 929b3–4 Cherniss)

F18 (DK 59B19; KRS 501) What we call a 'rainbow' is light in the clouds, shining opposite the sun. (Scholiast on Homer, *Iliad* 17.547, Dindorf 6.233)

T8 (DK 59A89) On earthquakes, Anaxagoras says that aither causes earthquakes because it naturally tends upwards, but is trapped inside the nether regions and hollows of the earth. For the upper layer of the earth gets clogged up by rainfall, despite the fact that all earth is in fact naturally porous. (Aristotle, *On Celestial Phenomena* 365ᵃ19–23 Bekker)

T9 (DK 59A42; KRS 502) Anaxagoras said that the earth is flat, and stays suspended because of its size, because there is no void, and because it is carried like a vessel by the air, which is extremely strong . . . The sun, moon, and all the heavenly bodies are fiery stones which have been taken up by the rotation of the aither.* Beneath the heavenly bodies are certain bodies, invisible to us, that are carried around along with the sun and moon.* We do not feel the heat of the heavenly bodies because of their distance from the earth; moreover, they are not as hot as the sun because the region they occupy is colder. The moon is lower than the sun and nearer to us. The sun is larger than the Peloponnese. The moon does not have its own light, but gains it from the sun. The stars in their revolution go under the earth. Eclipses of the moon occur when the earth gets in the way, but sometimes when the bodies beneath the moon get in the way; solar eclipses occur when the new moon gets in the way.   (Hippolytus, *Refutation of All Heresies* 1.8.3–9.2 Marcovich)

T10 (DK 59A81) Anaxagoras and Democritus say that comets are a conjunction of planets, when they come close enough to appear to touch one another.*   (Aristotle, *On Celestial Phenomena* 342ᵇ27–9 Bekker)

T11 (DK 59A80) Anaxagoras and Democritus say that the Milky Way is the light of certain of the heavenly bodies. They say that the sun, as it travels under the earth, does not look upon some of the heavenly bodies. The light of those which are in the line of sight of the sun is invisible, because it is impeded by the sun's rays, and the Milky Way is the light proper to those which are screened by the earth in such a way that they are not in the line of sight of the sun.*   (Aristotle, *On Celestial Phenomena* 345ᵃ25–9 Bekker)

T12 (DK 59A117) Anaxagoras and Empedocles say that plants are moved by desire, and they also assert that they feel sensations and experience sadness and pleasure. Anaxagoras' inference that plants are animals and feel happiness and sadness was based on the way they bend their leaves.* . . . Anaxagoras also held that plants breathe.   (Ps.-Aristotle, *On Plants* 815ᵃ15–19, 816ᵇ26 Apelt)

T13 (DK 59A1) Animals were generated out of what is moist, warm, and earthy, and then subsequently from one another.   (Diogenes Laertius, *Lives of Eminent Philosophers* 2.9.10–12 Long)

T14 (DK 59A117; KRS 506) Anaxagoras says that the air contains seeds of all things and that when these are carried down along with water they generate plants.   (Theophrastus, *Enquiry into Plants* 3.1.4.3–5 Hort)

T15 (DK 59A110) Anaxagoras and many others say that food comes to the foetus through the navel.   (Censorinus, *On Birthdays* 6.3.2–4 Jahn)

F19 (DK 59B17; KRS 469) Greek usage of the words 'generation' and 'destruction' is incorrect. Nothing is generated or destroyed; things are combined from already existing things and dispersed. It would therefore be correct to use 'combination' for 'generation' and 'dispersal' for 'destruction'.   (Simplicius, *Commentary on Aristotle's 'Physics'*, CAG IX, 163.20–4 Diels)

F20 (DK 59B21; KRS 509) The weakness [*of the senses*] means that we are incapable of discerning the truth. (Sextus Empiricus, *Against the Professors* 7.90.3–4 Bury)

T16 (DK 59A92; KRS 511) Anaxagoras says that perception occurs thanks to opposites, because similars are unaffected by one another. He undertakes to account for each sense separately. So we see, he says, thanks to the reflection in the pupil, but there is no reflection in pupils of the same colour, only in those of a different colour. In the majority of cases the pupil is differently coloured by day, but in some people it is differently coloured by night, and that is why they see well then; in general, however, night is more likely to be the same colour as the eyes.* . . .

The same goes for the way touch and taste discern their objects. For anything with the same degree of warmth or cold does not warm or cool us when it comes near us, and also we certainly do not recognize sweet or sour tastes by means of those same qualities. No, we discern something cold by something warm, something drinkable by something brackish, something sweet by something sour—in other words, depending on our deficiency in each quality. For everything, he says, is already in us. The same goes for smell and hearing . . . (Theophrastus, *On the Senses* 27–8 Stratton)

D. Bargrave-Weaver, 'The Cosmogony of Anaxagoras', *Phronesis*, 4 (1959), 77–91.

F. M. Cornford, 'Anaxagoras' Theory of Matter', in [26], ii. 275–322 (first pub. *Classical Quarterly*, 24 (1930)).

D. J. Furley, 'Anaxagoras in Response to Parmenides', in [32], 61–85.

M. Furth, 'A "Philosophical Hero"? Anaxagoras and the Eleatics', *Oxford Studies in Ancient Philosophy*, 9 (1991), 95–129; repr. in R.W. Sharples (ed.), *Modern Thinkers and Ancient Thinkers* (London: UCL Press, 1993), 27–65.

D. W. Graham, 'The Postulates of Anaxagoras', *Apeiron*, 27 (1994), 77–121.

B. Inwood, 'Anaxagoras and Infinite Divisibility', *Illinois Classical Studies*, 11 (1986), 17–33.

C. H. Kahn, 'The Historical Position of Anaxagoras', in [24], 203–10.

O. Kember, 'Anaxagoras' Theory of Sex Differentiation and Heredity', *Phronesis*, 18 (1973), 1–14.

G. B. Kerferd, 'Anaxagoras and the Concept of Matter Before Aristotle', in [30], 489–503 (first pub. *Bulletin of the John Rylands Library*, 52 (1969)).

D. Konstan, 'Anaxagoras on Bigger and Smaller', in M. Capasso *et al.* (eds.), *Studi di filosofia preplatonica* (Naples: Bibliopolis, 1985), 137–57.

A. Laks, 'Mind's Crisis: On Anaxagoras' Nous', *Southern Journal of Philosophy*, 31 (1993), suppl. vol., 19–38.

J. H. Lesher, 'Mind's Knowledge and Powers of Control in Anaxagoras DK B12', *Phronesis*, 40 (1995), 125–42.

W. E. Mann, 'Anaxagoras and the *Homoiomerē*', *Phronesis*, 25 (1980), 228–49.

J. Mansfeld, 'The Chronology of Anaxagoras' Athenian Period and the Date of his Trial', in [29], 264–306 (first pub. *Mnemosyne*, 32 (1979) and 33 (1980)).

A. L. Peck, 'Anaxagoras and the Parts', *Classical Quarterly*, 20 (1926), 57–62.

—— 'Anaxagoras: Predication as a Problem in Physics', *Classical Quarterly*, 25 (1931), 27–37, 112–20.

M. Reesor, 'The Meaning of Anaxagoras', *Classical Philology*, 55 (1960), 1–8.

—— 'The Problem of Anaxagoras', in [21], 81–7 (first pub. *Classical Philology* 58 (1963)).

C. D. C. Reeve, 'Anaxagorean Panspermism', *Ancient Philosophy*, 1 (1980/1), 89–108.

M. Schofield, *An Essay on Anaxagoras* (Cambridge: Cambridge University Press, 1980).

—— 'Anaxagoras' Other World Revisited', in K. Algra *et al.* (eds.), *Polyhistor: Studies in the History and Historiography of Ancient Philosophy* (Leiden: Brill, 1996), 3–20.

D. Sider, *The Fragments of Anaxagoras* (Meisenheim am Glam: Hain, 1981).

M. C. Stokes, 'On Anaxagoras', *Archiv für Geschichte der Philosophie*, 47 (1965), 1–19, 217–50.

C. Strang, 'The Physical Theory of Anaxagoras', in [30], 361–80 (first pub. *Archiv für Geschichte der Philosophie*, 45 (1963)).

S.-T. Teodorsson, *Anaxagoras' Theory of Matter* (Göteberg: Acta Universitatis Gothoburgensis, 1982).

S. S. Tigner, 'Stars, Unseen Bodies and the Extent of the Earth in Anaxagoras' Cosmogony: Three Problems and their Simultaneous Solution', in G. Bowersock *et al.* (eds.), *Arktouros: Hellenic Studies Presented to Bernard M. W. Knox* (Berlin: de Gruyter, 1979), 330–5.

G. Vlastos, 'The Physical Theory of Anaxagoras', in [26], ii. 323–53, and in [30], 459–88, and in [33], 303–27 (first pub. *Philosophical Review*, 59 (1950)).

EMPEDOCLES OF ACRAGAS

We have a large number of fragments from the poem (or poems) of Empedocles; more of his work survives than in the case of any other Presocratic. However, the doxographic tradition and other secondary sources attribute a huge, even encyclopedic range of teachings to him, and the resulting impression is that we may only have a small proportion of his work. Ancient sources credited him with a number of works, but almost all the extant fragments are nowadays invariably attributed to either *On Nature* or *Purifications*, the division depending on whether the subject of the fragment is Presocratic physical speculation or religious and spiritual claims and advice. In actual fact, though, the evidence for there being two separate poems, rather than two sections of a single poem, is surprisingly weak. It may be that we have the remains of a single work, which covered a variety of topics,[1] and some of which was addressed to the people of Acragas in the plural, while some was focused more sharply on a single individual, Pausanias, who is said to have been Empedocles' beloved. In any case, in what follows I shall speak of a single poem. The highly poetic and emotive language of his verse has led not only to problems of interpretation, but also to a number of textual difficulties. Like Parmenides, by writing in epic verse he was choosing to place himself within the epic didactic tradition.

Probably one of the best-known aspects of Empedocles' life is the supposed manner of his death, so although generally in this book I have focused on philosophy rather than biography, I here give the main testimonium regarding his death (**T1**). The story is, in any case, not irrelevant to understanding Empedocles. It is immediately clear that he was a wonder-worker, a man of magic, as much as what we would recognize as a philosopher, and there are clear strands in his poem which bear this out too: in **F1**, which must have come close to the start of the poem, he singles himself out from the rest of mankind as divine (see also the last line of

---

[1] No one claims that Heraclitus, for instance, wrote more than one work on the grounds that he covers both spiritual matters and scientific speculation. The conclusion that Empedocles probably wrote just the one major poem has recently been supported by the publication of some new papyrus fragments: see A. Martin and O. Primavesi, *L'Empédocle de Strasbourg (P. Strasb. gr. Inv. 1665–1666): Introduction, édition et commentaire* (Berlin: de Gruyter, 1999), especially pp. 114–19. If there were originally two poems, the most attractive division of their contents is that of Sedley 1989 (see bibliography below): *On Nature* contained all doctrinal material, on whatever topic, while *Purifications* contained no more than oracles and means of ritual purification.

F15), and **F2** too is definitely spoken in prophet mode; in **F3** (which probably comes from a stage of the poem when he was expounding the theory of reincarnation), he explains that godhood is the next incarnation up the scale from those who have become 'prophets, singers of hymns, healers, and leaders'; and in **F4** he promises Pausanias that he will learn from him all kinds of magical powers, including raising the dead.

But he also promises knowledge of the origin and constitution of the world (**F5**). We are lucky to have enough fragments to be able to reconstruct a great deal of Empedocles' thought in this area without having to rely on testimonia except to supplement the fragments. This is particularly fortunate because in the case of Empedocles, more perhaps than any other Presocratic, the doxographic tradition is tainted by Aristotelian errors. Aristotle was fascinated by Empedocles, and referred to him more than to any other Presocratic, but he failed to understand him, and the great majority of his reports are peevish and unsympathetic (e.g. **T2–4**). Anyway, Empedocles claims (**F6** and **F7**; see also **F20** ll. 61–70) that a judicious use of the senses, combined with a proper use of intelligence, can teach one the truth about the world.[2] Presumably the task of a teacher such as Empedocles, then, is to guide one's thinking until one can see the truth for oneself. **F8** is particularly interesting in this context. All we have to do with our insights about things, Empedocles teaches, is not interfere with them with our normal, associative mind; then, just as at the macrocosmic scale everything has intelligence, at least in the minimal sense that it has an innate impulse to seek its proper place in the universe (as it is the natural tendency of fire to move upwards), so on the microcosmic scale our insights will find their own proper place in our minds. In fact, it is quite likely (**F9**) that even our thoughts about the world have the same constitution as the world itself.

In his physics, Empedocles was a pluralist: he held that there was a plurality of original substances which together account for the physical world. He was the first to come up with the theory of the four elements— earth, water, fire, and air—which (after its revival by Aristotle) was to have such a long and significant history in the West, especially in medicine as the four humours.[3] Quite often, as in **F10**, he speaks about the four elements (or 'roots', as he called them) in allegorical terms, calling them by the names of divinities in order to suggest that even they have consciousness (just as the use of 'roots' implies their vitality). A comparison between Aëtius' remarks surrounding **F10**, and those of Hippolytus which make up **T5**, will reveal that even in ancient times there was controversy about

---

[2] Compare Heraclitus **F27** on p. 40.

[3] The deathblow to the four-element theory was not finally dealt until 1661, with the publication of Robert Boyle's *Sceptical Chymist*.

the precise allocation of Empedocles' allegorical figures. No one doubts that 'Nestis' is water, but of the other three Zeus, lord of the heavens, stands for aither, Empedocles' choice of word for 'air'; Hera, the 'life-bearing' mother, is earth; and Aidoneus, which is another word for 'Hades', must be fire. The idea of subterranean fire is recurrent in Empedocles' thought (see **F31**, **T28**, **T29**), and so the equation of Hades with fire is not so surprising. Each of the elements is also given other titles by Empedocles—water, for instance, may appear as 'sea' or 'rain'—and fire may appear as 'sun': again, the idea that the sun emerged from Hades, the source of its fire, renewed each morning, is traditional.[4]

As a pluralist, Empedocles faced a particular difficulty. Parmenides had apparently denied the possibility of the real existence of more than one thing, the totality of what-is. Empedocles accepted half of Parmenides' argument and ignored the rest. He agreed that what-is-not is impossible, but insisted that each of his four elements has an equal claim to existence, none of them being at all reducible to any of the others. So there were four basic existents, and all the things of the world[5] were explained as differently proportioned mixtures of these four elements. What we call 'change', 'generation', 'destruction', and so on, are really no more than the rearrangement of these elements. Nothing is generated out of or dies back into what-is-not, as Parmenides insisted; but things can be generated and die back into their constituent elements. Void or non-being does not exist, but motion is still possible if one regards it as one existent thing taking the place of another existent thing, which has just moved on. On these ideas, see **F11–17**, **F19** ll. 9–14, **F20** ll. 30–35, and **T6**. Empedocles' predecessors had come up with a picture of the universe which assigned different parts to the four substances (air, fire, water, and earth), but these were regarded as having more primary qualities—water being cold and wet, fire hot and dry, and so on—and often some were derived from others. Empedocles was the first to give these four equal status and the first to develop the concept of an element—an irreducible, imperishable, underived primitive form of matter.

In addition to the four 'roots', Empedocles posited two motivating factors, love and strife (**F20**, **T7**). Love's tendency is to unify things, that of strife to separate them; or, less simplistically and taking account of Empedoclean physics, love causes dissimilar things to come together, and strife causes similar things to come together. Thus, while any static object in the world could be explained as a proportionate mixture of the elements, many processes in the world can be explained as some kind of balance between

---

[4] See the opening chapters of Kingsley's 1995 book in the bibliography below.
[5] Some scholars think that this applies only to organic things such as bone (see **F16**), but **F15** speaks of the idea in all generality.

the action of love and the action of strife. Not all processes need be explained by the action of love and/or strife: fire, for instance, has a natural tendency to move upwards, and Empedocles does not rely on love or strife to explain it. Love and strife seem to be called on above all where the mixing and separation of elements are concerned. Like the elements, love and strife are sometimes given alternative, allegorical names: love, for instance, commonly appears as Aphrodite, Cypris, or Harmony, while strife may be 'discord' or 'wrath'. Like the elements, they too are eternal (**F18**). **F19** is a convenient summary of the basic importance of the four elements, and love and strife. In short, everything is a 'mortal' or temporary compound of the four elements, under the influence of more or less love and strife. Empedocles' clear recognition of the concept of elements and compounds represents an enormous scientific advance over his predecessors.

The action of love and strife on things is not just local. Empedocles saw the whole universe as subject to an endlessly repeating cosmic cycle, like a vast cosmic inbreath and outbreath. At one extreme love is totally dominant, with strife banished to the outermost reaches of the universe; at the opposite extreme, strife has become dominant, and has moved inwards to push love into the centre of the universe. Under the rule of love everything is unified into a mass with none of the four elements distinct; under the rule of strife the four elements are completely unmixed, and occupy four distinct layers or concentric spheres (from the outside: fire, air, water, earth). The way in which strife gradually separates the elements is by generating a rotational movement (the same we see in the whirling of the heavenly bodies), which would act (as Aristotle confirms at *On the Heavens* 295^{a}9–13) to sort things out according to their relative weights, with the lighter stuffs going towards the circumference and the heavier stuffs towards the centre. On the cosmogonic action of love and strife, see especially the important long fragments **F20** and **F21**, with **F22** and **F23**.

Details of the precise condition at the two extremes are controversial, and so are details of what happens in between, as the universe moves away from the rule of love, gradually towards increasing strife, and then away from total strife back towards the dominance of love again. It seems from **T8** that time moves faster during the period of increasing strife, and slower as the power of love increases and things begin to merge again into the sphere of love. The duration of each phase of the cycle is disputed: probably the sphere of love lasts as long as the sum of the two periods of increasing love and increasing strife, while the duration of the total dominance of strife is instantaneous; at any rate, that is one possible interpretation of the evidence of **T9**, though this could also mean that there are four equal time-periods—the rule of love, the period of increasing strife, the rule of strife, and the period of increasing love.

It seems that a world like ours is possible at two points in the cycle, both during increasing strife and during increasing love (**T10**).[6] However, it also seems likely that Empedocles saw our particular world as occurring during the rule of strife, since the elements are already well advanced in their separation into concentric spheres. He occasionally strikes a note of gloom and speaks of our birth in strife (e.g. **F34**).[7] Most strikingly, **F35** makes it clear, with a myth of original sin and fall, that even to be born on this world is a punishment.

Under the rule of love, everything comes together into a single stable sphere, which is described in terms reminiscent of the (probably metaphorical) sphericity of Parmenides' One (**F24**, **F25**). **F26** also seems to belong here, as a description of the sphere.[8] In the sphere all the elements are mixed in equal proportions, but it is unlikely that the sphere is a homogeneous blend or fusion of the four elements, because the elements are imperishable. On the microcosmic level, an equal proportion of the elements is responsible for clear thinking (**F43**, with note); so the sphere is described as total mind. Given its permanence and stability, what caused the sphere to begin to break apart? It must be the action of strife. Reminiscent of that aspect of Taoism which is summed up in the yin–yang symbol, even the sphere of love contains the seed of discord. At any rate, the 'limbs of the god were starting to quiver' (**F27**), and gradually the lineaments of our familiar universe began to emerge (**T11**). Empedocles illustrated the cycle as a whole, somewhat obscurely, by reference to what happens to a body in life and death: see **F28** with its note.

Empedocles was certainly not half-hearted in embracing the consequences of the cosmic cycle. If under the rule of strife things are totally disunited, then even while love's power is on the increase, there is no guarantee that things will be put together in a harmonious fashion. **F29–31** describe the various stages of zoogony. At first, while the love's influence is still strong, 'whole-natured' (i.e. undifferentiated) creatures arise. They resemble the description of love's sphere in **F24** and **F25**, and indeed may well be thought of as gods, suitable creatures to arise while love's blessed influence is still strong. There was a utopian world of peace

---

[6] Notice, then, a likely debt to Heraclitus: our world is born out of the struggle of opposites.

[7] Empedocles' pessimism has been strikingly confirmed by the d-group of fragments of *P. Strasb. gr.* Inv. 1665–1666 which speaks of rotting limbs and prophesies our pursuit by the vengeful Furies for the crime of eating meat.

[8] However, just conceivably this fragment belongs elsewhere, and is simply a description of an omnipotent Empedoclean deity. In this case, the 'thoughts' with which the deity rushes through the world may be the emotions of love and hatred or strife.

and harmony (**F32–3**), free from abominations such as blood sacrifices and the eating of meat. This is the Golden Age before the fall outlined in **F35**, and so presumably it was a time when spirits roamed the world not yet in human form, before the corruption of blood sacrifice and meat-eating had occurred. Then humans arise (that is, these spirits suffer corruption and are reborn as humans), and finally, as strife's power increases, monsters and separate limbs roam the earth. This was the age of legendary beasts such as the Minotaur. In all probability this sequence is reversed in the opposite half of the cosmic cycle, when love is gradually gaining dominance over strife. In our world strife still seems to be more dominant than Empedocles likes: **F34**.

Perhaps it was at this point in the poem that Empedocles found room for his theory of reincarnation (see the powerful fragment **F35**, with **F36** and also **F3**), since it connects with his dietary rules: the eating of meat is forbidden, bluntly, because you may be eating a reincarnated relative (**F37**, **F38**). Other dietary prohibitions included not eating beans, which were also banned by the Pythagoreans, for both practical and symbolic reasons (**F39**; see p. 97 for the Pythagorean prohibition).[9] Although it is punishment for the incarnated soul to be banished and born on earth, it is possible to re-ascend the ladder of incarnation and eventually to become a god again (**F3**).[10] The means of purification certainly included vegetarianism and abstention from blood sacrifice, but may also have included sexual continence (though not abstinence) and other moderative measures. It also included knowledge of the gods (**F40**) and presumably clear understanding of the nature of the universe, as Empedocles has taught it in his poem. Of course, given the circumstances, one could not hope to be united with the sphere of love in itself, since that is a thing of the past and the future, not of the present state of the world; but perhaps one could aspire to be united with the power of love that remains in the world.

During the description of the formation of our world, as the cycle

---

[9] Although it is likely that there is Pythagorean influence on Empedocles in this detail, the basic idea of transmigration of souls probably came to him from local Sicilian beliefs: see Demand's article in the bibliography below.

[10] Does this mean that the soul is immortal? If so, what becomes of the idea that *only* the four elements and love and strife are eternal? Perhaps Empedocles identified the soul with one or more of the elements, or perhaps he meant that the soul was relatively immortal, lasting as long as our universe lasted before being amalgamated into love's sphere or destroyed in the chaos of strife's separation (cf. 'long-lived' in F15 l. 7, F19 l. 11, F20 l. 40, F35 l. 5). After all, a theory of psychic transmigration by no means entails a theory of absolute immortality. It is also worth remembering that on Empedocles' theory, worlds recur cyclically; just possibly, then, he held (along with contemporary Pythagoreans; see T14, p. 99) that reincarnated souls were subject to eternal recurrence, which might confer a kind of immortality.

moved from strife slowly towards love, Empedocles digressed into an encyclopedic account of many features of the universe. Not only did he concentrate on typically Presocratic subjects such as the nature and behaviour of the heavenly bodies and meteorological phenomena, but he also went into botany and zoology, and especially human biology (remember that in F3 healers are one of the highest human incarnations). F41 is for its time a remarkably accurate description of the human eye; F42 a famous account of breathing as involving not just the nostrils and mouth (for those creatures which are equipped with them), but pores all over the body. Theophrastus preserves a long account of Empedocles' views on the senses, sense-perception, the perception of pleasure and pain, and understanding (T12), which can be supplemented by F9 and F43. Particularly noteworthy here is the idea that everything gives off emanations: T13 shows how this theory could also be used to explain other phenomena as well, and the last words of T14 suggest that all mixture and dissolution (that is, all apparent creation and destruction—see F13) was explained by means of these channels; Empedocles says in F19 l. 13 (and again in F20 l. 34 and F22 l. 3) that the elements 'run through one another', and the reason, Aristotle suggests,[11] they are able to do so is that they have channels which can accommodate emanations. He also went in some depth into embryology, a subject of perennial interest to the more mystically and numerologically inclined ancient Greek thinkers (T8, T15–17, F44, and a number of testimonia not here translated), and touched on digestion too (F45).

For Empedocles' astronomical theories, in so far as we can reliably reconstruct them, we have to rely largely on testimonia, since the relevant fragments tend to be no more than a line or two in length (e.g. F46, a true explanation of nightfall, and F47, which recognizes that the moon gets its light from the sun). T18–27 sketch some of the details. It seems that on Empedocles' view the outer heaven is made of a hard ice-like substance; despite its weight, it is prevented from falling down to join the earth at the centre of the universe by its whirling motion. The fixed stars are fragments of fire which remain in the aither after fire (in its property as a hardening agent) had crystallized the aither to create the outer periphery of heaven. This took place at an early stage of the formation of the universe, after which the remaining fire coalesced as our sun. It is clear that he also covered topics such as the nature and phases of the moon, but he may not have tried to explain the apparent motion of the planets.

---

[11] There are, however, difficulties with the idea that the elements themselves have pores or channels. What, for instance, would be the elemental status of such channels? They cannot contain air, because each element is in itself pure, so that earth cannot contain air. Are they void or empty space? But Empedocles denied the existence of void.

Finally, Empedocles explained life on earth as a result of heat trapped under the surface of the earth. Coming from Sicily, and living near Mount Etna, he was impressed by the presence of subterranean fire. In our finished world, fire, being light, has mostly moved outwards, towards the periphery, and even the fire trapped inside the earth has an upward tendency. This upward tendency causes life on earth to erupt (**F31**), and makes the earth 'sweat' and produce the sea (**T3**). The trapped heat is also responsible, in its function as a hardening agent (see also **F48** and **T24**), for other phenomena, such as solidifying stones out of water (**T28**, **T29**). Fire clearly had an important part to play in Empedocles' cosmogony, but it is going too far to complain, with Aristotle (*On Generation and Destruction* 330[b]), that in practice he relied on only two elements—fire and the other three. It is just that, as a hardening agent, fire had a particular part to play in the cosmogonical process.

———

T1 (DK 31A1) There are different accounts of his death. After telling the story about the woman who stopped breathing and how famous Empedocles became for having restored her corpse to life, Heraclides tells how once Empedocles was performing a sacrifice near Peisianax's farm, and he invited some of his friends, including Pausanias. After the feast everyone else took themselves off to rest (either under the trees of the nearby farm or elsewhere), but Empedocles stayed in the place where he had reclined for the meal. When they got up the next day, he alone was nowhere to be found. They looked for him and questioned the slaves, who said that they had no idea where he was; but one of them said that in the middle of the night he had heard a supernaturally loud voice calling out Empedocles' name, and then, when he had got out of bed, he had seen a light in the sky and torches shining, but nothing else. His friends were amazed at what had happened, and after Pausanias went home he organized a search party. Later, however, he stopped them from trying to interfere with events, suggested that prayer was the correct response to what had happened, and that they ought to sacrifice to Empedocles as though he had become a god. Hermippus, however, says that it was after Empedocles had cured a woman from Acragas called Pantheia, whom the doctors had declared to be a hopeless case, that he performed the sacrifice, and that there were almost eighty guests at the sacrificial feast. Hippobotus says that after he had got

up from his couch he made his way to Mount Etna, where he leapt
into the craters of fire and made himself disappear, because he
wanted to confirm what people were saying about him—that he had
become a god. Later, though, according to Hippobotus, he was found
out when one of his sandals was disgorged by the mountain, since
he had regularly worn bronze sandals.*   (Diogenes Laertius, *Lives
of Eminent Philosophers* 8.67.8–69.8 Long)

F1 (DK 31B112; KRS 399; W 102; I 1)

Friends, inhabitants of[†] the great city of the yellow river Acragas,
Dwelling on the heights of the city, filled with care for good
    deeds,
Havens of respect for strangers, innocent of hardship,
Greetings! Honoured, it seems,[†] as an immortal god,
Mortal no more, I come and go among all men,   5
Wreathed with ribbons and fresh chaplets.
No sooner do I arrive[†] in flourishing cities than by all
I am revered, both men and women, and they follow me
In their thousands, seeking directions to the path of benefit,
Some in need of prophecies, while others, afflicted by ailments 10
Of all kinds, ask to hear me utter words of healing,
Since they have long been pierced by cruel pains.

> (pieced together from: Diogenes Laertius, *Lives of Eminent
>   Philosophers* 8.61.3–6 Long; Diodorus of Sicily, *Universal
>   History* 13.83.1.9 Vogel; and Clement, *Miscellanies* 6.30.3
>   Stählin/Früchtel)

F2 (DK 31B114; W 103; I 2)

> My friends, I know that there is truth in the words
> I shall speak; but this truth is hard indeed for men,
> And the encroachment of trust is not welcome to them.

> (Clement, *Miscellanies* 5.9.1.3–5 Stählin/Früchtel)

F3 (DK 31B146; KRS 409; W 132; I 136)

> In the end as prophets, singers of hymns, healers, and leaders
> They come among the men of this world,
> And then they spring up as gods, highest in honour.

> (Clement, *Miscellanies* 4.150.1.3–5 Stählin/Früchtel)

F4 (DK 31B111; KRS 345; W 101; I 15)

All the potions there are that ward off ills and old age
You shall learn, since for you alone will I fulfil them all.
You will halt the energy of the untiring winds which blast
The earth with their gusts and wither the fields,
 And again, if you want, you will bring back compensatory winds. 5
After dark rain you will make dry heat, seasonable for men,
And after the dry heat of summer, to nourish the trees,
You will make streams, which flow through the aither.
And you will bring out of Hades the energy of a man who has died.

(Diogenes Laertius, *Lives of Eminent
Philosophers* 8.59.5–13 Long)

F5 (DK 31B38; KRS 368; W 27; I 39)

But come, and I will tell you of the source from which in the
  beginning
The sun and everything else which now we see became manifest†—
The earth and the surging sea and the moist air,
 Titan* and aither which encircles and holds everything together.

(Clement, *Miscellanies* 5.48.3.3–6 Stählin/Früchtel)

T2 (DK 31B53; I CTXT-29a, F42) Both alternatives are strange, then:
either our predecessors did not think there was such a thing as
chance, or they recognized its existence but ignored it. And this is
especially strange since they do sometimes rely on it, as Empedocles
does when he says that air is not always separated off towards the
highest region, but as chance would have it. At any rate, in the
cosmogonical section of his work, he says:

So chanced it then to run, but often otherwise.

And he also says that the parts of animals mostly came about by
chance.   (Aristotle, *Physics* 196ª17–24 Ross)

T3 (DK 31A25, B55; KRS 371; W 46; I CTXT-44, F59) It is equally
absurd for someone to think that in describing the sea as the 'sweat
of the earth' he has said something clear, as Empedocles does.
Although this statement may perhaps be sufficient for the purposes
of poetry (since metaphor is a poetic device), it is not sufficient for

the purpose of acquiring knowledge about nature.*   (Aristotle, *On Celestial Phenomena*, 357ᵃ24–8 Bekker)

T4 (DK 31A22; KRS 339) Homer and Empedocles have nothing in common except for their metre, which is why it is right to call Homer a poet, but Empedocles a natural scientist rather than a poet.   (Aristotle, *Poetics* 1447ᵇ17–20 Bekker)

F6 (DK 31B2; KRS 342; W 1; I 8)

For narrow are the means* spread over their bodies,
And many the afflictions that burst in and blunt their thinking.
In their lives they see a meagre portion of life, and then,
Doomed to a swift death, like smoke they fly away on high,
Trusting only in whatever each has encountered as he was driven   5
Here and there; yet he falsely† claims to have discovered the whole.
Not thus are these things to be seen by men, nor heard,
Nor grasped with the mind. But since you have withdrawn here,
You shall learn. Mortal wisdom has aroused no more than this.†*

> (pieced together from Sextus Empiricus, *Against the Professors* 7.123.3–10 and 124.5–6 Bury)

F7 (DK 31B3B; KRS 343; W 5; I 14)

Nor let it force you to take from mortal men the flowers
Of fair-famed honour. If you happen to speak more than is holy,
Have no fear, and then seat yourself on the heights of wisdom.
But come, consider by whatever means it takes to make anything
   clear.
Think not that sight is ever more reliable† than what comes to
   hearing,   5
Nor rate echoing hearing above the pores of the tongue, nor keep
Your trust from any of the other organs by which there is a channel
For understanding, but use whatever it takes to make things clear to
   the mind.

> (Sextus Empiricus, *Against the Professors* 7.125.7–14 Bury)

F8 (DK 31B110; KRS 398; W 100; I 16)

For if you plant them too† down under your agitated mind
And observe them kindly with episodes of untainted attention,
All of them will remain with you throughout your life, and from
   them

You will gain† many others.* For these things will themselves
Cause each thing to grow into its rightful place, according to its
    nature.   5
But if you reach out for things of a different kind, such as the
    countless
Afflictions there are among men which blunt their thinking,
Be assured that, as time goes around, they will suddenly leave you,
Since they desire to attain the family proper to themselves.
For know that everything has intelligence and a share of
    understanding.   10

      (Hippolytus, *Refutation of All Heresies* 7.29.26 Marcovich)

F9 (DK 31B109; KRS 393; W 77; I 17)

    For with earth we see earth, water with water,
    Bright aither with aither, and baneful fire with fire,
    Love with love, and strife with grim strife.*

      (Aristotle, *On the Soul* 404^{b}13–15 Ross)

F10 (DK 31A33, B6; KRS 346; W 7; I 12) Empedocles the son of
Meton, from Acragas, says that there are four elements—fire, air,
water, and earth—and two initiatory forces, love and strife, of which
the former is unificatory, the latter divisive. He speaks as follows:

    For hear first the four roots of all things:
    Bright Zeus, life-bearing Hera, Aidoneus,
    And Nestis, who soaks men's springs with her tears.*

'Zeus' is his name for the seething [*zesis*] of heavenly fire, 'life-
bearing Hera' for air [*aēr*], 'Aidoneus' for earth, and 'Nestis' and 'the
springs of mortals' for seed, so to speak, and water. (Aëtius,
Opinions 1.3.20 Diels)

T5 (DK 31A33) [*After quoting F10*] 'Zeus' is fire; 'life-bearing Hera'
is earth, which bears the crops necessary for life; 'Aidoneus' is air,
because although we look at everything through air the only thing we
do not see is air itself;* and 'Nestis' is water, because water is the
only thing which, while being a medium for nourishment for everything which is nourished, cannot nourish them by itself. For, he
says, if water did nourish creatures by itself, they would never have
died of starvation, since there is always plenty of water in the world.
And so he calls water 'Nestis' because although it is responsible for

nourishment it does not have the ability to nourish things which are
nourished.   (Hippolytus,   *Refutation   of   All   Heresies*   7.29.5–6
Marcovich)

F11 (DK 31B12; KRS 353; W 9; I 18)

> For there is no way for what-is-not[†] to be born,
> And for what-is to perish is impossible and inconceivable,
> Since wherever it is planted at any time, there it will always be.*

(Ps.-Aristotle, *On Melissus, Xenophanes,
and Gorgias* 975[b]1–4 Bekker)

F12 (DK 31B13; W 10; I 19)

> Nor in the totality is there anything empty or overfull.

(Aëtius, *Opinions* 1.18.2 Diels)

F13 (DK 31B8; KRS 350; W 12; I 21)

> Listen now to a further point: no mortal thing
> Has a beginning, nor does it end in death and obliteration;
> There is only a mixing and then a separating of what was mixed,
> But by mortal men these processes are named 'beginnings'.

(Aëtius, *Opinions* 1.30.1 Diels)

F14 (DK 31B9; KRS 351; W 13; I 22)

> But when fire meets with aither,* mixed in the form of a man,[†]
> Or in the form of the race of wild beasts, or in that of shrubs,
> Or in that of birds, then men talk of things 'being born';
> And again, when separation occurs, they talk of 'grim death'.
> Their language follows their rules,[†] and I too assent to convention. 5

(Plutarch, *Against Colotes* 1113a11–b2 Einarson/de Lacy)

F15 (DK 31B23; KRS 356; W 15; I 27)

> Consider two painters, men well versed by wisdom
> In their craft, at work decorating votive offerings:
> With their hands they take hold of the colourful pigments,
> And mix them harmoniously, using more of some, less of others.
> With these pigments there is nothing whose likeness   5
> They cannot reproduce: they give us trees, men and women,
> Animals, birds, and water-dwelling fish, and long-lived gods,
> Highest in honour.* In the same way let not your mind be cowed

Into accepting the falsehood that there is any other source
For all the countless mortal things that have become manifest;   10
But know this clearly, since you have heard the tale from a god.

> (Simplicius, *Commentary on Aristotle's 'Physics'*,
> CAG IX, 160.1–11 Diels)

F16 (DK 31B96; KRS 374; W 48; I 62)

And the kindly earth in her well-built† cauldrons
Received, out of a total of eight, two parts† of bright Nestis
And four of Hephaestus, and they became white bones
Put together with the divine† glues of Harmony.*

> (Simplicius, *Commentary on Aristotle's 'Physics'*,
> CAG IX, 300.21–4 Diels)

F17 (DK 31B22; KRS 388; W 25; I 37)

For all these things†—the flash of fire, earth, sky,
And sea—are one with those portions of themselves
Which have separate existence in the midst of mortal things.
And they, if strongly suited for blending, have likewise
Been made by Aphrodite to resemble and cleave to one another,   5
But if hostile,† they draw far apart from one another, especially
In their birth and their blending and the moulding of their forms,
In no way accustomed to union, and filled with misery
Under the influence of strife, because it was responsible for their
   birth.*

> (Simplicius, *Commentary on Aristotle's 'Physics'*,
> CAG IX, 160.28–161.7 Diels)

T6 (DK 31A78) Empedocles says that flesh is the product of an equal blend of the four elements and sinews of fire and earth mixed with double the amount of water; that creatures' nails and claws are the product of sinews which have been cooled down by meeting with air; that bones are the product of two parts of water and earth, and four of fire, when these parts have become mixed together inside earth; and that sweat and tears occur when blood dissolves and is diffused in addition to thinning out.   (Aëtius, *Opinions* 5.22.1 Diels)

T7 (DK 31A28; I CTXT-19b) Empedocles makes the corporeal elements four—fire, air, water, and earth. They are eternal, but change in respect of quantity and fewness by combination and separation. But the things which most deserve to be called principles, in the sense that these four elements are set in motion by them, are love and strife. For the elements are bound to be in constant alternating motion as they are at one time combined by love and at another separated by strife. The upshot is that, according to Empedocles, there are six first principles. (Simplicius, *Commentary on Aristotle's 'Physics'*, CAG IX, 25.21–6 Diels)

F18 (DK 31B16; W 11; I 20)

> For they are as they were† and will be, and never, I think,
> Will boundless time be emptied of the two of them.

> (Hippolytus, *Refutation of All Heresies*
> 7.29.10.4–5 Marcovich)

F19 (DK 31B21; KRS 355; W 14; I 26)

But come, consider this evidence for my former account,
If any aspect of it was left defective and unformed –
The sun, with its white appearance and pervasive warmth;
The immortals,* bathed in heat and bright light;
Rain water, dark and cold wherever it is found;   5
And from the earth there flow things dense† and solid.
Under wrath they are all distinct in form and separate,
Under love they come together and are desired by one another.
They are the roots of all that was and is and will be;
From them trees sprang, and men and women,   10
Animals, birds, and water-dwelling fish, and long-lived gods,
Highest in honour. For they are just themselves,
And by running through one another they gain
Different characteristics. So great is the change that mixing causes.*

> (Simplicius, *Commentary on Aristotle's 'Physics'*,
> CAG IX, 159.10.3–16 Diels)

F20 (DK 31B17; KRS 348, 349; W 8; I 25)

A double tale shall I tell. For at one time they grew to be one, alone,
Instead of many, and then again they divided into many instead of
one.
The birth of mortal things is twofold, and twofold their departure.
When the roots all meet the one is born and destroyed,

And when they divide again the other is nourished and dispersed. 5
The roots never cease from continuous alternation:
Now are they brought together by love until all are one,
Now all are borne asunder by the hostility of strife,
Until they grow together as one and the totality is overcome.[†]   8a
Thus, in that they have learnt to become one from many
And turn into many again when the one is divided,   10
In this sense they come to be and have an impermanent life;
But in that they never cease from continuous alternation,
They are for ever unchanging in a cycle.
But come, hear my words! For learning will extend your mind.
As I have already said, in explaining the limits of my words,   15
A double tale shall I tell. For at one time they grew to be one, alone,
Instead of many, and then again they divided into many instead of
    one—
Fire and water and earth and the boundless height of aither,[†]
And, separate from them, deadly strife, alike on every side,
And, among them, love,[†] equal in length and breadth.   20
Look on her with your mind; do not use your eyes and sit
    bewildered.
She is regarded even by mortals as inherent in their bodies,
And thanks to her they can feel affection and perform deeds of unity;
The names by which they call her are Joy and Aphrodite.
No mortal man has seen her whirling among the roots,   25
But I would have you attend to the true course of my account.
The roots are all equal and just as old as one another,
But each has a different domain and its own rightful place,
And they rule in turn, one after the other, as time goes around.
Nothing comes into existence or ceases to exist; there is only
    them.   30
For if they were constantly perishing, they would no longer exist.
What might increase this totality? Where might such a thing come
    from?
And how could it perish,[†] since there is nothing that lacks them?
No, they are just themselves, and by running through one another
They become now this and now that, and remain for ever the
    same.   35
But under love we unite into a single ordered whole,
Which under strife once again becomes, instead of one, many,

From which arise all that was and is and will be hereafter.
From them trees sprang, and men and women,
Animals and birds and water-dwelling fish, and long-lived gods,   40
Highest in honour. Under strife they never cease
From shooting up in frequent swirls . . .

[*some lines of fragmentary or disconnected text*]

Try to ensure that my tale reaches not just your ears,   61
And as you listen perceive the truth that is all around you.
I will show your eyes too that the elements meet a larger body.
First there is the gathering and the disclosure of the stock—
Of however many still remain today of this generation,   65
Not only among the wild beasts that roam the mountains,
But among human beings of both genders, and also among the
  crops
Of the root-bearing fields and the grapes that cluster on the vine.
Let these tales bring undeceitful proofs to your mind:
For you will see the gathering and the disclosure of the stock.   70

> (pieced together from: Simplicius: *Commentary on
> Aristotle's 'Physics'*, CAG IX, 158.1–159.4 Diels;
> *P. Strasb. gr.* Inv. 1665–1666, a(i)6–a(ii)4; and
> *P. Strasb. gr.* Inv. 1665–1666, a(ii)21–30)

F21 (DK 31B35; KRS 360; W 47; I 61)

But now I shall return to a part of my song whose course
I went through before, and I shall channel this account
From that one. When strife had come to the innermost depths[†]
Of the whirl, and love had reached the centre of the vortex,
Where all these things come together to be one, alone,   5
Not suddenly, but combining reluctantly[†] from various directions,
Their mixture caused countless species of mortal things to pour
  forth;
But among those being mixed were many which remained unmixed,
All those which strife still curbed from above; for not yet[†] had it
  moved
Entirely and blamelessly to the outer limits of the circle,   10
But partly it remained within and partly it had left the body of the
  universe.
Anywhere hastily abandoned by strife immediately saw the invasion

Of blameless love, the encroachment of the gentle and immortal one.
Suddenly there was a change of ways: things which before were
   immortal
Began to grow as mortal, things formerly unmixed as mixed.   15
As they were being mixed, countless species of mortal things poured
   forth,
Put together with all kinds of forms, a wonder to behold.

> (pieced together from: Simplicius, *Commentary on Aristotle's
>   'On the Heavens'*, CAG VII, 529.1–15 Heiberg; and
>   Simplicius, *Commentary on Aristotle's 'Physics'*,
>   CAG IX, 32.13–33.2 Diels)

F22 (DK 31B26; W 16; I 28)

One after another the roots prevail as the cycle goes around,
Fading into one another and increasing as their appointed turn
   arrives.
For they are just themselves, and by running through one another
They become men and all the other kinds of creatures,
Now being brought together by love into a single orderly
   arrangement,   5
Now being borne asunder by the hostility of strife,
Until they grow together as one and the totality is overcome.
Thus, in that they have learnt to become one from many
And turn into many again when the one is divided,
In this sense they come to be and have an impermanent life;   10
But in that they never cease from alternation,
They are for ever unchanging in a cycle.

> (Simplicius, *Commentary on Aristotle's 'Physics'*,
>   CAG IX, 33.19–34.3 Diels)

F23 (DK 31B36; W20; I 32)

   As the roots were coming together, strife was withdrawing to the
      extremity.

> (Aristotle, *Metaphysics* 1000[b]2a Ross)

T8 (DK 31A75; KRS 382) Empedocles said that when the human
race was first born from the earth, a day took as long to pass as a ten-
month period does now, because the sun's motion was slow. As time
went on, a day came to be as long as a present seven-month period.

That is why both ten-month and seven-month foetuses are viable, since the nature of the universe has seen to it that a baby grows in the single day on which it is also born.   (Aëtius, *Opinions* 5.18.1 Diels)

T9 [*In the course of a sustained criticism of Empedocles*] And then he needs an argument to support his contention that they [*love and strife*] occupy equal periods of time.   (Aristotle, *Physics* 252ª31–2 Ross)

T10 (DK 31A42) He also says that the universe is in the same state now under strife as it was before under love.*   (Aristotle, *On Generation and Destruction* 334ª5–7 Joachim)

F24 (DK 31B27; KRS 358; W 21; I 33)

> There neither the swift limbs of the sun are distinct
> <Nor . . .>†*
> And so it is kept fast by the firm lid of Harmony,
> A rounded sphere, delighting in its blessed† stability.

> (Simplicius, *Commentary on Aristotle's 'Physics'*,
>   CAG X, 1183.30–1184.1 Diels)

F25 (DK 31B29, 28; KRS 357; W 22; I 34)

For from its back no two branches spring and rush;
It has no feet, no nimble knees, no genitals for procreation,
But is equal to itself from every direction, and entirely boundless,*
A rounded sphere, delighting in its encircling solitude.*

(Hippolytus, *Refutation of All Heresies* 7.29.13.3–5 Marcovich)

F26 (DK 31B134; KRS 397; W 97; I 110)

> For its body is not equipped with a humanoid head;
> From its back no two branches spring and shoot,
> Neither do feet, nor nimble knees, nor hairy genitals,
> But it is only mind, sacred and inexpressibly vast,
> Rushing through the whole world with swift thoughts.*   5

(Ammonius, *Commentary on Aristotle's 'On Interpretation'*,
                                        CAG IV.5, 249.6–10 Busse)

F27 (DK 31B31; W 24; I 36)

> For one by one all the limbs of the god were starting to quiver.

> (Simplicius, *Commentary on Aristotle's 'Physics'*,
>   CAG X, 1184.4 Diels)

T11 (DK 31A49; I 40) For as aither was separated off, it was raised upwards by wind and fire, and it was what it came to be: the broad, vast, encircling heaven. As for the fire, it remained a short distance inside the heaven, and it grew to become the rays of the sun. Earth withdrew into one place and when solidified by necessity it emerged and settled in the middle. Moreover, aither, being much lighter, moves all around it without diversion.*   (Philo, *On Providence* 2.60)

F28 (DK 31B20; W 26; I 38)

> . . . First in the case of the glorious mass of the human body:
> Now we† are joined together and united by love as limbs
> Which have all obtained a body at the prime of life,
> Only later to be torn asunder by evil discord,
> And they each wander separately by the shore of life.   5
> And the same goes for shrubs, for fish in their watery homes,
> For mountain-dwelling wild beasts, and for winged gulls.*

> > (Simplicius, *Commentary on Aristotle's 'Physics'*,
> > CAG X, 1124.12–18 Diels)

F29 (DK 31B57; KRS 376; W 50; I 64)

> Here many heads sprang up without necks,
> Mere arms were wandering around without shoulders,
> And single eyes, lacking foreheads, roamed around.

> > (pieced together from Simplicius, *Commentary
> > on Aristotle's 'On the Heavens'*, CAG VII,
> > 586.12 and 587.1–2 Heiberg

F30 (DK 31B61; KRS 379; W 52; I 66)

> Many grew with faces and breasts on both sides,
> And man-headed bull-natured creatures, and again there arose
> Bull-headed man-natured creatures, and mixtures of male
> And female, equipped with shade-giving limbs.*

> > (Aelian, *On the Nature of Animals* 16.29.5–8 Hercher)

F31 (DK 31B62; KRS 381; W 53; I 67)

But now hear the account that follows of how the shoots
Of the wretched human race, men and women, were raised at night
By fire as it separated. The tale is true and informative.
First there arose from the earth whole-natured shapes

With a portion of both water and heat, 5
Their arising forced by the urge of fire to reach its kin.
Not yet did they display bodies fair with limbs,
Nor voices, nor again the human characteristic of speech.[†]

(Simplicius, *Commentary on Aristotle's 'Physics'*,
CAG IX, 381.31–382.3 Diels)

F32 (DK 31B128; KRS 411; W 118; I 122)

They did not worship Ares or the battle's rage,
Their gods were not Zeus and Cronus and Poseidon,
But the lady Cypris <. . .>
They sought her blessing with pious statues,
With animal paintings and infinitely varied fragrances, 5
With offerings of pure myrrh and scented frankincense,
And by pouring on to the ground libations of yellow honey.
No altar was bathed with the unspeakable[†] slaughter of bulls;
In fact, there was no greater abomination among men
Than to deprive a creature of life and to eat[†] brave limbs. 10

(Porphyry, *On Abstinence* 2.21.7–9, 2.27.39–41 Nauck)

F33 (DK 31B130; KRS 412; W 119; I 123)

Every creature and every bird was tame and amenable
To men, and everywhere kindness blazed forth.

(Scholiast on Nicander, *Creatures of the Wild* 452,
Keil 36)

F34 (DK 31B124; KRS 403; W 114; I 118)

Alas! Poor wretched race of mortal creatures!
What discord and grief have given you birth!

(Clement, *Miscellanies* 3.14.2.6–7
Stählin/Früchtel)

F35 (DK 31B115; KRS 401; W 107; I 11)

It is an oracle of Necessity, an ancient decree of the gods,
Eternal and securely sealed with broad oaths,
That when one goes astray and pollutes his body with murder—
One of the spirits to whom long life has been allotted[†]— 5
For thirty thousand seasons he wanders far from the blessed ones.
In time he assumes[†] all the various forms of mortal things

And exchanges one hard path of life for another.
For the power of aither pursues him into the sea,
And the sea spits him on to dry land, and the earth into the
   beams   10
Of the blazing sun, and the sun casts him into the whirling aither.
Each in turn receives him, but to all he is loathsome.
Now I too am one of these, an exile from the gods, a wanderer,
Putting my trust in the insanities of strife.*

> (pieced together from: Plutarch, *On Exile* 607c10–d1
> de Lacy/Einarson; and Hippolytus, *Refutation of
> All Heresies* 7.29.14–23 *passim* Marcovich)

F36 (DK 31B117; KRS 417; W 108; I 111)

For in the past I have already been a boy and a girl,
A shrub and a bird and the fish that leaps from the sea as it
   travels.†*

> (Hippolytus, *Refutation of All Heresies* 1.3.2.3–4 Marcovich)

F37 (DK 31B136; KRS 414; W 122; I 127)

Will you not end the terrible sounds of your murder? Do you not see
That in your thoughtlessness you are eating one another?

> (Sextus Empiricus, *Against the Professors* 9.129.2–3 Bury)

F38 (DK 31B137; KRS 415; W 124; I 128)

A father raises up his own son in a different form and slaughters him
With a prayer, the utter fool, while the son sheds bitter tears
And begs for mercy from the sacrificer.† Deaf† to his reproaches,
   the father
Slaughters the victim in his home and prepares a vile meal,
And likewise a son takes his father, children their mother,   5
Deprive them of life and consume their own flesh.

> (Sextus Empiricus, *Against the Professors* 9.129.5–10 Bury)

F39 (DK 31B141; KRS 419; W 128; I 132)

> Wretches, utter wretches, keep your hands off beans!

> (Aulus Gellius, *Attic Nights* 4.11.9.4 Marshall)

F40 (DK 31B132; W 95; I 4)

Prosperous is the man who has gained the wealth of divine thinking,

Wretched is he who cares not for clear thinking about the gods.

(Clement, *Miscellanies* 5.140.5.1–4 Stählin/Früchtel)

F41 (DK 31B84; KRS 389; W 88; I 103)

> Think of someone who plans a journey on a winter's night,
> And prepares a lamp, a burning source of fire's gleam;
> He attaches linen screens against winds from all quarters,
> And they scatter the breath of the winds as they blow,
> But as much of the light as is finer pierces through the screens   5
> And keeps shining with its untiring rays across the threshold.
> So at that time she* gave birth† to the round-faced eye,
> Primal fire enclosed within membranes and fine linens,†
> Which protected the fire against the depths of the surrounding
>   water,   10
> But let through to the outside as much of the fire as was finer.

(Aristotle, *On the Senses* 437ᵇ26–438ᵃ3 Bekker)

F42 (DK 31B100; W 91; I 106)

This is the way that all creatures inhale and exhale: spread over
The surfaces of all their bodies are thinly blooded channels of flesh,
And at the mouths of these channels the outer extremities of the skin
Have been pierced right through by numerous furrows,* so that the
    blood
Is contained, but a clear route has been cut with passages for
    aither.   5
Then, at the back-rush of the glistening blood from these furrows
There is an inrush of aither, turbulent in a surging swell;
And when the blood leaps back, aither is exhaled again. It is just like
    when
A young girl plays with a clepsydra of shiny bronze:
When she covers the mouth of the pipe with her pretty hand   10
And dips it into the glistening body of sparkling water,
No† water enters the vessel, but the bulk of the aither† from inside
Presses against the numerous holes and holds the water back,
As long as it covers the dense current. But then,
As the wind leaves, a due amount of water enters.*   15
It is the same when she holds water in the depths of the vessel,
With the mouth and the channel blocked by mortal flesh:
By its inward impulse the aither outside restrains the water

At the gates of the ill-sounding vessel whose extremities it controls,
Until she removes her hand, and then, contrary to what happened
    before,   20
As the wind pours in, a due amount of water rushes out.
Thus, when in its swift course along its paths[†] the glistening blood
Rushes back again towards the inner recesses, immediately
A current of aither enters in a seething swell, but when the blood
Leaps back, aither is exhaled back out again in equal measure.   25

(Aristotle, *On Breathing* 473^{a}9–474^{a}6 Bekker)

T12 (DK 31A86; KRS 391, 392) Empedocles gives a similar account
of all the senses, explaining perception by means of the accommodation of things into the channels of each sense organ. That, he says, is
why they cannot discern one another's proper objects: the channels
of some of the senses are too wide, of others too narrow, for the
object of perception, so that some objects of perception make their
way through without any contact, while others cannot enter at all.*

He also tries to describe the organ of sight. He says that its interior
is fire, and that this inner fire is surrounded by earth and air,[†] which
the fire can penetrate (think of the light in lanterns) because it is
rarefied. There are alternate channels of fire and water in the eye, and
we recognize pale things by means of the channels of fire and dark
things by means of the channels of water, since each of those kinds of
channels can accommodate each of those kinds of things. The colours
travel to the eye thanks to the emanations which objects give off.

Not all creatures' eyes have the same composition, but some are
made of the same elements, while others are made of the opposite
elements, and some have fire in the middle, while others have fire on
the outside. That is why some creatures can see better by day and
others at night; those which have less fire see better by day, because
the inner fire in their eyes is brought up to par by the external fire,
while those which have less of the opposite element see better at
night, because their deficiency too is supplemented. And under the
opposite conditions the opposite is true: those with an excess of fire
cannot see well in the daytime, because when their inner fire is
increased still further during the day it spreads and covers the channels of water; while those with an excess of water are in the same
situation by night, because the fire in them is covered by the water.
This goes on until, in the one case, the water is extracted by the

external light, and in the other case the fire is extracted by the external air. For in each case the opposite is the cure. The best blend for an eye is when it is a compound of both fire and water in equal proportions; this is the most effective eye. This is more or less what he says about vision.

He says that hearing is a result of noises from outside,[†] when the inside is set in motion by the voice and resonates.[†] For the organ of hearing (which he calls a 'fleshy offshoot') is like a bell for sounds of equal size,[*] and the air, when set in motion, strikes against the solid part of the ear and creates a sound.

Smell, he says, is due to the act of breathing, and that is why the people with the keenest sense of smell are those in whom the movement involved in breathing is strongest. The strongest odour emanates from rarefied and light objects. He does not devote separate analyses of how and thanks to what organs taste and touch occur, except in so far as he gives the account common to all the senses that perception occurs by the accommodation of objects to channels. And he says that we feel pleasure thanks to things which are similar in respect of both their parts and their blend, and pain thanks to things which are dissimilar.

He gives the same kind of account of thinking and ignorance as well, in the sense that he says that thinking occurs thanks to similars and ignorance thanks to dissimilars; in other words, he is assuming that thinking is either identical to or very similar to sense-perception. For after giving a list of how we recognize each element thanks to each element,[*] he adds at the end that from these elements[†]

> all things have been firmly fitted together,
> And by means of them they think and feel pleasure and pain.[*]

Hence, he says, it is principally thanks to blood that we think, because it is in blood, more than in any of the other bodily parts, that the elements are equally blended.[†]

Those people in whom the elements are equally or almost equally blended, and in whom they are not widely spaced, nor again small or too large, are the most intelligent and have the keenest senses; then those who most closely approximate to this condition are proportionately less intelligent and perceptive, and those who are in the opposite state are the most unintelligent. Those whose elements are in a widely spaced and loosely textured condition are slow and

laborious in their thinking, while those whose elements are compact
and broken up into fine particles are quick and throw themselves into
a lot of projects, but achieve little because of the rapidity of the
motion of their blood. Those who have a temperate blend in one part
only are clever in this one respect; so, for instance, some are good
speakers, while others are craftsmen, depending on whether this
blend occurs in their hands or in their tongues. And the same goes
for other abilities.   (Theophrastus, *On the Senses* 7–11 Stratton)

F43 (DK 31B105; KRS 394; W 94; I 96)

> The heart, nourished in the ebb and flow of seas of blood,
> Is the main seat of what men call understanding,
> For understanding is the blood around the heart.*

> (John of Stobi, *Anthology* 1.49.53 Wachsmuth/Hense)

T13 (DK 31A89) *On why the Heraclean stone attracts iron.** Empedocles says that iron moves towards the stone thanks to the emanations which flow from both the two objects, and thanks to the fact
that the stone's channels are commensurate with the emanations
from the iron. For the stone's emanations displace and stir the air
which is in the iron's channels, blocking them up, and once this air
has been removed the emanation flows all at once and the iron
follows. As these emanations travel from the iron to the stone's
channels, because they are commensurate with the channels and fit
in with them, the iron too follows and moves along with the emanations.   (Alexander of Aphrodisias, *Questions*, 2.23.1–8 Bruns)

T14 (DK 31A87) Some believe that anything that is acted upon is
acted upon when the agent (that is, the proximate agent, which is the
agent in the strictest sense of the word) enters it through certain
channels, and they say that this is how we see and hear and so on for
all the other senses, and moreover that things are visible through
transparent media such as air and water because such media have
channels which are too small to see, but of which there are many,
arranged in rows, and the more transparent a thing is, the more of
these channels it has. In addition to proposing this theory in certain
cases, those involving agents and the things they act upon, some,
including Empedocles, say[†] that mixture takes place between things
whose channels are mutually accommodating. (Aristotle, *On
Generation and Destruction* 324^{b}25–35 Joachim)

T15 (DK 31B69; W 141; I CTXT-61) That Empedocles too is aware that there are two periods of gestation is shown by the fact that he called women 'twice-bearing', mentioned the amount by which the number of days of one gestation exceeds the other, and described eight-month embryos as unviable.   (Proclus, *Commentary on Plato's 'Republic'* 2.34.25–8 Kroll)

T16 (DK 31A81) Others, like Empedocles, say that sexual differentiation happens in the womb. They say that seeds which enter the womb when it is warm become males, and those which enter a cold womb become females, and that the cause of heat or coldness in the womb is the menstrual flow, which can be either cooler or warmer, and either more in the past or more recent.   (Aristotle, *On the Generation of Animals* 764^{a}1–6 Bekker)

T17 (DK 31A81) Anaxagoras and Empedocles agree that males are born when the seed flows from the right side and females when it flows from the left side, but although they agree on this issue, they are at odds on the question of how children come to resemble their parents. On this matter Empedocles has the following to say, after discussing the subject:[†] If both parents' seeds* were equally warm, the offspring is a male which resembles the father; if both parents' seeds were equally cold, the offspring is a female which resembles the mother. However, if the father's seed is warmer and the mother's cooler, a boy will be born whose features resemble those of the mother; but if the mother's is warmer and the father's cooler, a girl will be born who resembles the father . . . [*On twins*] Empedocles did not state reasons why division takes place, but only said that separation occurs, and that if both seeds came to occupy equally warm locations, they would both be born male; if they came to occupy equally cool locations they would both be born female; and if they occupied locations of which one was warmer, the other cooler, the offspring would be of different sexes.   (Censorinus, *On Birthdays* 6.6–10 Jahn)

F44 (DK 31B98; KRS 373; W 83; I 98)

> And anchored in the perfect harbours of Cypris*
> Earth encountered, in more or less equal proportions,
> Hephaestus and water and bright-shining aither—
> Perhaps a little more of one or, relatively, less of another[†]—

Which gave rise to blood and the forms of flesh in general.*   5

> (Simplicius, *Commentary on Aristotle's 'Physics'*,
> CAG IX, 32.6–10 Diels)

F45 (DK 31B90; W 75; I 90)

> Thus sweet fastens on to sweet, bitter seeks out bitter,
> Sour goes to sour, and spicy quickly seizes on spicy.†
>
> (Plutarch, *Table Talk* 663a8–9 Hoffleit)

F46 (DK 31B48; W 42; I 55)

> The earth makes night by getting in the way of the sun's beams.
>
> (Plutarch, *Platonic Questions* 1006e13 Cherniss)

F47 (DK 31A55, B45; W 39; I CTXT-38, F52) There are some who
say that the sun is first [*in order from the earth*], the moon second, and
Saturn third. But the more usual view is that the moon is first, since
they say that it is in fact a fragment of the sun. Hence Empedocles
says:

> A round, derived light, it whirls around the earth.

(Achilles, *Introduction to Aratus' 'Phanomena'* 16.43.2–6 Maass)

T18 (DK 31A50) Empedocles says that the lateral distance of the
world is greater than the height from the earth to the sky—that is,
than the vertical extension from us here on earth, the sky being more
spread out in this direction, since the world lies very much like an
egg.*   (Aëtius, *Opinions* 2.31.4 Diels)

T19 (DK 31A50) Empedocles says that in its circuit the sun circum-
scribes the boundary of the world.   (Aëtius, *Opinions* 2.1.4 Diels)

T20 (DK 31A50) Empedocles says that the summer solstice lies to
the right of the world and the winter solstice to the left.   (Aëtius,
Opinions 2.10.2 Diels)

T21 (DK 31A51) Empedocles says that the heavens are ice-like as a
result of having been compounded from what is frost-like.
(Achilles, *Introduction to Aratus' 'Phanomena'* 5.34.29–30 Maass)

T22 (DK 31A49 *Nachtrag*) Nor, on the other hand, should we follow
Empedocles, who says that the heaven has been preserved for all this

time and still is because its rotational motion happens to be faster than its innate downward tendency. (Aristotle, *On the Heavens* 284ᵃ24–6 Allan)

T23 (DK 31A53) Empedocles says that the fiery nature of the heavenly bodies is a result of the fire-like stuff which the air contained within itself and then squeezed out at the time of the original separation. (Aëtius, *Opinions* 2.13.2 Diels)

T24 (DK 31A54) Empedocles says that the fixed stars are fastened to the ice, while the planets are free. (Aëtius, *Opinions* 2.13.11 Diels)

T25 (DK 31A59) According to Empedocles a solar eclipse is the result of the moon moving beneath the sun. (Aëtius, *Opinions* 2.24.7 Diels)

T26 (DK 31A60) Empedocles says that the moon is condensed cloud-like air, and is solidified by fire, with the result that it is impure. (Aëtius, *Opinions* 2.25.15 Diels)

T27 (DK 31A60) When the moon is in its first quarter it appears to be shaped not like a sphere but a lentil or a discus, and on Empedocles' view that is its basic shape. (Plutarch, *Roman Questions* 288b11–14 Babbit)

F48 (DK 31B73; W 62; I 76)

> Just as then Cypris, busy about the forms, after moistening
> The earth with water gave it swift fire to harden it up.

(Simplicius, *Commentary on Aristotle's 'On the Heavens'*, CAG VII, 530.6–7 Heiberg)

T28 (DK 31A68) Empedocles thinks water is heated by the fires which the earth keeps hidden inside itself in many places, if the fires are adjacent to ground through which a fiery flash can pass by means of the waters. We are accustomed to make 'snakes' and 'milestones'* and devices of all kinds of shapes, inside which we build pipes which are surrounded by thin bronze and which coil around in such a way that water, by repeatedly circling around the same fire, can flow for the distance needed to produce heat; and so the water enters cold and flows out hot. Empedocles thinks that the same thing goes on underground. (Seneca, *Questions about Nature* 3.24.1.4–3.2 Oltramare)

T29 (DK 31A69) Why are stones solidified by hot water more than they are by cold? Is it because stone is the result of the removal of moisture, and moisture is removed more thoroughly by heat than it is by cold? If so, petrifaction is a result of heat, and Empedocles is right when he says that rocks and stones are produced by hot waters.[†]   (Ps.-Aristotle, *Puzzles* 937ª11–16 Bekker)

H. E. Barnes, 'Unity in the Thought of Empedocles', *Classical Journal*, 63 (1967), 18–23.

M. van der Ben, *The Proem of Empedocles' Peri Physeos: Towards a New Edition of All the Fragments* (Amsterdam: Grüner, 1975).

—— 'Empedocles' Cycle and Fragment 17.3–5 DK', *Hermes*, 112 (1984), 281–96.

N. B. Booth, 'Empedocles' Account of Breathing', *Journal of Hellenic Studies*, 80 (1960), 10–16.

A. Chitwood, 'The Death of Empedocles', *American Journal of Philology*, 107 (1986), 175–91.

N. Demand, 'Pindar's *Olympian* 2, Theon's Faith and Empedocles' *Katharmoi*', *Greek, Roman and Byzantine Studies*, 16 (1975), 347–57.

D. J. Furley, 'Empedocles and the Clepsydra', in [26], ii. 265–74 (first pub. *Journal of Hellenic Studies*, 77 (1957)).

D. W. Graham, 'Symmetry in the Empedoclean Cycle', *Classical Quarterly*, 38 (1988), 297–312.

B. Inwood, *The Poem of Empedocles* (Toronto: University of Toronto Press, 1992).

C. H. Kahn, 'Religion and Natural Philosophy in Empedocles' Doctrine of the Soul', in [30], 426–56 (first pub. *Archiv für Geschichte der Philosophie*, 42 (1960)).

P. Kingsley, 'Empedocles' Sun', *Classical Quarterly*, 44 (1994), 316–24.

—— *Ancient Philosophy, Mystery, and Magic: Empedocles and Pythagorean Tradition* (Oxford: Oxford University Press, 1995).

H. de Ley, 'Empedocles' Sexual Theory: A Note on Fragment B 63', *L'Antiquité classique*, 47 (1978), 153–62.

A. A. Long, 'Thinking and Sense-perception in Empedocles: Mysticism or Materialism?', *Classical Quarterly*, 16 (1966), 256–76.

—— 'Empedocles' Cosmic Cycle in the Sixties', in [30], 397–425.

H. S. Long, 'The Unity of Empedocles' Thought', *American Journal of Philology*, 70 (1949), 142–58.

J. Longrigg, 'The "Roots of All Things"', *Isis*, 67 (1976), 420–38.

J. Mansfeld, 'Ambiguity in Empedocles B17, 3–5: A Suggestion', *Phronesis*, 17 (1972), 17–39.

E. L. Minar, 'Cosmic Periods in the Philosophy of Empedocles', in [21], 39–58 (first pub. *Phronesis*, 8 (1963)).

D. O'Brien, *Empedocles' Cosmic Cycle* (Cambridge: Cambridge University Press, 1969).

—— 'The Effect of a Simile: Empedocles' Theories of Seeing and Breathing', *Journal of Hellenic Studies*, 90 (1970), 140–79.

—— 'Empedocles Revisited', *Ancient Philosophy*, 15 (1995), 403–70.

C. Osborne, 'Empedocles Recycled', *Classical Quarterly*, 37 (1987), 24–50.

D. Sedley, 'The Proems of Empedocles and Lucretius', *Greek, Roman and Byzantine Studies*, 30 (1989), 269–96.

—— 'Empedocles' Theory of Vision and Theophrastus' *De Sensibus*', in W. W. Fortenbaugh and D. Gutas (eds.), *Theophrastus: His Psychological, Doxographical and Scientific Writings* (New Brunswick, NJ.: Rutgers University Press, 1992), 20–31.

F. Solmsen, 'Love and Strife in Empedocles' Cosmology', in [26], ii. 221–64 (first pub. *Phronesis*, 10 (1965)).

—— 'Eternal and Temporary Beings in Empedocles' Physical Poem', *Archiv für Geschichte der Philosophie*, 57 (1975), 123–45.

S. S. Tigner, 'Empedocles' Twirled Ladle and the Vortex-supported Earth', *Isis*, 65 (1974), 433–47.

F. A. Wilford, 'Embryological Analogies in Empedocles' Cosmology', *Phronesis*, 13 (1968), 108–18.

T. D. Worthen, 'Pneumatic Action in the Klepsydra and Empedocles' Account of Breathing', *Isis*, 61 (1970), 520–30.

M. R. Wright, *Empedocles: The Extant Fragments* (New Haven: Yale University Press, 1981).

G. Zuntz, 'Empedocles' *Katharmoi*', in id., *Persephone: Three Essays on Religion and Thought in Magna Graecia* (London: Oxford University Press, 1971), 179–274.

THE ATOMISTS

(LEUCIPPUS OF ABDERA, DEMOCRITUS OF ABDERA)

Together, Leucippus and Democritus are often called the 'early' atomists, to distinguish them from their famous later successors, Epicurus and his school, who took over and developed their teaching. We know so little of Leucippus, however, that there is no point in treating him separately from his colleague and contemporary, Democritus, and indeed even Aristotle often treated them simply as a doublet. Democritus was an extremely prolific writer, and the sheer volume of his work seems to have swamped that of his slightly older colleague. Because of the number of his writings, there are many implicit and explicit references to him; Aristotle's responses to him pervade works such as *Physics* and *On Generation and Corruption* at a deep and implicit level. The testimonia translated below are only a small proportion of the available evidence.

Although Diels/Kranz attribute nearly 300 fragments to Democritus (and two to Leucippus), they contain little of their most important work, for which we have to rely on testimonia. In fact, a great many of Democritus' fragments are ethical quips, and over eighty of these are attributed in our source to 'Democrates'. Since we know of no Democrates, and since a couple of the maxims are elsewhere attributed to Democritus by name, most scholars have long assumed that Democritus was meant. But for the atomic theory and its ramifications we are entirely dependent on testimonia, and it is clear from extant book titles and testimonia that Democritus covered not only familiar Presocratic chestnuts such as embryology and why magnets attract iron, but also wrote books on mathematics and geometry, geography, medicine, astronomy[1] and the calendar, Pythagoreanism, acoustics and other scientific topics, the origins of humans and animals, and even literature and prosody. Importantly, it is also clear that not only did he cover this wide range of topics, but he covered them in some depth—for instance, by raising and answering possible objections. He was therefore an important bridge between the dogmatism of many of the Presocratics and the fully fledged philosophy of Plato.

The basic premises of the atomic system are that all that exists is atoms and void, that (in response to Parmenides) both of these had always

---

[1] We know of some of the astronomical and meteorological views of both Leucippus and Democritus (they occasionally differ in this domain), but for reasons of space I have not given any of the relevant testimonia here, so as to focus on their more important contributions.

existed (that is, that void no less than atomic matter satisfies Parmenidean criteria for being), that atoms are in constant motion through the void, and that all things are made up of atoms and void. **T1–3** are good Aristotelian summaries of the basic atomist position, **T4** and **F1** reproduce some of their arguments for the existence of void,[2] and **T6** and **T7** outline a couple of arguments for the eternity of atoms and void. Since the atomists appear to have reached a conclusion about the fundamental structure of the world which echoes our own in naming invisibly minute particles as the basic building-blocks, and since they did this in an age long before microscopes and sophisticated science, we are faced first and foremost with the question how they arrived at this startling conclusion. It was, in fact, a deduction from Eleatic principles, mediated by the ideas of Empedocles that there can be a plurality of indestructible elements, and that all change is mixture. If what-is cannot move, then since the fact of movement is self-evident, there must, the atomists surmised, exist void or non-being (if it is not too paradoxical to say that it exists) to allow for movement. Equally evidently (or at least, evident to the senses), there is change, generation, and destruction, and these kinds of facts must be explained without contravening Parmenidean principles. If change and so on occur at the gross level of the senses, then the reality of things, the unchanging level of things, must be beyond the senses. And so the atomists came to posit a world in which the only two realities were atoms and the void.

Zeno had argued (see p. 78) that if any object is infinitely divisible, it must be divided ultimately either into parts with no finite size (but if so, even infinite parts of no finite size do not add up to an object of any finite size) or parts with finite size (but if so, infinite parts of finite size would add up to an object of infinite size). The atomist response was to deny that objects are infinitely divisible. One can divide them down to minute parts, but the process of division ends there. **T8** is Aristotle's summary of atomist thinking along these lines.

Anaxagoras had argued that the natural substances which are the basic building-blocks of things were infinitely divisible: however much you divide a piece of wood, it will remain wood all the way. But it was presumably Leucippus, as the earliest of the atomists, who made an intuitive leap of genius and proposed that the world was ultimately made up things which do not have qualities, as wood does. He said that if you were to

---

[2] 'Void' means 'empty space', and this is probably how we should understand the atomists. But Sedley (see bibliography below) makes a powerful and interesting case for 'void' and 'what-is-not' referring, for the atomists, not to empty space but to the 'negative substance' (anti-matter?) that occupies empty space. Hence, given the popular conception that to exist is to occupy space, the atomist paradox that what-is-not exists.

continue to divide anything, at some point you would reach things which are not further divisible—they are *atoma*, indivisibles. These atoms do not have qualities themselves (except size, shape, position, and arrangement), but the conglomerations of atoms that we recognize as the things of the world do have qualities. Thus only atoms are the fundamental realities of the world, and everything else is nothing but transient and random con-catenations of atoms.

The indivisibility of atoms is a deduction from the idea that only atoms and void exist (T5): since it is void that allows any kind of change to take place, including division, then if there is something solid to offset void, it must be totally solid—that is, entirely free of void—and so indivisible and indestructible. T9 adds that for the early atomists atoms were indivisible because they had no parts—division being division into parts—but if this is not an Epicurean contamination, it is probably only a restatement of the voidlessness of the atoms. A 'part' is at least theoretically separable from the whole of which it is part, and so if an atom had parts it would have something separable, which would introduce void into it. However, there is a potential difficulty for the early atomists here: given that the atoms have size and shape, then parts of them are distinguishable. One can talk about the jagged bits of a toothed atom, for instance, or the corners of a square one. It is possible, then, that while Leucippus and Democritus insisted on the actual indivisibility of atoms, they accepted their theor-etical divisibility, despite the talk in T9 about atoms having no parts.

The account of the formation of compound bodies in, for instance, T3 and T5 makes it clear that this is a random event, due to the accidental collisions of atoms as they fall through the infinite void.[3] How, then, can Leucippus say, at F2, that nothing happens at random? 'At random' here means 'in vain'; the kind of necessity Leucippus is referring to is sheer physical necessity: given their three basic qualities—shape, arrangement, and position—the atoms are bound to form compounds; and given that there are infinite compounds in an infinite void, all possible compounds will be formed. But any compounds will be temporary, however long-lasting, because each atom must retain its independence: being solid, it cannot merge with any other solid atom. Of the three basic qualities, as T2 clearly shows, 'shape' is self-explanatory, 'position' refers to the orienta-tion of the atom, and 'arrangement' refers to their situation relative to other atoms. To these three basic qualities, one could add size, which is not mentioned in many of the testimonia only because difference of size is

---

[3] This is presumably why the atomists felt the need to claim that there were infinitely many atoms. Given infinite space, there is no reason for atoms to be in one part of it rather than another (Aristotle, *Physics* 203[b]25–8), so there must be infinitely many atoms. On the likely prevalence of this kind of argumentation at all levels of atomism, see Makin [64].

taken for granted. As for the size of atoms, although as the basic and quality-less elements of things they are necessarily minute, an atom is not actually defined in virtue of its small size, but only in virtue of its freedom from void, and according to **T10** (and some other incidental testimonia) it is therefore theoretically possible for there to be vast atoms. But since atoms by definition have no secondary qualities such as colour (**T2**), and since the reason they have no such secondary qualities is presumably because of their minute size, it seems unlikely that the atomists held that there were enormous atoms, and certainly our earliest and best evidence is that all atoms fell below the threshold of perception (**T1**, **T3**).

Not unnaturally, given their views, the atomists were led to a deep suspicion of the evidence of the senses, and even to a kind of scepticism (**F4**). If **T11** is to be trusted, Democritus' reasons for this scepticism went further than just the contrast between the evidence of the senses and what reason tells us about the realities of the world. He also (like his fellow Abderite, Protagoras) pointed to the relativity of sense-impressions to justify his doubts about the senses; however, whereas Protagoras adopted the relativist position that, in cases of clashing perceptions, all perceptions are true, Democritus concluded that none of them is true. And from this it follows, as **F3** suggests, that to attribute any quality to anything is no more than a convenience and a convention. However, the continuation of **F3** shows that Democritus' began and ended his scepticism with the senses; he believed that we could reach the truth by means of our intellect. His doubts about the senses are also reflected in his account of their working and his important explanation of the objects of sense in **T12** and especially the long (and often obscure) **T13**.[4]

But this straightforward picture of scepticism is not the full story. **T13** contains an analysis of perceptible properties: we perceive something as salty, say, because of the shapes of the configurations of the atoms involved. It follows from this that the senses must give us access to the truth. Since atomic configurations of such-and-such a kind will always and inevitably produce on our tongues an impression of saltiness, then that impression of saltiness is reliable. Moreover, elsewhere (**T14**), and in apparent contradiction to **T11**, Aristotle bluntly says that according to Democritus the senses give us truth. On the one hand, then, Democritus found the evidence of the senses unreliable; on the other hand, he found them reliable. How can we resolve this dilemma? He must have made a distinction between the ontological or scientific statement 'X is sweet',

---

[4] For help with understanding the difficulties of **T13** see the articles by Baldes (1975 and 1978), Burkert, and von Fritz. At any rate, it is clear that Democritus was consistent in reducing everything to spatial properties, relations, and motions, so that his account of the senses was purely mechanistic and materialistic. For the sense in which the word 'mechanistic' applies to ancient atomism, see Furley [17], ch. 2.

which means that 'X has its atoms configured in such a way as to produce sweet taste on the tongue', and the empirical statement 'X is sweet', made by someone as a result of her subjective experience of eating strawberries. The first kind of statement is objectively true; the second is not true, but a product of convention.

In roughly the middle of **T13** Theophrastus tells us that for Democritus the atoms had weight. This is somewhat surprising in view of the traditional insistence that the atoms had only three properties—shape, position, and arrangement. However, it is supported by **T15** too. Perhaps Democritus and the doxographical tradition felt, as I have already suggested, that size was too obvious a property to stress, and also that weight was an obvious concomitant of size. Since the weight of compounds varies according to how much void there is in them, then two equal-sized atoms must have the same weight, since by definition they have no void in them, and therefore the larger an atom is the heavier it must be. It looks as though **T16** is wrong, then, in distinguishing Democritus from Epicurus on this score; certainly the report does not inspire confidence in claiming that Democritus attributed only two properties, size and shape, to atoms.

But if atoms had weight, can we also specify their motion in the void? In other words, should we say (as Epicurus did) that they had downward motion? But Epicurus had to introduce his doctrine of the 'swerve' to explain how atoms with the same motion could ever come into contact and form compounds, and there is no sign of any such doctrine in the early atomists. On the contrary, Aristotle complains in **T17** that they did not specify what motion the atoms had. In all likelihood, they thought of the atoms as having random motion, due to all the collisions and reboundings that were taking place between them (see e.g. **T5**); in other words, they may not have said what, if any, particular form of motion the atoms originally had, before the first collisions and reboundings caused them to have random motion. They stressed the eternity of atoms and void, and therefore the question of what first caused their motion, or what it was like 'before' they began to collide, does not really arise. And it is possible that they spoke of atoms having 'weight' only within a formed or forming world—that is, only once there is a context for the concepts of 'weight' and 'direction' to make sense.

Like all compounds, worlds are chance aggregates of atoms. With perfect consistency, given that there are infinite atoms in infinite void, Democritus held that there were innumerable worlds (**T22**, **T23**). But how were they formed? Or how, at any rate, was our world formed? There are some areas of unclarity in the picture given us by **T18–21**. First, the relevant number and kind of atoms have to become separated from the rest in a sufficient area of void (**T18**); then an Empedoclean or Anaxagorean whirl or vortex arises, which, through the principle of like to like, separates out the broad regions of the world into the familiar Presocratic concentric pattern, with the light elements of fire and air on the periphery outside water and earth (**T20**, **T21**). The whole world is protected by a kind of membrane around the outside (**T19**). However, there are clashes between our sources: talk of a membrane is explicit only in **T19** and has to be read into **T21**, and whereas **T19** has light atoms being 'sieved' out of the whole process of world-formation altogether, **T21** takes the more traditional line that light atoms form the lighter peripheral fire. Also, the account of the formation of the heavenly bodies is different in **T19** and **T21**. Nevertheless, although it is clear that none of our sources had the actual words of Democritus or Leucippus to guide them, the big picture does emerge.

One thing that is clear is that in their account of the origin of worlds, the atomists made considerable use of the principle that like attracts like (on which see **F5**). This is how the original regions of the cosmos were formed. However, generally, we are told that atoms stick together because their shapes allow them to 'become entangled'. It is not at all clear how the atomists reconciled these two processes. Perhaps 'like to like' provides the first impulse for similar atoms to come into contact, and then they form more stable compounds because they can become entangled. But even this cannot be the whole picture, because Democritus speaks of fire atoms as being spherical (**T12**, **T24**), and it is impossible to see how they could become entangled. This remains an area of mystery in the doctrine of the early atomists.

Leucippus and Democritus were thoroughgoing materialist scientists. Even things that we might think of as immaterial are for them no more than conglomerations of atoms. **T24** shows that they regarded soul or mind as atomic, made up of spherical, fiery atoms, because they are the most mobile, and the soul is what imparts movement to living creatures; Democritus also held that soul atoms were distributed evenly throughout the body, with one soul-atom adjoining each body-atom (**T25**). **T24** also shows how the atomists followed through their theory of the composition of the soul into an atomic theory of respiration and life. Even more remarkably, **T26** and **T27** inform us that Democritus regarded the gods as atomic compounds. True, they are particularly large and long-lived compounds, but they have lost their vital Homeric quality of indestructibility, since all compounds of atoms must be liable to dissolution. It was a common belief that dreams were the appearance of the gods to us, and so, just as ordinary vision is the taking in of 'images'—atomic emanations given out by all objects (**T13**)—the dreamt gods too are just such images, perceived while asleep (**T27**, **T29**). Although Democritus accepted that these gods have certain powers, such as foretelling the future,[5] **T28** shows that he deprived them of their traditional functions as bringers of rain and so on. Like his predecessors—and Democritus is in many ways a consummate Presocratic, the epitome of the scientific tendencies of his predecessors[6]—he explained all such phenomena by natural laws. **F6** and **T30–4** display a few interesting theories (and remember also **T10** and **T11** under Anaxagoras, p. 129). **F6** is a particularly interesting conundrum in the days before the concept of the dimensionless point entered mathematics.

Finally, we come to Democritus' ethics. As already remarked, the vast majority of the extant fragments are ethical in content, consisting mainly of sound and rather conservative advice, but stressing above all the good of the individual over the good of the state or group. There are occasional near contradictions within these fragments: in a couple of fragments, for instance, Democritus recommends involvement in the public life of one's community, despite the doubts about the value of this apparently expressed in **F7**. Or again, despite the praise for democracy in **F16**, another fragment appears to support the idea that 'might is right' (DK 68A267). However, a constant theme is the value of moderation in all things (e.g. **F7–11**), with oneself as responsible for one's own condition (**F10**, **F14**). He also stresses the importance of pleasure in various ways, most critically as a criterion (**T35**, **F12–14**). His importance in the history of ethics is that he was the first, as far as we know, to make a single aim—the attainment of 'contentment' (**T35**, **T36**, **F7**, **F8**)—the criterion to be followed when considering whether or not any particular action should be carried out, and, in a manner strongly reminiscent of Socrates, he located the goal of contentment in one's mind rather than in the acquisition of power or money. The contrast between mind (or soul) and body, with the mind taking the authoritative role, is clearly drawn (**F17**, **T37**). The mind is seen as the seat of happiness and misery, reason and emotion, character and intelligence (e.g. **T35**, **F8**). The relationship between contentment and pleasure is not perfectly clear, but it is likely that Democritus thought

[5] How, given Democritus' theory that perception is due to material emanations from the outside world, could he believe in precognition? **T29** shows that he also had a theory to account for telepathy: that a person's intention creates a certain motion among the soul-atoms that emanate from him along with body-atoms. Bicknell 1969 (see bibliography below) speculates that if those atoms from person A were to impinge and make an impression on person B, who later saw A doing what she had intended to do, then B may think he had seen into the future.

[6] This creates an irony in the history of the Presocratics. The first Presocratics turned to natural forces and laws to counter the fickleness of the Homeric gods, but by following this scientism as far as it could go Democritus has returned to a world dominated by chance.

that the most pleasant life overall was the life of moderation and content-ment, and therefore implicitly distinguished these mental or spiritual pleasures from the grosser pleasures of the body. **F18** suggests that he may also have expressed the contrast between physical and mental pleasures in terms of how fleeting and satisfying they were, and also shows that he anticipated Plato in linking pleasure and need (see also **F11**), with need perceived as a kind of pain. Gross hedonism is therefore self-defeating because its pursuit of pleasure leads it to value the pains or needs which will lead to subsequent pleasures.

It is a fascinating question whether there was any explicit connection between Democritus' atomic theory and his ethics. It is relatively easy to suggest that, because the soul is atomic, and because the soul-atoms are spread evenly throughout the body, major disturbances in the soul are to be avoided, as injurious both psychologically and constitutionally. It is also easy to see that in both fields, ethics and physics, Democritus would recommend critical examination of the evidence of the senses, so that (in ethics) one does not necessarily follow an immediate whim, without first seeing whether or not where it leads is truly conducive to one's long-term pleasure. Moreover, in **T22** Hippolytus reports, in effect, that Democritus saw the whole of human life as futile. Since he believed that we inhabit a world which is a chance concatenation of atoms, and may be destroyed at any moment by collision with another world (**T22**), and which is subject to bombardment by alien diseases (**T34**), he might well have encouraged us to achieve contentment, which is also glossed as 'composure', 'equa-nimity', and 'freedom from fear' (**T35**, **T36**). Otherwise his philosophy could easily induce a state of panic!

T1 (DK 67A7; KRS 545; T 48a) Leucippus and Democritus covered everything with a single explanation in a particularly systematic fash-ion, and came up with a first principle that was in accordance with the way things are. Some of the thinkers of old had decided that what-is is single and unmoving, on the grounds that void is non-existent, and that there could be no movement without a separately existing void, nor even a plurality of things without the existence of something to keep them apart . . . Leucippus, however, thought that he had come up with explanations which conformed with the evi-dence of the senses in that they would not do away with generation or destruction or movement, or with the plurality of existing things. But as well as conceding these things to appearances, he also agreed with the monists that there could be no movement without void, that the void is non-existent, and that nothing about what-is can not be. For what really and truly *is*, he said, is a plenum. Nevertheless, he said, this is not single, but there are numerically infinite existents, which are imperceptible because of their minute size. These things are in motion in the void (for the void exists), and their coming together constitutes generation, while their dissolution constitutes destruction. They act and are acted upon wherever they happen to come into contact, but their coming into contact does not make them a single entity. They generate things by combining and becoming entangled with one another, but no plurality, Leucippus said, could arise from what is truly single, nor could a singularity arise from what is truly multiple—that is impossible. Instead (similarly to how Empedocles and some others claim that things are modified and acted upon through their channels) he said that all alterations and all modifications happen in the following way: dissolution and destruction, and growth too, are the results of solid objects slipping in through the void.* (Aristotle, *On Generation and Destruction* 324^{b}35–325^{b}5 Joachim)

T2 (DK 67A6; KRS 555; T 46a) Leucippus and his companion Democritus say that the elements are the full and the void, by which they mean what-is and what-is-not, with what is full and solid being what-is, and what is void and rarefied being what-is-not. Hence they say that what-is has no more existence than what-is-not, because void exists just as much as solidity. These, according to them, are the material causes of things. And just as those thinkers who make the underlying substance single generate everything else by means of the modifications of this single substance, and posit rarefaction and condensation as the sources of these modifications, so Leucippus and Democritus say that differences are responsible for everything else. But they say that there are only three differences—in shape, arrangement, and position. For they say that what-is differs only 'by structure, contact, and inclination', of which 'structure' is shape, 'contact' is arrangement, and 'inclination' is position. So, for instance, A differs from N in shape, AN differs from NA in arrangement, and ⊟ differs from H in position. But just like the other thinkers we have been looking it, Leucippus and Democritus carelessly said nothing about the origin of movement and how things have movement. (Aristotle, *Metaphysics* 985^{b}4–20 Ross)

T3 (DK 68A37; KRS 556; T 44a) A few extracts from Aristotle's *On Democritus* will show the views of these men. 'Democritus thinks that the nature of the eternal existents consists in minute substances, infinite in number. To accommodate them, he assumes that there is an infinitely large place, different from them. He calls this place 'void' and 'no-thing' and 'infinite', and he calls each of the substances 'thing',* 'solid', and 'being'. He thinks that these substances are too small to be perceived by us, that they have all kinds of forms and shapes, and are variously sized. Treating these things as elements, he generates and compounds out of them things which are large enough to be visible and perceptible. These substances are moving in the void in a chaotic state. As a result of their dissimilarities and the differences I have just mentioned, as they move they collide and become entangled with the kind of entanglement that makes them in contact with and adjacent to one another, but fails to generate anything whatsoever with a truly single nature out of them, since it is perfectly stupid, according to Democritus, to think that something which was two or more could ever become one. He attributes the ability of the substances to stay together to the extent that they do to the ways in which they fit together and seize hold of one another. For they have countless differences—they may be crooked, for instance, or hooked or concave or convex. So he thinks that they hold on to one another and stay together for a certain amount of time, until some stronger force from around them comes along and shakes them and breaks them up.' The creation he speaks of, as well as its contrary, dissolution, happens not only to living creatures, but also to plants, worlds, and in short to all perceptible bodies. So if creation is the combination of atoms, destruction is their dissolution, and according to Democritus creation is just modification.   (Aristotle [fr. 208 Rose] in Simplicius, *Commentary on Aristotle's 'On the Heavens'*, CAG VII, 294.33–295.24 Heiberg)

T4 (DK 67A19; T 52b) Their arguments are, first, that without void it is inconceivable that there could be such a thing as change of place (i.e. movement and increase), since it is impossible for a plenum to be receptive of anything. If a plenum could receive something, two objects would be in the same place, and then you could have any number of bodies coinciding, since it would be impossible to specify

a point at which this coincidence would stop ... These considerations gave them one way to demonstrate that there is such a thing as
void, and a second argument is based on the observation that some
things contract and are compressed. For instance, they claim that a
wine-cask can hold not only the wine, but also the wineskins which
the wine is in,* and they explain this by claiming that a compressed
body contracts into the void which is within it. Third, they all use
void to explain the phenomenon of growth, the point being that food
is a body, and it is impossible for two bodies to coincide.* They also
cite as evidence what happens to ash: ash in a vessel can hold as much
water as an empty vessel can.*   (Aristotle, *Physics* 213^{b}4–22 Ross)

F1 (DK 68B156; T 178c) There is no more reason for thing to exist
than for no-thing to exist.*   (Plutarch, *Against Colotes* 1109a7–8
Einarson/de Lacy)

T5 (DK 67A14; KRS 557, 584; T 57) The opinion of Leucippus,
Democritus, and Epicurus on the first principles was that they are
numerically infinite, indivisible and atomic, and that nothing can
happen to them because they are 'solid' and have no void in them.
That is, they claimed that division takes place because of the void in
bodies. They said that these atomic bodies (which were separated
from one another in the infinite void, and differ from one another in
shape, size, position, and arrangement) are in motion in the void,
and that as they overtake one another they collide, and that while
some rebound in random directions, others become entangled, if
their shapes, sizes, positions, and arrangements are conformable,
and stay together, and so bring about the generation of compound
entities.   (Simplicius, *Commentary on Aristotle's 'On the Heavens'*,
CAG VII, 242.18–26 Heiberg)

T6 (T 69b) Those who say, as Democritus of Abdera does, that this
is just what has always happened, and regard this as a first principle,
are wrong and fail to state the necessity of the cause. They say that
nothing boundless has a beginning, but a cause is a beginning, and
what always exists is boundless, and therefore, he says, to ask for a
cause for anything of this kind is to look for a beginning for something that is boundless.   (Aristotle, *On the Generation of Animals*
742^{b}17–23 Bekker)

T7 (DK 68A71; T 64a) But with a single exception [*Plato*] everyone is clearly in agreement about time: they all say that time is not generated. In fact, Democritus even uses this to disprove the notion that everything is generated; after all, he says, time is not generated. (Aristotle, *Physics* 251ᵇ14–17 Ross)

T8 (DK 68A48b; T 49) The assumption that there exists a body that has magnitude, and that it is everywhere divisible, and that this division is possible, creates problems. For what will there be that survives the division? ... A magnitude? But that is impossible, because it means that there is still something that has not been divided, whereas *ex hypothesi* the body was everywhere divisible. On the other hand, if no body or magnitude remains, and yet the division will occur, then either the body consists of points and the things out of which it is made have no magnitude, or it will be nothing at all in the first place. If this is the case, then, the body in question would consist and be composed of nothing, and would itself be nothing at all, just an illusion ... This, then, is the argument which apparently forces one to conclude that there are atoms possessed of some magnitude. (Aristotle, *On Generation and Corruption* 316ᵃ14–317ᵃ1 Joachim)

T9 (DK 67A13; KRS 558; T 50a) Those who denied infinite divisibility, on the grounds that we are unable to divide anything infinitely, and therefore cannot prove the possibility of unceasing division, said that bodies are composed of indivisibles and are divisible into indivisibles. However, whereas Leucippus and Democritus attribute the indivisibility of the primary bodies not only to the fact that nothing can happen to them, but also to the fact that they are minute and have no parts, Epicurus later said that although they did have parts, the fact that nothing can happen to them still guarantees their indivisibility. (Simplicius, *Commentary on Aristotle's 'Physics'*, CAG X, 925.10–17 Diels)

F2 (DK 67B2; KRS 569; T L1) In his *On Mind* Leucippus says: 'Nothing occurs at random, but everything happens for a reason and because it has to.' (Aëtius, *Opinions* 1.25.4 Diels)

T10 (DK 68A43; KRS 561; T 63a) Epicurus and Democritus held these views [*the basic notions of atomism*], but they disagreed with each other in so far as one of them maintained that all atoms were minute and that this is why they are imperceptible, while the other,

Democritus, claimed that there could even be enormous
atoms. (Dionysius in Eusebius, *Preparation for the Gospel*
14.23.3.1–5 Dindorf)

F3 (DK 68B9a, 9b, 10, 6, 7, 8, 11; KRS 549, 550, 554; T 179a) Democritus occasionally does away with sensible phenomena, saying that
none of them really and truly presents itself to the senses, but is
only thought to do so, while the only truth in existing things is the
existence of atoms and void. He says: 'Sweet exists by convention,
and so does bitter, warm, cold, and colour; in reality there are atoms
and void.' . . . And in *Confirmations* . . . he says: 'In actual fact we
have no certain understanding, but our grasp on things changes
depending on the condition of our bodies, of the things that enter
into it, and of the things that impinge upon it.' Again, he says: 'That
we have no true understanding of what anything is or is not like has
often been demonstrated.' And in his *On Forms* he says, 'It is
important for a person to use this criterion to realize that he is
removed from reality'; and again, 'This is yet another argument
which demonstrates that in reality we know nothing about anything,
but that belief restructures things for each of us'; and again, 'However, the difficulty of knowing what anything is in reality will be
clear.'

   In these passages, then, he rejects apprehension more or less
entirely, even though his remarks are aimed in particular at the
senses. But in *Criteria* he says that there are two kinds of knowledge,
one which comes through the senses and the other which comes
through thinking, and he calls the one that comes through thinking
'genuine', and ascribes to it trustworthiness in the assessment of
truth, while the one that comes through the senses he calls 'bastard',
and denies that it is reliable in the discernment of truth. His actual
words are: 'There are two forms of knowledge, one genuine, the
other bastard. To the bastard kind belong all the following: sight,
hearing, smell, taste, touch. But the other kind is genuine and is far
removed from the bastard kind.'   (Sextus Empiricus, *Against the
Professors* 7.135.1–139.4 Bury)

F4 (DK 68B117; T D15) In reality we know nothing; for the truth
is hidden in an abyss.   (Diogenes Laertius, *Lives of Eminent Philosophers* 9.72.10 Long)

T11 (DK 68A112; KRS 548; T 177) Then again, along the same lines some thinkers have concluded that the truth about appearances depends on what is perceived. They think it wrong to assess the truth by majorities and minorities, and point out that the same thing appears sweet to some of those who taste it and bitter to others; the upshot of this, they claim, is that if everyone were ill or insane, except for two or three healthy or sane people, it is the latter who would be thought ill or insane, not the former. They also say that many other creatures perceive things in ways that directly contrast with the ways we perceive them, and even a single individual does not always perceive things the same way. It is unclear, then, which of these perceptions are true and which are false, since the one lot is no more or less true than the other. This is why Democritus, at any rate, says that either nothing is true or at least that the matter is unclear to us.   (Aristotle, *Metaphysics* 1009ª38–ᵇ12 Ross)

T12 Granted that sensible qualities are perceived by us but do not essentially inhere in bodies, some of them, according to Democritus, are inevitable consequences of the aggregation of certain kinds of atoms (as, for example, fire gains the sensible quality of heat as a result of the aggregation of spherical atoms—a sphere being mobile) . . . while others give an impression of change, thanks to the changing position and arrangement of the atoms, although the compounds are preserved. . . . For example, the same body seems now pale and now dark, or now cold and later hot, as a result of changes in the position and arrangement of the atoms in the compound. Fire, however, always appears the same, even if the atoms out of which it is composed change their positions, because spherical atoms always have the same effect on us.   (Philoponus, *Commentary on Aristotle's 'On Generation and Destruction'*, CAG XIV.2, 17.20–32 Vitelli)

T13 (DK 68A135; KRS 574, 589; T 113) Democritus says that sight is due to the manifestation of things in the eye, but he gives a peculiar account of this manifestation. He says that it does not occur immediately in the pupil, but that the air between the organ of sight and the seen object is compressed by the seen object and the seeing eye (for according to him everything is constantly giving off an emanation) and so gains an imprint of the object, and then, since the air is solid and is of a different colour to the pupil, it manifests in the eyes, which are moist.* A firm object cannot receive any such imprints, but a moist one lets them through, and that is why moist eyes have better sight than hard eyes—provided (a) that the outer membrane is particularly fine and firm, (b) that the inner parts of the eye are as spongy as possible, as free as they can be of firm, tough flesh, and filled† with thick, oily liquid; (c) that the channels in the eyes are straight and dry, so that they conform to the imprints, because everything finds it easiest to recognize what is akin to itself* . . .

His account of hearing closely resembles what others have said on the matter. He says that the air enters the empty part of the ear and causes a disturbance. Although in fact air is entering the whole body in the same way, it enters most easily and in the largest quantities through the ears, because there it finds the largest amount of empty space to pass through and so hardly lingers at all. That is why only this part of the body perceives sounds. Once the air is inside the body, it spreads out as a result of its speed, since sound occurs when the air is compressed and is forced into the body. In other words, just as he explains perception on the outside of the body as due to touch, so he also explains perception inside the body in the same way. People can hear best, he says, if (a) their outer membrane is firm, (b) their channels are empty, as dry as possible, and open over the whole body as well as the head and ears, (c) their bones are firm and their brain is well-tempered and the matter surrounding it is as dry as possible. These conditions ensure that the sound is not be broken up as it enters, since it passes through a considerable area that is empty, dry, and open, and spreads rapidly and evenly throughout the body, without escaping to the outside . . .

This is how he explains sight and hearing; his account of the remaining senses closely resembles what one finds in the majority of other authorities. On thinking, he says only that it happens when the mind's blend is moderate. Things change, however, he says, if the mind becomes too hot or too cold, and that is why in days past men were right to suppose that under these circumstances a person was not in his right mind. It is clear, then, that he attributes thinking to the composition of the body—which is perhaps not an unreasonable view for someone who makes the mind corporeal . . .

Democritus does not give the same account of all sensible qualities, but explains some by the size of their atoms, others by the shapes of their atoms, and others by the arrangement and position of their atoms . . . He explains heaviness and lightness in terms of size. For, he says, if every item were to be divided up, then even though there would be different shapes, nevertheless the weight of things is naturally related to their size. The same does not go for compounds, however, which are lighter if they contain more void, and heavier if they contain less. This is what he says at some points, but elsewhere he says that a thing is light simply because of its fineness.

He gives pretty much the same account of hardness and softness, saying that something compact is hard, and something loose is soft, and explaining degrees of hardness or softness along exactly the same lines. However, there is a difference between the position and accommodation of void spaces in things that are hard and soft, and in things that are heavy and light, which explains why iron is harder than lead, but lead is heavier than iron: iron has an irregular composition, consisting of considerable areas of void interspersed with some solidity, with generally more void than lead, whereas lead has less void and a regular composition, with an equal distribution of void and solidity throughout. Hence it is heavier, but softer, than iron.

That is what he has to say about heavy, light, hard, and soft. As far as the rest of the sensible qualities, he says that none of them really exists, but that they are all modifications brought about by changes in our sensory apparatus, which is what causes an impression to arise. He even denies real existence to heat and cold, claiming instead that changes in us are caused by changes in the configuration of atoms, on the grounds that only a tightly packed mass has the power to prevail, whereas something that is distributed over a wide area is imperceptible. And as proof of the fact that sensible qualities have no real existence he points to the fact that they do not appear the same to all creatures; what is sweet for us may be bitter for other creatures, and may be sour or pungent or astringent to yet others, and the same goes for other qualities.

Democritus also claims that people differ in composition according to their state* and their age. This too makes it clear, he says, that condition is responsible for impression, and in general that is how he would have us think about sensible qualities. However, as in other cases, so here too he attributes them also to the configurations.* He does not explain which configurations are responsible for all sensory qualities, but focuses on tastes and colours—and even where these are concerned he goes into more detail about the configurations responsible for tastes, while referring the actual impression to the person concerned.

Sour taste, then, is angular and twisted in its configuration, and small and light. Because of its sharpness it rapidly penetrates throughout the body, and because it is rough and angular it acts as a cohesive and contractive agent. That is why it warms the body by creating empty spaces within it; for the more void a thing contains the warmer it is.

Sweet taste consists of configurations that are rounded and not too small. Hence it serves basically to relax the body, and it gently and unhurriedly accomplishes all its work. It disturbs the other tastes, because as it makes its way through the body it pushes the others off course and moistens them. Once they have been moistened and moved from their usual arrangement they stream into the stomach, which is the easiest place for them to go since there is more void there than anywhere else.

Astringent taste consists of large, angular configurations, without the slightest roundedness. When these configurations enter the body, they clog and block the channels and stop their contents flowing, which is why astringent tastes cause constipation.

Bitter taste consists of configurations that are small, smooth, and rounded, but with a roundedness that also contains wrinkles; that is why it is viscous and sticky.

Saltiness is the taste made up of configurations which are large and, so far from being rounded, are only occasionally crooked,[†] so that they are not especially twisted. By describing them as crooked he means that they can interlock[†] and become entangled with one another. These configurations are large because saltiness comes to the surface of things, whereas if they were small and were in a position to be struck by things around them they would get mixed up with everything else. They are not rounded, because saltiness is rough, whereas roundedness is smooth. And they are not entirely crooked, because they do not readily become entwined,[†] which is why salt is friable.

Pungent taste is small, rounded, and angular, without crookedness. This is because pungent taste,[†] through being small, rounded, and angular, warms and relaxes the body with its roughness. After all, that is what angularity is like.

He also attributes all the other qualities a thing may have to configurations in the same way. But he does say that no configuration is pure—that is, free from admixture with others.† In every configuration there are many shapes, so that a single taste consists of configurations that are smooth and rough, rounded and sharp, and so on. It is the dominant configuration which prevails with regard to the sensory apparatus and determines which quality will be perceived. It also depends on what kind of condition it finds when it enters the body. For this makes quite a bit of difference too, since the same configuration can sometimes have opposite effects, and opposite configurations the same effect. Anyway, so much for what Democritus has to say about tastes . . .

He says that there are four simple colours. What is smooth is white, since that which is not so rough as to cast a shadow or be hard to penetrate is bright. But bright objects are bound also to have straight channels and to be translucent. White objects that are hard are formed from such configurations—like the inner surface of cockles—because that is what makes them free from shadows, shiny, and straight-channelled. However, white objects that are powdery and brittle are made out of configurations which are rounded and obliquely inclined in their position relative to one another and in their combination in pairs,* and whose general arrangement is highly consistent. Given this make-up, these objects are powdery because the configurations make contact with one another only tangentially, brittle because of their consistent structure, and free from shadows because they are smooth and flat. One object is whiter than another the more its configurations are exactly and purely as described, and the more the arrangement and positioning of the configurations conform to the above description.

That is the configuration of white objects. Something black is made up of the opposite kind of configurations—that is, those which are rough, crooked, and irregular. This is what makes them over-shadowed, with channels that are crooked and hard to penetrate. Moreover, their emanations are sluggish and disrupted. For the quality of the emanation also makes a difference to the impression received, which changes thanks to the air it contains.

The same kind of atoms that make something hot also make something red, except that it takes larger atoms to make something red. The larger the combinations of these same configurations, the more a thing is red. Proof of the fact that redness is composed of configurations of this kind is to be found in the fact that we get hot when we blush, and other objects get hot when placed in a fire, until they turn fiery-red. The larger the configurations, the redder the object—the flames, for instance, and coals of green wood are redder than those of dry wood; and when heated in a fire iron and so on are redder than other similar substances. The brightest objects, however, are those which contain the most fire and the finest fire, while objects are more red if they contain coarser fire and less of it. That is why redder objects are less hot, because only something fine is hot.

Green is a mixture of solidity and void, with the various shades of green dependent upon the position and arrangement of the atoms.

So much for the configurations of the simple colours. The less there are other colours blended in with it, the purer the colour is. The other colours are formed by the mixing of these simple colours. [*Theophrastus then goes on to explain how, according to Democritus, a range of other colours are formed by mixing two or more of the simple colours.*] (Theophrastus, *On the Senses* 50, 55–7, 60–7, 73–6 Stratton)

T14 (DK 67A9; KRS 562; T 42a) Democritus and Leucippus thought that the truth lay in appearance, but since they appreciated that appearances are contradictory and infinite, they made the shapes of the atoms infinite. The upshot of this is that, on their view, it is as a result of changes in the compound that the same thing has contradictory appearances to different people. (Aristotle, *On Generation and Corruption* 315^{b}9–12 Joachim)

T15 (DK 68A60; KRS 573; T 48a) Now, Democritus does say that each of the indivisibles is heavier the larger it is . . . (Aristotle, *On Generation and Corruption* 326^{a}9–10 Joachim)

T16 (DK 68A47; KRS 576; T 60a) Democritus said that the atoms had two properties, size and shape, while Epicurus added weight as a third. (Aëtius, *Opinions* 1.3.18 Diels)

T17 (DK 67A16; KRS 577; T 53) Hence Leucippus and Democritus, who claim that the primary bodies are in constant motion in the infinite void, should state what kind of motion they mean, and what kind of motion is natural to these primary bodies. (Aristotle, *On the Heavens* 300^{b}8–11 Allan)

T18 (DK 67A10; T 78) Leucippus was a companion of Zeno, but did not hold the same views as Zeno. He says that things are infinite in number and always in motion, and that generation and change are continually happening. He says that the elements are the full and the void. He explains the generation of worlds as follows: when many bodies congregate and rush together from the surrounding region into a large void, they collide and those with similar shapes and formations get entangled with one another; as a result of their entanglements the heavenly bodies are generated, and they wax and wane by necessity—but he fails to explain what this necessity might be.   (Hippolytus, *Refutation of All Heresies* 1.12.1–2 Marcovich)

T19 (DK 67A1; KRS 563; T 77a) Worlds are created as follows. A number of atoms with all kinds of shapes move 'by being cut off from the infinite' into a large void area, where they gather together and produce a single whirl. In this whirl they collide with one another and, as they move around in all kinds of ways, they begin to separate from one another, with atoms moving towards those to which they are similar. When there are too many of them for them any longer to rotate in equilibrium, the light atoms move out into the void, as if from a sieve, while the rest of them stay together and, as they become entangled, race along together with one another, and so create a first spherical composite body. This spherical body billows out like a membrane and encloses within itself all kinds of atoms. As these varied atoms whirl around with pressure provided by the centre of the system, the surrounding membrane becomes thinner, because atoms, connected by contact with the whirl, are constantly streaming together. So the earth was created, once those atoms that had moved down to the centre stayed together. Then again, the surrounding membrane (so to call it) grows by the influx[†] of atoms from outside, because as it is moved around by the whirl, it incorporates any atoms with which it comes into contact. Some of these incorporated atoms become entangled and form a composite body which at first is damp and muddy, but they dry out as they revolve along with the whirl of the whole system, and then ignite and form the heavenly bodies.   (Diogenes Laertius, *Lives of Eminent Philosophers* 9.31.3–32.11 Long)

T20 (DK 68A69; KRS 568; T 71a) Then there are others who even attribute this world of ours and all the worlds to spontaneity. They say that the rotation is a spontaneous event—that the motion which separated things out and established the orderly nature of the world began spontaneously.   (Aristotle, *Physics* 196ᵃ24–8 Ross)

T21 (DK 67A24; T 79a)   The world with its arched shape was formed as follows: atoms are moving continually and extremely fast with random and haphazard movements, and when a large number of bodies gather in the same place, they acquire a variety of shapes and sizes. Once they have gathered in one place, some (those which are larger and heavier) just settle down, while those which are small, round, light, and smooth are squeezed out by the convergence of the atoms and move up into the higher regions. When, as a result of this upward movement, the ability of the atoms to collide waned and their collisions were no longer driving atoms towards the upper regions, since these upper atoms were prevented from moving downwards, they were forced towards the regions that could receive them—that is, the surrounding periphery—and in addition the majority of the atoms took on an arched formation.* By becoming entangled with one another at this vault, they generated the heavens. Various kinds of atoms with the same basic nature, as I have said, formed the heavenly bodies once they were pushed out towards the upper regions. The majority of the bodies that rose up like vapour collided with the air and squeezed it out. Once the air was formed into wind by this movement and surrounded the heavenly bodies, it began to drive them around and to keep their present rotation up in the heavens. Next the earth was generated out of the atoms that were settling down, and the sky, fire, and air from those that were rising up. There was a great deal of matter contained within the earth and as this was thickened by the winds which buffeted it and by the slipstreams from the heavenly bodies, every tiny formation was squeezed out of the earth and generated moisture. Since it was in the nature of this moisture to be fluid, it was carried down into the hollows, and into those places that were able to contain and support it, or alternatively the water itself, just by standing there, hollowed out the places where it became established. This is how the principal parts of the world were generated.   (Aëtius, *Opinions* 1.4.1–4 Diels)

F5 (DK 68B164; KRS 570; T D6)   Democritus, however, bases his argument [*for the attraction of similars*] on animate as well as inanimate things. 'Even animals', he says, 'flock together with animals of the same kind—doves with doves, cranes with cranes, and so on for all other species of irrational animal. And the same goes for inanimate objects, as one can see in the case of seeds that are being sieved or pebbles on a beach. In the first instance, seeds are separated out by the whirling of the sieve—lentils fall with lentils, barley with barley, wheat with wheat; in the second instance, thanks to the motion of the waves, oblong pebbles are thrust into the same part of the beach as other oblong pebbles, and round ones end up with other round ones, as though the similarity in things possessed the ability to draw things together.' (Sextus Empiricus, *Against the Professors* 7.117–18 Bury)

T22 (DK 68A40; KRS 565; T 78) Democritus' views on the elements, the full and the void, are the same as those of Leucippus. He calls the full 'what-is' and the void 'what-is-not'. He spoke as if things were perpetually in motion in the void, and said that there was an infinite number of worlds of various sizes. Some of them do not have a sun or a moon, while others have a sun and a moon that are larger than ours, and others have more suns and moons than we do. He said that the intervals between worlds are unequal, so that in one part there are a larger number of worlds, while elsewhere there are fewer;* that some worlds are growing, while others are at their peak and others are decreasing in size; and that in some places worlds are arising, while elsewhere they are departing. Worlds are destroyed by colliding with one another. Some worlds are uninhabited by living creatures and have no plants or moisture. As for our world, the earth was formed before the heavenly bodies, and the moon is lowest, then the sun, and then the fixed stars. The planets too are not all at the same level. A world is at its peak until it is no longer capable of gaining material from outside. Democritus used to laugh at everything, since he regarded all human affairs as ridiculous. (Hippolytus, *Refutation of All Heresies* 1.13.2–4 Marcovich)

T23 (DK 67A21) Leucippus and Democritus said that there were numerically infinite worlds in the infinite void and that they were composed of numerically infinite atoms. (Simplicius, *Commentary on Aristotle's 'On the Heavens'*, CAG VII, 202.16–18 Heiberg)

T24 (DK 67A28; T 106a) Some say that the soul is above all and primarily that which causes movement, and because they believe that something which does not itself move is incapable of moving anything else, they suppose that soul is one of the things that move. Hence Democritus says that it is a kind of fire and is warm. Among all the infinite variety of shapes and atoms[†] he says that the spherical ones are fire and soul (and that they resemble the so-called motes in the air, which are visible in the sunbeams that come through windows). Like Leucippus, he says that the 'seed-aggregate' of atoms contains the elements of every kind of thing, but that the spherical ones are soul, because of the particular ability of such 'structures' to permeate everything and to move everything else by their own movement (for they suppose that soul is what imparts movement to living creatures). This also explains why they say that breathing is the mark of life. The surrounding atmosphere constricts bodies and squeezes out those atoms whose shape allows them, because they are never at rest themselves, to impart movement to living creatures; and then help comes from outside when other similar atoms enter the body in the act of breathing. These atoms stop the atoms which are inside living creatures from being removed from the body by supporting the effort to resist the forces of constriction and compression. And so, they say, a creature will remain alive as long as it is capable of doing this.   (Aristotle, *On the Soul* 403^{b}28–404^{a}16 Ross)

T25 (DK 68A108; T 110f)

In this context you could never affirm the following doctrine,
Originating with the revered mind of great Democritus:
That the principles of body and soul are arranged alternately,
One matching one, and so knit the body together.

(Lucretius, *On the Nature of the Universe* 3.370–3 Bailey)

T26 (DK 68A74; T 172c) Indeed, it seems to me that even Democritus, as great a man as ever lived, from whose springs Epicurus watered his own little gardens, faltered over the nature of the gods. At one point he holds that there are images endowed with divinity inherent in the world; at another he says that the elements of the mind, which are in this same world, are gods; at another that they are living images which may either help us or harm us; at another that they are certain enormous images, large enough to embrace the whole world from outside. All these ideas are more worthy of Democritus' homeland than of Democritus himself.* I mean, who can understand what he means by these 'images'? Who can revere them? Who can judge them worthy of worship or devotion?   (Cicero, *On the Nature of the Gods* 1.43 Plasberg)

T27 (DK 68B166; T 175b) Democritus says that there are certain images that are encountered by people, some of which are beneficent, others harmful. (That is why he prayed that he would meet propitious images.) These images, he said, are unusually large, and virtually, but not completely, indestructible; and they communicate the future to people when they are seen and by the sounds they make. When men in the old days, then, received an impression of these images, they took them to be a god, but the god, with his indestructibility, was in fact no more than these images.   (Sextus Empiricus, *Against the Professors* 9.19 Bury)

T28 (DK 68A75; T 173a) There are those who believe that our conception of the gods is due to the awesome things that happen in the world. Democritus seems to have been of this opinion, since he says that in ancient times men were frightened of celestial phenomena such as thunder, lightning, thunderbolts, conjunctions of heavenly bodies, and solar and lunar eclipses, and imagined that the gods were responsible for these things.   (Sextus Empiricus, *Against the Professors* 9.24 Bury)

T29 (DK 68A77; T 133a) But on this occasion Favorinus has taken down an ancient argument of Democritus, blackened with smoke, so to speak, and set about cleaning it and polishing it up. The basis of his argument was the familiar view of Democritus that images penetrate into our bodies through our bodily channels and, when they rise up, cause the visions we see when asleep. These images come to us from all over the place, since they are given off even by furniture and clothes and plants, but especially by living creatures, because of their constant restlessness and their warmth. They not only retain in outline the likenesses of the solid bodies which have been impressed upon them . . . but they also enlist and take along with them the reflections of a person's mental impulses and desires, and of his qualities and emotions. When the images strike with this baggage they speak as if they were living creatures, and tell those who receive them the opinions, thoughts, and desires of those whose emissions they are, provided that when they make contact the structure of the images has been preserved and not become jumbled up.   (Plutarch, *Table Talk* 734f7–735b6 Minar)

F6 (DK 68B155; T 164) Consider also how Chrysippus* responded to Democritus' scientific and vividly expressed† puzzle. The puzzle goes: If a cone is cut by a plain parallel to the base, how should one conceive of the surfaces of the segments? Are they equal or unequal? If they are unequal they will make the cone uneven, since it will gain many step-like notches and protuberances. If they are equal, the segments will be equal and the cone will turn out to have the qualities of a cylinder, since it will be composed of equal rather than unequal circles. But this is absurd.   (Plutarch, *On Common Conceptions* 1079e1–10 Cherniss)

T30 (DK 68A139; T 154b) Democritus of Abdera, however, thought that human beings were generated out of water and mud.   (Censorinus, *On Birthdays* 4.9.1–2 Jahn)

T31 (DK 68A143; T 138a) Democritus of Abdera agrees that differentiation into female or male happens in the womb, but denies that it depends on the warmth or coolness of the womb [*as Empedocles supposed*], claiming instead that it depends on the dominance of one or the other parent's semen, coming as it does from that part by which male and female differ from one another.*   (Aristotle, *On the Generation of Animals* 764ª6–11 Bekker)

T32 (DK 68A151; T 145) Democritus remarks that pigs and dogs produce more than one offspring and he explains this by saying that they have a plurality of wombs and places which are receptive of semen. The semen does not fill all these wombs with a single ejaculation, but these creatures mate two or three times, so that the places that are receptive of semen might be filled by the continuity of the emission. He says that mules do not bear offspring because their wombs are unlike those of other animals, being oddly shaped and quite incapable of receiving semen. The reason for this, he says, is that the mule is not a natural creation, but a product of human inventiveness and experimentation, so that you might describe it as an adulterous device or as a counterfeit. 'It seems to me', he says,* 'that an ass once happened to rape a horse, and men learnt from this act of violence and then went on to accustom them to this act of procreation.' (Aelian, *On the Nature of Animals* 12.16.1–15 Hercher)

T33 (DK 68A162) Democritus attributes the shorter life-span and earlier sprouting of straight trees compared with gnarled ones to the same constraints. He says that in straight trees the food, which nourishes the sprouting and the fruit, is quickly distributed, whereas in gnarled trees it is distributed slowly because the part of the tree that is above ground is not open-channelled, and instead the roots themselves consume the food, because gnarled trees have roots that are long and thick . . . He says that the roots of straight trees are weak, and that for both reasons they perish more quickly,[†] since because of the straightness of the channels both cold and heat pass rapidly from the upper part of the tree to the roots, and the roots are too weak to endure this. In general, he says, most straight trees begin to age from their lower parts upwards, because of the weakness of their roots. Moreover, because the parts of the tree above the ground are delicate, they are bent by the wind and disturb the roots, and when this happens the roots get broken and mutilated, and then death spreads from the roots to the whole tree. (Theophrastus, *On the Causes of Plants* 2.11.7.8–8.12 Einarson/Link)

T34 (T 153) All the same, we acknowledge the theory enunciated and written down by Democritus and his followers that it is the influx of alien atoms from the infinity of space, following the destruction of worlds out there, that causes plagues and unusual diseases to arise and assail us.[*] (Plutarch, *Table Talk* 733d6–11 Minar)

T35 (DK 68A167, B170, B171; T 189) Democritus and Plato both locate happiness in the mind. Democritus wrote: 'Happiness and misery are properties of the mind' and 'Happiness does not dwell in cattle or in gold: the mind is the dwelling-place of the guardian spirit.'[*] He calls happiness 'contentment', 'well-being', and 'harmony', and also 'concord' and 'composure'. He thinks that happiness consists in the determination and separation of pleasures, and that this is what is both finest and most beneficial for people. (John of Stobi, *Anthology* 2.7.3 Wachsmuth/Hense)

T36 (DK 68A169; T 188b) We are told (and we have no intention of asking whether or not the story is true) that Democritus blinded himself; at any rate, it is certain that so as to enable his mind to be distracted as little as possible from its contemplation, he neglected his ancestral estate and left his farm uncultivated, because he was searching for—what else?—happiness. Even if he located happiness in knowledge, still he wanted it to be a consequence of his enquiries that he should be of good cheer. After all, he calls the chief good 'contentment' and often 'equanimity', which is to say, a mind freed of fear.   (Cicero, *On the Goals of Life* 5.87.13–21 Mueller)

F7 (DK 68B3; KRS 593; T D27) Contentment comes from not doing too much, in either one's private or public life, and from keeping, in whatever one does, within one's own capabilities and nature. A man must be on guard, so that even if good fortune comes his way and leads him on to more, he can make a decision to lay it aside and not to take on more than he is capable of. A balanced load is safer than a heavy load. (John of Stobi, *Anthology* 4.39.25 Wachsmuth/Hense)

F8 (DK 68B191; KRS 594; T D55) Contentment comes to men from a moderate amount of enjoyment and a life of concord. Deficiencies and excesses have a habit of changing places and causing serious disruption in the mind, and minds which are being disturbed by large swings are neither well balanced nor content. So one should restrict one's intentions to what is within one's power and be satisfied with what is to hand, paying little heed to those who are objects of envy and admiration and certainly not dwelling on them in one's mind. Instead you should consider the lives of those who are badly off, and bear in mind their terrible sufferings, to help you appreciate the importance and desirability of what you have available and to hand, and to ease the mental torment that desiring more brings. The point is that anyone who admires people with possessions and the acclaim of the rest of the world, and who spends his whole time dwelling on them in his mind, is bound to be constantly devising novelties for himself and to be throwing himself, as a result of his desire, into doing something illegal—and then it will be too late to take it back. Hence one should not go in search of such innovations, but should be content with what is to hand. It is important to compare one's own life with the life of those who are worse off, and to count one's blessings by bearing in mind their sufferings and appreciating how much better than them one is doing and faring.

By sticking to this intention you will live with a greater degree of contentment and you will keep at bay quite a few things that can ruin a life—things such as envy, jealousy, and ill-will. (John of Stobi, *Anthology* 3.1.210 Wachsmuth/Hense)

F9 (DK 68B174; T D39) A man who is content, and undertakes actions which are just and legal, is happy asleep or awake, healthy, and carefree. But a man who ignores justice and fails to act as he ought is distressed by the memory of his actions, frightened, and self-reproachful. (John of Stobi, *Anthology* 2.9.3 Wachsmuth/Hense)

F10 (DK 68B234; T D98) In their prayers men ask the gods for health, but they fail to realize that this is within their own power. When their lack of self-control leads them to act in ways that run contrary to health, they themselves betray their health to their desires. (John of Stobi, *Anthology* 3.18.30 Wachsmuth/Hense)

F11 (DK 68B219; T D83) Unless a point of satiety is reached, the desire for money is far more cruel than the utmost poverty, because the greater the desire the greater the need. (John of Stobi, *Anthology* 3.10.43 Wachsmuth/Hense)

F12 (DK 68B188; T D26) The guides to what is good and bad for people are pleasure and pain. (John of Stobi, *Anthology* 3.1.46 Wachsmuth/Hense)

F13 (DK 68B211; T D75) Moderation increases pleasure and exaggerates enjoyment. (John of Stobi, *Anthology* 3.5.27 Wachsmuth/Hense)

F14 (DK 68B214; T D78) It takes courage not only to overcome an enemy, but also to overcome pleasure. Some men are masters of cities, but are slaves to women. (John of Stobi, *Anthology* 3.7.25 Wachsmuth/Hense)

F15 (DK 68B31; T D30) Medicine cures ailments of the body, wisdom removes negative emotions from the mind. (Clement, *The Pedagogue* 1.6.2.1–3 Marrou/Harl)

F16 (DK 68B251; T D115) Poverty in a democracy is as preferable to what is called prosperity under autocracy as freedom is to slavery. (John of Stobi, *Anthology* 3.40.42 Wachsmuth/Hense)

F17 (DK 68B187; T D52) It is fitting for people to regard the soul as more important than the body, because whereas perfection of soul corrects physical worthlessness, physical strength in the absence of reasoning does nothing to improve the soul.   (John of Stobi, *Anthology* 3.1.27 Wachsmuth/Hense)

T37 (DK 68B159; T D34) Democritus says that if the body were to take the soul to court for all the pain and trouble it had endured throughout its life, and he were to judge the validity of the accusation, he would not hesitate to find the soul guilty, first, of having ruined the body by neglect and weakened it by drinking, and, second, of having spoiled and wrecked it by pursuing pleasures, just as he would hold someone who made careless use of a tool or implement responsible for its poor condition.   (Ps.-Plutarch, *On Whether Desire and Grief are Mental or Physical Phenomena* 2.4–11 Sandbach)

F18 (DK 68B235; T D99) All those who derive their pleasures from their guts, by eating or drinking or having sex to an excessive and inordinate degree, find that their pleasures are brief and short-lived, in that they last for only as long as they are actually eating or drinking, while their pains are many. For the desire for more of the same is constant, and when they get what they desire, the pleasure passes rapidly. They get nothing good out of the situation except a fleeting pleasure—and then the need for more of the same recurs.   (John of Stobi, *Anthology* 3.18.35 Wachsmuth/Hense)

C. Bailey, *The Greek Atomists and Epicurus* (Oxford: Oxford University Press, 1928).

R. W. Baldes, 'Democritus on Visual Perception: Two Theories or One?', *Phronesis*, 20 (1975), 93–105.

—— 'Democritus on the Nature and Perception of Black and White', *Phronesis*, 23 (1978), 87–100.

—— '"Divisibility" and "Division" in Democritus', *Apeiron*, 12.1 (1978), 1–12.

—— 'Democritus on Empirical Knowledge: Reflections on DK 68B25 and on Aristotle, *Metaphysics* 4.5', *Ancient World*, 4 (1981), 17–34.

P. J. Bicknell, 'The Seat of the Mind in Democritus', *Eranos*, 66 (1968), 10–23.

—— 'Democritus' Theory of Precognition', *Revue des études grecques*, 82 (1969), 318–26.

I. M. Bodnár, 'Atomic Independence and Indivisibility', *Oxford Studies in Ancient Philosophy*, 16 (1998), 35–61.

W. Burkert, 'Air-imprints or Eidola: Democritus' Aetiology of Vision', *Illinois Classical Studies*, 2 (1977), 97–109.

K. von Fritz, 'Democritus' Theory of Vision', in E. Ashworth Underwood (ed.), *Science, Medicine, and History: Essays on the Evolution of Scientific Thought and Medical Practice*, vol. i (London: Oxford University Press, 1953), 83–99.

D. J. Furley, *Two Studies in the Greek Atomists* (Princeton: Princeton University Press, 1967).

—— 'Aristotle and the Atomists on Infinity', in [25], 103–14 (first pub. in I. Düring (ed.), *Naturphilosophie bei Aristoteles und Theophrast* (Heidelberg: Stiehm, 1969)).

—— 'Aristotle and the Atomists on Motion in a Void', in [25], 77–90 (first pub. in P. K. Machamer and R. J. Turnbull (eds.), *Motion and Time, Space and Matter* (Columbus: Ohio State University Press, 1976)).

P. S. Hasper, 'The Foundations of Presocratic Atomism', *Oxford Studies in Ancient Philosophy*, 17 (1999), 1–14.

C. H. Kahn, 'Democritus and the Origins of Moral Psychology', *American Journal of Philology*, 106 (1985), 1–31.

S. Makin, 'The Indivisibility of the Atom', *Archiv für Geschichte der Philosophie*, 71 (1989), 125–49.

D. McGibbon, 'The Religious Thought of Democritus', *Hermes*, 93 (1965), 385–97.

D. O'Brien, *Theories of Weight in the Ancient World*, vol. i: *Democritus: Weight and Size* (Leiden: Brill, 1981).

J. F. Procopé, 'Democritus on Politics and Care of the Soul', *Classical Quarterly*, 39 (1989), 307–31.

D. Sedley, 'Two Conceptions of Vacuum', *Phronesis*, 27 (1982), 175–93.

C. C. W. Taylor, 'Pleasure, Knowledge, and Sensation in Democritus', *Phronesis*, 12 (1967), 6–27.

—— *The Atomists: Leucippus and Democritus* (Toronto: University of Toronto Press, 1999).

G. Vlastos, 'Ethics and Physics in Democritus', in [26], ii. 381–408, and in [33], 328–50 (first pub. *Philosophical Review*, 54 (1945) and 55 (1946)).

DIOGENES OF APOLLONIA

Diogenes is something of a throwback—a Milesian kind of philosopher in a post-Parmenidean world. He is also an eclectic, borrowing not just from Anaxagoras and Leucippus (as **T1** says, though our evidence for Leucippus is so slight that it is hard for us now to detect his influence), but from Heraclitus too, while his most important debt is to Anaximenes. But he writes clearly, and makes some original contributions. Above all, in **F2** he announces his major new insight, which he thinks will allow him to reinstate monism instead of the pluralism of his immediate predecessors. This insight is that unless everything was essentially related (i.e. was made up of the same underlying stuff) nothing could interact and generation would be impossible.[1] It makes no sense to Diogenes to say that, for instance, Empedocles' four elements, randomly thrown together in certain proportions, can make up the things of this world: bone could not grow out of bone unless there was an underlying unity, and bone could not combine with other substances either unless there was an underlying unity. Like Empedocles and Anaxagoras, Diogenes believes that mixture and separation are responsible for the generation and destruction of things, but unlike them he holds that there is no plurality of elements or substances involved in the mixture and separation. It is tempting also to believe that Diogenes was attracted by the simplicity of his system, as opposed to the formidable complexity of Empedocles and Anaxagoras. We have no evidence as to how Diogenes got around the Eleatic strictures about change and motion, but he probably borrowed the concept of void from Leucippus.

Impressed (as Heraclitus and Anaximander were) with the regularity of large-scale events in the universe, Diogenes posited, like Anaxagoras, a guiding intelligence (**F3**), which he then went on to identify with air, for the reasons given in **F4**. Air turns out also to be his underlying stuff (**F5**).[2]

[1] It is precisely the fact that Diogenes seems to think that this is an innovation that makes one doubt that Anaximenes held the same view, whatever the Aristotelian doxographers said: see pp. 8–9.

[2] Strictly, however, it is a *deduction* from **F5** that air is the underlying matter, rather than just the principle of intelligence; this allows some scholars to deny testimonia such as **T1**, which clearly state that Diogenes' prime matter was air, and claim that Diogenes did not specify what his prime matter was: it was just 'matter' (Barnes [15] vol. ii, ch. 11). But if we start rejecting clear testimonia such as **T1** the study of the Presocratics becomes chaotic; and the fact that Diogenes identifies the governing intelligence with air could be evidence in favour of the view that his underlying stuff was air, since it was typically Milesian to divinize the *arkhē*, and Diogenes is, after all, a latter-day Milesian.

If air is responsible for life, Diogenes seems to have argued, then it is divine, and since life manifestly displays the workings of intelligence, then air is or has intelligence. Intelligence and warmth are related, presumably because a corpse is cold and has no intelligence. Presumably the most powerful intelligence, that of the divine air itself, is warmest. One may guess, then, that the air close to the sun to which Diogenes refers in **F5** is the primary, divine form of air; he may well, then, have been assuming a standard Presocratic universe of concentric spheres of the primary stuffs, with air on the outside controlling the universe as a whole, then fire, then water and earth. The idea that intelligence is warm air, combined with the idea that everything has air in different temperatures, cleverly allows Diogenes to distinguish not just between individuals, but between species, and between animate and (cold) inanimate objects. In **T1** Theophrastus reports that Diogenes attributed all different modifications of air to condensation and rarefaction, as Anaximenes had done, but we can see from Diogenes' own words that different temperature is of prime importance to him. If Theophrastus is right, then, perhaps Diogenes thought that compressed air was cooler or warmer than rarefied air.

Little is known of Diogenes' cosmogonical, cosmological, astronomical, and meteorological views. It is distinctly possible that he was far less interested in them than in the workings of the human body. But there are a few attributions of such views to him (**T2–6**), which are self-explanatory. The rest of the testimonia, and one long fragment, are concerned with human physiology in some way or another. I omit some incidental remarks about embryology, but his theories of perception (**T7**) are remarkable in recognizing the importance of the brain (rather than the heart, the traditional Greek seat of perception), although he was not the first to do so: earlier in the fifth century Alcmaeon of Croton, a physician with Pythagorean philosophical leanings, had pinpointed the brain as the core of perception. The consistency with which he explains everything by means of air is also worth noting. He even went so far as to say that male sperm carries air: since air is the source of life, it has to be essentially involved in conception. In considering **F8**, an account of the veins running through the body, it is worth not just reflecting on the passage as a piece of early medical science (although the principles of symmetry and division into two seem to be as important as observation), but also remembering that for Diogenes, of course, these veins did not just carry blood, but air as well: blood, like semen (which was a product of blood), was aerated. Hence (as we see from **T7**) the intelligence of adult humans: air could be transported all through their bodies.

Diogenes is indeed the last of the Presocratics. Dissatisfied with Parmenides and post-Parmenidean pluralism, he simply ignored what he wanted to ignore and borrowed what he wanted to borrow, to create a neat synthesis. But this opens the door only to further refinements, not to innovative work such as the Milesians or Parmenides or Empedocles had undertaken. Where now could Presocratic philosophy go? At the same time, his evident interest in the workings of the human body shows that Diogenes was truly a thinker of the late fifth century, emphasizing the individual over the cosmos, and the physical rather than the metaphysical.

─────────

T1 (DK 64A5; KRS 598) Diogenes of Apollonia was more or less the last of those who made a study of natural science. He cobbled together most of the ideas of his book from either Anaxagoras or Leucippus. He is another one who says that everything is made up of air, which is boundless and eternal, and that everything else is formed from it by its condensation and rarefaction and change of qualities. That is what Theophrastus records about Diogenes, and the book of his which has survived up to my time, *On Nature*, clearly states that air is that from which everything else comes into existence. (Theophrastus [fr. 226a Fortenbaugh *et al.*] in Simplicius, *Commentary on Aristotle's 'Physics'*, CAG IX, 25.1–8 Diels)

F1 (DK 64B1; KRS 596) This is how Diogenes starts his book: 'It is my opinion that at the start of any book a writer ought to make his starting-point indisputable, and his methodology straightforward and authoritative.'* (Diogenes Laertius, *Lives of Eminent Philosophers* 9.57.12–14 Long)

F2 (DK 64B2; KRS 599) In brief, then, it is my opinion that all existent things are modifications of the same thing and are the same thing. This is transparently obvious: if the things that exist in this universe—earth, water, air, fire and all the other things which plainly exist in this universe—if any of them was different, essentially different, from anything else, rather than being the same but changing and modifying in a number of ways, it would be completely impossible for things to mix with one another, or for one thing to help or harm another, or for a plant to grow from the earth or for a living creature or anything else to come into existence, unless they were all the same thing in terms of their composition. No, all these things are modifications of the same thing: they become differently qualified at different times and return back to the same thing. (Simplicius, *Commentary on Aristotle's 'Physics'*, CAG IX, 151.31–152.7 Diels)

F3 (DK 64B3; KRS 601) Without intelligence it is inconceivable that matters would be disposed in such a way as to contain measures of everything—of winter and summer, night and day, rain and warmth,[†] wind and sunshine. And anyone who cares to think about it will find that everything else too is in the best possible condition.[*] (Simplicius, *Commentary on Aristotle's 'Physics'*, CAG IX, 152.12–16 Diels)

F4 (DK 64B4; KRS 602) Moreover, here is powerful evidence in support of what I have been saying: human beings and all other living creatures are alive because of air, since they breathe. Air is for them both soul and intelligence, as will be explained in this book of mine, and in the absence of air they die and their intelligence fails. (Simplicius, *Commentary on Aristotle's 'Physics'*, CAG IX, 152.18–21 Diels)

F5 (DK 64B5; KRS 603) It is also my opinion that the possessor of intelligence is what men call air, and that everything is steered and controlled by air. I say this because it is my opinion that air is a god, and pervades everything, manages everything, and is present in everything. There is nothing that does not partake of air. However, there is nothing that partakes of air in the same way as anything else; there are many modes not only of air itself, but also of intelligence. For the modes of air are diverse: it may be warmer or cooler, drier or wetter, more or less mobile, and it contains the possibility of many, infinitely many, modifications in terms of taste and colour. In all living creatures soul is the same—air that is warmer than the outside air in which we live, but much cooler than the air near the sun—but in no two living creatures is this warmth identical. After all, even human beings differ from one another in this respect. The difference between creatures is not great, however, but small enough to allow them to be similar. It is impossible, though, for any of the things that undergo modification to become absolutely identical to anything else without actually being the same thing. In so far, then, as modification is diverse, living creatures are diverse too, and there is a plurality of them, with the diversity of modifications responsible for their dissimilar characteristics, ways of life, and kinds of intelligence.

Nevertheless, it is by means of the same one thing that all living creatures live and see and hear, and the rest of their intelligence too stems from the same one thing.   (Simplicius, *Commentary on Aristotle's 'Physics'*, CAG IX, 152.22–153.13 Diels)

F6 (DK 64B7; KRS 604) Although this very thing is an eternal and immortal body, it is thanks to this body† that some things come into existence and others depart.   (Simplicius, *Commentary on Aristotle's 'Physics'*, CAG IX, 153.19–20 Diels)

F7 (DK 64B8; KRS 605) But it seems clear to me that it is great, powerful, eternal, immortal, and possessed of wide knowledge. (Simplicius, *Commentary on Aristotle's 'Physics'*, CAG IX, 153.20–2 Diels)

T2 (DK 64A6; KRS 607) Diogenes of Apollonia supposes that air is the elemental stuff, that everything is in motion, and that there is an infinite number of worlds. His cosmogony is as follows: the universe was in motion and became rare in some places and dense in others; where a dense part coincided with rotational movement it created the earth, and all the other worlds were formed in the same way; but the lightest parts took the upper level and formed the sun.   (Ps.-Plutarch, *Miscellanies* 12 Diels)

T3 (DK 64A12; KRS 608) Diogenes says that the heavenly bodies are pumice-like, and he thinks of them as the breathing-holes of the universe.* The heavenly bodies are fiery, he says. Along with the visible bodies are carried around invisible stones which, being invisible, have gone unrecognized. They often fall to the earth and are extinguished, as happened to the rocky heavenly body that fell in a blaze of fire at Aegospotami.   (Aëtius, *Opinions* 2.13.5 Diels)

T4 (DK 64A13) Diogenes says that the sun is pumice-like, and that its beams are fixed into it from the aither.   (Aëtius, *Opinions* 2.20.10 Diels)

T5 (DK 64A13) Diogenes says that the sun is extinguished by cold which counteracts its warmth.   (Aëtius, *Opinions* 2.23.4 Diels)

T6 (DK 64A16) Diogenes says that fire impacts on moist cloud, and causes thunder by being extinguished and lightning by its brilliance; he also attributes these phenomena to wind.   (Aëtius, *Opinions* 3.3.8 Diels)

T7 (DK 64A19; KRS 612) Diogenes relates sense-perception to air, just as he does life and intelligence. Apparently, then, he attributes perception to similarity, because he says that there would be no action or being acted upon unless everything came from a single thing.*

He says that smell is caused by the air around the brain, there being an accumulation of air there which is commensurate with an odour, since the brain itself is open-textured because of its veins.† But then there are those creatures in whom the condition of the air is not commensurate and fails to mingle with odours—their brains are extremely fine. Obviously, then, perception occurs when there is commensurability with the blending.* Hearing occurs when the air inside the ears is set in motion by the air outside and passes through to the brain. Sight occurs when things are reflected on the pupil, and the pupil, by mixing with the air inside, produces perception. This is proved by the fact that if the veins become inflamed, there is no mixture with what is inside and seeing does not occur, even though the reflection is present just as much as before.* Taste occurs in the tongue, he says, because it is open-textured and soft. He completely fails to explain how touch occurs or what its proper objects are.

Next he tries to describe what is responsible for keener senses and what kinds of creatures have keener senses. Smell is keenest in those who have the least air in their heads, because then the mingling can take place most rapidly. Also, the longer and narrower the channel through which the air is drawn in, the better, because this enables the odour to be detected more quickly. That is why some creatures have a better sense of smell than humans do. All the same, if the odour were composed commensurately with the air in a man's brain, his sense of smell would be excellent.

Those creatures have the sharpest hearing whose veins are fine, and in whom the passages which are as relevant to hearing as to smell are short and fine and straight, and also in whom the ears are upright and large, because it is when the air in the ears moves that it sets in motion the air inside. But if the ears are rather wide, when the air in the ears moves there is an echo and an indistinct noise because the air inside which it meets is not still.

Those creatures see best whose inner air and veins are fine (which is also the case for the other senses too), and whose eyes are brightest. Opposite colours are reflected best, and so dark-eyed people see better in the daytime and see bright objects better, while people with the opposite kinds of eyes see better at night.

That it is the inner air that perceives, as being a fragment of the god, is shown by the fact that often when our minds are preoccupied with other matters we fail to see or hear.

Pleasure and pain occur as follows. When a lot of air mingles with the blood and makes it light, which is a natural occurrence, and pervades the whole body, pleasure is the result. When the unnatural happens and the air does not mingle, the blood gets heavier and weaker and thicker, and pain is the result. The same goes for confidence and health and their opposites. The tongue is what discerns pleasure most,* because it is particularly soft and fine and all the veins are connected to it. That is why so many symptoms of illness can be found on the tongue, and in other creatures their colours are revealed by the tongue; for the variety and quality of these colours are reflected on their tongues. Anyway, so much of how and under what circumstances perception occurs.

As for thinking, as I have already said, Diogenes attributes it to pure, dry air, since moisture impedes the mind. That is why thinking is impaired in people who are asleep or drunk or overfull. That moisture is detrimental to the mind is proved by the inferior intelligence of creatures other than man, which is due to the fact that the air they breathe arises from the earth and that the food they eat has a higher moisture content. As for birds, although they breathe pure air, in their constitution they resemble fish, in the sense that their flesh is firm and the air they breathe does not pervade the whole body, but halts in the region of the belly. That is why, although they digest food quickly, they remain stupid in themselves. Their mouths and their tongues also have a part to play in their stupidity, as well as their food, because they cannot understand one another. Plants have no intelligence at all, because they have no hollows and take in air.

This also explains why children lack intelligence: they have a great deal of moisture in their bodies, with the result that the air cannot penetrate deep inside their bodies, but gets no further than their chests before being excreted. That is why they are slow and stupid. They are liable to tantrums, and are emotionally unstable and fickle because a lot of air is excreted out of their small bodies. This is also why a child is forgetful, because the failure of the air to pervade the whole of its body means that it is incapable of comprehension. Proof of this is that when we try to remember something we feel a blockage in the chest, and when we remember it, the blockage clears and the pain is relieved.   (Theophrastus, *On the Senses* 39–45 Stratton)

F8 (DK 64B6; KRS 615) Here is what the veins in man are like. There are two particularly large ones which extend through the belly along the spine, one to the right of the spine and one to the left; each of these goes down to the leg on its side of the body and up to the head, going past the collar-bones and through the throat. Further veins spread from these two all through the body, those on the right of the body stemming from the one on the right, and those on the left from the one on the left. The largest of these secondary veins are two which enter the heart in the region of the spine, and two others a little higher up which run through the chest, under the armpits and down to the hands, each to the hand that is on its side of the body. One of these is called the spleen-vein, the other the liver-vein. Each of them divides into two at the end, with one branch going down to the thumb, and the other to the palm of the hand, and a number of fine, many-branched cuts stem off from these to the rest of the hand and the fingers. Other, even finer veins run from the primary veins, the ones on the right to the liver, and the ones on the left to the spleen and the kidneys. Those which run down into the legs divide at the groin and then run down the whole thigh. The largest of these runs down the back of the thigh and is readily visible as a thick vein, while the other, which runs down the inside of the thigh, is a little less thick. Then they extend past the knee to the shin and the foot, just like the ones which go down into the hands. They extend down to the sole of the foot and then their branches run to the toes. There are also a large number of fine veins which split off from these veins and run towards the belly and the flanks.

The veins which run into the head through the throat can be seen to be large in the neck. Each of them, at its end, divides into many veins which extend into the head, some passing from the left to the right and others from the right to the left. They end by the ears on either side. There is another vein in the neck, which runs alongside the large ones on either side. They are a little smaller than the large ones, to which the majority of the veins from the head are connected. They too run through the throat, but on the inside of the throat, and from each of them others run under the shoulder-blades and down into the arms, and are visible alongside the spleen-vein and the liver-vein, a little smaller in size; these are the veins doctors lance[†] to treat subcutaneous pain. For pain in the region of the belly, however, they lance the liver-vein and the spleen-vein. Other veins branch off from these and run under the breasts.

There are other fine veins which run on either side of the body through the spinal marrow and into the testicles; another pair runs through the flesh, under the skin, to the kidneys, and end in men in the testicles and in women in the uterus. These veins are called the spermatic veins.[†] The veins which run from the belly are at first fairly wide, but then they become finer, until they change over from the right to the left and from the left to the right. The thickest part of the blood is absorbed by the fleshy parts of the body, while the excess, which runs into the parts I have been talking about, becomes fine and warm and frothy.   (Aristotle, *Enquiry into Animals* 511[b]31–512[b]11 Bekker)

J. R. Shaw, 'A Note on the Anatomical and Philosophical Claims of Diogenes of Apollonia', *Apeiron*, 11.1 (1977), 53–7.

THE SOPHISTS

PROTAGORAS OF ABDERA

Protagoras was the first and greatest of the Sophists. **T1** is a list of 'firsts' attributed to him—in the domains of rhetoric, argumentation, semantics, and thought—which make him the founder of the Sophistic movement. Since this movement was essentially concerned with human progress and skill, his famous saying, embedded in **T1** and **T6**, that 'Man is the measure of all things'—that experience is comprehensible to anyone, just in virtue of the fact that he is a human being—may stand as a kind of maxim for the humanistic and democratic tendencies of the movement as a whole.[1]

Born in Abdera in northern Greece, Protagoras acquired fame particularly in Athens, where he was part of the intellectual circle surrounding the great Athenian statesman Pericles[2] and found a ready market for his skills, which were designed to help young men find fame and power in their communities (**T2**). Although it is undoubtedly true that the kind of rhetorical skills he introduced were morally suspect, or became used by less scrupulous speakers than himself, there is probably little truth to the story (e.g. Plutarch, *Life of Nicias* 23) that he was banished from Athens. Indeed, it is only later writers who tell this kind of story, while our earliest sources either do not mention it, or implicitly contradict it, as when Plato says at *Meno* 91e that Protagoras taught for forty years up to his death, and that his reputation remained consistently high. However, the ability to argue both sides of the case, which Protagoras taught (probably by writing and getting his pupils to write model speeches defending either side) as an objective means of evaluating complex situations was soon denigrated as the ability 'to make the weaker argument defeat the stronger'; this converts the neutral rhetorical claim, which Protagoras may indeed have made, to be able to take the two opposing arguments which are possible about anything (**T1**) and convert the weaker one into a winner,[3] into the morally dubious claim to make the worse or morally more

---

[1] A great many years later (in 1929), it became a clarion call for the rejection by the philosophers of the Vienna Circle of metaphysical speculation.

[2] See e.g. the stories in Plutarch, *Life of Pericles* 36, and Ps.-Plutarch, *Letter of Consolation to Apollonius* 118e–f. In particular, Protagoras was invited to draw up the constitution of the new colony of Thurii in 444—a nominally panhellenic colony which was actually the brainchild of Pericles.

[3] Some scholars water Protagoras down until all he said was that there are two opposing positions possible about anything, without making any claim that both of them were equally cogent.

unsound argument defeat the more sound one. This pejorative version of Protagoras' claim became a kind of slogan of the opponents of the Sophists, from comedians such as Aristophanes (*Clouds* 112–15)[4] to philosophers such as Aristotle (*Rhetoric* 1402ᵃ). Such responses ignore the clear value of the right to a good defence in court.

The Sophists often claimed to teach *aretē*, which means 'virtue' in general, or the ability to be good at some particular branch or branches of expertise. Though Protagoras was certainly alive to the possible moral overtones of *aretē*, it is likely that Plato is right in **T2** in having Protagoras claim that he really taught politics, or at any rate the art of political success. At its most general, he appears to have claimed to teach people to be good citizens, but this needs to be diluted by the consideration that he priced himself out of the reach of most people, and so his aim is not as democratic as it sounds.[5] He was (in fact, even if unwillingly) pandering to the political ambitions of the rich. Nevertheless, the very idea that good citizenship was something that could be taught, rather than something one inherited as a result of belonging to a family that had ruled for generations, was an important democratic innovation. A little later in *Protagoras*, at 323c–328c, Plato puts into Protagoras' mouth an extended justification of the teachability of civic virtue, which may be an imitation, or perhaps a development, of what Plato found in Protagoras' own writings. Its main features are (*a*) that civic virtue is teachable;[6] (*b*) a revolutionary, non-retributive, deterrent penology; (*c*) an emphasis on the role of rational argument within the state which effectively, for the first time in history, gives a theoretical basis for participatory democracy. These features too should probably be added to our picture of the historical Protagoras. However, it should also be noted that while Protagoras' ideal society may be democratic, it is not egalitarian, since he recognizes the need for experts in morality and politics.

In **T6** Plato immediately follows citation of Protagoras' most famous saying by explaining it as relativism. There is no reason to doubt the accuracy of this expansion, but although Plato also limits the meaning of the fragment to the equation of sense-perception with knowledge, the very broadness and vagueness of the saying militates against restricting its

---

[4] See also the famous clash between the two personified *logoi* at *Clouds* 889–1112.

[5] He was famous, however, for suggesting, at least on occasion, that his pupils paid him what they thought his teaching was worth, rather than a fixed fee: Plato, *Protagoras* 328b–c.

[6] Protagoras has to repeat this point, because in the intervening myth he had made it sound as though civic virtue was innately shared by everyone; in fact, his position probably is, according to Plato, that it is shared by everyone *because* it is taught. It is precisely the fact that civic virtue is teachable that underpins and justifies Protagoras' penology of deterrence.

meaning in this or any other way. Protagoras is saying that, whatever means we use, each of us is the authority where identifying or assessing things are concerned. The aphorism occurred at the beginning of Protagoras' modestly entitled book *Truth*; he began, then, by asserting a strong relativism. In cases of conflicting opinions, no one party is right while the other is wrong; both are equally 'measures', and both equally infallible. There is scholarly discussion about whether Protagoras might have held that the wind in itself is neither warm nor cold, or (in Heraclitean fashion) both warm and cold. In all likelihood, Protagoras would have resisted the very idea of a 'wind-in-itself', as opposed to a 'wind perceived as warm' and a 'wind perceived as cold'. In terms of the *nomos–physis* debate, in which many or all the Sophists participated, and which has had a rich later history in Western thought, the wind has no *physis*, no real nature; there is only *nomos* (law, convention—here, what appears to a person or group of people). **T7** also attributes this degree of scepticism to Protagoras.

For the achievement of political ambitions rhetorical skill was the key ingredient. Protagoras' rhetorical teaching, and all its ramifications (such as the correct use of terms (Plato, *Phaedrus* 267c; *Cratylus* 391b–c) and the distinction of the genders (**T14**), the tenses of verbs, and four grammatical moods (**T1**)), could be pressed into serving the aim of making a good impression on one's fellow citizens, though no doubt Protagoras was also interested in them for their own sake. In the direct democracy that prevailed in Athens at the time, speeches could make or break a political career, and the constitution almost guaranteed that every prominent figure was likely to find himself in court at some time or other, where again a good speech could save his life, or at least prevent the loss of property and prestige.

It is fairly easy to see the links between Protagoras' most important philosophical positions, and these connections are drawn for us by both Plato and Aristotle in **T3** to **T6**. If impressions are subjective and their truth cannot be denied by another person, then all impressions are equally true, the law of non-contradiction fails, and Protagoras' famous denial of the possibility of falsehood follows. However, Protagoras himself may have jumped straight to the denial of falsehood from his relativism, without using a denial of the law of non-contradiction as an intermediary. In fact, there is nothing in his relativism which breaks the law of non-contradiction, since he is a stickler for the subjective suffixes: the law of non-contradiction states that one cannot say both 'A is F' and 'A is not F' of the same thing at the same time, but once the Protagorean suffixes are added, the law remains intact. That is, there is no contradiction between 'A is F for person X' and 'A is not F for person Y, or for person X at another time.' Notice the emphasis on suffixes in **T10**, which is almost certainly a Platonic imitation of Protagoras. Hence Protagoras could acknowledge the appearance of contradiction in speech (and this is presumably how he recognized that there were two opposing or contrasting sides to any case), but claim that such contradictions were merely verbal, while nothing in reality would contradict anything else (because there is no such thing as 'external reality', only our subjective impressions).

Aristotle's response to all this is to claim that it destroys all sensible discourse; Plato's *ad hominem* response is to ask how Protagoras dared to set himself up as a teacher, if all his pupils already had a grasp on the truth (**T5**, **T8**). In **T11** he frames the beginning of a reply to this charge and attributes it to Protagoras, but it is very clear that he is here developing Protagoras' stated ideas, rather than paraphrasing anything he found in Protagoras' *Truth*. The starkest way to express the difference is that **T11** commits Protagoras to a denial that all statements are equally true, since by **T11** it is possible for someone to be mistaken about where their true advantage lies. Nevertheless, it is tempting to think that, if pushed, Protagoras would have taken the line Plato offers him (especially since it fits in with the claim to make a weaker argument stronger), that though all impressions are equally incorrigible and true, some are better (in a prudential sense—better for one) than others, and so teachers still have a role to play.

But if there is a straightforward connection between Protagoras' relativism and his denial of the possibility of falsehood, where did his relativism spring from in the first place? Perhaps it was just an axiom for him, but it is possible that reflection on the fact that, as his rhetorical teaching demonstrated, there are (at least) two sides to every question, led him to a relativist position. Thus, to paraphrase his famous dictum, the individual member of the Athenian Assembly is the one who is the measure of the rights and wrongs of the case being argued by an orator. Protagoras was, above all, a moderate sceptic; he withheld belief about the falsity of another person's thoughts and impressions; he denied the existence of a 'wind-in-itself' with objective properties, as distinct from the wind I feel and the wind you feel (this is somewhat clearer in **T9** than in **T8**; see also **T7**); he withheld assenting to the moral superiority of one side of the case over another; he remained somewhat agnostic about the existence of the gods. But if it is right to portray him as a moderate sceptic, this casts doubt upon the correctness of Plato's extension of his views in **T11**, since Protagoras there is made to express definite views about what is better and worse (and see also **T12**, where Plato portrays Protagoras as a utilitarian democrat). It is not impossible that Protagoras' scepticism was so moderate that he failed to apply it in certain areas, but we would have a more consistent thinker if we took these Platonic passages with a pinch of salt in terms of their historical veracity. We would then be left with a degree of consistency based on scepticism, but even here there are anomalies: the denial of the possibility of falsehood is actually quite an extreme position, whereas Protagoras' claim to teach political virtue, if 'political virtue' was not an entirely cynical paraphrase for 'whatever enables you to gain power in your particular society', does not suggest such an extreme position. After all, we can see why relativism might have become a suspect doctrine: it could be taken to mean that if a man believes it is right for him to kill his father, then, for him, it is right to do so. However, it is unlikely that Protagoras himself would have agreed with this: see **T11** on substituting better for worse ideas; and as a utilitarian democrat he would have upheld the greatest good of the greatest number, which means that people cannot just go around killing and stealing if they feel so inclined. So, in Protagoras' case, the idea that nothing is false must be modified: though nothing is false, some beliefs are better than others, and in the political sphere that means they are more conducive to utilitarian harmony. The noble purpose of the education Protagoras offered was presumably to bring about such an improved state of affairs.

T12 is another Platonic imitation of Protagoras, but there is no reason to doubt its essential veracity. The passage is central to two interlocking Sophistic or fifth-century concerns: a discussion of the origins of human beings, their societies, and their institutions; and the debate over the relative values of law or convention (*nomos*) and nature (*physis*). In **T12** Protagoras shows himself to be a champion of *nomos* over *physis*. In our primitive, natural state, we are relatively unprotected, and we therefore need society for our own protection.[7] But society is impossible without political expertise, which is glossed as 'justice and decency'—that is, the ability to respect and deal fairly with others, and to restrain one's own appetites in view of the demands of others.[8] Law is essential for the survival of the species, and so every human has (though no doubt in varying degrees) justice and decency. But the identification of political expertise simply as 'justice and decency' is puzzling, because surely more is required, and in particular Protagoras seems to ignore any intellectual or planning ability. But perhaps Protagoras assumes that humankind already possesses this (after all, mankind is contrasted right from the start with 'irrational animals'), so that only 'justice and decency' are required for

---

[7] As Thomas Hobbes was so memorably to put it, in our natural state there would be 'no knowledge of the face of the earth; no account of time; no arts; no letters; no society; and which is worst of all, continual fear and danger of violent death; and the life of man, solitary, poor, nasty, brutish, and short' (*Leviathan* part 1, ch. 13).

[8] The gloss of 'justice and decency' as 'political expertise' is problematic, as Socrates will go on to argue in *Protagoras*, because it controversially equates morality with skill.

people to put their intelligence to use in a social context. If so, then Protagoras' conception of political expertise, which he claims to teach, is a compound of intellectual and moral excellence. One puzzle arising out of **T12** is that it leaves us with a gap in Protagorean thinking: we have already seen that he supported democracy, but on the strict terms of the story told here, any political constitution would do as well as any other to restrain anarchy and provide protection. Moreover, in **T11** Plato has Protagoras say that whatever seems fine to a community is fine for it, for as long as that rule is in force. In other words, whatever *nomos* a state establishes is good for it, for as long as that *nomos* is in force. There is no objective standard of justice, but it is relative to each community. Perhaps we can bridge this apparent gap in Protagoras' thinking by a slight development of the idea in **T11** that a wise healer or politician substitutes better or more beneficial conditions or notions for worse ones. In that case, Protagoras might have made a distinction between constitutions on the basis of whether their laws are beneficial to the majority of the citizens, and clearly a democracy has the best laws by this criterion. If this is right, Protagoras is, again, a proto-utilitarian.

Protagoras was famous even in antiquity for his agnosticism about the existence of the gods (see his fragment 4, embedded in **T1**).[9] The classification of him later in antiquity (e.g. **T13**) as an atheist, however, is surely wrong: he does not seem to be denying the existence of the gods, but only our ability to gain certain knowledge of them, which may even be understood as quite a pious statement. There is such a gulf set between gods and men that we cannot know about them (compare Xenophanes). And certainly Plato apparently felt no qualms about having Protagoras, in the dialogue *Protagoras* at 323e–324a and 324e, praise piety as one of the important virtues. It is just possible, however, that if we had more of the context of this aphoristic saying, we would have to qualify our judgement of Protagoras' agnosticism. He might be saying, 'I cannot know what the gods are like, but I can say something about the origins of their worship.' This would fit in with Protagoras' general interest in origins, and would somewhat lessen the agnostic force of the bare saying. However, it is noteworthy that at *Theaetetus* 162d–e Plato has Protagoras express agnosticism.

T15–16 are somewhat less than startling evidence of a general interest in education, while **T17**, if it can be trusted,[10] with its suggestion that the

---

[9] Unless (as is just possible) Protagoras' statement of agnosticism were merely one half of an antilogical experiment, whose pious contradictory other half has been lost.

[10] Diodorus mistakenly attributes this and other reforms to a semi-legendary law-maker called Charondas, who probably lived in the early 6th cent., well before the foundation of Thurii, which Diodorus is here discussing.

basics of education should be available to all (that is, all young males, presumably) and paid for by the state, is truly remarkable. Finally, **T18** and **T19** look like the remnants of a typically Protagorean sceptical attack on geometry. In the real world a stick does not touch a hoop only at a point, so where is the evidence for what the mathematicians are talking about?

Protagoras was a Sophist, but he was also a philosopher. All the strands of his thought are interlinked, and based on moderate scepticism. If we cannot be certain about the truth of a matter, then we are justified in arguing either side of the case, we are justified in agnosticism, and we are even justified in denying the possibility of falsehood. It seems likely to me that if more of Protagoras' written work had survived we would be able to classify him more securely as a coherent and innovative thinker.

T1 (DK 80A1, B1, B4) Protagoras was the first to claim that there are two contradictory arguments about everything,* and he used them to develop the consequences of contradictory premises, being the first to use this argumentative technique. He began one of his books as follows: 'Man is the measure of all things—of the things that are, that they are, and of the things that are not, that they are not.'* He used to say that the mind was nothing but the senses, as Plato says in *Theaetetus*, and that everything is true. He began another of his books as follows: 'Where the gods are concerned, I am not in a position to ascertain that they exist, or that they do not exist.* There are many impediments to such knowledge, including the obscurity of the matter and the shortness of human life.' . . . He was the first to charge a fee of 100 minas, and the first to distinguish the tenses of verbs. He explained the potency of seizing the opportune moment,* he instituted debating competitions, and he introduced disputants to the tricks of their trade. Since he ignored meaning and focused in his talks on mere words, he was the forefather of the tribe of eristic speakers who are so common nowadays . . . He was also the first to develop the kind of argument known as 'Socratic'.* And, as Plato says in *Euthydemus*, he was the first to make use, in his talks, of the argument of Antisthenes which tries to prove that contradiction is impossible. He was also the inventor of methods of attacking any given position, as Artemidorus the dialectician reports in his *Against Chrysippus* . . . He was the first to distinguish the following

four kinds of speech: wishing, asking, answering, commanding.
(Diogenes Laertius, *Lives of Eminent Philosophers* 9.51–3 Long)

T2 (DK 80A5) [*Socrates is talking to Protagoras*] 'Hippocrates here
is an Athenian citizen; his father is Apollodorus. He comes from
an important and prosperous family, and is generally held to be the
equal of any of his contemporaries in terms of his natural endowments. I think he wants to acquire a name for himself in his community, and he thinks that this is most likely to happen to him if he
associates with you . . . He says, therefore, that he would like to hear
what will be the outcome for him if he associates with you.'

Protagoras' response was as follows: 'Young man, what will
happen to you, if you associate with me, is that on the first day of
that association you will go home better, and the same thing will
happen again the next day, and each day thereafter you will make
progress towards a better state.' . . .

[*Socrates spends some time trying to find out what Protagoras means
by 'better'—better at what?*] Protagoras listened to what I said and
then replied, 'These are good questions, Socrates, and I enjoy
answering those who ask good questions. If Hippocrates comes to
me, he won't experience what he would if he went to any of the other
Sophists. I mean, the others all treat young men in a disgraceful
fashion. They take people who have shunned the arts and crafts,*
turn them around again against their will, and get them involved in
arts and crafts, by teaching them mathematics and astronomy, geometry and music'—here he glanced at Hippias—'whereas if he comes
to me he will learn exactly what he came to learn. What I teach is the
art of making good decisions, both in one's domestic affairs, so that
one can manage his estate and household in the best possible way,
and in the affairs of the community, so that he can maximize his
potential to conduct political business and address political issues.'

'I just want to check that I've understood what you're saying,' I
said. 'You seem to me to be talking about political expertise, and to
be promising to make men good citizens of their community.'

'Yes, Socrates,' he said. 'That is exactly the profession I
make.'   (Plato, *Protagoras* 316b8–319a7 Burnet)

T3 (DK 80A19) Then again, if contradictories are all simultaneously true of the same object, the obvious consequence is that
everything will be one. The same thing will be a ship and a wall and a

person, if it is possible to either affirm or deny any attribute of anything, as those who argue as Protagoras did are bound to. After all, if a person is taken not to be a ship, then obviously he is not a ship; but if the contradictory is true, it follows that he also is a ship. (Aristotle, *Metaphysics* 1007^{b}18–25 Ross)

T4 (DK 80A19) Protagoras said that man is the measure of all things, by which he meant that any impression a person receives is also securely true. From this it follows that the same thing both is and is not the case, and is bad and good and all other contradictories, because it often happens that something can appear beautiful to one lot of people and the opposite to another lot, but on Protagoras' view it is what appears to anyone that is the measure. (Aristotle, *Metaphysics* 1062^{b}13–19 Ross)

T5 (DK 80A19) [*Socrates speaking*] Ctesippus made no reply, but I was astonished at the argument [*that it is impossible to contradict another person*], and I said: 'What do you mean, Dionysodorus? I'll have you know that I've heard this argument plenty of times from plenty of people, but it always surprises me. Protagoras' followers were particularly keen on it, and there were others even before them.* But what strikes me is its amazing capacity for destroying not only other arguments but itself as well . . . If neither speaking falsehood nor thinking falsehood nor ignorance are possible, then surely it is impossible, in any action, to make a mistake, because the agent cannot go wrong in what he does? . . . If action, speech, and thought are not wrong, then who on earth have you come to teach?' (Plato, *Euthydemus* 286b7–287a9 Burnet)

T6 (DK 80B1) *Socrates.* Whether or not you are aware of it, this statement of yours about knowledge [*defining it as perception*] is a substantial one; it's what Protagoras used to say as well, though he used different words to say the same thing. I mean, he says somewhere that 'Man is the measure of all things—of the things that are, that they are; of the things that are not, that they are not.' No doubt you've read this?

Theaetetus. Yes, often.

Socrates. And doesn't he mean by this that 'Each and every event is for me as it appears to me, and is for you as it appears to you'—you and I being 'man'?

Theaetetus. That's what he says.

Socrates. Now, he's a clever person, and unlikely to be talking nonsense, so let's follow in his footsteps. Isn't it possible that, when the same wind is blowing, one of us might feel chilly, while the other doesn't? Or one might feel slightly chilly, the other really rather cold?

Theaetetus. Certainly.

Socrates. So when that happens, are we to describe the wind *per se* as cold or not cold? Or should we follow Protagoras and say that it is cold for the one who feels cold, but not for the one who doesn't?

Theaetetus. That seems reasonable.

Socrates. And that is how the wind appears to each of us?

Theaetetus. Yes.

Socrates. Now, the phrase 'it appears to me' is the same as 'I perceive', isn't it?

Theaetetus. It is.

Socrates. So appearance is the same as being perceived, in the case of warmth and so on. I mean, as each person perceives events to be, so they also are, I suppose, for each person.

Theaetetus. That sounds reasonable.

Socrates. Perception, then, is always of something that is, and it is infallible, which suggests that it is knowledge.

(Plato, *Theaetetus* 151e8–152c6 Duke *et al.*)

T7 Protagoras says that the being of things that are consists in their being perceived. He says: 'If you are here with me, it is obvious that I am sitting, but this is not obvious to someone who is not here. Whether or not I am sitting is not clear.' And they say that everything that exists consists in being perceived. I see the moon, for example, while someone else does not see it; whether or not the moon exists is not clear. When I am healthy the apprehension of honey that arises is that it is sweet, but someone else who has a fever apprehends it as bitter; whether it is sweet or bitter is therefore not clear. In this way they intend to assert the lack of objective apprehension.* (A fragment of Didymus the Blind, *Commentary on the Psalms*; text first published by M. Gronewald in *Zeitschrift für Papyrologie und Epigraphik*, 2 (1968), 1–2)

T8 [*Socrates speaking*] I'm perfectly happy with the general theory, that what appears to each person is for that person, but the beginning of the argument puzzles me. Why didn't he start *Truth* off by saying, 'A pig is the measure of all things', or 'a baboon', or any sentient creature, however outlandish? That would have been a magnificently haughty beginning, showing that although we regard his wisdom as remarkable and almost divine, yet he is in fact no better off intellectually than a tadpole, let alone another human being. What else can we think, Theodorus? If a person's impressions, gained by perception, are true for that person; if no one else is a better judge of another person's experiences, in the sense of deciding authoritatively which are true and which false; if, in other words, as we have repeatedly said, each person alone makes up his mind about his own impressions, and all of them are correct and true; if all this is so, my friend, how on earth are we to distinguish Protagoras, whose cleverness was such that he thought he was justified in teaching others for vast fees, and ourselves, who are less gifted and had to go and be his students, when each of us is the measure of his own cleverness?*   (Plato, *Theaetetus* 161c2–e3 Duke *et al.*)

T9 (DK 80A13) [*Socrates speaking*] I think we should try to see, Hermogenes, whether you also think the same way about existing things. That is, does their being exist only in private for each person, as Protagoras used to assert with his saying that 'Man is the measure of all things'? Is it the case, then, that as things appear to me to be, so they are for me, and as they appear to you, so they are for you? Or do you think that things have some stable being in themselves?   (Plato, *Cratylus* 385e4–386a4 Duke *et al.*)

T10 (DK 80A22) [*Protagoras speaking*] I know of plenty of things which are harmful to people (they may be foods or drinks or drugs, or whatever), and others which are beneficial; and I know of things which are neither harmful nor beneficial to people, but which are to horses—or are only to cattle, or only to dogs. And then there are things which are neither harmful nor beneficial for any of these creatures, but are for trees; and things which are good for the roots of trees, but bad for their shoots, such as manure, which is good for all plants when it is applied to their roots, but deadly if put on their shoots and young branches. Or then there's olive oil, which is completely pernicious for all plants and ruins the hair of all non-human creatures, but is good for human hair and for the rest of their body too. Goodness is so diverse and varied that even in our case one and the same thing may be good for the outside of a human body, but awful for the inside.   (Plato, *Protagoras* 334a3–c2 Burnet)

T11 (DK 80A21a) [*Socrates is speaking for Protagoras*] I claim that the truth is as I have written: each of us is the measure of the things that are and are not. However, there is a great deal of inequality among people, precisely because there is so much variety in the things that are and appear to different people. In other words, so far from denying the existence of expertise and clever people, I actually define wisdom as the ability to make good things appear and be for someone instead of bad things.

. . . I will try to make my meaning even clearer to you. Remember, for instance, what was said earlier, that food appears and is unpleasant for someone who is ill, but appears and is the opposite for someone who is well. Now, there's no call for the unfeasible idea that either of these two people is *wiser*: that is, we shouldn't classify the sick person as ignorant because he thinks as he does, nor the healthy person as clever because he thinks differently. What we're after is a change from one state to the other, because one state is *better* than the other.

It's the same in education too: what we're after is change from one state to the better one. The only difference is that a doctor uses medicines to bring about the change, while a Sophist uses words. But it is never the case that a change is effected from earlier false belief to later true belief: it is impossible to believe something which is not the case—one can only believe what one is experiencing, and this is always true. What is possible, however, in my opinion, is that someone who is in an unsound mental state and whose beliefs are cognate with it can be made to think differently.[†] Now, these different impressions are naïvely called 'true', but what I am saying is that although they are *better* than the others, they are not more true at all.

I certainly do not equate wise people with frogs, my dear Socrates. On the contrary, I claim that each sphere of operation has its wise practitioners: there are doctors for bodies, farmers for plants (for I maintain that farmers can replace unsound perceptions in sickly plants with sound, healthy perceptions and affections[†]); and I claim that politicians who are wise and good at their job substitute sound for unsound ethical notions in their communities. It is true that whatever seems ethically fine to each community also is ethical for it, for as long as that rule is in force, but a wise person changes each unsound notion they have, and makes sound notions be and appear for them. By the same token, a Sophist, since he is capable of guiding his pupils in the same way, is wise and deserves to be paid a lot by his pupils.   (Plato, *Theaetetus* 166c9–167d2 Duke *et al.*)

T12 (DK 80C1) [*Protagoras speaking*] Once upon a time there were gods, but no mortal creatures. When the appointed time came for mortal creatures to be born, the gods moulded them inside the earth and made them out of a mixture of earth and fire, and out of all the stuffs that are compounded from earth and fire. When they were ready to bring them up into the light of day, they gave Prometheus and Epimetheus* the job of equipping them and distributing the appropriate abilities to each species. Epimetheus begged Prometheus to let him make the distribution by himself and said, 'After I've done the distributing, you can inspect them.' He got his way, and proceeded with the distribution. Some creatures he gave strength without speed, while he equipped weaker creatures with speed; to some he gave weaponry, while for others—those he gave an unarmed nature—he devised some alternative means of protection. If he made creatures small, he gave them winged flight or a home underground; if he made them big, their size itself was their protection. And all the other abilities he distributed on the same principle, balancing one against another, and taking pains to avoid the extinction of any species.* Once he had supplied them with means of escaping mutual destruction, he dressed them, as a way for them to remain comfortable whatever weather Zeus might send, in thick pelts and tough hides, which would not only be adequate protection against the cold of winter and effective against the heat of summer, but would also serve at the same time as innate and home-grown bedding for them when they went to sleep. And some he shod with hoofs, others with hard, bloodless claws. Then he went on to assign different creatures different things to eat. To some he assigned the grass that springs from the ground, to others the fruits of trees, and to others roots. There were those which he allowed to be nourished by eating other creatures, but he made them less prolific, while he made the species on which they preyed prolific, as a means of ensuring their survival.

Now, Epimetheus was not the most intelligent of beings, and he failed to notice that he had used up all the abilities on the irrational creatures. Eventually he found that he had left only the human species unequipped, and he didn't know what to do with it. While he was trying to think what to do, Prometheus arrived to inspect the distribution, and he saw that although all the other creatures were properly catered for in all respects, man was naked, unshod, uncovered, and unarmed. But the appointed day had arrived when man was supposed to emerge from the earth into the daylight. So, since he didn't know of any other way to find a means of protection for the human species, Prometheus stole from Hephaestus and Athena technical skill along with fire (for fire was essential to enable such skill to be acquired by anyone, or to be any use) and made these his gift to man. This is how man came by the skills required for the maintenance of life, but he did not yet have political expertise. This was in Zeus' domain, and Prometheus ran out of time before he could penetrate Zeus' palace, the acropolis; besides, Zeus' guards were terrifying. But he did break into the building where Athena and Hephaestus practised their arts together, stole Hephaestus' skill at working with fire and Athena's expertise too, and gave them to man.* As a result, man was well supplied with the necessities of life, but we hear that Prometheus was later punished for his theft.*

The consequences of man's acquisition of a portion of divinity were, first, that† humans were the only creatures to worship the gods and to set about establishing altars and images of the gods, and, second, that they soon used their skills to articulate speech and language, and discovered how to make houses, clothes, footwear, and blankets, and how to get food from the earth. Thus equipped, at first men lived all over the place, and there were no communities. And so they began to be killed by wild beasts, because they were weaker than them in all respects. Their creative skills were enough to support them where nourishment was concerned, but they lacked the ability to fight the wild beasts, because warfare is an aspect of political expertise, which they did not yet possess. They therefore tried to protect themselves by gathering together and forming communities, but once they had done so they began to wrong one another, because they did not yet possess political expertise; and so they scattered again and were killed by the wild beasts again.

Zeus was worried that our species might be completely annihilated, so he gave Hermes the job of taking humankind decency and

justice, to bring order to their communities and to bind men together
in friendship.* Hermes asked Zeus on what principle he should give
men justice and decency: 'In distributing them, should I follow the
way in which the skills have been distributed?' he asked. 'The principle there is that one person with skill as a healer suffices for many
laymen, and the same goes for all the other arts and crafts. So am I to
assign justice and decency in the same way, or shall I distribute them
to all men?' 'To all,' Zeus replied. 'Let all partake of them. For
communities would never be formed if only a few had justice and
decency, as they do the other skills. And make it a law, sanctioned
by me, that they are to put to death anyone who is incapable of
decency and justice, on the grounds that he is a plague on the
community.'   (Plato, *Protagoras* 320c8–322d5 Burnet)

T13 (DK 80A23) Protagoras of Abdera held a view that was identical in meaning to that of Diagoras,* but he did not express himself in
identical words, in order to avoid the excessive recklessness of the
view. So he said that he did not know whether there were gods—but
this is the same as saying that he knew there were no gods. For if in
contrast to his first statement he had said, 'I certainly do not know
that they do not exist' . . . *   (Diogenes of Oenoanda, fr. 11 Chilton,
col. 2)

T14 (DK 80A27) The fourth aspect of speaking proper Greek is to
follow Protagoras' distinction of the genders of words as masculine,
feminine, and neuter.   (Aristotle, *Rhetoric* 1407^{b}6–8 Ross)

T15 (DK 80B3) Teaching requires natural endowments and training; one should begin to learn when one is young.   (Anonymous,
On Hippomachus B3 (Bohler, *Sophistae Anonymi Protreptici*, p. 46.3))

T16 (DK 80B10) Protagoras said that skill was nothing without
practice, and practice nothing without skill.   (John of Stobi,
Anthology 3.29.80 Wachsmuth/Hense)

T17 That is why he used this piece of legislation to improve the
condition of illiterate people, on the grounds that they lack one of
life's great goods, and thought literacy should be a matter for public
concern and expense. (Diodorus of Sicily, *Universal History*
12.13.3.3–6 Vogel)

T18 (DK 80B7) No perceptible object is geometrically straight or curved; after all, a circle does not touch a ruler at a point, as Protagoras used to say in arguing against the geometers. (Aristotle, *Metaphysics* 998ª1–4 Ross)

T19 As Protagoras says of mathematics, the subject-matter is unknowable, and the terminology distasteful. (a fragment from Philodemus of Gadara, *On Poetry*; *PHerc.* 1676, col. 1.12–13)

A. W. H. Adkins, 'Ἀρετή, τέχνη, Democracy and Sophists: *Protagoras* 316b–328d', *Journal of Hellenic Studies*, 93 (1973), 3–12.

M. F. Burnyeat, 'Protagoras and Self-refutation in Plato's *Theaetetus*', *Philosophical Review*, 85 (1976), 172–95; repr. in S. Everson (ed.), *Companions to Ancient Thought*, vol. i: *Epistemology* (Cambridge: Cambridge University Press, 1990), 39–59.

—— 'Conflicting Appearances', *Proceedings of the British Academy*, 65 (1979), 69–111.

T. D. J. Chappell, 'Does Protagoras Refute Himself?', *Classical Quarterly*, 45 (1995), 333–8.

C. W. Chilton, 'An Epicurean View of Protagoras', *Phronesis*, 7 (1962), 105–9.

A. T. Cole, 'The Apology of Protagoras', *Yale Classical Studies* 19 (1966), 103–18.

—— 'The Relativism of Protagoras', *Yale Classical Studies*, 22 (1972), 19–45.

E. K. Emilsson, 'Plato's Self-refutation Argument in *Theaetetus* 171ac Revisited', *Phronesis*, 39 (1994), 136–49.

G. Fine, 'Protagorean Relativisms', *Proceedings of the Boston Area Colloquium in Ancient Philosophy*, 10 (1994), 211–43.

—— 'Relativism and Self-refutation: Plato, Protagoras, and Burnyeat', in J. Gentzler (ed.), *Method in Ancient Philosophy* (Oxford: Oxford University Press, 1997), 137–63.

D. K. Glidden, 'Protagorean Relativism and Physis', *Phronesis*, 20 (1975), 209–27.

G. B. Kerferd, 'Plato's Account of the Relativism of Protagoras', *Durham University Journal*, 42 (1949/50), 20–6.

—— 'Protagoras' Doctrine of Justice and Virtue in the *Protagoras* of Plato', *Journal of Hellenic Studies*, 73 (1953), 42–5.

R. J. Ketchum, 'Plato's "Refutation" of Protagorean Relativism: *Theaetetus* 170–171', *Oxford Studies in Ancient Philosophy*, 10 (1992), 73–106.

D. Loenen, *Protagoras and the Greek Community* (Amsterdam: Noord-Hollandische Uitgevers Maatschappij, 1941).

K. Marc-Wogau, 'On Protagoras' Homomensura-thesis in Plato's *Theaetetus*', in id., *Philosophical Essays* (Lund: Gleerup, 1967), 3–20.

D. Payne, 'Rhetoric, Reality, and Knowledge: A Re-examination of Protagoras' Concept of Rhetoric', *Rhetoric Society Quarterly*, 16 (1986), 187–97.

H. D. Rankin, 'Ouk Estin Antilegein', in [27], 25–37.

T. J. Saunders, 'Protagoras and Plato on Punishment', in [27], 129–41.

E. Schiappa, *Protagoras and Logos: A Study in Greek Philosophy and Rhetoric* (Columbia: University of South Carolina Press, 1991).

G. Vlastos, 'Protagoras', in M. Ostwald and B. Jowett, *Plato: Protagoras* (Indianapolis: Bobbs-Merrill, 1956), pp. vii–xxiv.

P. Woodruff, 'Protagoras on the Unseen: The Evidence of Didymus', in [23], 80–7.

GORGIAS OF LEONTINI

Gorgias, from Leontini in Sicily, was classified in antiquity (T1) and, if T2 is accurate, thought of himself too, as a rhetorician, a teacher of rhetoric and composer-speaker of model (epideictic) speeches. He was the most innovative orator of his time, and may be regarded as the first true prose stylist. But opinions about his style differed even in antiquity. In his own day, he seems to have been found very impressive, but even a generation later he began to acquire the reputation which has stayed with him ever since, of being over-florid and excessive in many ways. T1 and T3–5 mention some of the rhetorical techniques he introduced, and F1 and F2 display some of them at work.[1] And we hear elsewhere of ghastly figures of speech, such as avoiding the everyday word 'vulture' in favour of 'living tomb'.[2] Although most contemporary writers managed to avoid the excesses of his style and diction, certain features which he introduced or made popular were adopted, and are still with us today—things like antithesis, triplets, the gradual accumulation of numbers of syllables in phrases towards a climax, rhetorical questions. But the majority of the poetic features he introduced into prose have vanished.

His fame as a rhetorician should not make us hesitate to count him as a member—an important member—of the Sophistic movement. In the first place, rhetoric was one of the chief features of all the Sophists; most of them taught and/or displayed rhetoric, or some aspects of *logos*, the spoken word. Indeed, in T7 Aristotle makes Gorgias out to be a paradigmatic teacher of rhetoric. In the second place, Gorgias was not just a rhetorician, but a philosopher. We know this, despite the usual paucity of evidence about the Sophists, from casual asides such as those found in T13 and T14; from the fact that he not only practised rhetoric, but reflected on the subject too (T8–10, F1); from the jurisprudential relevance of some of F1 (particularly its sustained attack on the notion of responsibility, since it is a commonplace from Aristotle onwards that force excludes responsibility); and most particularly from the extraordinary work paraphrased in T11 and T12. So even if Plato is right to say (*Meno* 95b–c) that Gorgias scorned the other Sophists for claiming to teach virtue (*aretē*), a claim he never made himself, he still shares enough of the central concerns of the

---

[1] It should go without saying, though, that it is very hard to do justice to some aspects of Gorgias' style in translation. For instance, the English equivalents of words that rhyme in Greek rarely rhyme, and similar difficulties apply to alliteration, assonance, homoeoteleuton, and isocolon, to name just the first that come to mind.

[2] Athanasius, *Introduction to Hermogenes' 'Rhetoric'* 14.180.9 Rabe.

Sophistic movement to belong in this book.[3] And even his refusal to claim to teach virtue seems to have been philosophically based: **T15** suggests that he was a relativist (in a mild, non-philosophical sense of 'relativism') about virtue.

His reflections on the spoken word are pretty consistent (**T8–10, F1**). He stresses its persuasive power, whether that involves a kind of force, or something more gentle; he likens its effect on the mind to that of drugs on the body, argues for its emotive force, and by the very incantatory rhythms of his own prose bears out what he says about the spoken word having the power to bewitch and entrance. The spoken word has the power to persuade and to deceive, and there is a delightful ambivalence to **F1**, since it makes this point in defence of Helen, but the point also applies to itself. However, there is no reason to think that Gorgias believed that persuasion was necessarily bad. In *Gorgias* 456c–457c Plato attributes to the Sophist the view that rhetoric is in itself neutral, but may be used for good or ill, and this is probably the implication of Gorgias' analogy between the effect of rhetoric on the mind and that of drugs on the body. However, Gorgias did believe that words were essentially deceitful: they are not the things themselves that they are talking about (see **T11–12**). There is the real world, about which our usual condition is one of belief, rather than knowledge. As long as we have only beliefs, we are liable to manipulation by the spoken word.

I include both versions of the epitomes of Gorgias' treatise *On What Is Not*, or *On Nature* (**T11** and **T12**), since although **T12** is denser and more compressed, it supplements **T11** in important ways, and the two versions need to be put together to arrive at a more complete picture of what Gorgias originally wrote. Broadly speaking, **T11** tends to be clearer for the first part of the argument and is definitely clearer for the second, but **T12** is better for the third. In this treatise Gorgias claimed to prove that nothing has being (perhaps most naturally taken to mean that nothing exists), that even if it did have being it could not be comprehended, and that even if it could be comprehended it could not be communicated to anyone else. It used to be dismissed as a *jeu d'esprit* (see, perhaps, the concluding words of **F1**), but nowadays scholars are more inclined to take it seriously, and to think that it might even have been a work of philosophy in response to the monism of Parmenides and his followers; at any rate, it is a clear implication of Parmenides **F3** ll. 6–8 (p. 58) that if nothing is, it can neither be known nor communicated. In a number of ways **T11** and **T12** can be seen to complement a show piece such as his *Helen*; for instance, in *Helen*

---

[3] Note that Plato himself in *Meno* is not distinguishing Gorgias from Sophists, but making a distinction which is meant to be relevant within the Sophistic movement. And at *Apology* 19d–20c Plato definitely classifies Gorgias as a Sophist.

Gorgias argues that philosophers communicate beliefs about things that are unclear, while in *On What Is Not* he argues that communication is impossible precisely because things are unclear. Of course, just as *Helen* is self-referential, so is *On What Is Not*; indeed, it may even be self-refuting, because if Gorgias were to convince us of his theses, communication *would* have taken place, after all.

Whatever the intent of the piece, it is easy to see how reflections on the relations between existence, thought, and language could come to occupy a Sophist, with his preoccupation with speech and education. But it is legitimate to ask whether Gorgias himself believed in the outrageous theses for which he argues, or whether the piece is, like the *Helen*, a model, showing the kind of strategy a pupil could adopt. Some of the arguments are so blatantly fallacious that even in the infancy of logic it is hard to see how Gorgias could have intended them to form part of a seriously intended piece of philosophy. Alternatively, the very fact that it is so hard to pin down its intent may be the whole point of the piece. Is it philosophy, or parody, or a model speech? Perhaps it was deliberately intended to be impossible to categorize, and thus fulfils Gorgias' theory that the spoken word is or can be deceptive and tricky.

Nevertheless, some important philosophical points are made in the course of the argument—for instance, that it is possible to think of things that do not exist; that Eleatic argumentation can be used to 'prove' not just that what-is is, but that it is not too; that speech is a second-order phenomenon, arising as a result of our impressions of the sensible world. The third section, arguing for the inexpressibility of things, is the most compressed, but seems to proceed by establishing a series of unbridgeable gaps between things, such that communication is impossible. First, there is a gap between the proper objects of one sense and another: we cannot hear visible things, nor see audible things. Second, there is an ontological gap between the spoken word and the event which is being spoken of. Third, since sense-impressions are infallible (see also **T13**), then since there is a gap between the spoken word and the event, but there is no gap between the appropriate sense and the event, there is therefore a gap between the spoken word and sense-impressions. Fourth, there is a gap between sense-impressions and the corresponding thoughts. Fifth, from this it follows, since the spoken word expresses thoughts, that we cannot communicate our sensory experience, which is in any case entirely private to ourselves. And therefore, sixth, there is an unbridgeable gap between one person's thoughts and another. Hence communication is impossible.

A related philosophical issue concerning Gorgias arises with **F3**. It has been claimed that this shows that Gorgias is a relativist—that like Protagoras he holds that there is no such thing as real existence, only appearance. In actual fact, though, **F3** is bad evidence for this interpretation, since it seems to mean that we can know that something exists, since everything that exists has an appearance. This is not to equate existence with appearance in a relativistic fashion, because the second half of the fragment implies that appearance offers only feeble evidence for the existence of anything, and this means that Gorgias accepts a full-strength distinction between reality and appearance, such that reality must exist for him.[4]

Returning now to *On What Is Not*, it is relevant to note that its main topics—the existence of things, knowledge of things, and whether that knowledge can be communicated—are precisely topics with which Gorgias is concerned elsewhere. **F3** shows that he accepts the real existence of things, and **F1** explicitly talks of 'the nature each one actually has'; **F1** also implies that one can know the nature of things, but few do, and as long as people do not, but have only opinions, they are subject to manipulation by the spoken word; and one might well think that Gorgias' whole enterprise as an orator implies that he thought he could communicate—unless he was entirely sceptical, but we have found no evidence of that.

So the fact that the conclusions of *On What Is Not* contradict views Gorgias states elsewhere need some resolution. Perhaps the model for Gorgias' way of arguing in *On What Is Not* was Zeno's paradoxes. When Zeno argued, for instance, that Achilles could never overtake the tortoise, he was saying that this is so on a certain view of space and time. Given certain assumptions, paradoxical conclusions follow. The pattern of Gorgias' argumentation in *On What Is Not* could well be taken to be similar *reductiones ad absurdum*. For instance, on the assumption only perceptibles exist, it turns out to be impossible to communicate; remove the assumption, and the conclusion need have no force for you. This, I suggest, is what Gorgias is up to in **T11** and **T12**.

———

T1 (DK 82A4) The delegation [*from Leontini to Athens, in 427 BCE*] was headed up by the orator Gorgias, who was by far the most skilful person of his generation at speaking. He was also the inventor of rhetorical techniques and, as a Sophist, was so far ahead of everyone else that he was paid 100 minas by his pupils. After arriving in

---

[4] A sentence from Gorgias' *Palamedes* 35 has also been adduced in this context: 'If it were possible to make the truth about reality pure and clear to the audience through the spoken word, judgement would be easy, since it would simply follow from what was said; but since this is not so . . .' But again, this implies that there is truth; it is just that it is hard to communicate.

Athens, he went before the popular Assembly and spoke to them about the possibility of entering into an alliance, and his speech impressed the Athenians, who were an intelligent and cultured people, with its innovative use of language. For he was the first to make use of extravagant and extraordinarily contrived figures of speech, such as antithesis, isocolon, evenly balanced clauses, homoeoteleuton, and so on—things which were found acceptable in those days because of their artful novelty, but which nowadays seem futile and often appear ridiculous and excessively contrived. He eventually persuaded the Athenians to enter into an alliance with the people of Leontini, and then, once he had secured a high reputation in Athens for his rhetorical skill, he returned to Leontini. (Diodorus of Sicily, *Universal History* 12.53.2–5 Vogel)

T2 *Socrates.* Or rather, Gorgias, won't you tell us yourself what your area of expertise is, and so what to call you?

Gorgias. It's rhetoric, Socrates.

Socrates. We'd better call you a rhetorician, then?

Gorgias. A good one, Socrates, if you want to call me what (as Homer puts it) 'I avow I am.'

Socrates. I'll gladly do so.

Gorgias. Then that's what you can call me.

Socrates. What about training other people in rhetoric too? Should we attribute this ability to you?

Gorgias. Yes, that's what I offer to do, here in Athens and elsewhere as well.

(Plato, *Gorgias* 449a2–b3 Burnet)

T3 (DK 80A26) [*Socrates speaking*] And shall we leave Tisias* and Gorgias to their sleep, who saw that probabilities were to be preferred to truth, and by the power of their speech make small things seem large and large things small, and put new things in an old way and vice versa, and discovered how to express anything at all with concision or at infinite length?   (Plato, *Phaedrus* 267a6–b2 Burnet)

T4 (DK 82A25) Gorgias did the same, they say, in writing speeches designed to praise or criticize particular objects, because it was his opinion that it was especially relevant for an orator to be able to amplify a subject by praising it and, on the other hand, to deflate it by criticizing it.   (Cicero, *Brutus* 12.47.1–5 Friedrich)

T5 (DK 82A29) The poets were generally held to have gained their fame, despite speaking nonsense, because of their style, and so the first prose style to have been developed was poetic, like that of Gorgias. (Aristotle, *Rhetoric* 1404^{a}24–6 Ross)

T6 But to date no rhetorician or philosopher has produced the definitive treatise about timing; the person who first set about writing on the subject, Gorgias of Leontini, wrote nothing valuable about it. In fact, it is the nature of the subject itself that it is not liable to a comprehensive and systematic treatment: timing is, in general, not something that is susceptible to knowledge, rather than to one's personal judgement. (Dionysius of Halicarnassus, *On Literary Composition* 12.32–8 Roberts)

T7 (DK 82B14) The paid teachers of eristic argumentation used a form of training for their pupils which closely resembled Gorgias' approach. For they gave them speeches to learn, which were either rhetorical or those which questioned an opponent's position, and whichever kind of speech they gave their pupils they invariably supposed that the other kind was included among them. (Aristotle, *On Sophistic Refutations* 183^{b}36–184^{a}1 Ross)

T8 (DK 82A26) [*Protarchus, a pupil of Gorgias, speaking*] Well, Socrates, when I heard Gorgias speak he often used to say that the art of persuasion is easily the most outstanding science, the reason being that it enslaves everything in voluntary, unconstrained submission to itself; it is, in other words, the most noble science by a long way. (Plato, *Philebus* 58a7–b2 Burnet)

T9 *Gorgias.* I'm talking about the ability to use the spoken word to persuade—to persuade the jurors in the courts, the members of the Council, the citizens attending the Assembly—in short, to win over any and every form of public meeting of the citizen body . . .

Socrates. Gorgias, I think you've finally come very close to revealing what you think rhetoric does. If I've understood you correctly, you're saying that rhetoric is the agent of persuasion—that persuasion is the sum total and the fundamental goal of all its activity.

(Plato, *Gorgias* 452e1–453a3 Burnet)

T10 (DK 82C2) [*Socrates speaking*] But if the slaves drop for us frequent dew in goblets small (if you'll pardon the Gorgianism), then,

instead of being forced into intoxication by the wine, we shall reach a
more playful mood through gentle persuasion.   (Xenophon, *Symposium* 2.26.4–7 Marchant)

F1 (DK 82B11) *The Encomium of Helen*.* The glory of a city lies in
the quality of its men, of a body in beauty, of a mind in wisdom, of
an object in excellence, and of a speech in truth. The opposites of
these qualities constitute blemishes. If a man, a woman, a speech, a
deed, a city, and an object deserve praise one should honour them
with praise, but if they do not one should apply blame. For there is
no difference between the error and the ignorance of criticizing the
praiseworthy and praising the blameworthy. It is the job of one and
the same man to speak up when something must be spoken and to
refute† the detractors of Helen, a woman in whose case there is
unison and unanimity between the beliefs of those who heed the
poets and the omen of her name, which has become a reminder of
misfortune. I would like, by means of the logic with which I shall
inform my speech, to free both the slandered woman from the
charges against her and her detractors from their ignorance, by demonstrating the falsity of their views and by revealing the truth . . .

   She did what she did either because of the desires of Fortune, the
decisions of the gods, and the decrees of Necessity, or because she
was abducted by force, or because she was persuaded by the spoken
word, or because she was overwhelmed by love. Now, if it was
because of the first reason anyone who accuses her deserves to be
accused, since it is impossible for human premonition to impede
divine predilection. It is not in the nature of things that the stronger
should be impeded by the weaker, but that the weaker should be
ruled and guided by the stronger—that the stronger should lead and
the weaker follow. God is stronger than man in might and wisdom
and all other respects. Therefore, if responsibility is to be assigned to
Fate and to the gods, Helen is to be acquitted from her ill reputation.

   If she was abducted by force, unlawfully violated, and unjustly
assaulted, obviously it was her abductor who did wrong, since he
committed the assault, while she, the abductee, suffered misfortune,
since she was the victim of the assault. Therefore, it is the savage
who undertook an undertaking of verbal, legal, and actual savagery
who deserves to meet with verbal accusation, legal disenfran-
chisement, and actual punishment. But she, who was treated with

violence, deprived of her homeland, and robbed of her loved ones—would it not be reasonable to think that she deserves pity rather than defamation? He was the perpetrator of terrible crimes, she was the victim. By all rights, then, she should be pitied, and he should be hated.

But if it was the spoken word that persuaded her and deceived her mind, it is not hard to come up with a defence for this too and to dissolve the charge as follows. The spoken word is a mighty lord, and for all that it is insubstantial and imperceptible it has superhuman effects. It can put an end to fear, do away with distress, generate happiness, and increase pity. I will now prove that this is so, and I must also prove it to my audience with their beliefs.

'Speech with metre' is my designation and description of all poetry. When people hear poetry they are affected by fearful terror and tearful pity and mournful longing, and at the successes and setbacks of others' affairs and achievements the mind feels its own personal feelings, thanks to the spoken word. And now I shall turn from one argument to another.

Inspired incantations use the spoken word to induce pleasure and reduce distress. When the power of the incantation meets the beliefs of a person's mind, it beguiles, persuades, alters it by its sorcery. The twin techniques of sorcery and magic have been discovered—techniques which cause the mind to err and deceive beliefs. So many people have persuaded or do persuade so many others about so many things by forging false speech! For if everyone could remember everything that had happened in the past, could understand everything that was happening in the present, and could foresee everything that would happen in the future, the spoken word would not have the power[†] that it has. But as things are[†] it is not easy to remember the past or keep one's mind on the present or divine the future, and so in most cases most people make their beliefs the counsellors of their minds. But since beliefs are treacherous and insecure they bring those relying on them treacherous and insecure success. What is there, then, to rule out the idea that Helen, too, came under the influence of the spoken word just as unwillingly as if she had been abducted by the violence of violators? For thought is banished by persuasion. Indeed, persuasion may not have the appearance of compulsion, but it has the same power.[†] For the spoken word, the persuader of her mind (which is what it persuaded), compelled it both to obey what was being said and to approve what was being done. So it is the persuader who does wrong, since he wielded compulsion, while she, the persuaded, is falsely slandered, since she was the victim of compulsion by the spoken word.

The supervention of persuasion on the spoken word also moulds the mind as it wishes. To see this, one only has to appreciate, first, how words spoken by astronomers do away with one belief and instil another instead, and so make the eyes of belief see things which are unbelievable and unclear. Secondly, there are the inevitable conflicts which are mediated by means of the spoken word, where one of the arguments involved pleases and persuades a large crowd, not because it was spoken honestly, but because it was skilfully composed. Thirdly, there are philosophical debates, using the spoken word, which demonstrate how quick thinking makes the conviction on which beliefs rest fickle and changeable.*

The power of the spoken word bears the same relation to the arrangement of the mind as that of drugs does to the constitution of bodies. For just as various drugs expel various humours from the body, and some put an end to illness while others put an end to life, so some words cause distress, others pleasure, and others fear, while some arouse courage in those who hear them, and others drug and bewitch the mind by some evil persuasion.*

. . . If it was love that did all this, she will easily escape the charge of the crime she is alleged to have committed. For the things we see do not have the nature we want them to have, but the nature each one actually has, and through the organ of sight the mind receives an imprint even in its characteristics. For instance, when the organ of sight gazes† on hostile figures and an array, hostile with hostile weaponry,† of bronze and iron, some for attacking, some in the form of shields, it is disturbed and it disturbs the mind, and the upshot is that often people flee the danger which is looming as if it were actually present . . . So if Helen's eye found pleasure in Alexander's body and transmitted the eager flirtatiousness of love to her mind, why should that be found surprising? If Love is a god and has the divine power proper to the gods, how would the weaker party be able to repel it and ward it off? On the other hand, if it is a human ailment and a mental deficiency, it should not be regarded as a culpable crime, but as a misfortune. For when it comes, it comes as a result of Fortune's snares rather than planned decisions, and as a result of Love's compulsions rather than contrived preparations.

How, then, should one consider it fair to blame Helen, when she did what she did either because she was enamoured by what she saw[†] or persuaded by the spoken word or forcibly abducted or compelled by divine compulsion? Whichever of these is the case, she is not guilty of the charge brought against her.

By means of the spoken word I have saved a woman from infamy; I have kept to the plan[†] I set myself at the start of the speech; I have tried to dispel the injustice of blame and the ignorance of men's beliefs; I wanted to write the speech as an encomium of Helen and as an amusement for myself.

F2 (DK 82B6) In the second book of his *On Types of Style* the elder Dionysius says about Gorgias: ' . . . Here is an example of the style of his speeches, taken from a passage where he is praising those Athenians who displayed outstanding bravery in war: "For which of those qualities that men should possess was not possessed by these men? And which of those qualities men should not possess was possessed by them? May I be able to say what I want, and may I want to say what I should, while avoiding divine retribution and escaping human envy. For though the mortality of these men was human, their virtue was divine. Often they preferred gentle fairness to inflexible justice, often proper argument to legal precision, since it was their opinion that the most divine and universal law is to speak and to leave unspoken, to act and to leave undone, what one should and when one should. Above all they cultivated two essential qualities— intelligence and strength—using the one for planning and the other for achievement, as they tended the innocent losers and punished the guilty winners, inflexible about expediency but not over-rigid about propriety, using their intelligence to check stupidity,[†] treating the insolent with insolence, the decent with decency, the fearless with fearlessness, and grimly enduring grim situations. To bear witness to these qualities they set up trophies of victories over their enemies as tokens of Zeus' glory and tributes to their own honour. Not unversed were they either in native prowess or in legitimate passion or in armed strife or in noble peace. With their morality they showed reverence for the gods, with their care they showed respect for their parents, with their fairness they showed justice towards their fellow

citizens, with their trustworthiness they showed loyalty towards
their friends. Therefore, though they are dead, the example they set
has not died with them, but immortal in a world of mortal bodies
lives on, though they do not live." '   (Dionysius of Halicarnassus, in
Planudes, *Commentary on Hermogenes' 'Rhetoric'* 5.548 Walz)

T11 (DK 82B3) Gorgias of Leontini shared the starting-point of
those who did away with the criterion, but did not follow the same
line of attack as Protagoras. In his work entitled *On What Is Not* or
On Nature he constructs arguments under three headings, one after
another: (1) that nothing has being; (2), that even if it did have being,
no human being could apprehend it; (3) that even if it was apprehensible, still it could not be expressed or explained to our neighbour.*

(1) His reasoning for the conclusion that nothing has being is as
follows. If something has being, it is either something with being, or
something without being, or both something with being and something without being. But (*a*) he will go on to establish that it is not
the case that something with being has being; (*b*) he will show that
something without being has no being either; (*c*) he will demonstrate
that it is not the case that both something with being and something
without being have being.

(*b*) First, then, that nothing without being has being. If something without being has being, it will simultaneously have and not
have being, in the sense that *qua* conceived as not being it will not
have being, but *qua being* something without being it will, on the
other hand, have being. But since it is completely absurd for something simultaneously to have and not have being, it follows that
nothing without being has being. Besides, if something without
being has being, then something with being will not have being, since
they are opposites to each other, and if being turns out to be an
attribute of something without being, then not being will turn out to
be an attribute of something with being. But in fact it is not the case
that something with being does not have being, and so it is equally
not the case that something without being will have being.

(*a*) But then again, something with being does not have being
either. For if something with being has being, it must either be
eternal or created or both eternal and created. But it is neither eternal nor created nor both, as we will show, and from this it follows
that something with being does not have being. If it is eternal (taking

this proposition first), it has no beginning, because anything created has a beginning, but *qua* uncreated something eternal has no beginning. Since it has no beginning, it is infinite, and since it is infinite, it is nowhere, because if it is somewhere, then that in which it is is different from it, and so something with being will no longer be infinite, given that it is contained within something. For the container is greater than the contained, but there is nothing greater than what is infinite, which means that something infinite cannot be anywhere. But neither is it contained within itself. For if this is so, the container and the contained will be identical, and the thing with being will become two, both place and body (the container being place and the contained being body). But this is absurd, and therefore something with being is not within itself either. The outcome of all this is that if something with being is eternal, it is infinite, and if it is infinite, it is nowhere, and if it is nowhere, it has no being. And so, if something with being is eternal, it has no being at all.

But neither can something with being be created. For if it was created, it came into being either from something with being or from something without being. But it did not come into being from something with being, because something with being already has being and does not come into being. And neither did it come into being from something without being, because nothing without being is capable of generating anything, since in order for anything to generate anything else it necessarily has to partake of existence. Therefore, something with being is not generated either.

By the same token, it is not both eternal and created at the same time, because these two are mutually exclusive, so that if something with being is eternal, it did not come into being, and if it came into being, it is not eternal. And therefore, if something with being is neither eternal nor created nor both, then something with being has no being.

Besides, if it has being, it is either single or multiple; but since it is neither single nor multiple, as will be demonstrated, then something with being does not have being. For if it is single, it is either a discrete quantity or a continuum or a magnitude or a body. But if it is any of these, it is not single: if it is a quantity it will be divisible, and if it is a continuum it will be severable. Likewise, if it is conceived as a magnitude, it will not be indivisible. And if it is in fact a body it will be threefold, because it will possess length, breadth, and depth. But it is absurd to say that something with being is none of these things, and from this it follows that something with being has no being. Nor is it multiple, because if it is not single, it is not multiple either, because anything multiple is a compound of singles. Therefore, if there is nothing that is single, there is nothing that is multiple either.

And so it is evident that neither does something with being have being, nor does something without being have being. (*c*) And, next, it is easy to work out that it is not the case that both something with being and something without being have being. For if something without being has being and something with being has being, then in respect of being something without being it will be identical to something with being. And this is why neither of them has being. For it is a given that something without being has no being, and it has been shown that something with being is identical to something without being, and so something with being will therefore have no being. Moreover, if something with being is identical to something without being, the two of them cannot have being. For if there are the two of them, they are not identical, and if they are identical, they cannot be two.

From all this it follows that nothing has being. For since neither something with being has being, nor does something without being have being, nor do both have being, and since nothing else can be conceived except for these, then nothing has being.

(2) Next it must be demonstrated that even if something does have being, it is unknowable and incomprehensible to any human being. For, Gorgias says, if the objects of thought are not things with being, then something with being is not an object of thought. And this makes sense, because if it were the case that objects of thought were white, it would also be the case that only white things were objects of thought, and by the same token if it were the case that objects of thought were things without being, it would necessarily be the case that things with being would not be objects of thought. Therefore it is perfectly sound and logical to say: 'If the objects of thought are not things with being, then something with being is not an object of thought.' But objects of thought (to start with this) are not things with being, as we will show. And from this it follows that something with being is not an object of thought. Now, it is evident that objects of thought are not things with being. For if objects of thought were things with being, then everything that one thinks

of, however one thinks of them, would have being. But this is nonsensical. For it is not the case that if one thinks of a man flying or a chariot being driven in the sea, then there immediately is a man flying or a chariot being driven in the sea. And so it is not the case that objects of thought are things with being.

Moreover, if objects of thought are things with being, then things without being will not be objects of thought. For opposites are characterized by opposite attributes, and being is opposite to not being. Hence it inevitably follows that if being thought is an attribute of being, not being thought is an attribute of not being. But this is absurd, because Scylla and Chimaera* and plenty of things without being are thought of, and so it is not the case that something with being is the object of thought. Just as objects of sight are said to be visible because they are seen, and objects of hearing are said to be audible because they are heard, and it is not the case that we reject objects of sight because they are not heard, nor do we dismiss audible things because they are not seen (for each object should be assessed by its proper sense and not by any other), so also in the case of objects of thought, even if they are not seen by the eyes or heard by the ears, they will still have being, because they can be grasped by their proper criterion. So if one thinks of chariots being driven in the sea, even if one does not see them, one ought to believe that there are chariots being driven in the sea. But this is absurd. Therefore it is not the case that something with being is the object of thought and is apprehended.

(3) Even if it were to be apprehended, it could not be expressed to anyone else. If things with being are visible and audible and, in general, perceptible—that is, if they are external substances—and if those of them that are visible are apprehensible by sight and those of them that are audible are apprehensible by hearing, but not the other way round, then how could one communicate them to someone else? The spoken word is our means of communication, but the spoken word is not the same as substantial things and things with being. Therefore, it is not the case that we communicate things with being to our neighbours; what we communicate is the spoken word, which is different from these entities. Just as something visible cannot become something audible, and vice versa, so since something with being is an external substance, it cannot become our spoken words, and since it is not the spoken word it cannot be explained to anyone

else. Speech, according to Gorgias, is formed when external events—that is, perceptible things—impinge on us. It is from meeting with flavour that there arises in us the spoken word which is expressive of that quality, and the spoken word which is expressive of colour arises from encountering colour. But if this is so, it is not the spoken word that is indicative of something external, but something external that becomes revelatory of the spoken word. Moreover, it is impossible to claim that the spoken word is the same kind of substantial entity as things which are visible and audible,* and so that it is possible for substantial entities and things with being to be communicated as a result of its being a substantial entity and a thing with being. For even if the spoken word has substance, Gorgias says, it is still different from every other substantial entity, and there is an enormous difference between visible bodies and spoken words; that which is visible is grasped by one organ and the spoken word by another. Therefore, the spoken word cannot communicate most substantial entities, just as they too cannot demonstrate one another's natures. (Sextus Empiricus, *Against the Professors* 7.65.1–86.11 Bury)

T12 (DK 82B3a [Untersteiner]) Gorgias says (1) that nothing has being, (2) that if it did have being it would be unknowable, and (3) that even if it did have being and was knowable, it could not be communicated to others.

(1) In order to demonstrate that nothing has being, he gathers together the ideas of all the other thinkers who apparently contradicted one another in what they said about things with being (since some said that they were one and not many, others that they were many and not one, and some proved that they are uncreated, others that they have undergone creation), and draws up a conclusion in the form of a dilemma. He says that if there are things with being they must be neither one nor many, and neither uncreated nor created; and so there must be nothing with being, for if there were something with being, it would have one or the other of these attributes. And so, that they are neither one nor many, and neither uncreated nor created, he attempts to demonstrate along the lines of both Melissus and Zeno, after his first proof, which is peculiar to him, in which he claims that it is impossible for it either to have being or not to have being. For, he says, if not being *is* not being, then it has being just as

much as something with being does, in the sense that something without being *is* something without being just as much as something with being *is* something with being. And so things no more have being than they do not have being. But if not being *is*, then its opposite—that is, being—*is not*; for if not being *is*, then being must not be. Therefore, he says, it turns out that nothing has being, unless being and not being are the same. And even if they are the same, still there would be nothing with being, because not being has no being, and so if being is the same as not being, it too has no being. This is his first argument . . .

His next argument is as follows: if anything has being, it is either created or uncreated. If it is uncreated, he assumes, on the basis of Melissus' principles, that it is infinite. But what is infinite is not anywhere, since it is neither in itself nor in anything else, which is ruled out because in that case there would be two infinite things, the container and the contained. And since it is nowhere, it is nothing, as Zeno showed in his arguments about space. Hence it is not uncreated, but it is not created either, since nothing comes into being either from something with being or from something without being. For if something with being were to change, it would no longer be something with being, just as also if something without being were to come into being it would no longer be something without being. Nor, on the other hand, could it come to be except from something with being, since if something without being has no being, nothing could come to be out of nothing, and if something without being has being, it could not come to be out of something without being for the same reasons that it could not from something with being.

[*There follow some lines of corrupt text on unity and plurality, presumably arguing that something with being must be either one or many, but cannot be either one or many, and therefore there is nothing with being.*]

Nor, he says, can anything change, since if it were to change it would no longer be as it was before, but something with being would fail to have being, and something without being would come to have being. Besides, if it moves and, though one, changes location, then it is not continuous, and therefore something with being is divided and fails to have being in that place. And therefore, if it moves everywhere, it is divided everywhere, and if this is so, it fails to have being everywhere, since, he claims, it is defective just there, where it is divided . . .

(2) If there is nothing with being, then, he says, demonstrations are deceptive. For every object of thought must have being, and something without being, if it has no being, cannot be an object of thought. If this is so, there would be no such thing as a lie, not even, he says, if someone were to speak of chariots racing in the sea, because all such things would have being.[†] For instance, visible and audible things have being because they are objects of thought. But if this is not why they have being—if what we see does not have being any the more because we see it—then the same goes for what we think. For just as in the case of sight the objects seen by a plurality of people would be indistinguishable, so in the case of thinking the objects thought by a plurality of people would be indistinguishable [*a few corrupt words follow*], but it would be unclear which are the true objects of thought. And the upshot of this is that even if things have being, they are unknowable by us.

(3) And even if they are knowable, he says, how could anyone communicate them to anyone else? How could anyone use the spoken word to express what he has seen? How could what he has seen become clear to someone listening to him, who has not seen it? For just as sight does not recognize sounds, so hearing does not hear colours, but sounds. And a speaker speaks spoken words,[†] not colours or events. How, then, will a person gain a conception from someone else, either by means of the spoken word or some other form of communication, of something he does not have in his mind? This could only happen if it was colour and he saw it, or if it was noise and he heard it. But a speaker does not speak noise or colour, but the spoken word. And so it is not possible to think of colour, only to see it, and it is not possible to think of sound, only to hear it. Even if it is possible to know something and to speak what one knows, how could your audience gain the same conception? For it is not possible for the same thing simultaneously to be in more than one distinct place, since this would make what is single twofold. In any case, he says, even if it were possible for the same thing to be in more than one person, there is no reason why it would not appear different to them, since they are not the same people in all respects and do not occupy the same place; for if they did occupy the same place, they would be one person, not two. Besides, it looks as though not even a single person, on a single occasion, perceives things which are similar, because he perceives different things by means of sight and hearing,

and what he perceives now is different from what he perceived before. So it is hardly likely that two people perceive the same things.

And so nothing has being; even if something had being, it would be unknowable; and even if it were knowable, no one can communicate it to anyone else, because events are not spoken words, and because no two people's conceptions are the same. All these difficulties arise out of the work of earlier thinkers, so that in examining their views [*i.e. the views of Melissus and Xenophanes*] I have to investigate what Gorgias said too.   (Ps.-Aristotle, *On Melissus, Xenophanes, and Gorgias* 979^{a}12–980^{b}21 Bekker)

T13 (DK 82B5) When something is ignited by reflecting sunlight off a mirror or from specially polished bronze and silver surfaces, this does not happen, as Gorgias and some others think, because the fire is passed on through the channels.   (Theophrastus, *On Fire* 73.1–10, Gercke p. 20)

T14 (DK 82B4) *Socrates.* You and Gorgias believe in Empedocles' theory of emanations, don't you?

Meno. Certainly.

Socrates. And you maintain that there are channels into which and through which the emanations travel?

Meno. Yes.

Socrates. And some of the emanations fit some of the channels, while others are too small or too large?

Meno. That's right.

Socrates. Now, you acknowledge the existence of sight, don't you?

Meno. Yes.

Socrates. So you can use this to 'understand my meaning', to quote Pindar. Colour is an emanation from the surfaces of things which is commensurate with sight and is perceptible by it.

(Plato, *Meno* 76c7–d5 Burnet)

T15 (DK 82B18) The issue [*virtue, aretē*] is more likely to be illuminated by a piecemeal approach. To spout generalities and say that virtue is a good mental condition, or correct action, or something of this order, is to deceive oneself. Those like Gorgias who enumerate the virtues have a better case than those who come up with this kind of definition.   (Aristotle, *Politics* 1260^{a}24–8 Ross)

F3 (DK 82B26) Existence is unknown unless it acquires appearance, and appearance is feeble unless it acquires existence. (Proclus, *Commentary on Hesiod's 'Works and Days' 760–4*, Pertusi p. 232)

A. W. H. Adkins, 'Form and Content in Gorgias' *Helen* and *Palamedes*: Rhetoric, Philosophy, Inconsistency and Valid Argument in Some Greek Thinkers', in [22], 107–28.

J. D. Denniston, *Greek Prose Style* (London: Oxford University Press, 1952).

R. L. Enos, 'The Epistemology of Gorgias' Rhetoric: A Re-examination', *Southern Speech Communication Journal*, 42 (1976), 35–51.

B. E. Gronbeck, 'Gorgias on Rhetoric and Poetic: A Rehabilitation', *Southern Speech Communication Journal*, 38 (1972), 27–38.

E. L. Harrison, 'Was Gorgias a Sophist?', *Phoenix*, 18 (1964), 183–92.

G. Kennedy, *The Art of Persuasion in Greece* (London: Routledge & Kegan Paul, 1963).

G. B. Kerferd, 'Gorgias on Nature or That Which Is Not', *Phronesis*, 1 (1955), 3–25.

—— 'The Interpretation of Gorgias' Treatise Περὶ τοῦ μὴ ὄντος ἢ περὶ φύσεως', *Deucalion*, 9 (1981), 319–27.

D. M. MacDowell, *Gorgias: Encomium of Helen* (Bristol: Bristol Classical Press, 1982).

J. Mansfeld, 'Historical and Philosophical Aspects of Gorgias' *On What Is Not*', in [29], 97–125 (first pub. *Siculorum Gymnasium*, 38 (1985)).

J. Poulakos, 'Gorgias' *Encomium to Helen* and the Defense of Rhetoric', *Rhetorica*, 1.2 (1983), 1–16.

J. M. Robinson, 'On Gorgias', in [28], 49–60.

T. J. Saunders, 'Gorgias' Psychology in the History of the Free-will Problem', *Siculorum Gymnasium*, 38 (1985), 208–28.

W. J. Verdenius, 'Gorgias' Doctrine of Deception', in [27], 116–28.

R. Wardy, *The Birth of Rhetoric: Gorgias, Plato and their Successors* (London: Routledge, 1996).

PRODICUS OF CEOS

Our knowledge of Prodicus is (as is that of too many of the Sophists) severely limited. We know that he was a famous and popular Sophist—famous enough in Athens to be mentioned in the occasional Aristophanic comedy[1]—but we have only one extended paraphrase of his work, and our available evidence focuses only on two or three of his interests. This makes it very hard to build up an overall picture of his work and his contribution to the Sophistic movement.

Nevertheless, he counts as a Sophist because he shared some of the essential features of the Sophists: he was a paid educator who worked, no doubt among other places, in Athens (**T1**, **T2**), and he focused on *logos*, the spoken word (**T3–6**). Here it is clear that what impressed Plato and Aristotle most was his attempts to establish the correct meaning of words, which may be seen as the first attempts to develop a Greek dictionary. The importance of a dictionary in fixing a language and so enabling proper communication between different parts of a country cannot be overestimated. Prodicus therefore stands out as an important reformer. It is likely, given Prodicus' interest in words, that he also took part in the debate over whether the names of things were natural (i.e. that the word 'cow' somehow expresses the nature of cow-ness) or conventional (we have simply agreed to call a cow 'cow'),[2] but it is impossible now to reconstruct his position on this. In part it depends on whether he saw his work on words as having the passive aim of reflecting and sharpening distinctions that already existed in the Greek language, or the active aim of creating such distinctions, which would then definitely be conventional.

T7 has aroused some debate. The first Sophist, Protagoras, was a relativist, and some scholars regard relativism as one of the distinctive marks of the Sophistic movement as a whole. Is **T7**, then, evidence that Prodicus was a relativist? After all, he is made to say that wealth, for instance, is good for some and not for others. But in fact there is nothing in **T7** to suggest that Prodicus is a relativist; he might just as well be saying that there is a *right* way to use things, and that the goodness of a thing which is used rightly is independent of a person's knowledge about the right way to use it. When someone learns the right way to use a thing he does not *make*

---

[1] e.g. fragment 490 Kock (from the play *The Broilers*): 'This man has been corrupted by a book, or by Prodicus, or by some other babbler.'

[2] This debate is best reflected for us now in Plato's *Cratylus*, but we glimpse it also in contexts such as Ps.-Hippocrates, *The Art* 2.

the thing good; it is always good, as long as it is rightly used. These are not the ideas of a relativist.[3]

Of more interest is **T8**, showing that Prodicus denied the possibility of contradiction, (like Protagoras—see **T5**, p. 213; and see also Gorgias **T12**, p. 238, and *Double Arguments* at p. 294), and for the same reasons that Plato attributes to Euthydemus and Dionysodorus (see pp. 281–2). We have here a definite Sophistic motif. In the case of Prodicus it is possible to speculate that it might have been his interest in words that also led him to the denial of the possibility of contradiction. If he believed that in distinguishing near synonyms he was picking out real features of the world— if he believed, that is, that any name is a name of something—then he might well have also held, as **T8** suggests, that a true sentence also picks out facts in the world, while an untrue sentence corresponds to nothing in the world, and so says nothing. So, again, whereas for Protagoras the denial of the possibility of contradiction was part and parcel of his relativism, we have no real reason to call Prodicus a relativist.

Even Prodicus' forays into medical science may sometimes have been stimulated by his interest in words, as **T9** suggests. The description of professional speech-writers as occupying a domain halfway between philosophy and statecraft attributed to Prodicus in **T10** has often been thought a good description of a Sophist, as if Prodicus applied it to himself; but if Plato has preserved the saying in the right context, it is meant to be derogatory, and Prodicus himself would no doubt have described himself as a philosopher. The long **F1**, the famous 'Choice of Heracles', is difficult to assess. It is bound to seem rather banal to us, but it falls within the tradition of Greek wisdom literature, and as a defence of traditional Greek morality it is not only charming and memorable (with Heracles clearly serving as a typical person, caught in a moral dilemma), but serves to remind us that the reputation the Sophists acquired as subversives was not always justified. It reveals Prodicus as a champion of *nomos* over *physis*, and as believing that virtue can be taught, because Virtue insists that Heracles should cultivate his natural abilities, while Vice wants him to indulge his natural appetites. Finally, **T11** and **T12** testify that Prodicus' contribution to the fifth-century interest in origins was a cynical account of the origins of religion, and show that he extended this to a fully fledged atheism, at least as regards conventional Greek religion.[4]

[3] Indeed, they may not be the historical Prodicus' ideas in the first place. They are suspiciously similar to ideas Plato puts into the mouth of Socrates in *Euthydemus* 279a–282c.

[4] It is hard to assess the effect of Sophistic atheism on Greek society, and not least because Greek religion was non-dogmatic, which makes 'atheism' a more difficult concept than it is in the Judaeo-Christian tradition. One was required to perform certain ritual actions, and presumably these actions engaged one's emotions, but beyond this

T1 (DK 84A3) [*Socrates speaking*] Or take our eminent friend Prodicus, who often came here to Athens on public business, but the high point was his recent visit on public business from Ceos when he gained considerable fame in the Council as a speaker, as well as earning an incredible amount of money from giving lectures as a private individual and meeting with our young men. (Plato, *Hippias Major* 282c1–6 Burnet)

T2 (DK 84A3a) [*Socrates speaking*] As for people who strike me as not yet being pregnant [*with ideas*] and therefore as having no need of me, this is where my skills as a kindly match-maker come into play. Though I say so myself, I'm pretty good at guessing whose company would be beneficial for them. I have handed lots of them over to Prodicus' care, and plenty to other wise and remarkable men as well. (Plato, *Theaetetus* 151b1–6 Duke *et al.*)

T3 (DK 84A11) [*Socrates speaking*] There's an old saying, Hermogenes, that it is difficult to understand the nature of anything admirable, and it is certainly no small undertaking to come to understand the nature of words. Now, if I had heard Prodicus' 50-drachma exposition, which provides one (as he himself says) with a thorough education on the topic, there would be nothing stopping you from immediately knowing the truth about how to use words correctly; but in fact I've heard only the 1-drachma version. (Plato, *Cratylus* 384a8–c1 Duke *et al.*)

T4 (DK 84A13) When Critias had finished speaking, Prodicus said, 'I think you're right, Critias. Those who are present at a discussion like this should listen to the two speakers impartially, but not equally, the difference being that while one should listen to them both impartially, one should not assent to them equally, but should give more to the cleverer one and less to the less intelligent one. As for

---

one was not required to subscribe to a doctrinal position. However, there is an instructive passage in Thucydides (2.53.4), where he is describing the social effects of the plague in Athens: 'No fear of god or human law had a restraining influence. As for the gods, it seemed to make no difference whether or not one worshipped them.' This perhaps shows that agnosticism or atheism was near enough the surface to break out in a time of crisis. Truly orthodox people turn *to* the gods in times of crisis, not away from them.

me, Protagoras and Socrates, I think you should agree with each other to address the issue in an argumentative, but not disputative fashion—for friends argue among themselves without loss of affection, but disputes arise between people who have fallen out and are enemies. If you do this, our meeting will proceed best, because you, the speakers, will then gain the most respect, but not praise, from us, your audience (for respect is an unfeigned feeling in the minds of the audience, while praise is often confined to the level of words and runs contrary to their true opinion), and we, the listeners, will gain the most satisfaction, but not pleasure (for satisfaction comes from learning something or from participating in some intellectual activity in the mind, while pleasure comes from eating or from some other pleasant activity confined to the body).'*   (Plato, *Protagoras* 337a1–c4 Burnet)

T5 (DK 84A14) [*Socrates talking to Prodicus*] In fact, a proper defence of Simonides* requires the talent you have cultivated, which enables you to distinguish between 'wishing' and 'desiring', and to make all the other wonderful distinctions you made a short while ago [*in* **T4**]   (Plato, *Protagoras* 340a6–b2 Burnet)

T6 (DK 84A15) [*Socrates speaking*] Is there something that you call an 'end'? By this I mean, for example, a 'limit' or a 'boundary'— all three things being the same, as far as I'm concerned, though Prodicus might disagree.   (Plato, *Meno* 75e1–3 Burnet)

T7 [*Socrates is reporting a conversation between Prodicus and an unnamed young man*] The young man asked him under what circumstances he thought wealth was bad or good, and Prodicus replied as you did just now: 'It's good for people who are truly good, who know when to use their property, but it's bad for worthless people, who lack this knowledge. And the same goes for everything else as well: the nature of things is bound to depend on the nature of their users . . .'

   'It necessarily follows, then,' the young man said, 'that if someone were to make me an expert in the area of expertise at which truly good people are experts, he would simultaneously be making everything else good for me, despite the fact that those other things were not what he was concerned with at all, just because he has made me an expert instead of an ignoramus. And so, for instance, if someone were now to make me literate, he would also necessarily make everything else literate for me too; and if he made me musical, he would make everything else musical for me too. After all, when he made me good, he also made things good for me.'

Prodicus did not agree with these analogies, though he did concede the initial point. 'And do you think', the young man went on, 'that making things good is like making a house, in that it's something human beings are capable of doing? Or are things bound to remain in the same condition, good or bad, that they were originally in?'

I got the impression that Prodicus had an inkling of where their argument was heading, and so, in order to avoid being obviously defeated in argument by the young man in front of the assembled company (not that this would make any difference to him if he were alone with him), with extreme cunning he replied that it was something human beings are capable of doing.

'And do you think that excellence is teachable or innate?' the young man asked.

'In my opinion,' Prodicus replied, 'it can be taught.'

'Now, would you think it stupid of someone to imagine that he could become literate or musical by praying to the gods, or could use this method to acquire any other branch of knowledge which has to be gained either by learning it from someone else or by discovering it oneself?'

Prodicus agreed to this too.

'Therefore, Prodicus,' the young man said, 'when you pray to the gods for success, and to gain good things, what you're praying for is to become truly good, since good things are the property of truly good people and bad things are the property of bad people. Now, if excellence is teachable, it turns out that what you're praying for is to be taught what you don't know.'   (Ps.-Plato, *Eryxias* 397e3–398d8 Burnet)

T8 A paradoxical view of Prodicus has come down to us, to the effect that contradiction is impossible. What does he mean by this? It goes against the views and beliefs of all men, since in their daily lives and in the course of their intellectual pursuits everyone converses with people who contradict them. But Prodicus insists that contradiction is impossible, on the grounds that if two people are contradicting each other, they are both speaking, but they cannot both be speaking with reference to the same fact. Only the one who tells the truth, according to Prodicus, is speaking of facts as they are; the other person, who contradicts him, does not speak facts <. . .> (a fragment of Didymus the Blind, *Commentary on Ecclesiastes*; text in the article by G. Binder and L. Liesenborghs in C. J. Classen (ed.), *Sophistik* (Darmstadt, 1976))

T9 (DK 84B4) In *On the Nature of Man* Prodicus used the term 'phlegm' for the burnt and, so to speak, overcooked one of the four humours, since he derived the word from *pephlekhthai* ('to have been burnt'), so that he used a different word to refer to something whose existence he recognized as much as anyone else.* Anyway, his innovative use of words has been sufficiently demonstrated by Plato. But the white stuff which is universally called 'phlegm' Prodicus called 'mucus'.   (Galen, *On the Physical Faculties* 2.9.50.4–12 Kühn)

T10 (DK 84B6) *Socrates.* To which category does the man belong who approached you and criticized philosophy? Is he an orator, someone good at fighting cases, or is he one of their backroom boys, a writer of the speeches with which the orators do the fighting?

Crito. He's certainly no orator at all; in fact, I don't think he's ever entered a law court. But, as God is my witness, he is reputed to understand the pursuit, as well as to be clever and to compose clever speeches.

Socrates. Now I understand. I was on the point of bringing up the subject of these people myself not long ago. They are the ones, Crito, whom Prodicus described as sitting on the fence between philosophy and state affairs.

(Plato, *Euthydemus* 305b5–c7 Burnet)

F1 (DK 84B2) [*Socrates speaking*] The same view of moral goodness is also expressed by the Sophist Prodicus in his story about Heracles, which is one of his most popular displays; it runs like this, as far as I can remember. When Heracles was on the cusp between childhood and manhood, at the age when the young become independent and show whether they are going to approach life by the path of goodness or the path of wickedness, he went out to a quiet spot and sat down to consider which way he should take. While he was sitting there, he seemed to see two women approaching him. Both were tall, but one was handsome in appearance, with a natural air of distinction, clean-limbed and modest in expression, and soberly dressed in a white robe, while the other was well fed to the point of fleshiness and softness, made up to have a complexion too red and white to be real, held herself more upright than was natural, had a brazen expression, and was robed in a way that revealed as many as possible of her charms. She kept on examining herself, and watching to see if anyone was looking at her, and glancing at her own shadow. When they drew nearer to Heracles, the first of the two continued to advance in the same way, but the other, wishing to forestall her companion, ran up to him and said:

'Heracles, I see that you can't make up your mind which way of life to adopt. If you take me as your friend, I will lead you by the easiest and pleasantest road; you will not miss the taste of any pleasure, and you will live out your life without any experience of hardship. In the first place, you will not be concerned with wars or responsibilities; you will constantly consider what food or drink you can find to suit your taste, and what sight or sound or scent or touch might please you, and which lover's society will gratify you most, and how you can sleep most comfortably, and how you can achieve all these objects with the least trouble. And if there is ever any suspicion of a shortage of any of these benefits, you need not fear that I shall involve you in any physical or mental effort or distress in procuring them; you will enjoy the fruits of others' labours, and you will refrain from nothing from which you can derive any advantage, because I authorize my followers to benefit themselves from all quarters.'

When Heracles heard this, he asked, 'What is your name, lady?' She replied, 'My friends call me Happiness, but people who don't like me nickname[†] me Vice.'

Meanwhile, the other woman came forward and said, 'I too have come to meet you, Heracles, because I know your parents and I have carefully observed your natural qualities in the course of your education, and this knowledge makes me hope that, if you will only take the path that leads to me, you may become a very effective performer of fine and noble deeds, and I may win much greater honour still, and brighter glory for the blessings I bestow. I will not delude you with promises of future pleasure; I will give you a true account of the facts, exactly as the gods have ordained them. Nothing that is really good and admirable is granted to men by the gods without some effort and application. If you want the gods to be gracious to you, you must worship the gods; if you wish to be loved by your friends, you must be kind to your friends; if you desire to be honoured by a state, you must help that state; if you expect to be admired for your fine qualities by the whole of Greece, you must try to benefit Greece; if you want your land to produce abundant crops, you must look after your land; if you expect to make money from your livestock, you must take care of your livestock; if you have an impulse to extend your influence by war, and want to be able to free your friends and subdue your enemies, you must not only learn the actual arts of war from those who understand them, but also practise the proper way of applying them; and if you want to be physically efficient, you must train your body to be subject to your reason, and develop it with hard work and sweat.'

Here, Prodicus says, Virtue was interrupted by Vice. 'Do you realize, Heracles,' she said, 'what a long and difficult road to enjoyment this woman is describing to you? I will put you on a short and easy road to happiness.'

'Impudent creature!' cried Virtue. 'What good have you to offer, or what do you know of pleasure, when you refuse to do anything with a view to either? You don't even wait for the desire for what is pleasant: you stuff yourself with everything before you want it, eating before you are hungry and drinking before you are thirsty. To make eating enjoyable, you invent refinements of cookery and, to make drinking enjoyable, you provide yourself with expensive wines and rush about searching for ice in summer. To make going to sleep pleasant, you provide yourself not only with soft blankets, but also with bases for your beds, for it is not work but boredom that makes you want to go to bed. You force the gratification of your sexual impulses before they ask for it, employing all kinds of devices and treating men as women. That is the sort of training that you give your friends—exciting their passions by night, and putting them to sleep for the best part of the day. Although you are immortal, you have been turned out by the gods, and you are despised by decent men. You are robbed of hearing the sweetest of all sounds—praise of yourself—and you are robbed of seeing the sweetest of all sights, for you have never contemplated any act of yours that was admirable. Who would trust your word? Who would assist you if you needed someone? What sane person would have the face to join your devotees? When they are young they are feeble in body, and when they get older they are foolish in mind; they are maintained in their youth in effortless comfort, but pass their old age in laborious squalor, disgraced by their past actions and burdened by their present ones, because in their youth they have run through all that was pleasant, and laid up discomforts for their old age.

'I associate with both gods and good men, and no fine action, human or divine, is done independently of me. I am held in the highest honour among both gods and men who are akin to me. I am a welcome fellow worker to the craftsman, a faithful guardian to the householder, a kindly protector to the servant, an efficient helper in the tasks of peace, a staunch ally in the operations of war, and the best partner in friendship. My friends can enjoy food and drink with pleasure and without effort, because they abstain until they feel a desire for them. Their sleep is sweeter than the sleep of the easy-living, and they neither are vexed when they have to give it up, nor make it an excuse for neglecting their duties. The young enjoy the praise of their elders, and the older people bask in the respect of the young. They recall their past achievements with pleasure, and rejoice in their present successes, because thanks to me they are dear to the gods, loved by their friends, and honoured by their country. And when their appointed end comes, they do not lie forgotten in obscurity, but flourish celebrated in memory for all time.

'There, Heracles,' she said, 'child of good parents: if you work hard in the way that I have described, you can possess the most beatific happiness.'

That is roughly how Prodicus describes the education of Heracles by Virtue, except that he actually dressed up the sentiments in language still more splendid than I have used now.   (Xenophon, *Memoirs of Socrates* 2.1.21–34 Marchant)

T11 (DK 84B5) Prodicus of Ceos says, 'In the old days people regarded the sun, the moon, rivers, springs, and everything else which is helpful for life as gods, because we are helped by them, just as the Egyptians regard the Nile as a god.' And that, he says, is why bread is worshipped as Demeter, wine as Dionysus, water as Poseidon, fire as Hephaestus, and so on for everything that serves some useful purpose. (Sextus Empiricus, *Against the Professors* 9.18 Bury)

T12 He says that the gods worshipped by men neither exist nor have knowledge, but that the ancients exalted crops and everything else which is useful for life.*   (*PHerc* 1428 fr. 19.12–19)

A. Henrichs, 'Two Doxographical Notes: Democritus and Prodicus on Religion', *Harvard Studies in Classical Philology*, 79 (1975), 93–123.

G. B. Kerferd, 'The "Relativism" of Prodicus', *Bulletin of the John Rylands Library*, 37 (1954), 249–56.

HIPPIAS OF ELIS

Hippias was most famous as a polymath, who claimed to be able to answer any question on any topic (**T1**). Plato portrays him, for this reason and others, as somewhat big-headed, but if we remove that veneer, we glimpse a kind of fifth-century Renaissance man—a man of remarkable and wide-ranging accomplishments in subjects as diverse as mathematics and pottery (**T2**, **T3**; see also Protagoras **T2** on p. 212). His art of memory was particularly famous, though we do not know enough about it to begin to speculate what kind of system he might have used and taught.[1] Apart from all these other attainments, we are also told (**T2**) that he composed a model speech with a moral purpose, and we hear of a number of book titles whose subjects range from geography and history to Homeric criticism, taking in astronomy and cosmology on the way. And it is peculiarly relevant to this book to mention that he may (see **F1**) have been the first to create anthologies of passages from poets and philosophers, and to group them under certain headings of his own devising; this was effectively the start of the doxographic tradition which was continued by Aristotle, Theophrastus, and the later doxographers—and which so bedevils the study of the Presocratics. Even by the standards of the Sophists, our evidence for Hippias is unusually thin, but we can begin to glimpse a certain depth to his thought in **T4**, which is an important contribution to the fifth-century debate on the merits of *nomos* and *physis*. Hippias shows himself to be an advocate of nature over convention, and he may have been the first to speak (as in **T6**) of 'natural law', or, in his terms, the 'unwritten laws of nature', which have a greater claim on our obedience than man-made law (**T5**), and are supposed to be universal and unbreakable. A natural law, we may say, is descriptive—it states what simply and unalterably is the case—while a man-made law is prescriptive, since it states what should be the case. Heraclitus' **F12** (p. 39) is perhaps the ancestor of this view; compare also Antiphon **F18** (pp. 264–6), and the passage in Sophocles' *Antigone* (produced in 441 BCE) where Antigone proclaims and acclaims the permanence of the unwritten laws of the gods (450–60).[2] This is an emotively powerful, but legally dangerous argument, since it allows a defendant to claim that he was obeying a superior law in breaking a man-made one, and it had clearly gained

---

[1] On the subject in general, see F. Yates, *The Art of Memory* (London: Routledge & Kegan Paul, 1966).

[2] With a reference to *Antigone*, Aristotle provides a clear statement of the difference between written and unwritten law at *Rhetoric* 1373^b.

enough currency in Athens by the end of the fifth century for it to be found necessary to pass a law forbidding reference to unwritten laws in court (Andocides, *On the Mysteries* 87). Nevertheless, just as we have found reason to believe that the Sophistic movement in general was a democratic or liberal movement, appeal to unwritten laws (whether seen as stemming from a superior, divine realm, or as the unwritten code and customs of a given society) can play an important role within a democracy, to allow debate and prevent the laws becoming rigid and tyrannical. For instance, if a state's laws enshrine the death penalty, one might appeal to an unwritten law of humanitarian clemency or to the notion that only God has the right to take a human life, in order to stimulate debate about the death penalty.

Finally, **T7** affords us a tantalizing glimpse of a Hippian theory which has been called 'the continuity theory of reality'. Details are necessarily obscure, but it seems as though Hippias held that every whole has all the same properties as its parts: if you and I are both swarthy, we are a swarthy pair, and so on. This is an odd theory, and easy to demolish (a crowd of small people is not necessarily a small crowd), so what might have led Hippias to hold it? He possibly held that anything is no more than the sum of its properties (what we call 'kitten' is made up of 'small', 'furry', 'cute', 'playful', and so on), assimilated the relation between properties and the object possessing those properties to the relations between parts and wholes, and so inferred that any whole has the same properties as its parts. There is also a suggestion (at Plato, *Hippias Minor* 369b–c) that this continuity theory of reality was Hippias' justification for preferring long speeches and Sophistic displays to short, Socratic question-and-answer sessions: a long speech can more accurately represent reality, if reality is continuous and not to be chopped up into small pieces.

T1 (DK 86A8) *Socrates.* Well, Eudicus, it's true that there are some questions I'd like to ask Hippias in connection with what he was just saying about Homer . . .

Eudicus. Of course Hippias won't refuse to answer any question of yours. You'll answer Socrates' questions, Hippias, won't you?

Hippias. It would be monstrous of me to evade Socrates' questions, Eudicus. After all, every time the Olympic Games are on, I leave my home in Elis and go to Olympia, to the sacred precinct there, and make myself available to the assembled company of all the

Greeks, to expound any subject on which I've got a lecture prepared, and to answer any question: people only have to ask.*

Socrates. What a happy feeling, Hippias, to enter the sacred precinct at every Olympic festival with such confidence in your mental expertise. I very much doubt that any athlete goes there to compete with such sanguine confidence in his physical prowess as you claim you have in your intelligence.

Hippias. Naturally that's how I feel, Socrates: ever since I began to compete at Olympia, I have never been up against anyone who could beat me at anything.*

(Plato, *Hippias Minor* 363a6–364a9 Burnet)

T2 (DK 86A9, A11) *Socrates.* But what do the Spartans praise you for, and enjoy hearing about? I suppose it must be your special branch of knowledge, astronomy.

Hippias. Not at all. That's a subject they don't even tolerate.

Socrates. But does geometry give them any pleasure?

Hippias. No. It's barely an exaggeration to say that many of them can't even count.

Socrates. Then they won't put up with you lecturing on arithmetic.

Hippias. Certainly not.

Socrates. Then they must enjoy the subject in which your analytical abilities are so exceptional, the significance of letters, syllables, rhythms, and intonations.

Hippias. My dear Socrates! Intonations and letters! Ha!

Socrates. So which lecture-subject of yours gives them pleasure and wins you their praise? You'll have to tell me yourself, because I'm stuck.

Hippias. The genealogies of heroes and men, and how cities were founded in the distant past: in short, antiquarianism in general is what they most enjoy hearing about, and so I was obliged to make a thorough study of the whole subject until I'd mastered it.

Socrates. Well, Hippias, you're certainly lucky that the Spartans don't enjoy the enumeration of Athenian *arkhontes* from Solon onwards, otherwise you'd have had a job mastering it.*

Hippias. Why, Socrates? I can reel off fifty names after hearing them only once.

Socrates. You're right. I wasn't taking your mnemonic technique into account. Now I understand the situation: the Spartans treat you as children do old women, to tell them pleasant stories; so naturally they enjoy you and your vast store of knowledge.

Hippias. Yes, and I tell you, Socrates, I acquired quite a reputation by an exposition I gave there recently of the fine practices to which a young man ought to devote himself. I've got an exceedingly fine lecture composed on the subject; its choice of language is particularly good. The scene is subsequent to the sack of Troy and I start the lecture off with Neoptolemus asking Nestor which fine practices bring fame to a young man, and then Nestor gives him plenty of advice on the finest rules of life.*

(Plato, *Hippias Major* 285b7–286b4 Burnet)

T3 (DK 86A12) [*Socrates to Hippias*] In my hearing, you have bragged of being altogether more of an expert at more areas of expertise than anyone. I remember you in the city square by the bankers' tables enumerating your considerable and enviable expertise. You said that once you went to Olympia with nothing on your person which you hadn't made yourself. You started with the ring you were wearing, claiming to know how to engrave rings; not only it, but the rest of your jewellery too, and your strigil-and-flask set—all your own work, you said. Then you went on to the shoes you were wearing—cobbled by yourself, you claimed—and your cloak and tunic, woven by yourself. Then—and this struck everyone as most remarkable and as clear evidence of outstanding expertise—you said that although your tunic belt was in the Persian style of the expensive kind, you had braided it yourself. But that wasn't all. You had brought epic, tragic, and dithyrambic poetry, you said, and many prose speeches in a variety of styles. And you had come equipped not only with exceptional expertise in the areas I mentioned just before, but also in matters of rhythm, intonation, orthography, and very many other things besides, I seem to remember—oh, but I was forgetting what was apparently your technique of remembering, on which you really pride yourself. I reckon I've probably forgotten lots of other things too!   (Plato, *Hippias Minor* 368b2–e1 Burnet)

F1 (DK 86B6) Some of these things may perhaps have been said by Orpheus or, in a brief and scattered fashion, by Musaeus; some may have been said by Hesiod or Homer or other poets; some by Greek or foreign prose-writers. But from among all these sayings I will make a collection of the most important and closely related passages, and I will make out of them a new and multifaceted account. (Clement, *Miscellanies* 6.15.2 Stählin/Früchtel)

T4 (DK 86C1) After Prodicus, the wise Hippias spoke: 'Gentlemen,' he said, 'I regard you all as relatives and family and fellow citizens—by nature, not by convention.* For by nature like is akin to like, but convention is a tyrant over humankind and often constrains people to act contrary to nature.' (Plato, *Protagoras* 337c6–d3 Burnet)

T5 'But Socrates,' said Hippias, 'how can anyone take laws seriously or believe in them, when often the same people who established them repeal them and change them?' (Xenophon, *Memoirs of Socrates* 4.4.14.1–4 Marchant)

T6 'Do you know what is meant by "unwritten laws", Hippias?' Socrates asked.

'Yes, those which are observed in every country with respect to the same circumstances.'

'Can you claim that it was men who laid them down?'

'How could it be, considering that they couldn't all meet together and don't speak the same language?'

'Then who do you think are the authors of these laws?'

'I suppose that these laws were ordained for men by gods. At any rate, among all peoples the first established custom is to worship gods.'

'Isn't it a custom everywhere to honour parents?'

'Yes, that too.'

'And that parents shouldn't copulate with their children or children with their parents?'

'I don't think that this is a god-given law like the others, Socrates.'

'Why not?'

'Because I observe that some people break it.'

'In point of fact they break a good many other laws. But those who transgress the laws laid down by the gods pay a penalty which no man can escape in the way that some transgressors of man-made laws escape paying the penalty, either by escaping detection or by the use of force.' (Xenophon, *Memoirs of Socrates* 4.4.19–21 Marchant)

T7 *Socrates.* Are you sure, Hippias? I suppose you've got a point but I don't understand. Let me explain more clearly what I'm getting at: it seems to me that both of us together may possess as an attribute something which I neither have as an attribute nor am (and neither are you); and, to put it the other way round, that neither of us, as individuals, may be something which both of us together have as an attribute.

Hippias. Socrates, this is apparently even more preposterous than the response you made a little while ago. Look here: if both of us are just, then each of us must be too, surely? If each of us is unjust, aren't both too? If both are healthy, isn't each too? Or if each of us were tired, wounded, bruised, or had any other attribute, then wouldn't both of us also have this attribute? Or again, if both of us happened to be golden, silver, ivory, or well-born, if you like, or clever, or respected—yes, or old or young or anything else which a human being can be, isn't there an overwhelming necessity that each of us would be too?

Socrates. Yes, absolutely.

Hippias. The fact of the matter is, Socrates, that you and your usual interlocutors fail to take account of things at the general level: your method of analysis is to isolate fineness or whatever it may be, and dissect it verbally, so of course these obvious points pass you by, and you fail to take account of the continuity of physical reality. Your oversight in the present case is so great that you think there is some attribute or essential quality which obtains simultaneously for both the things we've been talking about, but not for each individually—or, conversely, for each but not for both. How mindless, careless, senseless, and thoughtless can you get!

Socrates. That's in keeping with the saw one is always hearing, Hippias: ability, not desire, dictates human achievement. But your constant criticism is helpful. I mean, just now, before your scolding about how foolishly we were behaving—well, shall I tell you even more of what we thought on this issue, or should I keep quiet?

Hippias. Go ahead, if you want, Socrates, just so long as you understand that you'll be speaking to an expert: I know all the ways discussions are conducted.

Socrates. Yes, I do want to. You see, before you spoke, my friend, we were so inane as to believe that each of us—you and I—is one, but that both of us together, being two not one, are not what each individual is. See how stupid we were! But now we know better: you've explained that if both together are two, then each individual must be two as well; and if each individual is one, both must be one as well. For this necessarily follows from Hippias' theory of 'continuous' reality.

(Plato, *Hippias Major* 300e1–301e5 Burnet)

M. L. Morgan, 'The Continuity Theory of Reality in Plato's *Hippias Major*', *Journal of the History of Philosophy*, 21 (1983), 133–58.

ANTIPHON THE SOPHIST

The question whether Antiphon the Sophist and his contemporary Antiphon of Rhamnus, the eminent Athenian speech-writer and orator, are one or two people will probably never be resolved. Since the title of this book is *The First Philosophers*, and since I incline to the view that they are two people, I have not here included any of Antiphon of Rhamnus' excellent speeches, but reproduce the evidence for the philosophical activities of Antiphon the Sophist and fragments from his famous books *On Truth* and *On Concord*, though he also wrote a number of other books, including *On the Interpretation of Dreams*. Indeed, some of the book-titles and testimonia testify to an interest in rhetoric, which makes him particularly hard to distinguish from his namesake,[1] but also shows that he shared the common interest of his fellow Sophists. He wrote a handbook on rhetoric, and also a collection of introductions which could be used to preface legal speeches.

On Concord seems basically to have consisted of often wry or humanitarian aphorisms on various aspects of human life. I translate a few as **F1–14**. Despite ancient charges of obscurity (e.g. by Hermogenes, *On Kinds of Literary Composition* B 399.18.9 Rabe), the clarity of Antiphon's insights and expression is pleasing. But the tone of *On Truth* is quite different, as if written for a more specialist philosophical audience. An attempt to reconstruct a coherent argument from the scattered fragments might go like this. The senses are our windows on to reality and our means of knowledge (**F15, F16**), but words are deceptive (**F16**); for instance, we call people 'Greeks' or 'foreigners', when in fact all human beings are akin (**F17**), we differentiate between 'tree' and 'bed', when in fact they are both wood (**T1**), and we differentiate between 'circle' and 'straight-sided figure', when in fact they share the same area (**T2**). So we need to be careful when we make up words (**T3**): mind is the ruler of the body (**F20**), but it needs the correct starting-point (**F21**). This starting-point is conformity with nature, not convention. But nature is just brute reality: it is not made by God (**T4**), nor does God have any need of us (**F22**). At some point Antiphon also managed to slip in Presocratic theories about the origin and nature of the heavenly bodies, embryology, and so on (**F23–4, T5–8**), and a criticism of Homeric poetry and society's reliance upon it (**F25**).

---

[1] Antiphon of Athens, the orator, wrote model speeches showing how one could both prosecute and defend certain charges. Even if the orator and the Sophist are different people, these speeches are consummate examples of the Protagorean ability to argue both sides of a case.

The radical nature of much of what Antiphon says in **F17–19** needs to be emphasized. The fragmentary nature of the evidence has led to a number of different interpretations in recent years; in particular, it is difficult to tell sometimes whether Antiphon is advocating a point of view, or just reporting a case. But what follows is an orthodox view, and the most natural reading. In terms of the fifth-century debate about nature and convention, he shows himself to be a champion of nature over law and convention, and he uses this to arrive at some conclusions that, however familiar in today's liberal and pluralistic Western societies, would have seemed highly shocking and unusual to Antiphon's contemporaries—that there is nothing essential or natural to distinguish Greeks from foreigners, and that all such distinctions are matters of convention;[2] that natural law is so much more essential than man-made law that one should obey man-made laws (or at least those which contravene natural law) only in order to avoid punishment and stigmatization, while if one can get away with it, one should transgress man-made laws in favour of the laws of nature; that the whole judicial process is self-contradictory and fails to help those it should help. Antiphon is going much further than simply criticizing the legal system: he says that most laws are hostile to nature, which is to say they do us harm, and that even when they do stand a chance to be beneficial they are weak and governed by a concept of justice which fails in practice.

These are remarkable conclusions for a fifth-century Greek. Self-preservation, Antiphon implies, is the ultimate natural law, and a great deal of his critique of society stems from this: self-preservation requires one to obey unnatural laws when others are watching; pain and discomfort are criteria by which we can judge that something is bad for us, and tends against self-preservation, and by these criteria human laws are bad, since they cause us pain. Like Hippias, he maintains that natural laws are unbreakable, or at least unbreakable without dire consequences to oneself: the kinds of laws he has in mind, however, are less the moral laws on which Hippias appears to have focused than physical demands such as hunger, tiredness, and so on. If you are hungry, you have to eat, or you will die; the pain of hunger is nature's way of telling you that something is wrong; the pleasure of eating is good, and so Antiphon is some kind of hedonist.

Two thoughts on Antiphon as a hedonist. First, is there, then, a clash between *On Truth* and *On Concord*? Many scholars have thought so. In **F5**, for instance, Antiphon seems to advise against hedonism, and in

[2] Contrast Sophocles, *Ajax* 548–9, which implies exactly the opposite: men are born different and law makes them similar.

general *On Concord* seems less radical than *On Truth* (see the conservative tone of **F1** and **F2**, for instance). But in fact, in **F5**, self-interest is still the dominant motive; restraint is counselled in order to avoid the pain of retribution from someone you injure. Instead of looking to short-term pleasure, Antiphon suggests, we should look to the overall pleasure guaranteed by self-interest and self-preservation. This, I think, may also adequately explain the value Antiphon finds in self-discipline in **F2**. Second, if Antiphon is a hedonist, he is not a partisan of *physis* in the straightforward sense that *physis* is for him the *summum bonum*. Rather, it is a criterion—perhaps the only valid criterion—of what is right and wrong. Your nature will tell you what is right and wrong, and so steer you towards pleasure. In this sense *On Concord* complements *On Truth*, and may even be mined as a source for more positive, less destructive, comments on law.

Antiphon shares with Thrasymachus a focus on self-interest, but makes a different use of it. For Thrasymachus advantage lies in always being unjust, but Antiphon counsels a more moderate, though more hypocritical stance: it is advantageous to be seen to obey the law, but when there are no witnesses you can do what you like, as your nature judges best, not as the law judges best. But the main thrust of the surviving fragments is his criticism of *nomos* as incoherent. For instance, he argues that a part of the common notion of justice is that it is just to bear witness against a criminal. But often it is not the case that the criminal wronged you personally, merely that you happened to see him carrying out his crime. If the criminal is convicted and suffers some unpleasant punishment because of your testimony, it follows that though he did not wrong you, you are causing him harm—that is, doing injustice to him. Moreover, in a law court, the instrument of *nomos*, it is not necessarily the case that justice is done. It depends on one's skill at persuading a jury rather than on the justice of one's case. Besides, the legal process comes into play only after the act: it does nothing to prevent injustice in the first place.

These are the kinds of arguments Antiphon brings against *nomos*. Perhaps he believed that there should be an ideal of justice where these incoherencies do not obtain, a justice which is in accordance with *physis*, with one's pleasure, advantage, and self-preservation. This humanitarian and moral ideal is opposed to Thrasymachus' radical interpretation of the theory of natural right, but is in keeping with the humanitarianism of Antiphon's comments on the natural and essential identity of Greeks and foreigners, free men and slaves.

F1 (DK 87B60) There is nothing more important for men than education, since any business that is started correctly is likely to end correctly too. After all, it is the kind of seed one sows in the ground that determines the kind of products one should expect. So when one sows a sound education in a young body, it lives and flourishes throughout that person's lifetime, and neither rain nor drought destroys it.   (John of Stobi, *Anthology* 2.31.39 Wachsmuth/Hense)

F2 (DK 87B61) There is nothing worse for men than lack of discipline. It was recognition of this fact that led earlier generations of men to accustom their sons to discipline, and to doing what they were told, right from the start. The idea was that when they were grown up they should not be upset by any serious changes they met. (John of Stobi, *Anthology* 2.31.40 Wachsmuth/Hense)

F3 (DK 87B62) Whatever kind of person one spends the majority of the day with, one is bound to come to resemble him oneself in respect of his characteristics.*   (John of Stobi, *Anthology* 2.31.41 Wachsmuth/Hense)

F4 (DK 87B49) Well, then, let's move on through his life and have him wanting marriage, wanting a wife. That day, that night, is the beginning of a whole new direction for him,* a new destiny, because marriage is a serious trial of a man's strength. For if she turns out to be unsuitable, how can he deal with this unfortunate situation? Divorce is troublesome, in that it makes enemies of his friends, men with the same ideas and the same qualities, men who have found him acceptable and have accepted him. But it is also troublesome to keep a possession of this kind, to marry pain when one expected to acquire pleasure. Well, then, let's not speak of such a grim possibility; let's say that she is completely suitable. What could be more pleasant for a man than a compatible wife? What could be more delightful, especially when he is young? But in exactly the same place, precisely where pleasure is to be found, pain too lies close at hand. For pleasures do not travel unaccompanied, but pain and hard work attend them. All the pleasures of life—the acquisition of knowledge, even victories at the Olympic and Pythian Games and so on—tend to arrive as a result of great pains. Prestige, prizes, all the lures which the gods have given men, involve them in the necessity of hard work and an enormous quantity of sweat. Thinking of myself, for instance, if I had another body to look after as I do the one I have, life would become impossible, since my body's health, the daily business of scraping together enough to keep it alive, and maintaining its reputation, regard, fame, and esteem, already occupy so much of my time and efforts. What would happen, then, if I had another similar body, which I had to look after in the same way? And it obviously follows from this that even a compatible wife provides a man with just as much affectionate attention and trouble as he gives himself, since now he has to think of the health of *two* bodies, and of scraping together a livelihood for *two* bodies, and of the regard and fame of *two* bodies. Now, then, suppose they have children. Straight away he is beset by nothing but worries, the youthful buoyancy leaves his thinking, and his features change. (John of Stobi, *Anthology* 4.22.66 Wachsmuth/Hense)

F5 (DK 87B58) The more sensible option, when a man is poised to attack his neighbour with the intention of doing him harm, is for him to be afraid of failing to carry out his intentions and achieving the opposite result instead. For fear leads to hesitation, and hesitation leaves him an interval in which to change his mind, as often happens. This is impossible once the action has already taken place, but it can happen while he is hesitating.[†] Anyone who imagines that he will do harm to his neighbour and remain unscathed himself is not being sensible. Hopes are not always good: hopes of this kind have often brought men low and involved them in irreparable disasters, and they have ended up experiencing what they had been expecting to do to their neighbours. The most accurate criterion by which to judge if a man has good sense is to see whether he resists his heart's immediate impulses towards pleasure and has proved capable of self-control and self-mastery. But the man who tends to gratify his heart's impulses is the man who tends towards the worse, not the better, course of action. (John of Stobi, *Anthology* 3.20.66 Wachsmuth/Hense)

F6 (DK 87B59) The man who has never desired or experienced anything base and bad is not a man of restraint, because he has never had to master anything to compose himself. (John of Stobi, *Anthology* 3.5.57 Wachsmuth/Hense)

F7 (DK 87B56) A coward is someone whose tongue is full of confidence and whose will pushes him forward when the danger is absent and impending, but draws back when faced with the actual event. (*The Suda* s.v. *oknō*, 3.514.24–6 Adler)

F8 (DK 87B57) Illness is a holiday for cowards. (John of Stobi, *Anthology* 3.18.8 Wachsmuth/Hense)

F9 (DK 87B50) Life is like a day watch and the length of life is like a single day, so to speak: once we have looked up at the light we pass the duty on to others, who come after us. (John of Stobi, *Anthology* 4.34.63 Wachsmuth/Hense)

F10 (DK 87B51) It is incredibly easy to find fault with life, my friend: it contains nothing remarkable or important or significant, but everything is petty, feeble, ephemeral, and bound up with terrible grief. (John of Stobi, *Anthology* 4.34.56 Wachsmuth/Hense)

F11 (DK 87B52) It is impossible to take back one's life like a move at backgammon. (Harpocration, *Lexicon* s.v. *anathesthai*, 31.1–2 Dindorf)

F12 (DK 87B53a) Some people do not live the life they have, but thoroughly occupy themselves with plans, as if they had another life to live, not the one they have. And meanwhile time passes them by. (John of Stobi, *Anthology* 3.16.20 Wachsmuth/Hense)

F13 (DK 87B54) There's a story about a man who saw another man winning a lot of money and asked whether he could borrow it, at interest. The man with the money refused, being a mistrustful kind of person, the kind who doesn't help anyone else, and he took the money and stored it somewhere. But word got around, and the money was stolen. Later, the man who had stored the money came and found that it had gone. He was very upset at what had happened, and not least because he hadn't lent the money to the man who had asked him for it, because then his money would have been safe and he would gained the interest as well. He happened to meet the man who had previously wanted to borrow the money and complained about his misfortune, saying that he had made a mistake and that he regretted not having done him a favour and having turned him down, because he had lost all his money. The man told him not to worry, but to imagine that he still had the money and hadn't lost it, and to put a stone in the place where he had stored the money. 'After all,' he said, 'you didn't make the slightest use of the money when you had it, and so now you needn't imagine that you've lost anything.' For if a person hasn't made use of something he has, and has no intention of doing so in the future, there's no difference at all between owning it and not owning it: in either case, he suffers no more or less harm. When the gods want to benefit a man, but to qualify their blessings, they give him financial wealth but poverty of good sense, so that his lack of the one asset causes him to lose the other as well.   (John of Stobi, *Anthology* 3.16.30 Wachsmuth/Hense)

F14 (DK 87B65) People with friends often fail to recognize them, and go around instead with those who flatter wealth and fawn on good fortune.   (*The Suda* s.v. *thōpeia*, 2.723.25–6 Adler)

F15 People believe what they see with their eyes more than they do those things the evidence for whose genuine existence comes from what is unseen.   (*The Suda* s.v. *atta*, 1.397.15–17 Adler)

F16 (DK 87B1) No single thing uttered by someone has a single meaning, and neither is it one of those things which a far-seer sees with his eyes nor one of those things which a far-knower knows with his mind.[†]   (Galen, *Commentary on Hippocrates' 'On the Doctor's Workshop'* XVIIIB.656.14–15 Kühn)

F17 (DK 87B44B)[†] <. . .> we know and respect,* but those who dwell far away we neither know nor respect. This has led to our behaving like foreign savages towards one another, when by nature there is nothing at all in our constitutions to differentiate foreigners and Greeks.* We can consider those natural qualities which are essential to all human beings and with which we are all equally endowed, and we find that in the case of all these qualities there is nothing to tell any of us apart as foreigner or Greek. For we all breathe the air through our mouths and nostrils, laugh when our minds feel pleasure or cry when we are distressed; we hear sounds with our ears; we see with our eyes thanks to daylight; we work with our hands, and walk with our feet <. . .>   (pieced together from *Oxyrhynchus Papyrus* 1364, fr. B, cols. 1–3 Grenfell/Hunt, and *Oxyrhynchus Papyrus* 3647)

F18 (DK 87B44A)[†] Justice, therefore, is conforming to the rules and regulations of the community of which you are a citizen.* The way to gain maximum advantage for yourself from justice, then, is to treat the laws as important when other people are present, but when there is nobody else with you to value the demands of nature. For the laws' demands are externally imposed, but those of nature are essential, and while agreement, not nature, has produced the laws' demands, nature, not agreement, has produced those of nature. So if your transgression of regulations escapes the notice of those who have made the agreement, you avoid both shame and punishment, but incur them if it doesn't; however, if you achieve the impossible and violate one of the inherent demands of nature, the harm you suffer is not decreased if what you do goes totally unnoticed, and not increased if everyone sees you, because it is genuine harm, not a result of what others think of you. This is exactly what this investigation of mine is concerned with—to show that most of the actions sanctioned by law are inimical to nature. For laws dictate what the eyes may and may not see, what the ears may and may not hear, what the tongue may and may not speak, what the hands may and may not do, where the feet may and may not go, and what the mind may and may not desire. There is no difference between the things the laws deter us from doing and the things the laws encourage us to do: both are equally inimical to nature. For what is natural is life and death, and life comes about through things which are advantageous, while death comes about from things which are disadvantageous. The advantages offered by the law are fetters on nature, but the advantages offered by nature bring freedom. Properly speaking, it is not the case that discomfort benefits one's nature more than comfort, pain more than pleasure; for things which are genuinely advantageous should help, not harm. Therefore, things which are naturally advantageous <. . .>

<. . .> and people who defend themselves after having become the victims but do not themselves instigate any action, and people who are good to their parents even if their parents are bad to them, and people who allow others to swear an oath when they themselves have not sworn an oath.* Many of the things I've mentioned will be found to be inimical to nature, and they bring with them more pain, when less is possible, and less pleasure, when more is possible, and suffering, when suffering is unnecessary. So if support was available from the laws for those who surrender their rights† in this way, and degradation for those who choose to resist rather than surrender their

rights, then obedience to the laws would serve some useful purpose. But as things are, it looks as though justice under the law does not offer sufficient support to those who surrender their rights in this way. In the first place, it allows the victim to suffer and the agent to act: not only did it not prevent the victim suffering or the agent acting at the time, but also when it comes to punishment it does not favour the victim over the perpetrator. For the victim has to convince those who would punish him that he has been a victim, and he has to be able <. . .> But it is still possible for the perpetrator to deny <. . .>　　(*Oxyrhynchus Papyrus* 1364, fr. A, cols. 1–6 Grenfell/ Hunt)

F19 (DK 87B44C)[†] <. . .> for all parties to tell the truth in court is generally regarded not only as just, but also, and equally, as useful for human customs. But anyone who does this will not be just, given that it is just not to commit injustice against or injure anyone when one has not been injured or had injustice committed against oneself. For anyone who testifies in court is bound to injure another person in some way or other, even if his testimony is true . . . while because of his testimony the person he testifies against is convicted and loses either property or his life thanks to the testimony of a man he never injured. So he commits an injustice against the person he testifies against, because he is injuring someone who didn't injure him, and then he too is injured by the person he testified against, because he is hated by him for having told the truth in court. And he is injured not only by the other man's hatred, but also because he has to spend his whole life watching out for the man against whom he testified. So he gains the kind of enemy whose words and actions will be designed to do him harm, if he possibly can. Now, these injustices—those he suffers and those he commits—are clearly not insignificant, since there is no way (1) that the situation just described is just *and* (2) that it is just to avoid injuring others and being injured oneself. On the contrary, it necessarily follows either that some other situation is just or that both (1) and (2) are unjust. It is clear, then, that the judicial process, the verdicts, and arbitration to a conclusion, are not just, since in trying to help some people one harms others, and so although those who are helped are not injured, those who are harmed are injured <. . .>　　(*Oxyrhynchus Papyrus* 1797, cols. 1–2 Grenfell/Hunt)

T1 (DK 87B15) Some people take the nature and substance of any natural thing to be its primary component, something which is unformed in itself. They say, for instance, that wood is the 'nature' of a bed, bronze the 'nature' of a statue. Antiphon cites as evidence the fact that if you bury a bed and, as it rots, it manages to send up a shoot, the result is wood, not a bed. He concludes from this that the arrangement and design of the bed, which are due merely to human convention, are coincidental attributes, and that the substance is that which persists throughout, however it is affected. (Aristotle, *Physics* 193ª9–17 Ross)

T2 (DK 87B13) At the same time, it is not our business [*as conducting an enquiry into the principles of nature*] to correct all mistakes, but to do so only where someone has drawn false inferences from principles, and not otherwise. Similarly, it is a geometer's job to refute the attempt to square the circle by means of segments, but it is not up to a geometer to refute Antiphon's method of squaring a circle.* (Aristotle, *Physics* 185ª12–17 Ross)

T3 That every single one of those whose professional interest lay in the spoken word felt entitled to make up new words is sufficiently and clearly shown by the fact that Antiphon taught the best way to make them up. (Galen, *Glossary of Hippocratic Terminology*, XIX.66.12–14 Kühn)

F20 (DK 87B2) For all men it is the mind that leads the body to health, illness, and everything else. (Galen, *Commentary on Hippocrates' 'On the Doctor's Workshop'*, XVIIIB.656.15–17 Kühn)

F21 (DK 87B14) Deprived of a starting-point it would have made the condition of many good things bad.* (Harpocration, *Lexicon* s.v. *diathesis*, 92.2–3 Dindorf)

T4 (DK 87B12) Even if one person were to be a Demosthenes . . . and another an Antiphon, who was taken to be an orator and, in his book called (like that of Celsus) *On Truth*, did away with Providence, these people would still be worms wallowing in a muddy corner of ignorance and stupidity. (Origen, *Against Celsus* 4.25.9–15 Koetschau)

F22 (DK 87B10) That is why he needs nothing and has no

expectations, but is without limits or needs.*   (*The Suda* s.v. *adeētos*,
1.46.20–22 Adler)

T5 (DK 87B26) Antiphon says that the sun is fire which consumes
the moist air around the earth, and whose risings and settings
are caused by the fact that it is constantly leaving the scorched air
and instead pursuing the damp air.*   (Aëtius, *Opinions* 2.20.15
Diels)

T6 (DK 87B27) Antiphon says that the moon has its own light, but
that the hidden part of the moon is obscured by the sun's light
falling upon it, just as the light of a stronger fire will obscure a
weaker one. And he says that this happens in the case of the other
heavenly bodies too.   (Aëtius, *Opinions* 2.28.4 Diels)

F23 (DK 87B30) By scorching and melting the earth it makes it
wrinkled.*   (Harpocration, *Lexicon* s.v. *grupanion*, 82.1–2 Dindorf)

T7 (DK 87B32) Antiphon says that the sea is the sweat of the hot
substance, from which the remaining moisture was secreted, and
that it became salty† as a result of being boiled away, which is how all
sweat becomes salty.   (Aëtius, *Opinions* 3.16.4 Diels)

T8 (DK 87B34) 'Headache' and 'heaviness of the head' . . . and food
or drink which causes heaviness of the head: Antiphon says that
what causes this is 'stupefaction'.   (Pollux, *Lexicon* s.v. *kephalaion*
(4), 2.41 Dindorf)

F24 (DK 87B36) The word for what the embryo grows and is nourished in is 'placenta'.   (Pollux, *Lexicon* s.v. *kephalaion* (4), 2.223
Dindorf)

F25 < . . . > or to regard it as bad. A young man ought to have
nothing to do with an occupation of this kind. I will explain my
opinion about the poets, since I have in the past heard a lot of people
saying that it is beneficial to spend time over the poems which men
of old have left us. The benefit they afford, they say < . . . > about
things good and bad, and right and wrong; about supernatural phenomena; about what happens in Hades; about human birth and
funerals < . . . > for someone who does not already know about men
of previous generations to listen to the poet. Moreover, I think that
one poet can improve on another < . . . > *   (*Oxyrhynchus Papyrus*
414, cols. 1–3 Grenfell/Hunt)

H. C. Avery, 'One Antiphon or Two?', *Hermes*, 110 (1982), 145–58.

J. Barnes, 'New Light on Antiphon', *Polis*, 7 (1987), 2–5.

J. Dillon, 'Euripides and Antiphon on Nomos and Physis: Some Remarks', in [23], 127–36.

D. J. Furley, 'Antiphon's Case Against Justice', in [27], 81–91.

G. B. Kerferd, 'The Moral and Political Doctrines of Antiphon the Sophist: A Reconsideration', *Proceedings of the Cambridge Philological Society*, 4 (1956–7), 26–32.

R. D. Luginbill, 'Rethinking Antiphon's *Peri Aletheias*', *Apeiron* 30 (1997), 163–87.

J. S. Morrison, 'Antiphon', *Proceedings of the Cambridge Philological Society*, 7 (1961), 49–58.

—— 'The *Truth* of Antiphon', *Phronesis* 8 (1963), 35–49.

C. Moulton, 'Antiphon the Sophist, *On Truth*', *Transactions of the American Philological Association*, 103 (1972), 329–66.

M. Ostwald, 'Nomos and Physis in Antiphon's *Peri Physeos*', in M. Griffith and D. Mastronarde (eds.), *Cabinet of the Muses* (Atlanta: Scholars Press, 1990), 293–306.

G. Pendrick, 'Once Again Antiphon the Sophist and Antiphon of Rhamnous', *Hermes*, 115 (1987), 47–60.

M. Reesor, 'The Truth of Antiphon the Sophist', *Apeiron*, 20 (1987), 203–18.

T. J. Saunders, 'Antiphon the Sophist on Natural Laws (B44 DK)', *Proceedings of the Aristotelian Society*, 78 (1977/8), 215–36.

A. Wasserstein, 'Some Early Greek Attempts to Square the Circle', *Phronesis*, 4 (1959), 92–100.

THRASYMACHUS OF CHALCEDON

Thrasymachus was evidently a famous and well-respected orator in his own day, who like all the major Sophists made his name in Athens. Although **T1–4** testify to his fame in this respect, we have only a few phrases from his speeches, and one extended fragment from a model speech, which I translate despite its lack of philosophical interest (**F1**). As well as composing speeches, it looks as though he also taught others to defeat opponents through argumentation in speeches, if the title of a book of his, preserved by Plutarch in **T5**, is genuine. But his lasting fame has come about because of his memorable place in the first book of Plato's *Republic*. Were it not for **T6**, however, we would have cause to wonder about the veracity of Plato's use of Thrasymachus, since we would know of the Sophist only as an orator. But **T6** shows that he was also a philosopher, and was a critic of culture along with many other Sophists. **T6** is a trace of a common agnostic or atheistic argument that there is injustice in the world, but the gods would not tolerate injustice, from which it follows either that the gods do not exist,[1] or that even if they do they are not interested in human affairs. The latter conclusion seems to have been the one Thrasymachus arrived at.

Although, as usual, it is not clear how much Plato is embellishing any genuine views of the historical Thrasymachus, I have included the most relevant parts of his speeches from Plato as **T7**, since they are certainly representative of a trend of thought current in the last quarter of the fifth century. However, the precise interpretation of what Thrasymachus meant is controversial. In particular, he makes two claims which are not entirely consistent with each other. At one point he says that 'Justice is nothing other than the advantage of the stronger party'; at another that 'Justice is the promotion of someone else's good.' For the weaker party in a transaction, the two statements are equivalent; but for the stronger party they are contradictory, since if a strong person acts to his own advantage he is acting justly according to the first statement, but unjustly according to the second statement.

One interpretation privileges the first of these statements and makes Thrasymachus an ethical nihilist, in the sense that there is no such thing as justice beyond what rulers lay down as just; another privileges the second and makes Thrasymachus a supporter of natural right. But the

---

[1] This was the consequence drawn from these premises by an earlier atheist, Diagoras of Melos, who lived *c.*430 BCE. See also Euripides fr. 286, from *Bellerophon*.

ethical nihilist view cannot be right, because it limits justice to being something only the ruled do, whereas Thrasymachus clearly wants it to be something rulers do as well. Moreover, the ethical nihilist view focuses on political justice, whereas the terms of Thrasymachus' whole speech are not confined only to politics, but also to business transactions and human intercourse in general. And finally, if justice is only the advantage of the stronger, then it would be a good and praiseworthy thing for Thrasymachus, but in fact he praises injustice.

I believe that the first statement is meant to be a shocking entrée into the discussion (the Sophists often played to the crowd and sought applause), while the second statement represents the view of the character Thrasymachus in Plato's dialogue (and most probably that of the historical Sophist too). Thrasymachus believed, then, that justice was the promotion of someone else's good. It is only because the other party is invariably the stronger party that the two statements coincide.

Leaving aside this controversy, what is important for our purposes about Thrasymachus' position in *Republic* is that it illustrates a trend of fifth-century thought. Although it is hard to say whether the Sophists were symptoms or causes,[2] conventional moral standards were under attack, and the reasons for the attack were well and forcefully formulated, as here by Thrasymachus, or by Callicles in Plato's *Gorgias* (**T1**, pp. 303–5). Only a fool, Thrasymachus says, would adhere to the norms of Greek culture, since they bring no advantage to oneself. Natural right demands that one follows one's own advantage wherever it may lead, and whoever might get trampled on in the process. Years of unthinking acceptance of what in **F1** (and with apparent approbation) Thrasymachus calls 'the ancestral constitution' came to an end with these attacks, and in the future the norms of society required argued justification. This is the kind of justification which Plato was to give in the following century.

T1 (DK 85A2) Today's celebrities [*in rhetoric*] are the heirs of a long succession of people whose piecemeal advances gradually made the subject grow, with Tisias following in the footsteps of the first pioneers, Thrasymachus following Tisias, Theodorus following

---

[2] For instance, was the parade of eastern gurus in the West in the 1960s and 1970s a symptom or a cause of the increasing interest in eastern religion and religious practices? De Romilly [103] argues that the earliest and greatest Sophists played no part in the attack on conventional morality, but that the techniques and argumentation they taught were later put to this kind of use by people such as Thrasymachus.

Thrasymachus, and a lot of people making partial contributions.
(Aristotle, *On Sophistic Refutations* 183^b29–33 Ross)

T2 (DK 85A11) [*Of the kinds of rhythm employed in speeches*] there
remains the paean, which speakers have used since the time of Thrasymachus, but without being able to define it.*   (Aristotle, *Rhetoric*
1409^a2–3 Ross)

T3 (DK 85B6) [*Socrates speaking*] Then there are speeches filled
with lamentation and dwelling at length on the miseries of old age
and poverty. It seems to me that the power of the Chalcedonian has
scientifically mastered this technique, and also that he has become
expert at rousing a crowd to anger and then, when they are angry, at
soothing them with incantations, as he put it. And there is no one
better than him both at casting aspersions and at dispelling them,
whatever their source.   (Plato, *Phaedrus* 267c7–d2 Burnet)

T4 (DK 85A13) Of those with a professional interest in accuracy of
expression and who trained themselves in argumentative rhetoric . . .
Thrasymachus was clear and refined, and was particularly inventive
and good at expressing himself in a terse and striking fashion.
But his surviving works are all examples of technique and show-
pieces, with none of his forensic speeches extant.   (Dionysius of
Halicarnassus, *Isaeus* 20.4–6, 16–20 Usener/Radermacher)

T5 (DK 85B7) [*In the course of a debate about whether dinner-guests
should be allowed to take any old place at table, or should be placed by the
host*] In any case, the decision is hard, given how guests differ in age,
power, intimacy, and kinship. One would have to have available, like
someone studying a problem of comparison, Aristotle's *Topics* or
Thrasymachus' *Overwhelming Arguments*.   (Plutarch, *Table Talk*
616d1–6 Clement)

F1 (DK 85B1) The third kind of diction was the mixed, a compound
of the previous two [*the 'severe' and the 'simple'*]. I am not in a
position to say whether it was (as Theophrastus says) Thrasymachus, or whether it was someone else, who originally formed and
arranged it in its current form . . . Anyway, Thrasymachus' diction,
if it really was one of the sources of the intermediate style, seems to
have a claim on our interest even if only for his principles, because it
is a good blend of the other two and has taken over from them

exactly what is useful. But that his abilities fell short of his intentions is shown by the following example, from one of his political speeches:

'Gentlemen of Athens, I wish I had been alive in the old days, when the younger generation could happily remain silent, since matters did not force them to make speeches and their elders were looking after the city in an appropriate manner. But since it is our fate to find ourselves alive now, at a time when we submit to others ruling the city, but endure its disasters ourselves, and since the greatest of these disasters are due not to the gods or to fortune, but to those who are in charge, I have no choice but to speak. It takes either insensitivity or extraordinary patience to keep allowing oneself to suffer wrong at the hands of all and sundry and to take the blame oneself for the treachery and cowardice of others, because what has already happened in the past is enough for us. Instead of peace, we are now at war; we have fought our way through danger to a time when our hearts go out to the day that is past and we face the day to come with terror; instead of concord we have reached a state of mutual hostility and chaos. Insolence and discord, for everyone else, are consequent on an abundance of blessings, but we behaved with moderation in the good times, and it is during the bad times, which usually teach people moderation, that we have gone insane. Why, then, should a man hesitate to speak his mind when he is distressed at the present situation and thinks he has a solution to prevent this kind of thing happening again?

'In the first place, then, I will show that those people—and they include some of our politicians—who have spoken out against one another have simply experienced what people who thoughtlessly strive to outdo one another are bound to experience. That is, although they think they are contradicting one another, it has escaped their notice that they are pursuing the same policies and that their own ideas incorporate those of their opponents. I mean, take a step back and consider what the aims of both sides are. In the first place, the ancestral constitution is a source of confusion for them, although it is very easy to understand and is shared by every citizen. Whatever lies beyond our own understanding requires us to listen to our ancestors' words, and whatever our elders have seen of their own accord we must learn from their firsthand knowledge.'

This will serve to illustrate Thrasymachus' expression, which was intermediate between the other two, a good blend of them both, and a valuable starting-point for approaching both styles.   (Dionysius of Halicarnassus, *Demosthenes* 3 Usener/Radermacher)

T6 (DK 85B8) In one of his own books, Thrasymachus said something along the following lines: 'The gods pay no attention to human affairs; if they did, they would not have ignored justice, which is the greatest good for men; for we see that men do not act with justice.'   (Hermias, *Notes on Plato's 'Phaedrus'* 239.21–4 Couvreur)

T7 'All right, then, listen to this,' Thrasymachus said. 'My claim is that justice is nothing other than the advantage of the stronger party. Well, why aren't you applauding?' . . .

[*Socrates then proceeds to argue against this idea, until* . . .]

Once we'd reached this point in the discussion, it was perfectly clear to everyone that the definition of justice had been turned upside down. Thrasymachus didn't respond to my last remarks, but instead said, 'Tell me, Socrates, do you have a nurse?'

'What?' I asked. 'Shouldn't you come up with some response rather than this question?'

'The point is,' he said, 'that she takes no notice of your runny nose and lets it dribble on when it needs wiping, when you can't even tell her the difference between sheep and shepherd.'

'I haven't the faintest idea what you're getting at,' I said.

'What I'm getting at is your notion that shepherds or cowherds consider what is good for their sheep or their cows, and fatten them up and look after them, with any aim in mind other than what is good for their masters or for themselves; and also at your supposition that the attitude which people with political authority—who are the real rulers—have towards their subjects differs in the slightest from how one might feel about sheep, and that what they consider day and night is anything other than their own advantage and how to gain it. You're so far off understanding right and wrong, justice and injustice, that you don't even realize that justice and right are actually good for someone else—they are the advantage of the stronger party, the ruler—and bad for the underling at the receiving end of the orders. Nor do you realize that the opposite is true for injustice: the wrongdoer lords it over those moral simpletons—that's what they are, really—while his subjects do what is to his advantage, since he is stronger, and make him happy by doing his bidding, but don't further their own happiness in the slightest.

'You fool, Socrates, don't you see? In any and every situation, a just person is worse off than an unjust one. Suppose, for instance, that they're doing some business together, which involves one of them entering into association with the other: by the time the association is dissolved, you'll never find the just person up on the unjust one—he'll be worse off. Or again, in civic matters, if there's a tax on property, then a just person pays more tax than an unjust one even when they're equally well off; and if there's a handout, the one gets nothing, while the other makes a lot. And when each of them holds political office, even if a just person loses out financially in no other way, his personal affairs deteriorate through neglect, while his justice stops him making any profit from public funds, and moreover his family and friends fall out with him over his refusal to help them out in unfair ways; in all these respects, however, an unjust person's experience is the opposite.

'I'm talking about the person I described a short while ago, the one with the power to secure huge advantages for himself. This is the person you should consider, if you want to assess the extent to which injustice rather than justice is personally advantageous—and this is something you'll appreciate most easily if you look at injustice in its most perfect form and see how it enhances a wrongdoer's life beyond measure, but ruins the lives of his victims, who haven't the stomach for crime, to the same degree. It's dictatorship I mean, because whether it takes stealth or overt violence, a dictator steals what doesn't belong to him—consecrated and unconsecrated objects, private possessions, and public property—and does so not on a small scale, but comprehensively. Anyone who is caught committing the merest fraction of these crimes is not only punished, but thoroughly stigmatized as well: small-scale criminals who commit these kinds of crimes are called temple-robbers, kidnappers, burglars, thieves, and robbers. On the other hand, when someone appropriates the assets of the citizen body and then goes on to rob them of their very freedom and enslave them, denigration gives way to congratulation, and it isn't only his fellow citizens who call him happy, but anyone else who hears about his consummate wrongdoing does so as well. The point is that injustice has a bad name because people are afraid of being at the receiving end of it, not of doing it.

'So you see, Socrates, injustice—if practised on a large enough scale—has more power, licence, and authority than justice. And as I said at the beginning, justice is really the advantage of the stronger party, while injustice is profitable and advantageous to oneself.' (Plato, *Republic* 338c1–3, 343a1–344c8 Burnet)

T. D. J. Chappell, 'The Virtues of Thrasymachus', *Phronesis*, 38 (1993), 1–17.

G. B. Kerferd, 'The Doctrine of Thrasymachus in Plato's *Republic*', *Durham University Journal*, 9 (1947), 19–27.

P. P. Nicholson, 'Unravelling Thrasymachus' Arguments in the *Republic*', *Phronesis*, 19 (1974), 210–32.

EUTHYDEMUS AND DIONYSODORUS OF CHIOS

Plato (who was to be followed in this by Aristotle) believed that one of the things that characterized the Sophists, or some of them, was bad argumentation. The word 'sophism' has come to mean an argument which has the appearance of a valid argument, but is invalid. In fact, at any rate in his earlier dialogues, before his thorough treatment of the subject in *Sophist*, Plato was probably less concerned about this than about the fact that they were explicitly or implicitly wedded to a set of standards and goals which he found superficial at best, and at worst downright immoral. However, these two aspects of sophistry—bad argument and misplaced ethics—were connected by their contemporaries and critics. When Aristotle defined a Sophist (*On Sophistic Refutations* 165ª) as 'someone who makes money by apparent but not genuine wisdom', it should be remembered that wisdom was an important part of what constituted virtue in ancient Greece. Therefore, to pretend to have wisdom was immoral. For Aristotle, the demonstration that they only pretend to have wisdom is the demonstration that their arguments are invalid. Their immorality is subsidiary to their weakness at arguing. This is less true for Plato, because he is less clear at distinguishing logical fallacies (at any rate, he puts quite a few into the mouth of Socrates, who is generally reckoned to be Plato's own mouthpiece). For Plato their immorality lay in their raising money by argumentative displays which treated the interlocutor as an opponent to be dazzled and defeated, rather than encouraged to change his life for the better. So in *Euthydemus* Plato has the Sophist brothers *exploit* bad arguments deliberately: that is, they are not arguing badly because they can do no better; they are arguing badly because they choose to do so, to confound their opponents. They are masters of the art of what Plato calls 'eristic', arguing to win.

Euthydemus contains a marvellous parody of bad and eristic arguments, a few of which are included here, concentrating on those which are most accessible in English translation. In formal terms the fallacy in each case is a form of equivocation. But it is also important to note that the Sophists' arguments are driven by theory too; their fallacies run deeper than mere punning or equivocation. Lurking behind **T2**, for instance, may be the Eleatic denial of change, in such a way that to want Cleinias to change is to want him to cease to exist; and Eleaticism is explicitly brought out, by Socrates, as underlying **T4**. Protagoras may also be invoked behind **T4**:

my knowledge at any given time is irrefutable, according to Protagoras, but if time consists of a series of such 'given times', then at any time in my life I have knowledge. Nevertheless, one is left with the feeling that explaining the sophisms with this degree of sophistication misses the point: *Euthydemus* is a sophisticated comedy, and the bad argumentation of the Sophists is the main joke.

The two Sophists are otherwise virtually unknown (their obscurity perhaps reflecting their mediocrity), but the fact that Euthydemus gains another mention by Plato at *Cratylus* 386d, and crops up briefly in Aristotle at *On Sophistic Refutations* 177[b] and *Rhetoric* 1401[a], while Dionysodorus is mentioned by Xenophon at *Memoirs of Socrates* 3.1.1, is sufficient to guarantee their historical existence. According to Plato in *Euthydemus* 273c–d, the two Sophist brothers had originally taught military skills (one of the rarer Sophistic accomplishments) before turning to the verbal and argumentative pyrotechnics Plato illustrates.

T1 [*Socrates speaking*] Euthydemus started in from roughly this direction, I think: 'Tell me, Cleinias, are clever or ignorant people those who learn?'

Faced with this momentous question, the lad blushed and looked at me in puzzlement. I saw that he was flustered and said: 'Don't worry, Cleinias. Just pluck up courage and give whichever answer you think is right. Remember, you'll probably benefit enormously.'

While I was saying this, Dionysodorus had leaned over to me with a big grin on his face, to whisper briefly in my ear. 'In fact, Socrates,' he said, 'I can tell you now that whichever answer the lad gives, he will be proved wrong.'

As luck would have it, Cleinias gave his answer at the same time as Dionysodorus was telling me this, so I didn't have time to warn him to be careful; he replied that clever people are the ones who learn.

'Do you or do you not acknowledge the existence of teachers?' asked Euthydemus.

He agreed that he did.

'And teachers teach learners—for instance, you and your school-mates had a music-teacher and a writing-teacher, from whom you used to learn?'

He agreed.

'So wasn't it the case that when you were learners, you didn't yet know what you were learning?'

He agreed that they did not.

'And were you clever when you didn't have this knowledge?'

'Of course not,' he said.

'In fact, if you weren't clever, you were ignorant, weren't you?'

'Yes.'

'So, while learning what you didn't know, you were learning because you were ignorant.'

The lad nodded.

'Therefore, Cleinias, it is ignorant people who learn, not clever people, as you imagine.'

As if these words were a prompt by a director to a chorus, Dionysodorus' and Euthydemus' followers broke out into cheers and laughter. And before the lad could draw a proper breath, Dionysodorus took over and said, 'Now, Cleinias, when the writing-teacher was reciting a piece, was it the clever or the ignorant children who learnt it?'

'The clever ones,' said Cleinias.

'So clever people learn, not ignoramuses: you gave the wrong reply to Euthydemus just now.'

At this point, the pair's admirers, delighted with their heroes' cleverness, laughed and cheered very loudly, while the rest of us were speechless with amazement. Euthydemus recognized our amazement and, in order to astound us even more, kept on relentlessly questioning the lad, and in good choreographic style began to turn his questions back around the same spot. 'Do those who learn learn what they know,' he asked, 'or what they do not know?'

Dionysodorus had another brief word in my ear: 'This is another one just like the first, Socrates,' he said.

'Heavens!' I exclaimed. 'I can assure you that we were impressed by the *first* question.'

'All our questions of this sort are designed to trap people, Socrates,' he said.

'That, I think,' I said, 'is why your pupils look up to you.'

Cleinias had meanwhile replied that those who learn learn what they do *not* know, and Euthydemus' questions employed the same method as before. 'But surely you know the alphabet, don't you?' he asked.

'Yes,' he said.

'Right through?'

He agreed.

'Now, doesn't a recitation consist of letters?'

He agreed.

'So, if you know the whole alphabet, then a recitation consists of what you know, doesn't it?'

He agreed to this too.

'Well, then,' he said, 'do you *not* learn a recitation, while someone ignorant of the alphabet does?'

'No,' he replied, 'I do learn it.'

'Therefore, you learn what you know,' he said, 'if you know the alphabet.'

He agreed.

'So your answer was wrong,' he said.

These words were hardly out of Euthydemus' mouth when Dionysodorus took over the argument, as if it were a ball to catch and throw at the lad: 'Euthydemus is having you on, Cleinias,' he said. 'I mean, wouldn't you say that learning is the acquisition of knowledge of what is being learnt?'

Cleinias agreed.

'And knowing is the current possession of knowledge, surely?'

He agreed.

'Ignorance, therefore, is not yet possessing knowledge?'

He agreed with him.

'Well, do people acquire something they already possess or something they lack?'

'Something they lack.'

'And you have agreed that ignorant people are among those who have a lack?'

He nodded.

'And those who learn are acquirers, not possessors?'

He agreed.

'Therefore, Cleinias,' he concluded, 'it is ignorant people who learn, not knowledgeable ones.'   (Plato, *Euthydemus* 275d2–277c7 Burnet)

T2 'Tell me,' Dionysodorus said, 'Socrates and all the rest of you who say you want this young man to become wise, is this a joke or do you really mean it? Are you serious?'

Now, the explanation, I assumed, for this banter and lack of seriousness was that, in spite of all, they had got the impression that our earlier request for them to speak with the lad had not been serious, so I said in no uncertain terms that we were incredibly serious.

'Look out, Socrates,' Dionysodorus rejoined. 'You may end up taking your words back.'

'I *have* looked,' I said. 'There's no way that I shall ever take them back.'

'All right, then,' he said. 'Now, you say that you want him to become wise?'

'Yes.'

'Is Cleinias wise at the moment or not?' he asked.

'Well, he says he isn't yet,' I said, 'and he's not given to idle talk.'

'And you want him to become wise,' he said, 'and not to be ignorant?'

We agreed.

'So you want him to become someone else and to stop being the person he now is.'

This took me aback, and before I could recover, he cut in: 'In other words, since you want him to stop being the person he now is, you apparently want him to die, don't you? Of course, it's those who place supreme value on their beloved dying that make sterling friends and lovers!'

Ctesippus, nervous about his beloved, got annoyed when he heard this, and said: 'If it wasn't a bit impolite—after all, you're a visitor, all the way from Thurii—I would have said "Go and die yourself!", for getting it into your head to slander me and the others like that. I think it's blasphemous to suggest that I could wish him to die.'

'Oh, I see, Ctesippus,' said Euthydemus. 'You think it's possible to lie, do you?'

'Good heavens, of course!' he said. 'I'm not crazy!'

'Do lies occur when someone mentions the thing which he mentions, or when he does not?'

'When he mentions it,' he said.

'So if he mentions it, then, out of all facts, he is mentioning precisely the one which he is mentioning, isn't he?'

'Of course,' said Ctesippus.

'Then at least *this* thing which he mentions is one out of all facts, distinct from all other facts, isn't it?'

'Yes.'

'So in mentioning this thing, he is talking about the fact of the matter?' he asked.

'Yes.'

'But if he mentions the fact of the matter, if he mentions fact, then he is speaking the truth. So if Dionysodorus mentions facts, he is speaking the truth and not slandering you at all.'   (Plato, *Euthydemus* 283b4–284a8 Burnet)

T3 'Do animate or inanimate things have ideas?' asked Dionysodorus.

  'Animate.'

  'Do you know an animate sentence?' he asked.

  'Good heavens, no!'

  'Why, then, did you just ask me what the idea of my sentence was?'   (Plato, *Euthydemus* 287d7–e1 Burnet)

T4 Euthydemus started with a very generous offer. 'Socrates,' he said, 'you've both been puzzling over this knowledge [*the science of happiness*] for a while now. Shall I instruct you in it or demonstrate that you have it?'

  'You marvellous man,' I said. 'Can you do that?'

  'Certainly,' he said.

  'Then please, please demonstrate that I have it,' I said. 'For someone my age that's easier than learning about it.'

  'All right, then,' he said. 'You answer my questions. Do you know anything?'

  'Yes,' I said, 'lots of things—unimportant things, though.'

  'That doesn't matter,' he said. 'Now, do you think it possible for anything not to be what it is?'

  'Of course I don't. What a question!'

  'And you know something?'

  'Yes.'

  'So, if you know, you are in possession of knowledge?'

  'Yes, of that thing, anyway.'

  'That's irrelevant. Aren't you bound to know everything, if you are in possession of knowledge?'

'Good heavens, no!' I said. 'There are plenty of other things I don't know.'

'Well, if you don't know something, you are not in possession of knowledge.'

'Of *that*, my friend,' I said.

'But that doesn't alter the fact that you are not in possession of knowledge, does it?' he asked. 'But just now you said you were. So you both are what you are, and again are not what you are, in the same respect and at the same time.'

'All right, Euthydemus,' I said. '*Touché*, as they say. So how do I have that knowledge we were looking for? Because (*a*) it is impossible both to be and not be the same thing; (*b*) if I know one thing, I know everything, since I cannot at the same time both be and not be in possession of knowledge; (*c*) since I know everything, then I possess that knowledge too. Is that what you're saying? Is that the bright idea?'

'You are refuting yourself out of your own mouth, Socrates,' he said. (Plato, *Euthydemus* 293a8–e1 Burnet)

T5 'Tell me,' said Dionysodorus, 'do you have a dog?'

'Yes, a real scamp,' said Ctesippus.

'And has he got puppies?'

'Yes, regular chips off the old block,' he said.

'So your dog is their father?'

'Yes, I myself saw him mounting the bitch,' he said.

'Well, now, the dog is yours?'

'Yes,' he said.

'He is a father, and he is yours—so he turns out to be your father, and you are brother to puppies!' (Plato, *Euthydemus* 298d8–e5 Burnet)

T6 'Oh, so you know what each craftsman's function is, do you?' Dionysodorus asked. 'Do you know, firstly, whose job it is to hammer metal?'

'Yes, a smith's.'

'And to make pots?'

'A potter's.'

'And to slaughter, skin, chop meat up, boil it, and roast it?'

'A cook's.'

'Now, doing one's proper job is right, isn't it?' he asked.

'Very much so.'

'And, as you agree, the proper thing for a cook is chopping and skinning? Did you admit that or not?'

'I did,' I said, 'but please don't hold it against me.'

'The proper thing to do, then, obviously, is to slaughter cooks, chop them up, boil them, and roast them. Likewise, the proper thing is to hammer smiths and make pots out of potters!' (Plato, *Euthydemus* 301c6–d8 Burnet)

T. H. Chance, *Plato's Euthydemus: Analysis of What Is and What Is Not Philosophy* (Berkeley: University of California Press, 1992).

M. M. McCabe, 'Persistent Fallacies', *Proceedings of the Aristotelian Society*, 94 (1994), 73–93.

DOUBLE ARGUMENTS

To judge by the Greek dialect this anonymous treatise uses, it was perhaps written in southern Italy round about 400 BCE (though it is impossible to date with any certainty), by someone of wide reading who was familiar with Athenian culture. This second-rate treatise shows more clearly than anything else why Plato and Aristotle thought that one aspect of Sophistry was bad argumentation. I call it 'second-rate' because it is demonstrably an amalgam of the work of other Sophists, and because of its intellectual poverty. Most of the other Sophists whose work survives in sufficient quantity for us to attempt a reconstruction all made genuine and interesting contributions to ancient philosophy, but the main, if not the entire interest of *Double Arguments* is historical. However, its interest in this respect is considerable, since it is a sustained piece of genuine fifth-century Sophistic writing. Moreover, the writing is generally clear, if unpolished.

As far as concerns its derivative nature, it is often connected only with the rhetorical work of Protagoras. That there is Protagorean influence is undeniable, but Protagoras is not alone. Protagoras taught his pupils to be able to argue both sides of any case,[1] and this is essentially what much of *Double Arguments* does; indeed, an alternative translation of its title, *Dissoi Logoi*, would be *Contrasting Arguments*. So, for instance, in the first section, 'On Good and Bad', we find arguments like: 'Illness is bad for the sick, but good for doctors', or 'Death is bad for those who die but good for undertakers and grave-diggers.' By a whole string of such arguments, if they are worthy of the name, the author seeks to show that the good and the bad are the same. He then goes on to argue, to the contrary, that the good and the bad are different, by taking the obvious tack that if they were the same any case of goodness could be called a case of badness, which is absurd. And in the following sections he performs the same antilogical trick for acceptable and unacceptable behaviour, right and wrong, and truth and falsity—in each case presenting antinomies about their identity and difference.[2]

In these first four sections, the form of the argumentation is Protagorean, but this is not to say very much. Are the ideas also Protagorean? In

---

[1] But after Protagoras, there were other Sophists who produced similar handbooks, according to Aristotle, *On Sophistic Refutations* 183^b.

[2] However, since it is likely that Protagoras wrote extended speeches arguing both sides of a case, truer repositories of his influence are the debates in both Euripides and Thucydides.

part, they are. For instance, our anonymous author is often concerned
with the important Protagorean suffixes: A is good for X, but bad for Y.
But if this pattern of the arguments by which he claims to prove that
'good' and 'bad' are identical is Protagorean, it follows that the antithetical
replies, where he demonstrates that 'good' and 'bad' are different, cannot
be Protagorean. This is particularly clear in the fourth section, about truth
and falsehood. Having argued that they are identical,[3] the author goes
on to give substantially the same objection to the Protagorean denial of
falsehood that Plato brought against Protagoras (T5 and T8 in the section
on Protagoras, pp. 213 and 215). *Double Arguments* probably predates
Plato, but he is still not being original: we know that Democritus too,
brought the same argument to bear against his fellow Abderite (Plutarch,
Against Colotes 1108f–1109a).

Properly speaking, we should not call the ideas of these first four
sections 'relativist': they are too banal to deserve a philosophical title. A
true relativist (such as Protagoras) denies the possibility of reaching
objective judgements about things. For Protagoras in Plato's *Theaetetus*, it
is impossible to decide whether the wind in itself is warm or cold. The
author of *Double Arguments*, however, is merely insisting that in different
circumstances different judgements are possible, which falls short of
denying that there may be objective standards.

Another thinker whose influence may be traced in these early sections
of *Double Arguments* is Socrates: if the dialogue form is peculiarly
Socratic, then the inclusion of a short dialogue in the first section is
significant. But although the Sophists were generally known for their long
speeches, they did engage in question-and-answer sessions as well, so this
may not be conclusive evidence of Socratic influence. And apart from
Protagoras and Socrates, we can sometimes recognize other influences,
some of which are annotated below.

With the fifth (untitled) section, the author adopts a new approach.
First, it is no longer the identity of values that is in question; second,
instead of the antilogical structure of the previous section, we find little
more than an argument against one of a possible antilogical pair.[4] He
mentions some opposites that could be identified, such as 'sane' and
'insane', but shows that he comes down firmly on the side of the partisans
of *physis*, with the claim that everything has its own nature, its own separate existence. The straightforward structure of this section is blurred,

[3] If this section is based on Protagoreanism, it is ill considered, because our author
assumes that there is an objective basis to truth and falsity, whereas for Protagoras all
such things were relative and subjective.

[4] Unless, just possibly, there is enough text missing at the beginning of the section to
have contained the whole of the other antilogical half.

however, by the fact that he raises a powerful argument against the identity of sane and insane people (that even if they say the same things, only sane people say them at the appropriate time), only to dismiss this argument. As elsewhere in the tract, our author sides with the wrong argument.

Sections 6–9 of the work are again different: the sixth section argues that virtue is teachable, the seventh that public officers should not be elected by lot; the eighth that a good speaker knows everything; and the ninth breaks off in the middle of describing a mnemonic technique. In none of these sections is there more than the faintest hint of any antilogical structure (e.g. at the very end of section 6). There is less Protagorean influence here, then, but more of others. It is worth mentioning Gorgias on the importance of the window of opportunity to an orator (see Gorgias T6), and Hippias on the possibility of omniscience and on memory techniques. The question whether or not virtue was teachable was a debating point in the fifth century,[5] with most of the Sophists naturally coming down in favour of its teachability, since that was what they professed to do. And so this sixth section explicitly becomes a (brief) defence of the Sophistic movement in general. The seventh section is relevant to the theme of the treatise because if Sophists like Protagoras claimed to teach political skill, that would tend to undermine the Athenian system of election by lot. The eighth section consists of a thumbnail sketch of an ideal Sophist-politician. The ninth section is relevant to the Sophistic movement because mnemonic techniques were an important part of rhetorical training.

———

F1 (DK 90)

1. On Good and Bad

In Greece, thanks to the intellectuals, there are double arguments about the good and the bad. Some say that the good and the bad are different,* others that the same thing can be either good or bad, in the sense that it may be good for some people but bad for others, or good for the same person at one time and bad for him at another time.*

I myself side with the latter group. I will base my investigation of the matter on human life, with its concern with food, drink, and sex, since these things are bad for someone who is sick, but good for

———

[5] The debate is also reflected in Plato's *Protagoras* and *Meno*.

someone who is healthy and who needs them. Moreover, over-indulgence in these things is bad for those who over-indulge, but good for those who sell these products and make money from them. Illness is bad for the sick, but good for doctors. Death is bad for those who die, but good for undertakers and grave-diggers. When farming produces good crops it is good for the farmers, but bad for shopkeepers. If merchant ships are broken up and wrecked, that is bad for the owner, but good for ship-builders. Furthermore, if a tool gets corroded or blunted or broken, that is bad for everyone else, but good for the smith. And if a pot is smashed, that is bad for everyone else, but good for potters. If shoes are worn out and fall apart, that is bad for everyone else, but good for the cobbler. Then consider athletic contests, musical competitions, and warfare: for instance, in an athletic competition—a foot-race, say—victory is good for the winner, but bad for the losers. The same goes for wrestlers, boxers, and all musicians too: for instance, victory at playing the lyre is good for the winner, but bad for the losers. In warfare (and taking the most recent cases first), the Spartan victory over the Athenians and their allies was good for the Spartans, but bad for the Athenians and their allies;* and the Greek victory over the Persians* was good for the Greeks, but bad for the invaders. The capture of Troy was good for the Achaeans,* but bad for the Trojans. The same goes for what happened to the Thebans and the Argives.* And the battle of the Centaurs and Lapiths was good for the Lapiths, but bad for the Centaurs. And in the legendary battle between the gods and the giants victory was good for the gods, but bad for the giants.

But there is an alternative argument which claims that the good and the bad are different, and that the difference in words points to a difference in actual fact. I myself also distinguish them in this way, because I think we would not be able to tell good and bad apart if it were somehow the case, extraordinarily, that they were the same and not different. And I doubt that anyone who holds that they are identical would be able to respond to someone who said: 'Tell me, have your parents in the past ever done you any good?' 'Yes,' he would answer, 'they have often done me a great deal of good.' 'So, if the good and the bad are the same, you ought to repay them often with a great deal of bad. Also, did you ever do good to your relatives?† Then you were doing them bad. And have you ever in the past done bad to your enemies? Then you often did them a very great deal of good. But tell me this too: if the same thing is good and bad, don't you simultaneously feel sorry for paupers because of all the bad things they suffer, and count them happy because of all their great good fortune?' The king of Persia must be in the same condition as paupers, since all his great goods are so many great evils, if the same thing is both good and bad. Let's assume that I have covered every instance; nevertheless, I shall go through particular instances too, beginning with food, drink, and sex. For if the same thing is good and bad, then these things are not only bad for sick people, but are also good for them. And illness is both bad and good for people who are ill, if the good and the bad are the same thing. The same goes for all the other topics that I brought up earlier.* I am not here defining the good, but I am trying to explain that the bad and the good are not the same, but different.

2. On Acceptable and Unacceptable

There are also double arguments about the acceptable and the unacceptable. Some say that the acceptable and the unacceptable are two separate things, and that the difference in words points to a substantial difference, others say that the same thing is both acceptable and unacceptable. I will attempt an exposition too, along the following lines. For instance, for a good-looking boy to gratify a lover is acceptable, but for him to gratify someone who is not his lover is unacceptable.* And whereas it is acceptable for women to bathe indoors, it is unacceptable for them to bathe in the wrestling-school (although it is acceptable for men to bathe in the wrestling-school or the gymnasium). And whereas it is acceptable for a woman to have sex with her husband unobtrusively, in the privacy of their own home, it is unacceptable to do so in public, where people will see them. And whereas it is acceptable for a woman to have sex with her husband, it is totally unacceptable for her to have sex with someone else's husband. And, of course, whereas it is acceptable for a man to have sex with his own wife, it is unacceptable for him to have sex with someone else's wife. And whereas beautifying oneself, putting on make-up, and wearing golden jewellery is unacceptable for a man, it is acceptable for a woman. It is acceptable to do good to one's friends, but unacceptable to do good to one's enemies. It is unacceptable to run away from one's enemies, but acceptable to run away from one's rivals in a foot-race. It is unacceptable to kill one's friends and fellow citizens, but acceptable to do so to one's enemies. And so on and so forth. I go on to what states and peoples have come to regard as unacceptable. For instance, Spartans find it acceptable for young women to exercise and walk about with bare arms and no outer garment, whereas Ionians* find it unacceptable. And although they† find it unacceptable for their sons to learn music, reading, and writing, Ionians find it unacceptable for their children *not* to learn all these things. Thessalians find it acceptable for someone to take horses and mules from their herds and break them in himself, or to take a cow and slaughter it, skin it, and chop it up himself, but in Sicily this is unacceptable, and these jobs are given to slaves. Macedonians find it acceptable for young women to have love affairs and sex before marriage, but unacceptable for them to do so after marriage, whereas Greeks find both unacceptable. Thracians think that tattooing enhances a girl's beauty, whereas for everyone else tattooing is a punishment for a crime. Scythians regard it as acceptable for someone who has killed an enemy to skin his skull and carry the scalp on his horse's forelock, and to drink and pour libations to the gods from the skull, which is covered in gold or silver; but no Greek would willingly even find himself in the same house as someone who had done that. The Massagetae chop up their parents and eat them, and think that being buried in their children's insides is the most acceptable form of burial, but if anyone did this in Greece he would be expelled from the country and would die an ignominious death, as one who had committed unacceptable crimes. The Persians regard it as acceptable for men to beautify themselves just as much as women, and also for them to have sex with their daughters, mothers, and sisters, but the Greeks regard this behaviour as unacceptable and aberrant. The Lydians find it acceptable for their daughters to work as prostitutes to raise money for getting married, but no one in Greece would be prepared to marry such a girl. Egyptian views about what is acceptable differ from everyone else's:* for instance, while it is acceptable here for women to weave and work in the fields,† there it is acceptable for the men to do that, and for the women to do what men do here. It is acceptable for them to knead clay with their hands and dough with their feet, but for us it is the other way round. I think that if one were to get all the people in the world to gather together the things they found unacceptable, and then to take from this pile the things they found acceptable, not a single custom would remain, but in the end they would all have been distributed among the peoples of the world. The point here is that people have different customs. Here is a relevant piece of verse too:*

If you discern things in this way, you will find the other law
That holds for mortal men: there is nothing that is universally
Either acceptable or unacceptable, but circumstances take hold of things
And make them unacceptable or, conversely, acceptable.

In brief, then, anything may be acceptable under the right circumstances and unacceptable under the wrong circumstances. What have I achieved? I said I would show that the same things are unacceptable and acceptable, and I have shown that this is so in all these cases.

But the other position that is held on the unacceptable and the acceptable is that they are different. After all, if one were to ask those who claim that the same thing is both unacceptable and acceptable whether they have ever performed an acceptable action, they will have to admit that they have also performed an unacceptable action, if the unacceptable and the acceptable are identical. And if they know an acceptable man, he is also unacceptable to them—which is to say that if they know a pale man, he is also swarthy! Now, it is of course acceptable behaviour to worship the gods—and also unacceptable to do so, if the same thing is both unacceptable and acceptable. Let's assume that I have covered every instance; now I shall turn to the particular points made by the proponents of this view. If it is acceptable for a woman to beautify herself, it is unacceptable for a woman to beautify herself,† if the same thing is unacceptable and acceptable; and the same goes for all other cases. In Sparta it is acceptable for girls to exercise, in Sparta it is unacceptable for girls to exercise; and so on. And they say that if one were to gather from all the peoples of the world everything that is unacceptable, and then convene all the peoples and get them to take what they regarded as acceptable, everything would be taken away, as falling into the category of the acceptable. As for me, though, I would be astonished if things introduced as unacceptable were to turn out to be acceptable, rather than remaining what they were when they came. At any rate, if they had brought horses or cows or sheep or people, that is exactly what they would have taken away as well. After all, if they had brought gold, they wouldn't have taken bronze away, and if they had brought silver, they wouldn't have taken lead away. So do they take away acceptable things instead of unacceptable ones? Well, then, if they had brought an unacceptable man, would they have taken away an acceptable man?[†] They adduce poets to testify to the validity of their position, but poets write for pleasure, not for truth.

3. On Right and Wrong

There are also double arguments about right and wrong. Some say that they are two different things, others that the same thing is both right and wrong. For my part, I will try to support the latter view. My first claim will be that it is right to tell lies and deceive others. It might be objected that it is unacceptable and bad to do these things to one's enemies, but not to one's nearest and dearest, such as one's parents.[†] For instance, if your father or mother is supposed to drink or eat some medicine, but doesn't want to, isn't it right to give them the medicine in their food or drink, without telling them that it is in there? So under these conditions it is right to lie and to deceive one's parents. Moreover, it is right to steal from one's friends and treat one's nearest and dearest with violence. For instance, if a member of your household is so miserable or upset that he is planning to kill himself with a sword or a rope or something, isn't it right to steal these things from him, if possible, or to snatch them violently from him if you are late and come upon him with the object in his hand? And how could it not be right to enslave one's enemies and, if possible, conquer their state and sell the population into slavery? It is also obviously right to break into the public buildings of one's community: if your father is in prison, awaiting execution after having lost out in a feud with his political rivals, isn't it right to dig through the walls and smuggle your father safely away? It is also right to break a solemn promise: if a man has been taken prisoner by his enemies and promises under oath that if he is set free he will betray his state, does this man do right to keep his promise? I don't think so. It is more likely to be right for him to break his promise and save his state, his friends, and his ancestral shrines.[†] Under these circumstances, then, it is right even to break a solemn promise. And to rob temples too.[*] Never mind the temples belonging to particular states, but consider just the panhellenic temples at Delphi and Olympia:

suppose the invader is on the point of conquering Greece and Greece's preservation depends on money, is it not right to take the money and use it for the war effort? And it is right to murder one's nearest and dearest—after all, that's what both Orestes and Alcmaeon did,* and the god pronounced through his oracle that they acted rightly. Now I will turn to the arts and crafts, and especially to poetry, for in drama and painting the best craftsman is the one who deceives his audience the most by making his composition resemble the real thing. I'd also like to introduce the testimony of some lines written quite a long time ago by Cleoboulina:

> I saw a man of violence, a thief and a cheat,
> And his violence was perfectly right.*

Those lines were written long ago, but these are from Aeschylus:

> The god does not withhold himself from rightful deceit.

and:

> There are times when the god accepts that it is time for lies.

But there is also the contrary position, that right and wrong are distinct, and that just as there are different words for them, so they are different things. After all, if one were to ask those who claim that the same thing is right and wrong whether in the past they have ever done right by their parents, they would say yes, and so they have wronged their parents, because they maintain that the same thing is wrong and right. Here is another example: if you know that a man habitually does right, you also know that the same man habitually does wrong (and by the same token that he is both tall and short). And yet if a man has done wrong let him die for what he has done!† But that is enough on this topic. I shall go on to address the arguments adduced by those who want to show that the same thing is both right and wrong. The very fact that stealing enemy property is right proves that it is also wrong, if their argument is true, and the same goes for all the other cases. And they introduce arts and crafts which have nothing to do with right and wrong. And poets' compose their poems for pleasure, not for truth.

4. On True and False

There are also double arguments about true and false. One position is that a false statement is different from a true statement, while others say that there is no difference.* For my part, I am one of those who take the latter position. My reasons are, first, that both true and false statements use the same words, and, second, that when a statement is made, if the facts are as the statement says, the statement is true, whereas if they are not, the same statement is false.* Let's say, for instance, that a statement accuses someone of temple-robbery. If the deed actually took place, the statement is true; if it didn't, it is false. Moreover, the defendant uses the same argument. And, of course, the law courts judge the same statement to be both false and true. Then again, suppose we are sitting in a row and we each say, 'I am an initiate':* we will all be saying the same thing, but I am the only one telling the truth, because I *am* an initiate. It is evident, then, that one and the same statement is false when falsehood attaches to it, and true when truth attaches to it, just as a man is the same when he is young, youthful, mature, and old.

But there is also the argument that a false statement is different from a true statement, because there are two different words involved.[†] For if one were to ask those who claim that the same statement is both false and true whether this statement of theirs is false or true, then if it is false, it obviously follows that a false statement and a true statement are two separate things, and if it is true, it follows that their statement is simultaneously false.* And if[†] anyone ever made a true statement or deposition in court, his statement and deposition were also false. And if anyone knows that a man is truthful, he also knows that he is a liar. From this they deduce that a statement is true if it corresponds to the facts and false if it doesn't.[†] This is what makes it important to ask[†] the members of the jury, in their turn, to make an assessment—an assessment only, because they were not eyewitnesses to the events. Even the proponents of the view in question agree that a statement is false when it is bound up with falsehood and true when it is bound up with truth. But it makes all the difference in the world <. . .> [*some words or sentences are missing*]

5. [*Untitled*]

'Whether they are insane or sane, clever or stupid, people say and do the same things. In the first place, they use the same words: "earth", "man", "horse", "fire", and so on and so forth. Also, they do the same things: they sit, eat, drink, lie down, and so on. Moreover, the same thing is both larger and smaller, more and less, heavier and lighter. And so all things are the same. A talent is heavier than a mina and lighter than two talents.* So the same thing is both lighter and heavier. And the same person is both alive and dead, and the same things both are and are not:* for the things which are here are not in Africa, and the things that are in Africa are not in Cyprus. And the same goes for everything else. Therefore, things both are and are not.' This view, that the insane and the sane, the clever and the stupid, do and say the same things, is incorrect both in itself and in its consequences. After all, if one asks its proponents whether insanity differs from sanity, and cleverness from stupidity, they say yes. For the actions of either group make it clear that they have to say yes. So if their actions were the same, clever people would be insane and insane people would be clever, and everything would be in a total muddle. It is also worth asking whether it is sane or insane people who speak at the appropriate time. For when one asks this question, the proponents of this view admit that although the two groups say the same things, clever people do so at the appropriate time, while insane people do so at an inappropriate time. And when they say this, it rather looks as though they have added the suffixes 'at the appropriate time' and 'at an inappropriate time', which destroys the identity they were arguing for.* Actually, I don't think that things are altered by the addition of such qualifications, though they are by a change of accent [*There follow a number of examples where a change of accent on a Greek word gives it a different meaning: for instance*, sákos *(shield) is different from* sakós *(enclosure)*], and others are by a change of lettering [*e.g.* onos *(ass) and* noos *(mind)*]. So since considerable differences can occur when nothing is subtracted, what about cases where some addition or subtraction does occur? I will go on to show what I mean, as follows: if one is subtracted from ten,[†] there would no longer be ten or even one, and so on and so forth.* As for the assertion that the same person both is and is not, I ask the following question: 'Does this person have being in some respect, or in all respects?'—the point being that the denial that the person has being is false, because it implies that a person has to be in all respects. So all these things exist in *some* respect.[†]

6. On Whether Knowledge and Virtue are Teachable

There is an argument, which is neither true nor new, that wisdom and virtue cannot be taught or learnt. The evidence offered to support this claim is as follows. First, that if you pass something on to someone else, you cannot still have it yourself. Second, that if they were teachable there would be recognized teachers of them, as there are for music. Third, that the wise men of Greece would have taught their children and their friends.[†] Fourth, that people have in the past gone to the Sophists without being helped at all. Fifth, that plenty of people have become remarkable without having associated with the Sophists. I think this position is extremely naïve. For instance, I know that schoolteachers teach literacy, which is their branch of expertise, and that music-teachers teach music. As for the second piece of evidence, that there are no recognized teachers, what do the Sophists teach, if not wisdom and virtue? And what about the fact that there are followers of Anaxagoras and Pythagoras? As for the third point, Polyclitus taught his son to sculpt.[*] It is irrelevant that a given person has not been a teacher, but as long as any one individual has been a teacher, that is evidence that teaching is possible. Fourthly, if some people have failed to acquire wisdom from skilled[†] Sophists—well, plenty of people have failed to become literate too, in spite of taking lessons. There is in fact a certain natural ability, thanks to which a person may become good enough (at any rate, if he has natural talent), without having studied with Sophists, to grasp most things easily once he has learnt a little from those who teach us the language—at least some of which we learn from our fathers or mothers. If someone doesn't believe that we learn the language, but thinks we are born knowing it, he can come to know the truth by considering the following: if a new-born child were sent to Persia and raised there, without ever hearing Greek, he would speak Persian; and if a new-born child were brought here from there, he would speak Greek.[*] So we do learn language, and we don't know who teaches us it. So much for my argument; you have its beginning, middle, and end. But note that I am not saying that virtue is teachable, only that[†] I am satisfied with these pieces of evidence.

7. [*Untitled*]

Some public speakers claim that political positions should be filled by lot, but this view of theirs is rubbish. After all, suppose one were to ask such a person, 'Why, then, do you not use a lottery to give your slaves jobs, so that if the lot chose your muleteer to be the cook, he would cook, and if it chose your cook to drive your mules, he would drive your mules, and so on and so forth? And why don't we convene the smiths, cobblers, builders, and jewellers, and assign them their jobs by lot, having them work at whatever craft each obtained in the lottery rather than the one he knows?' Likewise, in musical competitions, we could have the contestants draw lots and take part in whichever competition each of them was assigned by the lottery: the pipe-player will play the lyre, perhaps, and the lyre-player the pipes. And in battle an archer or a hoplite will be a cavalryman, while a cavalryman will be an archer. And the upshot will be that everyone will be doing what they are not experts or competent at. They say that election by lot is not only good but also democratic. For my part, I think that democratic is the last thing it is, since every state contains people who are anti-democratic, and if the lottery chooses them, they will destroy the democracy. No, the people themselves should elect those whom they have observed to be well disposed towards democracy, and they should choose suitable men as their military commanders, and other suitable men to serve on the law-and-order committee, and so on.*

8. [*Untitled*]

I think it is the job of the same man and the same skill to be able to talk succinctly,* to know the truth about things, to know how to judge cases correctly, to be able to deliver public speeches, to have mastered the various skills relevant to the spoken word, and to be able to explain the nature and origin of all things.* In the first place, if someone knows the nature of everything, how could he fail to be able also to act correctly in every case?[†] Secondly, someone who has mastered the various skills relevant to the spoken word will also know how to speak correctly on any matter, since in order for anyone to speak correctly, he must speak about what he knows. He will therefore know about everything.* For he knows the skills relevant to all words, and the totality of all things is covered by the totality of all words. And if someone is going to speak correctly he must, whatever his topic, know <. . .> [*There is a gap of a few lines in the text*] and how to give sound advice to his community on how to act well, and how to avoid doing wrong. If he knows these things, he will also know other things, things which are different from the things he knows, because these different things are likewise among all things, and the exigency of the situation will, if needs be, provide him with them to the same end of knowledge.† And if he is capable of playing the pipes, he knows how to play the pipes whenever he has to. Someone who knows how to judge legal cases has to have correct knowledge of justice, since that is what legal cases are concerned with. Because he knows what is just, he will also know the opposite of justice, and things which are different from justice and injustice. He must also know all the laws, but if he doesn't know the facts, he doesn't know the laws either. After all, it is the man who knows music who also knows the laws of music, and anyone who doesn't know music doesn't know its laws either. Now, if someone knows the truth about things, it is easy to argue that he knows everything. And anyone who is capable of speaking succinctly† must when questioned give answers, whatever the topic. So he has to know everything.

9. [*Untitled*]

No discovery is more important or admirable than memory; it is universally useful for intellectual pursuits and for skill.† This is what it consists in: first, if you pay attention, your mind advances by these means until it perceives what it has learnt in a more holistic fashion.† Second, you must study whatever you hear, because if you hear and repeat the same things over and over again, they reach your memory. Third, relate everything you hear to something you already know: for instance, if you have to remember 'Chrysippus', relate it to 'gold' (*chrysos*) and 'horse' (*hippos*); or relate 'Pyrilampes' to 'fire' (*pyr*) and 'shining' (*lampein*). These are examples to do with names, but this is what you do for things: relate 'courage' to Ares and Achilles, metal-working to Hephaestus, cowardice to Epeius <. . .> *

T. M. Conley, 'Dating the So-called *Dissoi Logoi*: A Cautionary Note', *Ancient Philosophy*, 5 (1985), 59–65.

A. Levi, 'On Twofold Statements', *American Journal of Philology*, 61 (1940), 292–306.

T. M. Robinson, *Contrasting Arguments: An Edition of the Dissoi Logoi* (New York: Arno Press, 1979).

A. E. Taylor, 'Socrates and the *Dissoi Logoi*', in id., *Varia Socratica* (Oxford: Parker, 1911), 91–128.

ANONYMOUS AND
MISCELLANEOUS TEXTS

Included in this section are a number of texts, from various authors, which illustrate two interlocking debates that flourished in the fifth century, largely under the influence of the Sophistic movement. The first and main debate concerns the relative value of *nomos* and *physis*, the second the origins of humankind and its institutions. We have already met the debate over *nomos* and *physis*, law (or custom, or convention) and nature, when discussing certain passages in Protagoras, Hippias, Thrasymachus, and Antiphon; and both Protagoras and Prodicus also had something to say about origins.

Callicles (the evidence for whose views constitutes **T1**) was a historical figure from the end of the fifth century in Athens, but as usual we have no way of knowing how far Plato is embellishing his views. Nevertheless, the impassioned speech Plato gives him, denouncing conventional morality and singing the praises of the slogan that 'Might is right', is one of the great pieces of rhetoric from the ancient world, and a clear expression of one way in which the terms 'nature' and 'convention' could be used to make a point. According to Callicles nature and convention are invariably opposed (Antiphon agrees). The case at issue is that doing wrong, understood as having more than one's fair share or gaining an advantage over others, is shameful and wrong according to convention, but (so Callicles claims) is right according to nature. Convention, custom, and law are the means by which the weak keep the naturally strong subdued. Thrasymachus and Callicles both subvert standard morality, but whereas Thrasymachus agrees with morality that the pursuit of one's own interest and advantage is unjust (but thinks that the natural ruler will follow this unjust course), Callicles claims that the pursuit of one's own interest and advantage is natural justice. That this doctrine of 'Might is right' was not unknown towards the end of the fifth century is chillingly shown by passages from the historian Thucydides (1.75–7; 3.37–50; 5.84–114): the deadpan way in which the historian records this element of Athenian politics, and the way he subtly portrays a progression in Athenian arrogance throughout the first few books, are indictments of the terrible uses to which the conviction that might is right could be put, such as deciding to slaughter the whole population of a town which had rebelled against Athens' rule.

Critias was a famous oligarchic politician and associate of Socrates from the end of the fifth century. Whether or not he should be counted as a

Sophist in his own right is unclear, but at any rate, in both his dramas and his speeches he was strongly influenced by Sophistic ideas (as was the playwright Euripides too). The fragment from his *Sisyphus* translated as **F1** need not, then, represent Critias' personal views, as opposed to those he put in the mouth of one of his characters, but it is a clear account of a possible position within the fifth-century debate over law and nature.[1] What this piece of verse shows clearly is that a defence of the value of law against the attacks of thinkers such as Antiphon need not make one any less radical; for Critias combines such a defence with the view that the gods are fictions, created by a clever man to stop people doing wrong even when they are not overlooked by other people. The inventor's cleverness lies in his preying on people's fears: they were already in awe of the power of certain meteorological phenomena, so this storyteller makes the sky the home of the gods.

The *Anonymus Iamblichi* (**T2**) is a stretch of prose from the end of the fifth century embedded in the *Exhortation to Philosophy* of the late Platonic philosopher, Iamblichus. Although Iamblichus does not tell us who the author of the piece is, and does not even signal that it is not by him, in *Exhortation to Philosophy* he does include a number of sections from other writers, and scholars are unanimous in believing that these words genuinely date from the Sophistic period of the fifth century. The anonymous author shows himself, in a rather tedious fashion, to be a utilitarian democrat, and a champion of law and order, whose virtues he sings at some length, in awkward Greek, and in a very derivative fashion.[2] A very similar view, similarly expressed, may be found briefly stated in Euripides' play *The Suppliant Women*, at lines 429–38; this play was produced in the late 420s, which may not allow us to date *Anonymus Iamblichi* more precisely, but does show that the discussion was in the air. The most interesting aspect of the treatise is that just as Callicles could appeal to law, understood as natural law, to justify his view of nature, so our anonymous author includes an appeal to nature to justify his view of the importance of law; that is, our natural inability to live alone compels us to form societies, and

---

[1] Some scholars believe the fragment should be attributed to Euripides.

[2] For instance, the idea that success depends on both natural talent and practice is a commonplace found in Protagoras **T15** (p. 219) and in several fragments of Democritus; the injunction to work hard is found in many conventional moralists, such as Prodicus **F1** (p. 248); the *Anonymus*' utilitarianism may have its roots in Protagorean ideas; the importance of law and justice in a community is found in Protagoras **T12** (p. 219) and elsewhere; the anonymous author adumbrates the idea found in Protagoras, Critias, and others of a primitive state for humankind, from which we have progressed; much of the praise of obedience to the law towards the end of the piece is reminiscent of Democritus' stress on the importance of tranquillity. Cole 1967 (see bibliography below) believes that the treatise is an epitome of a work by Democritus, which was influenced by Protagoras.

societies require law and order (compare Protagoras **T12**). It is also tempting to see a response to Callicles in the middle and at the very end of the
treatise, where the author denies that there could ever be a superman
strong enough to wrest power from an unwilling population.

T3 was written in the fourth century, and is part of a speech attributed
to the fourth-century orator Demosthenes, but the speech contains
material which certainly goes back to fifth-century Sophistic debate.
Because of the difficulty of differentiating the original fifth-century text
from the speech surrounding it, I have translated little of the relevant
sections of the speech (15–35, 85–91, 93–6), concentrating on those bits
which are most clear and relevant, and which are more likely to contain
genuine fifth-century material. Like *Anonymus Iamblichi* the author
defends the importance of law; the interest of the piece is that whereas the
partisans of *physis* had been inclined to argue that man-made laws necessarily change according to the whims of different governments or the
same governments at different times, and so that we should look to nature
or 'natural law' for stability (see Hippias **T5** and **T6**, p. 255), our author
turns this on its head by arguing that nature changes from individual to
individual, whereas law is stable. However, there are also hints in the
speech (although these may not be original to the fifth-century tract) of a
reconciliation between *nomos* and *physis*: the last couple of sentences translated suggest that the desires and objectives inherent in the nature of a
perfectly good man, a paragon of virtue, coincide with the goals of the
laws.

The debate on origins continues in **T4**, which combines an account of
origins with the terminology of the debate over *nomos* and *physis*. Though
writing in the fourth century, Plato is clearly reflecting earlier debate when
he has Glaucon challenge Socrates in *Republic* to prove that justice benefits a moral person more than injustice benefits an unjust person. Glaucon
expresses the challenge with an account of the origin of legal codes and
political constitutions as necessary to curb the lawlessness of men's
natures. Glaucon's account of justice as a compromise is no less cynical
than that of Callicles in **T1**, but his conclusions are different: as far as
Callicles is concerned, it is the fact that laws were invented as such a curb
that proves their perniciousness, whereas for Glaucon (as for Critias in
F1) it proves their value. This is a clear example of how different thinkers
could employ similar arguments towards opposite ends.

We have already met theories of progress and origins in Protagoras and
Prodicus. In this section, **F1** as well as **T4** fit into this context. Those
theories which are actually theories of *progress* are naturally part of the
nomos-physis debate because, 'progress' being a term of approval, they
assume that the way we live now is better in various respects from how we

lived in the distant past, in a supposed 'natural' state. The idea that there was progress and development was important, because previously the tendency in Greek thought had been to locate a Golden Age in the past, and trace a decline from then up to the present.[3] A number of passages from both prose-writers and poets could illustrate the wide spread of the idea of progress in fifth-century Greece,[4] but the one which is broadest in its scope, despite its brief length, and contains more than just enthusiasm for technical advances, is **T5**. This is another anonymous tract embedded in the work of a later author, in this case the historian Diodorus of Sicily, who is explicitly reproducing an earlier account of origins and progress.

Summarizing the *nomos-physis* debate is not straightforward, since the broadness of the terms allowed various thinkers to exploit them in various ways. But one thing that characterizes it is its emotive quality. *Nomos* and *physis* each had champions or partisans; the terms were not merely tools of cool, rational analysis, as, for instance, the related contrast between appearance and reality was for Democritus (in **F3**, p. 176). The partisans of *nomos* include all those who see humankind progressing from a bestial and vulnerable state to one where law and society offer protection, but also those like *Anonymus Iamblichi* who, without committing themselves to a theory of progress, simply see in law and order our best hope for survival and life with some kind of dignity, and, at a personal level, for getting on in the world. Ranged against them were the partisans of *physis*, who vary from radicals like Callicles and Thrasymachus, who value self-interest above all (a view which is apologetically reflected in **T4**), to Antiphon, who uses the facts of *physis* to argue for a kind of liberal cosmopolitanism and argues that the natural law of self-preservation shows how defective man-made laws are; and to Hippias, who probably argued that the laws of nature, so far from sanctioning Calliclean self-interest, simply provide us with a more objective moral code.

T1 [*Callicles speaking to Socrates*] To be specific, where I think Polus was at fault was in agreeing with you that doing wrong is more

[3] The *locus classicus* for this kind of thinking being Hesiod, *Works and Days* 90–201.

[4] See e.g. Aeschylus, *Prometheus Bound* 442–68, 478–506; Sophocles, *Antigone* 332–71; Euripides, *Suppliant Women* 201–13; Ps.-Hippocrates, *On Ancient Medicine* 2–3, 14. Other works celebrating progress, but written later than the 5th cent., certainly reflect 5th-cent. terms and issues: Isocrates, *Panegyricus* 28–42; Plato, *Laws* 676a-683a; Moschion, fr. 6 Nauck; Lucretius, *On the Nature of the Universe* 5.783–1457. On these and other relevant texts, see Cole 1967, pp. 1–10; several of the later texts are discussed in more detail in subsequent chapters of Cole's book, in order to establish the likelihood that Democritus was the common source for many of them.

shameful than suffering wrong. It was this admission of his which enabled you to tie him up in logical knots and muzzle him; he was just too embarrassed to voice his convictions. You pretend that truth is your goal, Socrates, but in actual fact you steer discussions towards this kind of ethical idea—ideas which are unsophisticated enough to have popular appeal, and which depend entirely on convention, not on nature. They're invariably opposed to each other, you know—nature and convention, I mean—and consequently if someone is too embarrassed to go right ahead and voice his convictions, he's bound to contradict himself. This in fact is the source of the clever, but unfair, argumentative trick you've devised: if a person is talking from a conventional standpoint, you slip in a question which presupposes a natural point of view, and if he's talking about nature, you substitute convention.* On this matter of doing and suffering wrong, for instance—to take the case at hand—Polus was talking about what was more shameful from a conventional standpoint, but you adopted the standpoint of nature in following up what he said, because in nature everything is more shameful if it is also worse (as suffering wrong is), whereas convention ordains that doing wrong is more shameful. In fact, this thing—being wronged—isn't within a real man's experience; it's something which happens to slaves, who'd be better off dead, because they're incapable of defending themselves or anyone else they care for against unjust treatment and abuse.

In my opinion it's the weaklings who constitute the majority of the human race who make the rules. In making these rules, they look after themselves and their own interest, and that's also the criterion they use when they dispense praise and criticism. They try to cow the stronger ones—which is to say, those who are capable of increasing their share of things—and to stop them getting an increased share, by saying that to do so is wrong and shameful and by defining injustice in precisely those terms, as the attempt to have more than others. In my opinion, it's because they're second-rate that they're happy for things to be distributed equally. Anyway, that's why convention states that the attempt to have a larger share than most people is immoral and shameful; that's why people call it doing wrong. But I think we only have to look at nature to find evidence that it is *right* for better to have a greater share than worse, more capable than less capable. The evidence for this is widespread. Other creatures show, as do human communities and nations, that right has been determined as follows: the superior person shall dominate the inferior person and have more than him. By what right, for instance, did Xerxes make war on Greece or his father on Scythia, not to mention countless further cases of the same kind of behaviour? These people act, surely, in conformity with the natural essence of right and, yes, I'd even go so far as to say that they act in conformity with natural *law*, even though they presumably contravene man-made laws.

What do we do with the best and strongest among us? We capture them young, like lions, mould them, and turn them into slaves by chanting spells and incantations over them which insist that they have to be equal to others and that equality is admirable and right. But I'm sure that if a man is born in whom nature is strong enough, he'll shake off all these limitations, shatter them to pieces, and win his freedom; he'll trample all our regulations, charms, spells, and unnatural laws into the dust; this slave will rise up and reveal himself as our master; and then natural right will blaze forth.   (Plato, *Gorgias* 482d7–484b1 Burnet)

F1 (DK 88B25)

> There was a time when human life was chaotic,
> As subject to brute strength as the life of beasts,
> When not only did the good go unrewarded,
> But neither was there any punishment for the bad.
> And then, or so it seems to me, men introduced   5
> The restraint of law, so that justice would be the tyrant
> Of the human race,† the master of abuse
> And punisher of any transgression.
> Next, since the laws made it impossible
> For people to commit obvious crimes by force,   10
> They began to act in secret, this was the point, I think,
> At which some shrewd and clever man first
> Invented fear of the gods for mortal men, so that
> The wicked might have something to fear, even if
> Their deeds or words or thoughts were secret.   15
> So that is why he introduced the divine, saying:
> 'There is a god, and he teems with life undying.†
> He will hear all that is said among mortals,   20
> And he will be able to see all that is done.

Your evil schemes, plotted in silence,
Will be noticed by the gods. For intelligence
Is one of their qualities.'† With these words
He introduced the crucial† doctrine   25
And covered up the truth with a fictional story.
He claimed that the home of the gods is the place
Whose merest mention would fill men with utter terror,
Knowing that this place is the source of fears for mortal men
And of things which support them in their wretched life—   30
The revolving sky above, where, as he observed,
There were flashes of lightning, terrifying thunderclaps,
And the brilliance† of the stars in the heavens,
The fair embroidery of the wise craftsman, Time.
Also from the sky heavenly bodies come in a gleaming mass,* 35
And moist rain proceeds from there into the earth.
These are the kinds of fears with which he enveloped† men,
And by means of these stories† he not only settled
The gods properly in an appropriate place,
But also quenched lawlessness by means of law.   40
[*there is a gap of a few lines in the text*]
This, I think, is how in the first place someone persuaded
Mortal men to worship the race of gods.

        (Sextus Empiricus, *Against the Professors* 9.54 Bury)

T2 (DK 89) The final completion and perfection of anything—it
may be skill or courage or eloquence or virtue (in whole or in part)—
is a possible attainment under the following circumstances. The first
prerequisite is natural ability, and while one may think that this is
due to fortune, the following qualities are up to the individual himself: he must be eager to achieve noble and admirable things, work
hard at them, learn them as quickly as possible, and persevere at
them for a long time. If a person lacks even one of these qualities, it
is impossible for him to bring anything to the peak of perfection, but
if he has them all, no one will be able to surpass his achievements,
whatever his speciality.

    A person who wants to gain prestige among men and to let them
know what kind of man he is must begin from an early age and apply
himself consistently, without starting and stopping. For any of the
qualities I mentioned—provided it has been around for a long time

after an early start and has grown to perfection—acquires a stable reputation and fame. The reason for this is that by then people know without a doubt that they can rely on the person for this quality, and they do not envy him for it. Envy is what either stops people praising someone and not giving him the exposure that he might reasonably expect, or makes them find fault with him and tell unfair lies about him. The point is that people resent giving someone else respect, because they think it takes something away from themselves, but if they are left with absolutely no choice and have slowly and gradually been won over, they are prepared to praise someone else, even if grudgingly. However, it must also be said that they do not stop to wonder whether a man is as he appears to be, or whether he is setting traps and deceitfully chasing a good reputation by leading people on with a display of fine deeds. But if virtue is cultivated in the way I have already mentioned, it imbues itself with trustworthiness and fame, because once people have become firmly convinced, they stop being capable of deploying envy or thinking that they are being duped.

Besides, the passage of time—if a good long time is spent over any endeavour and business—confirms the quality that is being cultivated, whereas a short period cannot do this. It is true that verbal skill can be acquired and learnt in a short time, so thoroughly that the pupil becomes just as good as his teacher, but as far as concerns the virtue which is formed as a result of the performance of a lot of deeds, it is impossible for someone to start late at this and rapidly bring it to perfection; no, he has to grow and develop with it, by avoiding bad arguments and habits, and taking a lot of time and care over practising and attaining the opposite. Moreover, there is another drawback to the rapid acquisition of prestige, and that is that people resent those who have suddenly and rapidly acquired wealth or skill or virtue or courage.

When a person has set his sights on one of these qualities, has brought it to perfection, and has attained it, whether it is eloquence or skill or strength, he must next employ it for good and lawful purposes. There is nothing more pernicious than for someone to use the good quality he has gained for immoral and criminal purposes, and it would be better for him not to have it than to have it. Just as a person who has any of these qualities and uses it for good purposes is completely good, so the converse is also true, and there is no one worse than the man who uses them for bad purposes.

We should also consider what kind of speech and behaviour supports the intention of someone who is aiming for complete virtue, given that what would enable him to attain this aim is helping large numbers of people. Now, if someone does his neighbours a favour by lending them money, he will be forced to do them a bad turn later when he collects the money. In the second place, he could not accumulate such unlimited wealth that he could go on and on giving gifts and favours without it running out. In the third place, there is also an additional disadvantage, once he has accumulated his wealth, if he spends his money and becomes poor, losing what he had and ending up with nothing. What else might someone do, then, to be a benefactor to others, which does not involve handing out money? And, whatever it is he does, how can he avoid the bad and keep to the good? Moreover, if he keeps giving presents, how can he not exhaust his ability to give? He can avoid this by supporting the laws and justice, because it is justice that unites and joins communities and individuals.

Now, every man should be exceptionally self-disciplined. The best tests of self-discipline are the ability to resist that universal corrupting agent, money; and not sparing one's soul in the effort to do what is right and pursue the goal of virtue. It is in regard to these two that most people lack self-discipline. This happens because they love their souls (which is to say, their lives), and so this clinging to life and the familiar feel of something they have known all their lives make them protect and cherish their souls. And they love money because there are certain things they fear. What are these things? Illness, old age, unexpected penalties—by which I do not mean penalties imposed by the courts, which one can anticipate and take precautions about, but things like fires, the death of relatives or livestock, and other disasters, which afflict either their bodies or their minds or their wealth. So every man desires money to ensure that he is in a position to use it should any of these disasters arise. And there are other factors too, which just as effectively impel men towards making money—things like competitiveness, the desire to emulate others, and political power, which cause people to regard money as important, because of the help it affords in such situations. But the man who is truly good does not rely on the cloak of someone else's ornaments to chase after prestige, but on his own virtue.

Where love of the soul is concerned, the following argument might be found persuasive. If men could resist the onset of old age and could remain undying for all time, unless killed by someone else, that might be a valid reason for someone to protect his soul. But since what happens if life is prolonged is not immortality, but baneful old age, then it is sheer stupidity, and suggests over-exposure to bad arguments and objectives, to preserve the soul for infamy, rather than exchanging it for immortal fame—eternal and everlasting esteem in exchange for something mortal.

The next point to note is that one should not desire to gain an advantage over others, nor should one count as virtue the power that accompanies such an advantage, while calling a law-abiding man a coward. There is nothing worse than this frame of mind, and it is the cause of everything that is, so far from being good, bad and pernicious. Since men are constitutionally incapable of living alone and have been compelled to join together with one another, since they have come up with their whole way of life and invented the skills to support it, and since it is impossible for them to live with one another without law (which would be an even worse penalty for them than living alone), it is these necessities that have enthroned law and justice as kings over men,* and they will never be dislodged, because they have been securely bound in place by nature. Now, if a person were born who was invulnerable, enjoyed nothing but good health, never suffered any setbacks, had a supernatural constitution, and was physically and mentally as hard as nails, one might perhaps think that the power that accompanies advantage over others would be all right for such a man, because he could get away with refusal to submit to the law. But one would be wrong to think that, because if (what is impossible) there were to be such a man, it is only by allying himself with the laws and with justice, and by confirming them, and by using his strength to reinforce them and their supports, that he could be safe. Otherwise, he would never survive, because it is likely that everyone would come out against such a man, and because of their conformity to the law and their numbers their skill or power would be superior to his, and they would get the better of him. It therefore turns out that power—what really deserves to be called power—is maintained by law and justice.

The first result of conformity to the law is trust, which brings enormous benefits for everyone and is one of the great blessings of the world. For instance, it is as a result of conformity to the law that property is shared, and this means that even a little property is sufficient, since it is shared around; but without conformity to the law even a great deal of property is never enough. Also, the changes of fortune that affect property and life either adversely or the opposite are managed in a way that maximizes their benefit as a result of conformity to the law; for those who are successful can enjoy their good fortune in safety and without worrying about others' intriguing against them, while those who fail are supported by the successful ones because, thanks to their conformity to the law, there is interdependence and trust between them. Then again, because of conformity to the law people's time is not filled with public business, but with the business of daily living, and under law-abiding conditions people avoid the extreme distress brought on by a concern with public business and gain the great pleasure of concerning themselves with their daily work.* Moreover, sleep is the way men find relief from their troubles, and under law-abiding conditions when they go to sleep they do so without fears and without any distressing worries, and they feel similar feelings when they wake up. Fear does not come upon them out of the blue, nor after an extremely pleasant rest do they expect the day to be extremely distressing.† No, they pleasantly† occupy their minds with untroubled concerns about their daily work, and lighten their efforts to gain the good things of life with high and confident hopes, all of which are the product of conformity to the law. As for war, the source of men's worst evils, because it brings downfall and enslavement, this too is more likely to afflict lawless people than those who conform to the law.

Conformity to the law entails many other benefits too, which make life easier and offer relief from the difficult aspects of life, but the consequences of lawlessness are the following evils. First, men are too busy to attend to their jobs and occupy themselves instead with public business, which is the least pleasant of all tasks, and because they do not trust and depend on one another they hoard their money, rather than sharing it, which means that money is hard to come by even if there is plenty of it. Also, the outcome of success and failure is the opposite to what we found it was for those who conform to the law. Under conditions of lawlessness, success is insecure and is the object of intrigues, while so far from being repelled, failure is confirmed by lack of trust and interdependence. These two factors also make both war from abroad and internal discord more likely to occur, and even if they were unknown before, they start to happen then. And all the plots and intrigues going on among them mean that people constantly have to be involved in public business, and that they spend their time looking over their shoulders and meeting plots with counter-plots. They pass their waking hours with unpleasant concerns and in sleep they find no pleasant haven but a place of terror, while waking up induces fear and terror and serves only to remind an individual of his troubles. These and all the evils I have already mentioned are the consequences of lawlessness.

Furthermore, the sole cause of that unspeakably terrible evil, tyranny, is lawlessness. Some people have reached the wrong conclusion and attribute tyranny to other factors, claiming that the responsibility for loss of freedom does not lie with the people themselves, who have, on this account, been forced to submit to the tyrant, once he has become established. But this idea is wrong. It is idiotic to think that the emergence of a king or a tyrant is due to anything other than lawlessness and trying to gain an advantage over others. It is simply a result of a general involvement with evil, because it is impossible for men to live without law and justice, so when these two things, law and justice, are abandoned by the general populace, then care and responsibility for them end up in the hands of a single person. After all, how could autocracy devolve on to a single person unless law, which benefits the general populace, had been banished? For anyone to do away with justice and abolish law, the common benefactor of everyone, he would have to be as hard as nails: how else could he deprive the general run of mankind of these things, when he, as a single individual, is vastly outnumbered by the general populace? This would be impossible for a normal flesh-and-blood person, who could become an autocrat only by re-establishing the abandoned opposite qualities. That is why some people have failed to notice that this is what happens.   (Iamblichus, *Exhortation to Philosophy* 95.13–104.14 Pistelli)

T3 The whole of human life, gentlemen of Athens, whether the community in which they live is large or small, is governed by nature and by laws. Of these, nature is disorderly and private to each individual, while laws are shared, ordered, and the same for all. Now, nature may be bad, and then it often has bad objectives; that is why you find this kind of person committing crimes. But the objectives and goals of the laws are justice, morality, and benefit. Once achieved, these qualities are published as a regulation, which everyone shares in alike and equally, and this is what we call a 'law'. Among the many reasons why everyone should obey the laws are, above all, that every law is a discovery and a gift of the gods, a decree issued by wise men, a means of correcting both deliberate and involuntary crimes, and a compact entered into by the whole community, giving guidelines for the kind of life everyone in the community should live . . . There are two reasons why laws are made: the first is to stop anyone committing any unjust acts, and the second is for the rest of the community to make those who transgress better by punishing them . . . I am not about to say anything new or strange or peculiar, but only what you all know just as well as I do. For if any of you is prepared to look into why and for what reason the Council convenes, the Athenian people gather in the Assembly, the courts are filled, and the outgoing officers happily give way to the new ones— why, in short, everything which enables the city to be well governed and safe happens—you will find that all this is due to the laws and to the fact that everyone obeys them. If the laws were abolished, and it was open to everyone to do what he pleased, not only would the constitution come to an end, but there would be no difference between the way we humans lived and the way wild beasts live.

. . . All men have altars dedicated to justice, law and order, and decency: the finest and most sacred of these altars are in the mind and nature of each individual, but others are built in public so that all may worship at them . . . For in fact, gentlemen of Athens, where people in general are concerned, it is noticeable that in the case of the best and most disciplined of them the impulse to carry out all their duties comes from their very nature . . .   (Ps.-Demosthenes, *Against Aristogeiton* 15.1–16.8, 17.4–7, 20.1–11, 35.1–4, 93.1–3 Butcher)

T4 'Well,' Glaucon said, 'I promised I'd talk first about the nature and origin of justice, so here goes. The idea is that although it's a fact of nature that doing wrong is good and having wrong done to one is bad, nevertheless the disadvantages of having it done to one outweigh the benefits of doing it. Consequently, when people have experienced both committing wrong and being at the receiving end of it, they see that the disadvantages are unavoidable and the benefits are unattainable, so they decide that the most profitable course is for them to enter into a contract with one another, guaranteeing that no wrong will be committed or received.* They then set about making laws and decrees, and from then on they use the terms "legal" and "right" to describe anything which is enjoined by their code. So that's the origin and nature of justice on this view: it is a compromise between the ideal of doing wrong without having to pay for it, and the worst situation, which is having wrong done to one while lacking the means of exacting compensation. Since justice is a compromise, it is endorsed because, while it may not be good, it does gain value by preventing people from doing wrong. For any real man with the ability to do wrong would never enter into a contract to avoid both wronging and being wronged: he wouldn't be so crazy . . . As for the fact that justice is only ever practised reluctantly, by people who lack the ability to do wrong, this would become particularly obvious if we performed the following thought-experiment. Suppose we grant both types of people—just and unjust—the scope to do whatever they want, and we then keep an eye on them to see where their wishes lead them. We'll catch our moral person red-handed: his desire to gain the advantage over others will point him in the same direction as the unjust person, towards a destination which every creature naturally regards as good and aims for, except that people are compelled by convention to deviate from this path and respect equality.' (Plato, *Republic* 358e1–359c6 Burnet)

T5 (DK 68B5.1) So much for the traditional account of the origins of the universe.* And they say that the first men to be born lived a chaotic and bestial life, setting out one by one to find their food, and eating only the least tough plants and those fruits which grow of their own accord from trees. Since they were under attack from wild beasts, they let themselves be taught by expediency and began to come to one another's help; and once fear had made them gather together they gradually came to recognize one another's characteristics. At first the sounds they made were meaningless and confused, but gradually they began to develop articulate words, and by agreeing among themselves which symbols stood for which objects they established a means by which they could communicate with one another and pass on knowledge about everything in the world. But since these kinds of groups were scattered throughout the inhabited world, they did not all speak the same language, since each group had organized its speech just as it occurred to them to do so. That is why there are now so many different languages; and these first groups were also the ancestors of all the various peoples in the world.

Now, since none of the things useful for life had yet been discovered, the life these first humans lived was full of trials and tribulations: they wore no clothing, houses and fire were alien to them, and they knew nothing about cultivating food. In fact, since they didn't even know how to harvest the food they got from the wild, they didn't lay up a store of their fruits to cater for the hard times, with the result that many of them died in the winters of cold and shortage of food. As a consequence of this their experience gradually taught them to take refuge in caves during the winter and to store any fruits that would keep. And once they had acquired knowledge of fire and other practical aids, they gradually also invented the arts and crafts and everything else which serves to support living together. Generally speaking, need was the teacher in everything and gave appropriate instruction in each branch of knowledge to a creature endowed with natural talent, hands to help him in everything, reason, and a shrewd intellect.   (Diodorus of Sicily, *Universal History* 1.8.1–9 Vogel)

A. T. Cole, 'The Anonymus Iamblichi and his Place in Greek Political Theory', *Harvard Studies in Classical Philology*, 65 (1961), 127–63.
—— *Democritus and the Sources of Greek Anthropology* (American Philological Association Monograph, 25, 1967).
W. K. C. Guthrie, *In the Beginning: Some Greek Views on the Origins of Life and the Early State of Man* (London: Methuen, 1957).
C. H. Kahn, 'The Origins of Social Contract Theory in the Fifth Century B.C.', in [27], 92–108.
M. J. O'Brien, 'Xenophanes, Aeschylus, and the Doctrine of Primeval Brutishness', *Classical Quarterly*, 35 (1985), 264–77.
G. Vlastos, 'On the Pre-history in Diodorus', in [33], 351–8 (first pub. *American Journal of Philology*, 67 (1946)).

EXPLANATORY NOTES

12 *made use of this theorem*: for details of this practical application of the theorem, see McKirahan [12], p. 26.

13 *as the poets call it*: the river Styx was one of the dread rivers of the underworld. Examples of the gods swearing by this river can be found in Homer (*Iliad* 14.271, 15.37). Ocean was supposed to be the primordial water, which still surrounds the continents of the world; Tethys was the wife of Ocean personified. At *Iliad* 14.201 (again at 302), Homer spoke of 'Ocean, whence gods are generated, and mother Tethys.' Aristotle was not the first to suggest a cosmogonical interpretation of this line: Plato had done so at *Theaetetus* 152e.

14 *passage of the hours*: the *gnomon* is simply an upright stick which casts a shadow which can be used to determine the sun's height and direction.

a thing of wonder: Hecataeus of Miletus was an early geographer and ethnographer, a forerunner of Herodotus, who is heavily indebted to his work in the first four books of his *Histories*. Hecataeus' *Circumnavigation of the Known World* was written in the late sixth century, so that he was more or less a contemporary of Anaximenes. Although not strictly a Presocratic philosopher, he was influenced by the new thinking to the extent that he rationalized and systematized his discoveries, and was pleasantly sceptical about many of the 'travellers' tales' he came across. He apparently began his *Genealogies* with the words: 'What I write here is the account I consider to be true; for the stories of the Greeks are numerous and, in my opinion, ridiculous.' However, the extent to which he lived up to this promise may be doubted. More generally, both he and Herodotus conform to the spirit of the Ionians in that they undertook *historia* ('research' or 'investigation'), which is also what the Ionians were trying to do. (It is because Herodotus called his work *Investigations* that the word 'history' in our language means what it does.)

the first principle: an important alternative translation of this sentence would read: 'It was he who originally introduced this word *arkhē* [first principle].'

15 *infinity is predicated*: in this and the following testimonia, Aristotle does not actually name Anaximander as the exponent of the view that the source of all things is intermediate between the recognized elements, but scholars universally believe that Anaximander is the thinker Aristotle has in mind. If correct, this on its own is sufficient to refute the recent claim (by Finkelberg 1993) that Anaximander's originative stuff was actually air.

18 *Anaximenes of Miletus*: it will be noticed that Diels/Kranz gave **T30** and **T31** 'B' numbers (see Note on the Texts, p. xli), since they (along with

other scholars) took these testimonia to preserve some of Anaximenes' original words. However, since we know that Anaximenes wrote in Ionic dialect, the semi-quotation in **T30** is ruled out (except, of course, as a close paraphrase); and in **T31** only the one word 'loose' may originate with Anaximenes.

18 *synonyms*: if the 'ice-like' substance of which the outer periphery of the universe is made (according to **T39**) is as solid as it sounds, it is hard to see how air might surround it and yet be a vital component of the universe. Some scholars therefore reject or reinterpret this testimony of Aëtius, while others conceive of the surrounding periphery as a permeable membrane. If Aëtius is to be reinterpreted, air might be imagined as inside the periphery, rather than outside it.

felting: without going into all the technical details of felting, it is a process that involves *compression* of the cloth. See also Xenophanes **T6**. It is likely that this use of the term goes back to Theophrastus.

19 *clepsydra*: Aristotle's reference to the clepsydra is somewhat obscure. A clepsydra was shaped like an inverted funnel, with the narrow opening at the top and a wider bottom. The opening at the top was narrow enough to be stopped by a thumb (as we do a pipette), and the bottom was solid, but perforated with a number of holes. The use of the instrument was that it was dipped into a large bowl of water and wine; the liquid entered the clepsydra through the perforated bottom, and then, when the thumb was placed over the top hole, the liquid could be carried over to another vessel, where the thumb was released, so that the liquid would flow out through the holes in the bottom. So Aristotle seems to think that somehow the water does not escape through the holes in the bottom because of the pressure of the air outside the clepsydra. For another Presocratic analogy with the clepsydra, see Empedocles **F42**, p. 155.

27 *blue eyes and red hair*: the Thracians lived in what is now north-eastern Greece, Bulgaria, and on up into Romania and beyond; the Ethiopians occupied from southern Egypt southward through Sudan and into Ethiopia. The Thracians were commonly regarded as the most northerly race, and the Ethiopians as the most southerly. Xenophanes is therefore saying, in effect, 'All peoples everywhere, from north to south, portray their gods like themselves.'

30 *their discoveries improve*: or, just possibly: 'But in time, through seeking, men discover what is better.'

37 *once they have heard it*: the introductory 'but' suggests that the very first words of Heraclitus' book have been lost. The most attractive suggestion is that the first words were: 'One thing is common' (Osborne [80], p. 155).

while asleep: 'punctuating the work of Heraclitus is difficult because it is unclear whether a given word goes with the word that precedes it or the one that follows it. At the beginning of his treatise, for instance, where he says "Of this principle which holds forever men prove ignorant", it is unclear which of the two the word "forever" goes with' (Aristotle, *Rhetoric* 1407ᵇ14–18). What Aristotle apparently could not imagine is that the word goes with both at once. This is not untypical of Heraclitus' style.

38 *private universe*: despite Diels's numbering of this as a fragment, it is in fact a paraphrase (albeit a good one) of whatever it might have been that Heraclitus originally said. It is often difficult to distinguish between actual fragments and paraphrases in the case of Heraclitus.

'Most men are bad, few good': the saw quoted at the end of this fragment is a popular saying, attributed to Bias of Priene.

Archilochus as well: not only the Homeric epics, but also shorter lyric poems such as those of Archilochus were recited by rhapsodes in public competitions.

39 *common to all*: there is an untranslatable pun in the Greek: the two words translated 'with intelligence' are *xun noōi*, while the word for 'common' is *xunōi*. For Heraclitus, similarity of sound was significant, and implied similarity of meaning. So what is common or universal is what can be apprehended with intelligence.

still the same road: for a cosmological interpretation of this fragment, see the beginning of **T8**.

40 *strife and necessity*: note the echo and implicit correction of Anaximander **T15** (p. 14).

41 *I searched for myself*: given that in fr. 64 DK the same verb is used of mining for gold, it is tempting to introduce a Heraclitean kind of pun here, and translate: 'I mined myself.'

we are and are not: it is quite possible that there was originally a single river fragment, from which the last three entries derive more or less accurately.

42 *in regular measures*: note the hint of Milesian mechanism in this, which is only partially mitigated by Heraclitus' divinization of fire.

lightning: it is not absolutely clear what meteorological phenomenon Heraclitus had in mind for *prēstēr*. But the word is cognate with 'fire', and at *Histories* 7.42.2 Herodotus says it can kill people, so 'lightning' seems a reasonable choice. It also seems to mean 'lightning' in another early occurrence, at Hesiod, *Theogony* 846.

43 *new each day*: Plato puts this idea to amusing use at *Republic* 498a6–b1, arguing that dilettante philosophers are, with a few exceptions, when they die, 'snuffed out more thoroughly than Heraclitus' sun, since they are never rekindled later'.

will find it out: interestingly, the Derveni papyrus, discovered in 1962, whose text dates from about 420 BCE, at column IV, combines both **F42** and **F43** into a single fragment, while claiming to quote Heraclitus directly: 'The sun by its own nature is as broad as a human foot, and does not overstep its boundaries; for if it oversteps its own breadth, the Furies, the allies of Justice, will find it out.'

43 *heavenly bodies*: the idea that the sun, at any rate, was contained in a bowl, predates Heraclitus. In a traditional myth, the sun sailed around Oceanus, the river of water surrounding the world, in a bowl.

44 *the principle it contains*: an interesting conjunction of ideas is gained by placing this fragment in the context of **F9** and **F30**. Heraclitus would be calling on us to search ourselves, as he did himself, without hope of ever reaching a conclusion, and without prejudging what we will find on the way.

he contacts sleep: another Heraclitean pun: the word for 'kindles' is the same as the word for 'contacts'.

45 *die through illness*: this line is a verse adaptation of a lost original of Heraclitus.

the better the portion: the fragment is an extreme example of Heraclitean assonance: *moroi mezones mezonas moiras lankhanousi*. The structure of the sentence is chiastic as well.

46 *chatting to a house*: or, taking the sarcastic sting out of the fragment: 'They purify themselves in an unusual way.'

the same as Hades: the Lenaea was one of the most important festivals in honour of Dionysus. The point of this fragment is contained in a pun. The word for 'disgraceful', *anaides*, could punningly be parsed as 'not-Hades' (*Aides*); moreover, the word for 'phallus' is *aidoia*. Hades and Dionysus are presumably identified because Hades represents death, and Dionysus drunkenness: it is death for souls to become moist (**F44**).

with her voice: the Sibyl was an oracular prophetess, inspired by Apollo.

57 *with their hands*: this is a significant gesture. A modest Greek maiden would be expected to veil her face when away from home. Parmenides' guides unveil their faces on reaching the threshold of day and night, indicating that they have returned home. Since Homeric and Hesiodic echoes by Parmenides guarantee that he is locating this gateway in the underworld, it follows that Parmenides' journey is to the underworld, not towards a transcendent upper realm of light.

alternating locks: this is a compressed way of saying that she opens the doors to let out day and night alternately. The idea that justice regulates the length of day and night is reminiscent of Anaximander **T15** (p. 14).

as they altogether are: the goddess's promise at this point is obscure, but presumably refers to the second half of Parmenides' poem (now largely irrecoverable), in which he constructed a cosmology to explain the phenomenal world. I take it that these final lines of the prologue mean that since appearances pervade or penetrate everything, mortals were bound to fit them into an acceptable system. But the last words of the prologue are so difficult in Greek that others emend the text and read: ' . . . since they are, in fact, thoroughly everything'.

58 *no end to it*: there is no end to this way because, for any positive predicate F, there are infinite things which are not F.

can be thought and can be: an alternative translation of this fragment is 'Thinking and being are the same.' If this translation is correct, and mind and being are identical for Parmenides, a whole new light is shed on his poem. Its subject would not so much be being *per se* as thinking about being; and what-is would be a living, sensible entity, somewhat akin to Xenophanes' god.

turns back on itself: Parmenides uses the same word, *palintropos*, that Heraclitus had used in **F21** (p. 40), and, of course, his description of this way as identifying opposites is reminiscent of Heraclitus too. Though 'mortals' in general are Parmenides' target here, Heraclitus in particular is probably not far from his mind.

are present: or, perhaps: 'Gaze unshaken on things which, though absent, are present to the mind.'

59 *whether it comes together*: I take this puzzling fragment to be the goddess's instructions as to how we are to listen to what she has to say. That is, I take the ordering mentioned to be the arguments she orders or marshals in what follows: see **F8** ll. 52 for a similar use of the word 'ordering' (*kosmos*). In both places I have attempted to capture the ambiguity of the word with the English 'composition/compose'. Then the point of the fragment is that we are not to worry if language necessarily appears to separate things which are not really separable; we have to bear in mind that this is an illusion. But I admit that this would be an unusual meaning of the word *kosmos*, which basically just means 'ordering', and hence, in particular, 'world-order'. However, Parmenides would not agree that what-is can scatter or come together in the world.

60 *contact with what-is*: these lines are not necessarily as materialistic as they sound. Try reading them thinking of the denial that what-is forms lumps as a denial that it varies in *intensity* at all.

lies: the careful translator notices that the 'Way of Appearance' contains far more poetic ambiguities than the 'Way of Truth'. The polar nature of Parmenides' cosmology is reflected in the polar ambiguities of his text. Unfortunately, these cannot be captured in any translation, short of providing two or three variant translations of certain lines or passages.

should not be named: one of the two forms should not be named, because in any pair of opposites, one is defined as the negation of the other, and yet Parmenides has already forbidden us from saying 'X is not F'. This does not mean, as Aristotle seems to have assumed (**T5**), that Parmenides is leaving us with the other of the pair of opposites as a single cosmogonic factor: he is saying that the whole idea of a cosmology based on opposites is fundamentally mistaken. An alternative translation might be 'one of which should not be named alone', which looks like direct criticism of Parmenides' cosmogonic predecessors, in so far as they had relied on a single stuff (e.g. Anaximenes' air) to generate the universe; Parmenides would be saying that you need two primary stuffs, with opposite attributes. But I do not think this alternative translation can be right, since no one, as far as we know, had named either of Parmenides' pair alone as his cosmological principle. Yet others translate 'of which not even one should be named', but this is not a possible translation of the Greek.

62 *the name 'to be'*: despite the differences in translation, this could be an inaccurate reminiscence of F8 l. 38; however, since Simplicius also records this line in exactly this form on two occasions (*Commentary on Aristotle's Physics* 29.18 and 143.10), it may be an independent fragment.

they say: Aristotle does not name any of the thinkers he has in mind, let alone Parmenides, but in Philoponus' commentary on this passage he records the view of Alexander of Aphrodisias that 'Parmenides was of this opinion'.

the signs in the aither: that is, the heavens and all the heavenly bodies.

63 *the narrower ones*: there is no doubt that this is a reference to the 'rings' with which Parmenides filled the heavens and explained the motions of the heavenly bodies: see T8.

64 *mixture of light and dark*: this looks like a misunderstanding of F13 ll. 1–2, where in his own words Parmenides seems to posit a number of fiery rings followed by a number of mixed rings (basically dark, but with some flame in them too). Though Aëtius' account of the rings is suspect, the rest of his report may be treated with less circumspection.

felting: on 'felting' as a term for 'compression', see note to p. 18 above.

74 *is this what you mean?*: any reconstruction of Zeno's argument from this flimsy evidence is highly speculative. It seems to be another argument against the notion of plurality (see T3). Perhaps it went as follows: 'If there are many things, they must be both similar and dissimilar to one another; they must be similar because, after all, they all exist—they all share the property of existence; they must be dissimilar because otherwise the whole notion of plurality is meaningless; therefore they are both similar and dissimilar; but similars cannot be dissimilars.'

76 *slowest thing in the world*: that is, Achilles and the tortoise.

78 *not to reject singularity*: in this passage Simplicius is concerned to refute the view of Alexander and Eudemus that Zeno argued against Parmenidean monism.

97 *magistrates by lot*: in actual fact the prohibition on beans was more probably due to the fact that the flatulence they cause was supposed to disturb the mind, and specifically to impede prophetic dreams. Alternatively, there might have been experiential familiarity with a genetic tendency towards favism.

101 *the sun and moon*: since the 'Isles of the Blessed' are where enlightened people go after death, this may be a hint of the eastern teaching of astral immortality, which was beginning to enter Greece in the fifth century.

104 *the counter-earth*: this dry, factual report disguises the astonishing leap of the imagination which led the Pythagoreans (or, more probably, Philolaus) to displace the earth from the centre of the universe.

106 *what is being sought will be the result*: equality is 'what is being sought'; 'all the parts which are at a fifth remove from the excessive parts are 1, 2, 3, 4—respectively at a fifth remove from 6, 7, 8, 9. So if the sum of 1, 2, 3, 4—that is, 10—is subtracted from the sum of 6, 7, 8, 9, and added to the sum of 1, 2, 3, 4, the result is equality: 20 = 20.

107 *exceeding and falling short*: see the commentary in Heath, pp. 150–4.

the cosmic figures: the five regular or 'Platonic' solids—the tetrahedron (pyramid), cube, octahedron, icosahedron, and dodecahedron. It is unlikely that the early Pythagoreans had formulated a method of theoretical construction of the solids, but they may well have 'constructed' them as Plato does in *Timaeus* 53c–55c, by forming solid angles out of equilateral triangles, squares (or isosceles triangles), or pentagons.

108 *and the added line*: see Euclid, *Elements* 2.10. The importance of this theorem is that it gave the Pythagoreans a method of finding successive approximations to the value of $\sqrt{2}$. See the commentary by Heath, pp. 91–3 or Thomas, pp. 138–9. However, it remains unlikely that the early Pythagoreans had developed a *theory* of irrationals, although they may have discovered some particular cases of incommensurability: see Heath, pp. 154–7. Basically, however, they conceived of numbers as whole numbers, and fractions as ratios between whole numbers.

act of impiety: a parallel tradition says that Hippasus was killed for discovering the existence of irrational numbers. Since the faces of the dodecahedron are regular pentagons, and the construction of the regular pentagon requires the golden section, which involves irrationals, the two traditions may plausibly be linked.

109 *light and heat to us*: the word 'filters' is odd, until we read in the parallel testimony of Achilles Tatius (*Introduction to Aratus' 'Phaenomena'* 46.13 Maass) that it filters its light to us 'through certain interstices'. In the fifth century a burning-glass was imagined to have channels through which the sun's heat and light were concentrated and transmitted.

110 *distinguishes one number from another*: the Pythagoreans conceived of numbers as arrays of dots (see n. 6 on p. 93); the dots are the limiting principle, the space between them the unlimited void.

111 *plainly unlimited*: note that the argument of this fragment is blatantly self-contradictory if the 'true existents' of the beginning of the fragment are the same as the 'things' of the second half. For then Philolaus would first have argued that they cannot be unlimiteds, and then have argued that they can be unlimiteds. In his edition of Philolaus, pp. 102–7, Huffman must be right, then, to claim that at the beginning 'all the things that exist' are 'true existents'—that is, the elemental sources of the world—

while the 'things' later are the things of the world which are made up of these elements.

111 *positions are reversed*: this 'fragment' of Philolaus is actually written in the wrong dialect—Ionic, rather than Doric—to count as a fully genuine fragment of his writings. Nevertheless, the amount of rewriting involved in the change of dialects would be slight, and I am confident (unlike the parallel case of Anaximenes **T30** on p. 18) that we have a perfectly accurate transcript of the original.

123 *the bright and the dark*: three points on this list. First, we should not take it to be exhaustive, but representative. Second, we should not follow Aristotle (at any rate in **T4**) in regarding the opposites as Anaxagorean principles, along with the 'seeds': Anaxagoras is only stressing the absoluteness of his original mixture by saying that *even opposites* were mixed together so thoroughly as to be indiscernible. Third, note that Anaxagoras lacks the philosophical vocabulary to distinguish between stuffs and qualities, and so that the warm and the cold, for instance, are material items conceived as carriers of these primary qualities.

dissimilar to one another: Anaxagoras specifically mentions earth and seeds together because, as **T13** and **T14** show, he believed that these were the prerequisites for the generation of animals and plants. Animal and plant seeds were, initially, carried down by the air to earth, where they grew.

flesh from not-flesh: though printed in DK as a B-fragment, this final sentence is far more likely to be a paraphrase, along with the preceding sentences.

125 *mind is present too*: that is, all animate creatures, which for Anaxagoras includes plants as well as humans and animals (**T12**).

mind is limitless: in what sense is mind limitless? Perhaps because it never stops initiating actions; perhaps because it comprehends the universe, which is infinite; perhaps because it is our means of intellectual enquiry, but can never fully comprehend itself (compare Heraclitus **F48** on p. 44).

initiating the rotation: this is presumably what led Plato to have Socrates make his famous complaint (*Phaedo* 97b–99c) that although Anaxagoras held out the hope of explaining how mind ruled all things for the best, in fact he made little use of mind—except, as we see here, as a cosmogonic initiatory force. See also Aristotle, *Metaphysics* 985^{a}18–21: 'Anaxagoras uses mind as a *deus ex machina* for his cosmogony, and when he finds it impossible to explain why something necessarily is as it is, he drags mind in, while elsewhere he uses anything rather than mind to explain how things happen.'

wider area still: Anaxagoras places no limits, in time or space, on the expansion of the universe. Empedocles' universe, by contrast, has a spatial outer limit, and is temporally limited too, in that things are moving towards the rule of either love or strife, either of which will put an end to the universe.

127 *everything that was in motion*: or, possibly: 'Mind began to separate off from all that was in motion.' But if this translation were correct, there would be an obvious clash with **F13**, where Anaxagoras says that mind is still present in things.

these things: probably the opposites enumerated in **F12**—or at any rate the dark, heavy, moist opposites, because these are implied in the use Anaxagoras immediately goes on to make of water and clouds.

128 *more than water*: compare Anaximenes' sequence in **T29** on pp. 17–18. It is likely (see **T9**) that Anaxagoras thought of the heavenly bodies as fragments of the earth that had been thrown off by the rotation of the earth and ignited in the upper sky.

rotation of the aither: see the end of **F16**, with its otherwise puzzling idea that stones have a tendency away from the centre and towards the periphery.

the sun and moon: the falling of these invisible bodies was Anaxagoras' explanation of meteorites; and see also what he says a few lines later about lunar eclipses.

129 *touch one another*: the commentary by Alexander of Aphrodisias on this passage of Aristotle adds that the planets in question are Saturn, Jupiter, Venus, Mars, and Mercury—that is, all the known planets. Such a conjunction would be extremely rare, so perhaps Anaxagoras was connecting two phenomena because of their common rarity.

line of sight of the sun: it is worth remembering that Anaxagoras thought the sun smaller in size than the earth; hence on this theory only a narrow band—the Milky Way—would be lit up. Presumably, those stars outside the Milky Way whose light is visible are especially strong—strong enough to be visible despite the light of the sun.

bend their leaves: there are certain plants (e.g. *Mimosa pudica*) which, if touched, close up their leaves and bend away from the contact in a way remarkably reminiscent of delicate shyness.

130 *same colour as the eyes*: on this theory dark-eyed people will see better by day and find night sight difficult, blue-eyed people the opposite.

141 *bronze sandals*: a single bronze sandal was a token of a shaman, who could pass to the underworld. Volcanoes such as Etna were considered gateways by which a magician might descend to the underworld to be reborn as a hero or god: see Kingsley 1995.

142 *Titan*: the sun.

143 *knowledge about nature*: a little earlier in *On Celestial Phenomena*, at 353^{b}11, Aristotle had remarked that those who liken the sea to sweat noted also that both sweat and the sea are salty.

narrow are the means: that is, the sense organs.

no more than this: assuming the addressee (who is singular) is Pausanias (rather than Empedocles himself, addressed by a deity), Empedocles is saying that what he has to teach Pausanias is the best that human wisdom has to offer.

144 *gain many others*: the method is familiar from meditation techniques, but precisely what Empedocles was talking about—the 'them'—is lost. Perhaps they are his teachings.

strife with grim strife: as Aristotle objects (*On the Soul* 409^{b}26–410^{a}13) this theory makes it difficult to explain how we perceive compounds. Most things are compounds of all four elements, but unless our eyes were compounded in the same way, they could not, on this theory, see the compounds. But then in order for the eyes to see bones they would have to be bone.

with her tears: Zeus and Hera are husband and wife; since Aidoneus is another name for Hades and Nestis is probably a local Sicilian cult name for Persephone, they too are a couple, linked in legend. She is subterranean water to Hades' subterranean fire.

air itself: Hippolytus is suggesting that 'Aidoneus' is derived from the Greek from 'invisible' (*aïdes*). Likewise, a few lines later, he suggests, with considerable implausibility, that 'Nestis' is derived from *eutonein* ('have the ability'). In actual fact, her name means 'fasting'.

145 *will always be*: echoes of Parmenides are particularly evident in this fragment.

fire meets with aither: these two elements are merely examples; of course, all four elements are involved in fact.

Highest in honour: this list repeats a few lines of **F19** and **F20** where all these things, including the gods, are said to be the product of the mingling of the four elements. It makes better sense of Empedocles' analogy with painting if we think of the ancient technique whereby pigments were not mixed together exactly, but placed side by side: so the elements do not fuse with one another, but in different proportions appear as different things. At *On Generation and Destruction* 334^{a}26–31 Aristotle also talks of Empedocles' elements being 'placed next to one another'. Empedocles' image is even more exact if the technique of four-colour painting, which certainly became popular in the next century, was already extant and was in his mind.

146 *glues of Harmony*: there is a lot of fire in bones. This is surprising until one realizes that fire is a hardening agent in Empedocles' thought: see especially **T26** and **F48**. As for Empedocles' basic idea that everything can be explained as different proportions of the four elements, he appears never to have explained what was responsible for the elements coming together in these particular proportions rather than any others. He may have left it to chance, but Aristotle, as a teleologist, was very critical of this aspect of Empedocles' theory: see e.g. *On Generation and Destruction* 333^{a}35–^{b}22.

responsible for their birth: the text of this last line is irredeemably corrupt. I translate the text of DK, but without much confidence.

147   *the immortals*: the heavenly bodies.

the change that mixing causes: the idea that the elements 'run through' one another is Empedocles' explanation not only of mixture and change, but of locomotion. Each element replaces another in a circle, and, as Plato says in *Timaeus* 80c, on this theory there is no need of void to explain locomotion.

151   *under love*: note that when Aristotle says 'under love' and 'under strife', he means, strictly, 'under increasing love' and 'under increasing strife'.

<Nor . . . >: further examples of the indistinctness of things under the rule of love would have followed.

entirely boundless: note the echo, and partial contradiction, of Parmenides F8 l. 49 (p. 60).

encircling solitude: Empedocles uses the same word here for 'solitude' as he did for 'stability' in **F24**; he chose the word for its radical ambiguity.

with swift thoughts: the influence of Xenophanes on this fragment is immediately noticeable.

152   *without diversion*: this fragment is preserved only in Armenian. DK's A49 consists of a translation back into Latin of the original Armenian; however, the translations of both Abraham Terian, published in Inwood's edition, and of Kingsley differ significantly from the text of DK. I am not in a position to judge the merits of the two versions by referring to the original Armenian. I have preferred Kingsley's version as the most authoritative, and I here simply reproduce it, supplemented by Terian.

winged gulls: this is supposed to be an illustration on the familiar, microcosmic scale of the macrocosmic processes of unification under love and separation under strife. But it is not entirely clear what Empedocles is getting at. If in the prime of life we can be said to have a body that is well put together, how in old age, or at other times of life, is our body torn apart by discord? How do our limbs wander separately? Perhaps it is a reference not to a single body, but to two bodies: in the prime of life they come together in love (i.e. for sex and living together), but then people quarrel and the bodies separate. Most likely, if a single body is involved (as it seems to be), it is a tale of life and death: in death (poetically, 'on the shore of life'—that is, not swimming in the sea of life) our limbs, formerly part of a single body, will become separated from that body in the sense that, for Empedocles, nothing perishes and everything is recycled.

shade-giving limbs: for a famous borrowing from this fantasy of Empedocles' see Aristophanes' speech in Plato's *Symposium* (189c–193d), which imagines primeval double-sided humans, whose method of locomotion was to cartwheel along on their eight limbs. This perhaps helps explain Empedocles' 'shade-producing limbs', but it is more likely to be a reference to the famous legendary Skiapods, just as we also get references to other figures from Greek myth and legend: the Minotaur, Hermaphroditus, and other hybrids.

154 *insanities of strife*: notice that since Empedocles says 'I have suffered corruption' where previously he had said that it is spirits (*daimones*) that fall, he is identifying the person with his *daimōn*. Then see, for instance, the teaching about *daimones* contained in the myth with which Plato ends *Republic*.

the fish that leaps from the sea as it travels: a dolphin.

155 *she*: the subject is presumably Aphrodite or Love.

numerous furrows: on the higher animals, as opposed to plants, insects, and so on, the two most obvious of these 'furrows' are the nostrils. The word Empedocles uses for 'skin' is deliberately ambiguous: it could also mean 'nose'.

water enters: for a description of the operation of a clepsydra, see note to p. 19.

156 *cannot enter at all*: there is tension between the idea here that sense-perception is a result of emanations coming from the external object to the sense-organ, and the idea implied in **F41** that it is light proceeding from the eye that causes sight. But it is clear from the next paragraph of **T12**, as well as from **F9**, that Empedocles certainly did hold that the eye contained fire. Probably what **F41** means is that the fire in the eye must correspond to the fire outside (i.e. daylight), which is just to say that there must be light for vision to take place. Just as the sense-organs must be in the right condition to accommodate and receive external emanations and generate sensation, so the elements in the body must be in the right condition to receive the input of data from outside.

157 *sounds of equal size*: this very condensed report presumably refers to Empedocles' explanation of why we can hear only certain sounds (i.e. not those from far away): just as all the sense organs can accommodate only certain objects, so the ears can accommodate only sounds which are somehow the same size as the ears.

thanks to each element: see **F9**.

pleasure and pain: these lines form B107 in Diels/Kranz [1], F92 in Inwood's edition, and F78 in Wright's edition.

158 *blood around the heart*: see also the note to p. 160 on *the forms of flesh in general*. In blood the elements are in more or less the perfect proportion—that is, $1:1:1:1$. Thus what makes blood responsible for understanding is presumably the fact that it can give an undistorted view of things.

stone attracts iron: the Heraclean stone, sometimes also called the Magnesian stone, is our 'magnet'. Heraclea and Magnesia were both places in Lydia where lodestones occurred naturally.

159 *both parents' seeds*: earlier, at 5.4, Censorinus has explained that in Empedocles' view both parents produce seeds.

harbours of Cypris: Cypris is another name for Aphrodite. Her 'perfect harbour' is probably the womb.

160 *the forms of flesh in general*: the proportion 1 : 1 : 1 : 1 for the elements is the most perfect proportion, since it is the one which subsisted under the rule of love. Blood is thought to have this proportion, or a good approximation to it, because it is the circulation of blood around the heart that is responsible for intelligence, according to Empedocles (see **F43**). And intelligence, or knowledge, must have this proportion if it is to understand the world, because there are equal amounts of the four elements in the universe.

very much like an egg: in actual fact, Empedocles may have likened the world more specifically to an egg, whose shell is the earth, albumen the subterranean waters, and yolk subterranean fire. See Kingsley's 1995 book, pp. 56 ff. But it is noteworthy that **T18** does not say that the earth is shaped like an egg, but 'lies' like an egg. Its shape, according to Empedocles, was probably an oblate spheroid, and the point of the comparison with an egg is only to say that the broadest section of the spheroid is where the celestial equator lies, just as when an egg is placed on a table its 'equator' is at its broadest section.

161 *'snakes' and 'milestones'*: as the context shows, these are water-heating devices. If cold water flows through a heated pipe, there is not enough time for the water to heat up; but if secondary pipes are coiled around inside the main pipe, so that the water remains near the source of heat for a longer time, it has enough time to heat up.

172 *through the void*: it has even been claimed, on no good grounds, that this extract should count as an actual fragment of Leucippus.

173 *'thing'*: the Greek is a made-up word. The Greek for nothing is *ouden*, and the sixth-century poet Alcaeus coined the word *den* by removing the prefix *ou*, which means 'not': so 'not-thing' became 'thing'. In Democritus, the word recurs in **F1**.

174 *wine is in*: this is the fallacious result of an experiment, or supposed fact, that if all the wine from a cask is poured into wineskins, the cask can later receive not only the original amount of wine, but the skins too. The atomists plainly took this to show the presence of void in the wine, so that it could be compressed.

two bodies to coincide: that is, since two bodies cannot coincide, the food we take in must go into void spaces inside our bodies.

empty vessel can: this looks like a variant of the second argument, about compression.

no-thing to exist: the phrase *ou mallon* (translated here as 'There is no more reason . . .' became a standard ploy in sceptical arguments. It is possible that Plutarch is paraphrasing rather than directly quoting Democritus.

177 *which are moist*: one of the chief difficulties in reconstructing Democritus'

theory of vision is that whereas here there is no hint that air impedes vision (in fact, it is probable that he thought that one of the functions of light in vision was to compress the air until it was thick enough to receive imprints, which were then conveyed by the light along a narrowing cone to the eye), there is elsewhere: see Theophrastus below on blackness, and also Aristotle, *On the Soul* 419^a.

178 *akin to itself*: one important point Theophrastus does not immediately make clear (but does in section 54, when he turns to criticism of Democritus' views) is that all the soul-atoms, which are distributed evenly throughout the body, are involved in sight (and presumably in all cases of perception). The visible object makes an impression in the eye, but it is only when all the soul-atoms have been disturbed that recognition and perception take place.

179 *according to their state*: that is, especially, whether they are healthy or ill.

configurations: these 'configurations' are not individual atoms, but tiny atomic aggregates with structures which create certain appearances to the human senses.

181 *in pairs*: a most puzzling clause, which few interpreters pretend to understand.

184 *arched formation*: I think this is a somewhat garbled record of the following idea. The atoms which are in the upper regions still have a slight downward tendency—natural to all atoms—but are being pushed at from below by those that are being squeezed upwards. Thus the crust, as it were, of upper atoms curls round and forms a rounded shape, just as a cloth enfolds a fist which is pushed up into it.

185 *there are fewer*: this has been strikingly confirmed by modern astronomy.

186 *Democritus himself*: Abdera was (and still is) a sleepy backwater, whose inhabitants were thought to be somewhat dense.

188 *Chrysippus*: an eminent Stoic philosopher of the third century BCE.

differ from one another: Democritus, then, held two theories that would strike us today as unusual: (1) that both men and women secreted semen ('seeds'); (2) that the whole of a parent's body contributes to the composition of the semen (see also DK 68A141). Thus Democritus says that a male child is the result of the prevalence of the man's semen over the woman's, in so far as part of the man's semen is made up of that part of himself that makes him male rather than female. (As a matter of fact, although the second thesis may be unusual today, it closely resembles Darwin's theory of pangenesis.)

he says: Aelian is probably paraphrasing rather than quoting.

189 *assail us*: a remarkable anticipation of the theory proposed in this century by astronomer Fred Hoyle.

guardian spirit: compare Heraclitus **F60** on p. 46.

196 *straightforward and authoritative*: the modern eye glides easily over this—

to us—self-evident statement, but Diogenes was the first to show clear awareness of the point, as opposed to the dogmatism of many of his predecessors.

197 *best possible condition*: this is the first extant statement of the famous Argument from Design; then see Xenophon, *Memoirs of Socrates* 1.4 and 4.3.

198 *breathing-holes of the universe*: pumice stones are pitted with holes.

199 *a single thing*: see **F2** above.

the blending: these are a puzzling couple of sentences. Since we will shortly be told that it is those who have the least air whose sense of smell is keenest, the idea here seems to be something like this: brains have veins for the passage of air. Some brains have so many channels that there is too much air swirling around the brain and the odour is too diffuse to be smelled. Smelling occurs when the air in and around the brain is compact enough to mingle with the relatively dense odour.

just as much as before: that is, if the air in veins in the eye cannot transmit the reflection back to the brain (or, rather, the air around the brain), then perception fails to occur.

200 *discerns pleasure most*: the word for 'pleasure' can also mean 'taste'.

211 *two contradictory arguments about everything*: it is not clear if, as some maintain, this statement also amounts to an ontological claim about reality—that reality is such that there are always possible two arguments or positions about any aspect of it. This Heraclitean interpretation of Protagoras stems from Plato's *Theaetetus*, but it seems more likely that Plato is being innovative in combining Protagorean relativism with Heraclitean ontology in that dialogue.

that they are not: there is actually considerable ambiguity in the Greek of this famous saying of Protagoras (his fragment 1). It could be translated by any combination of the following elements: '[A] man is [a]/[the] measure of all things, of the things that [are the case]/[are . . .]/[exist], [that]/[how] they [are the case]/[are . . .]/[exist], of the things that [are not the case]/[are not . . .]/[do not exist], [that]/[how] they [are not the case]/[are not . . .]/[do not exist].' Given the likely aphoristic nature of his books he probably did not go on to make things much clearer even for his original readers. At any rate, it is clear that, contrary to Parmenides' denial of 'is not', Protagoras is insisting that we are the measures of what-is-not, as much as of what-is.

that they do not exist: a possible alternative translation is: '. . . in what manner they exist, or in what manner they do not exist.'. This is fragment 4 of Protagoras.

the opportune moment: probably in the context of rhetoric.

known as 'Socratic': that is, arguing by question and answer, or dialectical argument.

212 *shunned the arts and crafts*: probably on the grounds that they are beneath the dignity of these high-born young men.

213 *others even before them*: it is far from clear whom Plato might have in mind as Protagoras' predecessors in this respect.

214 *lack of objective apprehension*: this passage contains Sceptic technical vocabulary and is unlikely to contain any actual words of Protagoras.

215 *his own cleverness*: this *ad hominem* claim that Protagoras' thesis is self-refuting is the same as in **T5**. However, later in *Theaetetus*, at 169d–171c, Plato develops a more sophisticated self-refutation: There are people who do not believe the same as Protagoras, but Protagoras must hold that their beliefs are as true as anyone else's, therefore it is true that Protagoras' thesis is false. In actual fact, Protagoras could respond by insisting on his usual suffixes and claiming that this is only true *for these people*.

217 *Prometheus and Epimetheus*: Prometheus occurs in a number of Greek myths as a benefactor of mankind; his name means 'foresight' or 'providence'. His brother, Epimetheus, is 'hindsight'.

     the extinction of any species: Herodotus, who undoubtedly knew Protagoras, since they would have coincided in the early years of the new colony at Thurii, developed this idea in the case of hares and lions at 3.108.

218 *gave them to man*: Hephaestus was the blacksmith god, and therefore the god of fire; the relevant skills of Athena are weaving, spinning, and pottery. Hephaestus appears as a direct benefactor of humankind in the Homeric hymn to him, and in Diodorus of Sicily, *Universal History* 1.13.

     punished for his theft: he was condemned to eternal torture in the Caucasus. Spread-eagled on a rock, by day an eagle came and ate his liver, which grew again during the night, in time for the eagle to eat it again the next day.

219 *together in friendship*: Protagoras was almost certainly an agnostic. The use made in this story of Prometheus and Zeus is either allegorical or a Platonic accretion on to a more mechanistic original.

     Diagoras: Diagoras of Melos (*fl.* 420 BCE) was the most famous atheist of classical antiquity.

     that they do not exist . . .: the block of stone on which this fragment of Diogenes is preserved is badly broken; the reconstruction of the remaining text is uncertain and controversial. However, that Diogenes went on to try to justify the blatant illogicality with which the translated text ends is certain, given the final incomplete sentence.

     Tisias: Tisias and Corax, from Syracuse (and so fellow Sicilians of Gorgias), were said to have written the first technical handbooks on rhetoric, but nothing reliable is known about them.

228 *The Encomium of Helen*: there is also extant, not translated here, a defence of Palamedes, a Greek hero who in legend was put to death as a result of a false accusation by Odysseus. Helen's reputation in the fifth

century was as the woman who had betrayed her husband for an effete
easterner and had caused countless Greek deaths.

230 *fickle and changeable*: two of Gorgias' cases for proving the instability of
belief are drawn from Presocratic ('the astronomers') and Sophistic
argumentation. The third, the middle one, is a reference to the law courts.
Gorgias finds grist for his mill in his immediate intellectual environment.

by some evil persuasion: some scholars have found traces of Protagorean
scepticism here: no knowledge is possible, and people have only opinion;
nothing truly exists, but everything merely seems to be. But there is no
suggestion in Gorgias that people cannot have knowledge, only that as
long as people have only opinion, they can be pushed around by the
power of *logos*.

232 *explained to our neighbour*: it is very likely that the 'it' Gorgias talks about
throughout the treatise is 'anything at all'.

235 *Scylla and Chimaera*: mythical monstrous creatures.

236 *visible and audible*: compare *The Encomium of Helen* on the spoken word
being 'insubstantial and imperceptible'.

244 *confined to the body*: this distinction between 'enjoyment' and 'pleasure'
was evidently famous, because something similar is ascribed to Prodicus
by Aristotle at *Topics* 112^b—a distinction between 'joy', 'delight', and
'satisfaction'.

Simonides: a famous Greek lyric poet of the late sixth and early fifth
centuries BCE, one of whose poems is being analysed at this stage of
Plato's *Protagoras*.

246 *as much as anyone else*: the usual view was that phlegm was cold and wet.

250 *useful for life*: the text of this fragment is most conveniently found in
Henrichs's article.

253 *only has to ask*: at *Meno* 70b–c Plato attributes this same ability, to answer
any question, to Gorgias too.

beat me at anything: the agonistic tone of this claim is striking. Many of
the Sophists do seem to have been concerned with public acclamation
and defeat of opponents. They may have undertaken public debates, with
the winner being decided by the acclaim of the audience. The best surviving example of such a debate is the famous Constitutional Debate in
Herodotus 3.80–2.

mastering it: each year in Athens nine *arkhontes* ('leaders') were elected by
lot, with mainly administrative duties. One of them, the eponymous
arkhōn, gave his name to the year. Socrates is referring to a list of these
eponymous *arkhontes*. The office had been in existence before Solon
(*arkhōn* 594/3), but his reforms lessened its power, so Socrates takes him
as the founder of the democratic office.

254 *the finest rules of life*: on this lecture of Hippias, compare perhaps
Prodicus **F1** on pp. 246–9.

255 *not by convention*: how sweeping a statement is this? Does Hippias mean that everyone is an equal member of the community of humankind, in which case he prefigures Antiphon, or at least of the Greek community (panhellenism was a fifth-century topic), or does he only mean that the present company are akin, as all being intellectuals? The generality of the rest of his words incline one to prefer the first option.

261 *characteristics*: some scholars believe that this maxim refers to children, but adults are often as impressionable themselves, and the generality of most of Antiphon's sayings suggests that his target is everyone, adult or young.

   whole new direction for him: literally, 'a new guardian spirit for him', the guardian spirit (*daimōn*) being considered as that which navigates one through life.

264 *we know and respect*: the remnants of **F17–19** have been found on papyrus fragments. The reconstruction of the text is sometimes contentious. I have concentrated on those sections where we can be reasonably sure of the reading, but some guesswork is involved. In addition to Diels/Kranz [1] and Untersteiner [3], it is important to consult the edition of these fragments of Antiphon in F. Adorno *et al.*, *Corpus dei papiri filosofici greci e latini*, vol. i (Florence: Olschki, 1989). The text of *POxy* 3647 is also easily available in Barnes's article in *Polis*, 7 (1987).

   foreigners and Greeks: Greeks tended to be highly xenophobic, regarding everyone outside the confines of Greek civilization—all foreigners—as *barbarous* (that is, those whose language sounded like *bar-bar*). Even Gorgias said, 'Victory over foreigners calls for praise, victory over Greeks for mourning' (DK 82B5b). But later, in the following century, one of Gorgias' pupils, Alcidamas, said, 'God has set all men free; nature has made no man a slave.' Evidence for fifth-century debate about the equality of women is scattered: Plato seems to imply at *Republic* 450a–b that there had been some debate about the issue, and we glimpse it reflected in a number of fifth-century contexts, but most noticeably Aristophanes' comedy *The Assembly Women*.

   you are a citizen: some interpretations of Antiphon depend on reading this sentence as expressing approval of justice. But there is nothing to warrant such a reading, which goes against the tenor of everything else Antiphon says. Antiphon is here simply defining man-made justice, as opposed to natural justice. Compare the famous fragment of the philosopher Archelaus of Athens, earlier in the fifth century: 'Right and wrong are conventional, not natural standards' (DK 60A2). The fact that Antiphon uses the emphatic expression, 'the community of which one is a citizen', rather than simply saying 'one's community', suggests an implicit contrast with the universality of natural law.

265 *an oath*: these are examples of situations where the natural response is disallowed by law or convention, when it would be advantageous to one, and the sanctioned response is disadvantageous. So, to take Antiphon's first example, if someone wants to kill me, it is to my advantage (and it

conforms to the natural law of self-preservation) to make a pre-emptive strike against him, but society disallows that. The oath-taking example is obscure, but what Antiphon may have in mind is this. In court, to offer someone the opportunity to swear under oath that his testimony was true is also to create the opportunity for yourself to swear that your testimony is true too, even though it may contradict the other testimony. Thus if a man is constrained by convention to allow his opponent in court to swear to the truth of his testimony, but does not resort to such a captious tactic himself, he is not taking the advantage offered him.

267 *squaring a circle*: the problem of how to construct a square or a polygonal figure with an equal area to a given circle (partly as a way of determining the area of the circle) exercised a good many minds until it was shown to be impossible in 1882. Antiphon's method was one of approximation: he constructed a series of triangles (or, in another report, squares) inside the circle, and maintained that if he constructed enough triangles, perhaps an infinite number, the whole area of the circle would be exhausted.

good things bad: the sentence lacks a subject, but it may well have been 'mind'. Others think it might have been 'nature'.

268 *without limits or needs*: the only conceivable subject of this sentence is God.

pursuing the damp air: a delightful picture of the sun, like an orderly Pacman, chasing damp air through the skies, and leaving behind the scorched air it has already 'consumed' or dried out.

makes it wrinkled: the subject is presumably the sun, or heavenly fire at some early stage of the cosmogonic process.

improve on another: not all scholars are convinced that this papyrus fragment is to be attributed to Antiphon. I translate the text given in Untersteiner [3]; it can also be found in S. Luria, *Classical Quarterly*, 22 (1928), 176–8.

272 *without being able to define it*: Aristotle goes on to define the rhetorical paean as one where the phrase either starts with a long syllable and ends with three short syllables or, on the contrary, starts with three shorts and end with a long.

287 *the good and the bad are different*: e.g. Socrates.

at another time: our author appears to be unaware of the difference between saying that the good and the bad are the same, and that the same thing is both good and bad. *Mutatis mutandis*, the same criticism applies to the following sections.

288 *Athenians and their allies*: this is an unmistakable reference to the Peloponnesian War, which ended in 404; however, we cannot say with any certainty how long after the end of the war the treatise was written.

victory over the Persians: that is, in 479.

the Achaeans: the author uses the usual Homeric word for the Greeks.

288 *the Argives*: the reference is probably to the legendary conquest of Thebes by Argos in the expedition known as the Seven against Thebes.

289 *brought up earlier*: in actual fact, though, the author has failed to address the issues of the first half of this section. In the first half of this section, the thesis was that an object may be both good and bad in different respects. This is (*a*) unobjectionable, and (*b*) a thesis about predication. But when the author attacks this specific thesis in the second half, he makes out that it is (*a*) objectionable, and (*b*) a thesis about the identity of goodness and badness. It is hard to escape the view that our author is muddled.

unacceptable: homosexuality was an accepted aspect of (usually upper-class) Greek society.

290 *Ionians*: on mainland Greece the Ionians were chiefly the Athenians.

everyone else's: see Herodotus 2.35–6 on Egyptian customs which are opposite to those of everywhere else. Quite a few of our author's ethnographic facts or fables are similar or the same to stories found in Herodotus; this may be coincidence, in the sense that they may both be drawing on a common stock of stories, but it is hard to resist the idea that our author is indebted in this section to Herodotus 3.38 given the similarity of his conclusions, that there are as many customs as there are peoples, and that what is acceptable in one place is unacceptable in another.

291 *piece of verse too*: from an unknown tragic poet.

292 *rob temples too*: temples were often the repositories of both private and public valuables.

293 *Orestes and Alcmaeon did*: legendary characters who killed their mothers in retribution for crimes against their fathers.

perfectly right: Cleoboulina was a sixth-century poet; this was a famous riddle whose solution may be that the man was a wrestler.

294 *no difference*: compare Euthydemus and Dionysodorus T2 (pp. 281–2), which has a Protagorean provenance (see Protagoras T5 and T8 on pp. 213 and 215, with the refutation our anonymous author will shortly produce).

the same statement is false: I suppose the author's meaning is that the truth or falsity of the sentence is somehow accidental or non-essential, whereas what is essential to the statement is the way it is expressed, the words in which it is spoken.

'I am an initiate': that is, an initiate of the Eleusinian Mysteries, the popular Athenian cult.

simultaneously false: compare the famous Liar Paradox, which was well known to the Greeks: a liar says, 'This statement is true.'

295 *two talents*: 'talent' and 'mina' are units of weight.

both are and are not: the influence of Gorgias may be detected here.

they were arguing for: the addition of the suffixes is a Protagorean tactic.

and so on and so forth: similarly, Plato argues (*Cratylus* 432aff.) that if something is added or subtracted from an image, it remains an image, whereas if something is added or subtracted from a number, it is no longer that number. Now, it looks as though Plato should have said, not 'it is no longer that number', but 'it is no longer number', otherwise the numerical example does not provide a proper contrast with the image example. And that is why our author says not just that ten no longer exists, but that even the one no longer exists. He is saying not just that if one is subtracted from ten, you get a different number, but that if one is subtracted from ten you get no number at all. The argument trades on an ambiguity in 'number': it can be thought of either distributively or collectively. Considered collectively, 'number' resembles other collective words such as 'team'. If one member drops out of a cricket team, you no longer have the (full) team (although you have only subtracted one from eleven, distributively speaking): the team no longer exists. Aristotle identified trading on this ambiguity as a Sophistic argument at *On Sophistic Refutations* 178ᵃ, and Sextus Empiricus refers to it or employs it several times (*Outlines of Pyrrhonism* 3.90; *Against the Professors* 4.23–30, 9.312–20, 10.308–9).

296 *taught his son to sculpt*: Polyclitus of Argos was one of the greatest sculptors of the late fifth century.

would speak Greek: a somewhat similar argument occurs in the fifth-century Ps.-Hippocratic treatise, *Airs, Waters, and Places*, section 12: Greek emigrants to the Middle East end up as effete as the original inhabitants.

297 *and so on*: Socrates certainly criticized election by lot on these grounds, and claimed that (at least in an ideal world) moral and political experts would form our governments; but this may not establish Socratic influence on this section of *Double Arguments*, since it is likely that such criticisms of election by lot were common.

talk succinctly: Plato not infrequently has Socrates tease the Sophists for relying too much on long speeches (*makrologia*), but in fact they prided themselves on being able to talk succinctly as well, which meant being able to enter into question-and-answer dialogue with others, and, like Socrates, gradually leading their interlocutor towards a conclusion.

nature and origin of all things: it is noteworthy that our author's paragon includes among his skills at least two of the known titles of Sophistic books—*On Truth* (Protagoras, Antiphon), *On Nature* (Gorgias, and most of the Presocratics).

298 *know about everything*: Plato's parodied Sophists, Euthydemus and Dionysodorus, also claim to be omniscient—but then they also claim that everyone is always omniscient (*Euthydemus* 293a–297a, part of which is **T4** on pp. 282–3). Hippias claimed to be able to answer any question on any subject (Hippias **T1**, pp. 252–3).

cowardice to Epeius . . .: the text breaks off at this point. Memory techniques such as the one our author is recommending only work if they are vivid. Thus, when he says that if we need to remember something about courage we should connect it to Ares and Achilles, he means us to have in our minds a vivid picture of Ares and/or Achilles. These pictures serve as focuses: concepts, passages of text that we need to remember, whatever, accumulate around these pictures, and are there to be recalled the next time we visit these pictures in our minds.

304 *you substitute convention*: with a reference to this passage of *Gorgias*, Aristotle says (*On Sophistic Refutations* 173ᵃ) that, so far from being typical of Socratic argumentation, as Callicles claims, the switch from *nomos* to *physis* and back again was typically Sophistic.

306 *bodies come in a gleaming mass*: this presumably means meteors.

309 *kings over men*: as opposed to Hippias' dictum (**T4**, p. 255) that *nomos* is a tyrant.

310 *daily work*: there may here be an implicit criticism of Athenian democracy, where every male citizen had the right directly to participate in the political process.

313 *committed or received*: this (and Plato again, in *Crito* 50c–53a) is the first clear statement in history of the social contract theory that was later to be developed by Hobbes, Locke, Rousseau, Kant, Rawls, and others. The idea of a social contract may, however, be implicit in **F1** above, and it recurs in **T3** and is briefly alluded to by Antiphon in **F18** (p. 265). We can be certain, then, that it predates Plato, and belongs to the era of the Sophists.

origins of the universe: Diodorus has just reproduced a supposedly traditional cosmogony, which may be an amalgam of Presocratic thought, or Egyptian or pseudo-Egyptian in origin.

TEXTUAL NOTES

Note that since the punctuation of many Presocratic fragments, particularly those of Heraclitus and Parmenides, is difficult and variable, I have not here indicated places where I punctuate the text differently from DK, but only those where I adopt a different reading of the Greek text itself.

XENOPHANES

27 **F8.1.** It does not substantially alter the translation, but I prefer the form of this first line given e.g. by Edmonds and Lesher to that found in DK.

28 **F14.2–3.** Reading ἦν ἄνεμος κεν (Edmonds) for the unmetrical and nonsensical MSS ἐν νέφεσιν ἔσωθεν, and therefore omitting Diels's addenda.

29 **T6.** I conjecture <διὰ τὸ> διατμίζειν τὰ πνεύματα.

T7. Reading φυκῶν (Gomperz) for the MSS φωκῶν ('seals'), and then a little later καταβολήν (Lloyd-Jones) for the nonsensical MSS καταβάλλειν.

F16.1. I marginally prefer γένετ', as found in Plutarch's citation of the fragment at *On Listening to Poetry* 17e, to Sextus' ἴδεν. Sextus' reading would give the sense: 'No man has seen the truth, nor will there ever be one who knows about the gods . . .' I cannot see that this reference to the sense modality of sight is relevant here.

HERACLITUS

38 **F3.** The text is uncertain. The best reading seems to me to be that of Gigon: ὅκη κυβερνᾶται πάντα . . . With an alternative text, the fragment could be translated '. . . to know the judgement which guides . . .', thus referring the 'judgement' to the divine *logos* rather than to human intellect.

F6. Reading, with recent editors: διὸ δεῖ ἔπεσθαι τῷ <ξυνῷ> [τουτέστι τῷ κοινῷ. ξυνὸς γὰρ ὁ κοινὸς.] τοῦ λόγου . . .

F8. I agree with Robinson that only this much of what DK print as fr. 72 is genuinely Heraclitean.

40 **F20.** Reading ψυχρὰ θέρεται, θερμὰ ψύχεται, ὑγρὰ αὐαίνεται, καρφαλέα νοτίζεται with Dilcher.

41 **F32.** Omitting (τἀναντία ἅπαντα· οὗτος ὁ νοῦς) with all recent editors, and then a little later reading, with Pfleiderer, ὅκως πῦρ instead of ὅκωσπερ.

41 **F35**. Reading εὕδοντες ὁρέομεν ... ἐγερθέντες ὕπνος with Mansfeld.

42 **F36**. Omitting τὸν αὐτὸν ἁπάντων as part of the context from Clement.

F37. Omitting Burnet's <γῆ>. For a parallel use of διαχεῖσθαι, see Herodotus, *Histories* 6.119.

F38. Retaining ἀνταμείβεται πάντα with the MSS.

43 **T8**. Reading κινεῖσθαι with Reiske.

44 **F47**. Reading αὐγὴ ξηρὴ, σοφωτάτη ... with the majority of the ancient authors who preserve this fragment.

F49. Reading, with Mouraviev: ἄνθρωπος ἐν εὐφρόνῃ φάος ἅπτεται ἑαυτῷ· ἀποθανὼν ἀποσβεσθεὶς ὄψεις, ζῶν δὲ ἅπτεται τεθνεῶτος· εὕδων, ἀποσβεσθεὶς ὄψεις, ἐγρηγορὼς ἅπτεται εὕδοντος.

46 **F61**. Retaining the MSS ἄλλως.

PARMENIDES

56 **F1.3**. Retaining δαίμονος with the MSS.

F1.3. Reading ἀσινῆ with Meineke.

57 **F1.24–5**. Reading ἀθανάτῃσι συνήορος with Brandis, and then ἵπποις θ' αἵ with MSS NL.

58 **F3.1**. Retaining εἰ δ' ἄγε, τῶν ἐρέω with the MSS.

F3.4. Retaining Ἀληθείη with the MSS.

F5.3. Reading ἄρξω with Nehamas (instead of Diels's conjectured εἴργω), and taking the elided pronoun as dative.

F5.5. Reading πλάζονται with the Aldine edition.

59 **F8.2**. Reading ἔπι rather than ἐπι, since the preposition follows what it governs.

F8.4. Retaining the majority reading οὖλον μουνογενές.

F8.4. Reading ἠδὲ τέλειον with Owen.

F8.7. Retaining οὔτ' with the MSS.

F8.12. Reading οὔτε ποτ' (Reinhardt) ἐκ τοῦ ἐόντος (Karsten).

F8.19. Retaining the MSS πῶς δ' ἂν ἔπειτα πέλοι τὸ ἐόν;

60 **F8.22**. Reading ἔστιν with Owen.

61 **F8.55**. Reading ἀντία with the MSS.

F8.61. Reading γνώμῃ with Stein.

62 **T6**. Reading οἷον with Karsten.

63 **F13.4**. Reading πάντων with MS Moscow State Historical Museum 3649.

65 **F18.1–2**. Reading κρᾶσις with Stephanus, and then παρέστηκεν with Theophrastus.

ZENO

76 **T3.** Omitting ἢ κινεῖται with MS T and Zeller.

77 **T3.** Retaining ἴσον . . . ὥς φησιν with Aristotle's MSS.

79 **F1.** I read εἰ δὲ <πολλά> ἐστιν.

MELISSUS

86 **F8.** Bracketing ὥστε συμβαίνει μήτε ὁρᾶν μήτε τὰ ὄντα γινώσκειν as a gloss, with Barnes.

PYTHAGORAS AND FIFTH-CENTURY PYTHAGOREANISM

95 **T4.** Reading ἐτύμως σοφός, ὅς with Burkert.

96 **T5.** Transposing the second and third lines with Zuntz.

104 **T30.** I have silently incorporated a couple of minor changes to de Falco's text: see my article in *Classical Quarterly*, 38 (1988), at p. 227.

109 **T40.** Retaining the MSS reading οὐρανόν, πλανήτας.

111 **F7.** Retaining the MSS reading, largely: τοῖς γὰρ κάτω τὸ κατωτάτω μέρος (Wachsmuth) ἐστὶν ὥσπερ . . .

ANAXAGORAS

122 **F1.** I agree with Sider that the fragment ends here, without the explanatory sentence: 'For these [air and aither] are the greatest ingredients, in terms of both number and size, in the mixture of all things.'

F2. Reading πόλου with MS F and Sider.

F5. Omitting ταῦτα with Sider.

124 **F7.** Reading τομῇ μή with Jöhrens.

125 **F10.** Omitting οὐδενί with Wasserstein.

127 **F12.** Supplying the one missing definite article before ψυχρόν, with recent editors.

F12. Reading καὶ τὸ λαμπρόν with Schorn.

F13. Reading ὅσα ἐστί τ' ἐκράτησε with Sider.

F13. Retaining πολλά with the MSS.

EMPEDOCLES

141 **F1.1.** Reading κάτα with recent editors.

F1.5. Reading ὥσπερ ἔοικε with recent editors.

F1.7. Reading πᾶσι δ' ἅμ' εὖτ' ἂν ἴκωμαι with Wright.

142 **F5.1–2.** Reading πρῶτ' ἐξ ὧν ἥλιος ἀρχὴν | τἆλλά τε δῆλ' ἐγένοντο with Wright.

143 **F6.**6. Reading μάψ with Stein.

F6.9. Retaining οὐ πλεῖόν γε with the MSS, and punctuating with Bollack.

F7.5. Reading πιστήν with Bergk.

F8.1. Reading καὶ [ἐν] with Wright.

144 **F8.**4. Reading τῶνδε κτήσεαι with Marcovich.

145 **F11.**1. Reading ἐκ γὰρ τοῦ μὴ ἐόντος with Wright.

F14.1. Reading μιγὲν φῶς αἰθέρι <κύρσῃ> with Burnet.

F14.5. Reading ᾗ σφι θέμις καλέουσι with Karsten.

146 **F16.**1. Reading εὐτύκτοις with some MSS.

F16.2. Retaining τὰς . . . μοιράων with the MSS.

F16.4. Reading θεσπεσίῃσιν with Sider.

F17.1. Retaining ἑαυτά ἑαυτῶν with the principal MSS.

F17.6. Reading ἐχθρὰ <δὲ> πλεῖστον with Karsten.

147 **F18.**1. Reading ἐ<στ>ι γὰρ ὡς πάρος ἦν with Lloyd-Jones.

F19.6. Reading θέλυμνα (or θελυμνά) with Diels.

148 **F20.**8a. Following O'Brien, I repeat this line too (as well as line 9) from DK B26.

F20.18. Reading αἰθέρος with some of the ancient sources.

F20.20. Reading καὶ φιλίη μετὰ τοῖσιν with Sextus Empiricus, *Against the Physicists* 2.317 and Athenagoras 22.

F20.33. Reading κῆρ' ἀπόλοιτο with Bollack.

149 **F21.**3. Reading ἐνέρτατα βένθε' ἵκηται with *P. Strasb. gr.* Inv. 1665–1666.

F21.6. Reading ἀλλ' ἀθελημά with Kingsley.

F21.10. Reading πω instead of τῶν, with some MSS and recent editors.

151 **F24.**2. Diels's conflation of two fragments to make up his B27 is not necessary, and makes bad sense grammatically. It is best to keep them apart, as two incomplete sentences.

F24.4. Reading περιγηθεί with the MSS.

152 **F28.**2. Reading συνερχόμεθ' with *P. Strasb. gr.* Inv. 1665–1666.

153 **F31.**8. Reading οὔτ' αὖ ἐπιχώριον ἀνδράσι γῆρυν with the Aldine edition.

F32.8. Reading ἀρρήτοισι with Fabricius.

F32.10. Retaining ἐέδμεναι with the MSS.

F35.4. Omitting line 4 of this fragment, with Knatz.

F35.7. Reading φυόμενον with Wilamowitz.

154 **F36.**2. Retaining ἔμπορος with the MSS.

F38.2–3. Reading οἰκτρὰ τορεῦντα | λισσόμενον θύοντος (Zuntz, Hermann).

F38.3. Reading ὁ δὲ νήκουστος with Bergk.

155 **F41.**7. Reading λοχεύσατο with Förster.

F41.8. Omitting, with recent editors, the line made up by Blass and inserted by DK as l. 9 of this fragment.

F42.12. Reading οὐδέ τις with Bollack.

F42.13. Reading αἰθέρος with Stein.

156 **F42.**22. Reading δι' ἀγυιῶν with some MSS and Bollack.

T12. Omitting Diels's addition <ὕδωρ καί>.

157 **T12.** Retaining ἔξωθεν with the MSS.

T12. Reading ὅταν γὰρ ὑπὸ τῆς φωνῆς κινηθὲν ἠχῇ τὸ ἐντός with the MSS and Bollack.

T12. Along with recent editors I count ἐκ τούτων as part of Theophrastus' text, not of the Empedocles fragment, and so exclude Karsten's additional γάρ.

T12. Reading ἴσα for ἐστί, with Frenkian.

158 **T14.** Reading φασιν with some MSS.

159 **T17.** Reading *Super qua re Empedocles disputata ratione talia profatur* with the MSS and Jahn.

F44.4. Reading εἴτ' ἐν πλεόνεσσιν ἐλάσσων with Dodds.

160 **F45.**2. Reading δαερὸν δαεροῦ λάβετ' ὦκα, after the MSS of Plutarch.

162 **T29.** Reading διὰ τὰ θερμά with Forster.

ATOMISTS

178 **T13.** Reading μεστά instead of ἔτι, with Diels.

180 **T13.** I see no reason to assume a lacuna at this point, as Diels did.

T13. Reading ἐπάλλαξιν with McDiarmid.

T13. Reading περιπλέκεσθαι with McDiarmid.

T13. I delete πολυγώνιον ποιεῖν.

181 **T13.** I omit τοῖς.

183 **T19.** I read ἐπίρρυσιν.

186 **T24.** There seems no good reason to delete the rest of this sentence.

188 **F6.** Reading ἐμψύχως with Cherniss.

189 **T33.** Reading θᾶττον [apparently omitted by accident in DK] γίγνεσθαι τὴν φθοράν with Wimmer.

DIOGENES

197 **F3.** Reading <καὶ ἀλεῶν> with Solmsen.

198 **F6.** Reading τῷ δέ with MSS DE.

199 **T7.** I read διὰ τὰ φλεβία.

202 **F8.** Reading ἀποσχάζουσιν with Peck.

F8. Transposing these words with Thompson.

PROTAGORAS

216 **T11.** I read αὐτῆς [χρηστή].

T11. Reading καὶ πάθας with Richards.

218 **T12.** I omit διὰ τὴν τοῦ θεοῦ συγγένειαν as a reduplicated gloss.

GORGIAS

228 **F1.** There seems no urgent need to assume that the text contains a lacuna here.

229 **F1.** Reading δυνατός with MacDowell.

F1. Reading ἀλλά νῦν γε with MacDowell.

F1. For the last three sentences I read MacDowell's text, which contains conjectures by Diels, Blass, Croiset, and himself: τίς οὖν αἰτία κωλύει καὶ τὴν Ἑλένην ὑπὸ λόγους ἐλθεῖν ὁμοίως ἄκουσαν οὖσαν, ὥσπερ εἰ βιατήρων βίᾳ ἡρπάσθη; ὑπὸ γὰρ τῆς πειθοῦς ἐξηλάσθη νοῦς· καίτοι πειθὼ ἀνάγκης εἶδος ἔχει μὲν οὔ, τὴν δὲ δύναμιν τὴν αὐτὴν ἔχει.

230 **F1.** Reading καὶ πολέμιον ἐπὶ πολεμίᾳ ὁπλίσει κόσμον with Sauppe.

F1. Reading ἐπιθεάσηται with MacDowell.

231 **F1.** Adding ὄψει with Immisch.

F1. Reading τῇ γνώμῃ with MacDowell.

F2. Deleting Sauppe's addition at this point.

238 **T12.** Reading ταῦτα with Mansfeld.

T12. Reading καὶ λέγει ὁ λόγων λόγους.

PRODICUS

247 **F1.** Retaining ὑποκοριζόμενοι with the MSS.

ANTIPHON

262 **F5.** I see no particular reason to include the supplementary text of Diels and Bücheler.

264 **F16**. Reading ἓν τῷ λέγοντι οὐδὲ γε νοῦς εἷς, ἔν τε οὐδὲν αὐτῷ οὔτε ὧν ὄψει ὁρᾷ ὁ ὁρῶν μακρότατα οὔτε ὧν γνώμῃ γιγνώσκει ὁ μακρότατα γιγνώσκων with Morrison.

F17. I have translated the text to be found in *Corpus dei papiri filosofici greci e latini*, i. 184–6.

F18. I have translated the text to be found in *Corpus dei papiri filosofici greci e latini*, i. 192 ff.

265 **F18**. Retaining προιεμένοις with the papyrus, here and in the next few lines.

266 **F19**. I have translated the text to be found in *Corpus dei papiri filosofici greci e latini*, i. 215–17.

268 **T7**. I read παραλυκίσασαν.

DOUBLE ARGUMENTS

288 **1.13**. There is no need to supplement the text with Diels's additions here or in the next line.

290 **2.10**. Again, there is no need for Diels's supplement.

2.17. There is no need for Valckenaer's supplement.

291 **2.24**. There is no need for Diels's καί.

292 **2.28**. Reading Diels's text but without ἄνδρα and with the last word as ἀπάγαγε (MS P).

3.2. As usual, Diels's additions are unnecessary.

3.7. Reading σώσαι ἂν τά with Robinson, and therefore omitting Diels's supplementary material.

293 **3.14**. Reading καίτοι πολλὰ ἀδικήσας ἀποθανέτω πραξάμενος with the MSS.

294 **4.6**. Omitting Diels's addition.

4.6. Reading καὶ <αἱ> with Blass.

4.7. Omitting Diels's λέγοντι.

4.8. Reading οὐκῶν διαφέρει ἐρέσθαι. αὖθις . . . with Robinson.

295 **5.13**. Diels's addition is unnecessary.

296 **5.15**. Reading ψεύδεται 'τὰ πάντα' εἰπών. ταῦτα πάντα . . . with Robinson.

6.4. Reading τὰ αὐτῶν τέκνα ἂν ἐδίδαξαν καὶ τὼς φίλως with the MSS.

6.10. Retaining σοφῶν with the MSS.

297 **6.13**. Retaining ἀλλ' ὅτι ἀποχρῶντί μοι with the MSS.

8.2. Omitting Diels's addition.

298 **8.7**. I read ἔστι γὰρ κατὰ τωὐτὸν τῆνα, τῆνα δὲ ποτὶ τωὐτὸν τὰ δέοντα παρέξεται, αἱ χρή.

298 **8.13.** Reading ὃς δὲ and δεῖ with the MSS, but otherwise including Diels's first addition, and Blass's second addition. In other words, I follow Robinson's text here.

9.1. Retaining ἐς φιλοσοφίαν καὶ σοφίαν with the MSS.

9.2. Retaining σύνολον ὃ ἔμαθες with the MSS at this point rather than at the end of the next sentence.

ANONYMOUS AND MISCELLANEOUS TEXTS

305 **F1.7.** Reading γένους βροτείου with Grotius.

F1.18–19. Omitting these lines as superfluous, with Blaydes.

306 **F1.24.** Reading ἔνεστιν αὐτοῖς with Heath.

F1.25. Reading κύδιστον with Diggle.

F1.33. Reading σέλας with Aëtius.

F1.37. Reading πέριξ ἔστησεν with Meineke.

F1.38. Reading τῶν λόγων with Diggle.

310 **T2.** I read ἀηδεστάτην.

T2. Retaining ἡδέως with the MSS.

CONCORDANCE WITH DIELS/KRANZ

DK	WATERFIELD	DK	WATERFIELD	DK	WATERFIELD
Milesians		21A32	T3	22B13b	F18
11A3a	T5	21A33	T7, 8	22B14	F62
11A4	T2	21A40	T5	22B15	F63
11A5	T1	21A46	T6	22B16	F41
11A6	T3	21B8	F1	22B18	F9
11A9	T7	21B11	F6	22B21	F35
11A12	T8	21B14	F7	22B25	F51
11A14	T9	21B15	F8	22B26	F49
11A15	T10	21B16	F9	22B27	F52
11A17	T4	21B17	F20	22B29	F50
11A20	T6	21B18	F19	22B30	F36
11A22	T11	21B23	F3	22B31	F37
12A1	T12	21B24	F4	22B32	F4
12A6	T13	21B26	F5	22B33	F54
12A9	T15	21B27	F10	22B34	F5
12A10	T22	21B28	F13	22B36	F44
12A11	T24	21B29	F11	22B41	F3
12A15	T20	21B30	F14	22B42	T2
12A16	T17, 19	21B32	F15	22B43	F58
12A21	T25	21B33	F12	22B44	F53
12A23	T26	21B34	F16	22B45	F48
12A26	T23	21B35	F17	22B49	F55
12A27	T21	21B38	F18	22B49a	T3
12A30	T27, 28	21B45	F2	22B50	F10
13A5	T29	*Not in* DK: T4		22B51	F21
13A6	T34			22B53	F23
13A7	T35			22B54	F24
13A10	T32, 33	**Heraclitus**		22B55	F28
13A14	T36, 39	22A1	T8	22B60	F14
13A15	T38	22A6	T4	22B61	F15
13A17	T40	22A10	T5, 6	22B64	F39
13A20	T37	22A16	T9	22B66	F40
13A21	T41	22B1	F1	22B67	F32
13B1	T31	22B2	F6	22B72	F8
13B2	T30	22B3	F42	22B78	F2
Not in DK: T14, 16, 18		22B5	F61	22B79	F19
		22B6	T7	22B80	F22
Xenophanes		22B7	F29	22B85	F46
		22B9	F17	22B88	F13
21A13	T2	22B11	F59	22B89	T1
21A29	T1	22B12	F33	22B90	F38

DK	WATERFIELD	DK	WATERFIELD	DK	WATERFIELD
22B91	F34	28B15	F16	31B129	T5
22B92	T11	28B17	F17	36B4	T4
22B93	F26	28B19	F12	44A12	T46
22B94	F43			44A16	T40
22B96	F64	*Not in* DK: T4, 10		44A19	T42
22B101	F30			44A20	T43
22B104	F7			44A23	T48
22B107	F27	**Zeno**		44A27	T49
22B108	F11	29A10	T7	44B1	F2
22B110	F16	29A12	T1	44B2	F3
22B114	F12	29A24	T4, 5	44B4	F4
22B116	F31	29A25	T2, 3	44B6	F5
22B117	F45	29A26	T3	44B7	F6
22B118	F47	29A27	T3	44B13	F8
22B119	F60	29A28	T3	44B14	F1
22B121	F56	29A29	T6	44B17	F7
22B123	F25	29B1	F1	45A3	T51, 52
22B125a	F57	29B2	F1	47B1	T21
22B126	F20	29B3	F1	58A8	T26
22B136	T10			58B1	T34
				58B4	T25
		Melissus		58B9	T28
		30B1	F1	58B20	T33
Parmenides		30B2	F2	58B21	T32
		30B3	F3	58B30	T44, 45
28A24	T5	30B4	F4	58B35	T41
28A25	T3	30B6	F5	58B37	T38
28A28	T1	30B7	F6	58B39	T7
28A35	T7	30B8	F8	58B40	T47
28A37	T8	30B9	F7	58C3	T10
28A40a	T9			58C4	T22
28A46	F18			58C6	T11
28A52	T11	**Pythagoreans**		58D2	T13
28B1	F1	14A1	T6, 9	*Not in* DK: T15, 16, 17,	
28B2	F3	14A2	T3	23, 27, 29, 30, 35, 37, 39	
28B3	F4	14A4	T18		
28B4	F6	14A7	T12		
28B5	F2	14A8	T8	**Anaxagoras**	
28B6	F5	14A8a	T14		
28B7	F7	14A10	T20	59A1	T13
28B8	F8, T6	14A16	T19	59A41	T7
28B9	F11	16A1	T50	59A42	T9
28B10	T2, F9	18A4	T36	59A43	T4
28B11	F10	18A12	T24	59A45	T6
28B12	F13	18A15	T31	59A46	T3
28B13	F14	22B40	T2	59A52	T5
28B14	F15	22B129	T1		

DK	WATERFIELD	DK	WATERFIELD	DK	WATERFIELD
59A63	T1	31A60	T26, 27	31B111	F4
59A80	T11	31A68	T28	31B112	F1
59A81	T10	31A69	T29	31B114	F2
59A89	T8	31A75	T8	31B115	F35
59A92	T16	31A78	T6	31B117	F36
59A110	T15	31A81	T16, 17	31B124	F34
59A117	T12, 14	31A86	T12	31B128	F32
59B1	F1	31A87	T14	31B130	F33
59B2	F2	31A89	T13	31B132	F40
59B3	F7	31B2	F6	31B134	F26
59B4a	F4	31B3b	F7	31B136	F37
59B4b	F5	31B6	F10	31B137	F38
59B5	F15	31B8	F13	31B141	F39
59B6	F8	31B9	F14	31B146	F3
59B7	F3	31B12	F11		
59B8	F6	31B13	F12	*Not in* DK: T9	
59B9	F11	31B16	F18		
59B10	T2	31B17	F20		
59B11	F9	31B20	F28	**Atomists**	
59B12	F10	31B21	F19	67A1	T19
59B13	F14	31B22	F17	67A6	T2
59B14	F13	31B23	F15	67A7	T1
59B15	F12	31B26	F22	67A10	T18
59B16	F16	31B27	F24	67A13	T9
59B17	F19	31B29	F25	67A14	T5
59B18	F17	31B31	F27	67A16	T17
59B19	F18	31B35	F21	67A19	T4
59B21	F20	31B36	F23	67A20	T23
		31B38	F5	67A24	T21
		31B45	F47	67A28	T24
Empedocles		31B48	F46	67B2	F2
31A1	T1	31B53	T2	68A9	T14
31A22	T4	31B57	F29	68A37	T3
31A25	T3	31B61	F30	68A40	T22
31A28	T7	31B62	F31	68A43	T10
31A33	F10, T5	31B69	T15	68A47	T16
31A42	T10	31B73	F48	68A48b	T8
31A49	T11	31B84	F41	68A60	T15
31A49b	T22	31B90	F45	68A69	T20
31A50	T18, 19, 20	31B96	F16	68A71	T7
31A51	T21	31B98	F44	68A77	T29
31A53	T23	31B100	F42	68A108	T25
31A54	T24	31B105	F43	68A112	T11
31A55	F47	31B109	F9	68A135	T13
31A59	T25	31B110	F8	68A139	T30
				68A143	T31

DK	WATERFIELD
68A151	T32
68A162	T33
68A167	T35
68A169	T36
68B3	F7
68B6	F3
68B7	F3
68B8	F3
68B9a	F3
68B9b	F3
68B10	F3
68B11	F3
68B31	F15
68B117	F4
68B155	F6
68B156	F1
68B159	T37
68B164	F5
68B166	T27
68B170	T35
68B171	T35
68B174	F9
68B187	F17
68B188	F12
68B191	F8
68B211	F13
68B214	F14
68B219	F11
68B234	F10
68B235	F18
68B251	F16

Not in DK: T6, T12, T34

Diogenes

DK	WATERFIELD
64A5	T1
64A6	T2
64A12	T3
64A13	T4, 5
64A16	T6
64A19	T7
64B1	F1
64B2	F2
64B3	F3

DK	WATERFIELD
64B4	F4
64B5	F5
64B6	F8
64B7	F6
64B8	F7

Protagoras

DK	WATERFIELD
80A1	T1
80A5	T2
80A13	T9
80A19	T3, 4, 5
80A21a	T11
80A22	T10
80A23	T13
80A27	T14
80B1	T1, 6
80B3	T15
80B4	T1
80B7	T18
80B10	T16
80C1	T12

Not in DK: T7, T8, T17, T19

Gorgias

DK	WATERFIELD
80A26	T3
82A4	T1
82A25	T4
82A26	T8
82A29	T5
82B3	T11
82B4	T14
82B5	T13
82B6	F2
82B11	F1
82B14	T7
82B18	T15
82B26	F3
82C2	T10

Not in DK: T2, T6, T9, T12

Prodicus

DK	WATERFIELD
84A3	T1

DK	WATERFIELD
84A3a	T2
84A11	T3
84A13	T4
84A14	T5
84A15	T6
84B2	F1
84B4	T9
84B5	T11
84B6	T10

Not in DK: T7, T8, T12

Hippias

DK	WATERFIELD
86A8	T1
86A9	T2
86A11	T2
86A12	T3
86B6	F1
86C1	T4

Not in DK: T5, T6, T7

Thrasymachus

DK	WATERFIELD
85A2	T1
85A11	T2
85A13	T4
85B1	F1
85B6	T3
85B7	T5
85B8	T6

Not in DK: T7

Antiphon

DK	WATERFIELD
87B1	F16
87B2	F20
87B10	F22
87B12	T4
87B13	T2
87B14	F21
87B15	T1
87B26	T5
87B27	T6
87B30	F23

DK	WATERFIELD	DK	WATERFIELD	DK	WATERFIELD
87B32	T7	87B58	F5	*Double Arguments*	
87B34	T8	87B59	F6	90	F1
87B36	F24	87B60	F1		
87B44A	F18	87B61	F2		
87B44B	F17	87B62	F3		
87B44C	F19	87B65	F14		
87B49	F4	*Not in* DK: T3, F15,		**Anonymous and**	
87B50	F9	F25		**Miscellaneous**	
87B51	F10			**Texts**	
87B52	F11				
87B53a	F12			68B5.1	T5
87B54	F13	**Euthydemus and**		88B25	F1
87B56	F7	**Dionysodorus**		89	T2
87B57	F8	*Not in* DK		*Not in* DK: T1, T3, T4	

INDEX OF TRANSLATED PASSAGES